NONVIOLENT INTERVENTION ACROSS BORDERS

A Recurrent Vision

edited by

Yeshua Moser-Puangsuwan
and
Thomas Weber

Spark M. Matsunaga Institute for Peace
University of Hawai'i
Honolulu, Hawai'i
2000

© 2000 Spark M. Matsunaga Institute for Peace
All rights reserved
Printed in the United States of America

Library of Congress Cataloging-in-Publication Data
Nonviolent intervention across borders : a recurrent vision / edited by Yeshua
Moser-Puangsuwan and Thomas Weber.
p. cm.
Includes bibliographical references and index.
ISBN 1-880309-11-4 (alk. paper)
1. Nonviolence. 2. Peace movements. 3. Intervention (International law)
I. Moser-Puangsuwan, Yeshua, 1954– II. Weber, Thomas, 1950–

JZ5574.N66 2000

341.5'23—dc21   99-088960

This book is printed on acid-free paper and meets the guidelines for
permanence and durability of the Council on Library Resources.

Distributed by
University of Hawai'i Press
Order Department
2840 Kolowalu Street
Honolulu, Hawai'i 96822

CONTENTS

Foreword
  Narayan Desai — v
Acknowledgements — ix
Contributors — xi

Introduction
  1. The Recurrent Vision and the Peace Brigade Movement
     Yeshua Moser-Puangsuwan and Thomas Weber — 3

Maude Royden and Beyond
  2. A History of Nonviolent Interposition and Accompaniment
     Thomas Weber — 15

Toward a Comprehensive Typology
  3. Cross-border Nonviolent Intervention: A Typology
     Robert J. Burrowes — 45

Mobilization Actions
  4. The Voyage of the Lusitania Expresso
     Andrew McMillan — 73

Nonviolent Humanitarian Assistance
  5. "Wave After Wave They Went Crossing the Border":
     Friendshipments by Pastors for Peace
     Robin Hayes — 103

Nonviolent Reconciliation and Development
  6. Cyprus Resettlement Project: An Instance of International
     Peacemaking
     A. Paul Hare — 115

Nonviolent Witness and Accompaniment
  7. Peace Brigades International: Nonviolence in Action
     Liam Mahony — 133
  8. Project Accompaniment: A Canadian Response
     Beth Abbott — 163

9. Christian Peacemaker Teams
   Kathleen Kern   175
10. Balkan Peace Team International in Croatia:
    Otvorene Oci (Open Eyes)
    Dave Bekkering   191
11. Cry for Justice in Haiti, Fall 1993
    Ed Kinane   207

Nonviolent Intercession
12. The Sahara Protest Team
    April Carter   235

Nonviolent Solidarity
13. One Million Kilometers for Peace, Reconciliation and Hope:
    The Dhammayietra Movement in Cambodia
    Yeshua Moser-Puangsuwan   257
14. Mir Sada: The Story of a Nonviolent Intervention that Failed
    Christine Schweitzer   269

Nonviolent Interposition
15. Witness for Peace
    Ed Griffin-Nolan   279
16. The Persian Gulf War and the Gulf Peace Team
    Robert J. Burrowes   305

Conclusion
17. Nonviolent Humanitarian Intervention: A Framework for
    the Future
    Yeshua Moser-Puangsuwan and Thomas Weber   319

Appendices
A. From the Peace Army to SIPAZ: A Chronology of Grassroot
   Initiatives in Unarmed Peacekeeping
   Yeshua Moser-Puangsuwan   341
B. Nongovernmental Organizations Currently Seeking Volunteers
   and Placing Peace Teams   357

Index   361

FOREWORD

For the last six or seven decades men and women all round the world have attempted to intervene nonviolently in situations of international conflict. Accounts of these attempts have been published from time to time. The two editors of this book have done a commendable job in putting these accounts together and analyzing them. These efforts of intervention have more often failed than succeeded. But even so the attempts have been most interesting to activists and researchers alike. People learn by their mistakes. Each account of a partial or a total failure has contributed significantly to the endeavor to bring an end to war between and within countries. The graphic account as well as the careful analysis presented in this book will be of lasting value both practically and theoretically to those who endeavor to find solutions to violent conflict.

The book makes fascinating reading even in its description of failures, because it tells us about a vision that has been recurrent, a vision that has defied all failures.

In introducing the book, I will take the liberty of adding two more stories to the scores that have been given here, even at the risk of being a bit subjective. They may perhaps help in understanding this vision which is global and which raises its head again and again after every failure.

My first story is at an individual level, which may not be considered to be a part of the concern of this book, which is confined to conflicts between large groups of people. But it is a story of a success. I was in my early teens, spending a few days of holiday at my ancestral village. I heard some loud voices outside the little mud hut that was my "home." I also saw a lot of people collecting in the street outside. At the center of the crowd there were two of my distant uncles, both using foul language, both were armed with lethal staves, and were bent upon striking each other. One of them was drunk and was creating a nuisance in the vicinity, the other was trying to prevent him from doing so, but by using the same violent means. The crowd was watching, screaming and yelling, but scared to intervene in any way. Instinctively I jumped into the fray, between the two brawling uncles, who were physically much stronger than I and who were burning with rage. "What are you doing, uncle?" I asked loudly, not pointing at any one particularly from among them. "Can't you see?" answered the one who was sober, "He is completely drunk and I want to bring some sense to him!" "Yes, that is obvious," said I, "but he behaves like that because he is drunk. Why are you, who is sober, behaving exactly like him?" That argument worked. Upon hearing me, the sober uncle put down his staff, whereupon the uncle who was drunk also put down his staff proclaiming that he had won, because the other uncle could not harm him a bit! Hearing this, the watching crowd laughed and gradually the foul language on both sides also subsided.

In this case the crowd was scared and was also passive. The person who intervened, was physically weak and was no match for any one of the warring parties. All that I did was instinctive and almost instantaneous. My strength was moral, though I was not conscious about it, and my argument was persuasive enough to force one party to abstain from going ahead with his violence. My sudden intervention had prevented both of them escalating their violence and my argument brought some sense to the mind of the uncle who was sober.

My first exposure to the idea of "Shanti Sena" (peace army) was also very personal. Late one evening at Sevagram, Mahatma Gandhi's ashram, I overheard my parents whispering to each other, thinking that I, whose bed was in between the two, was fast asleep. Gandhi had collected all the inmates of his ashram that afternoon and had given them some idea of his plan to defend a country nonviolently in case of aggression against it, as at the time this was an actual possibility. The Japanese army had been knocking at India's doors after overrunning Singapore, Malaya and Burma. One of Gandhi's ideas was to physically face the invading army and act as "cannon-fodder" to their guns. The discussion that was going on that night between my two parents was about this idea.

Gandhi had asked his ashram inmates whether they would be willing to go with him in the front, and both my parents were anxious to go. The problem was myself. Who would take care of me? My mother was arguing that she had taken care of me all these years, and it was time for my father to give me a proper education. It would be better, therefore, for her to go to the front and leave my father behind to take care of me. My father argued that even if he decided to remain at home, he simply could not do so, because it was impossible for him to think of Bapu (Gandhi) going to the front to die while he remained at home. The decision that my parents ultimately arrived at was that they would both join Gandhi's army, go to the front and act as "cannon-fodder" if need be, and leave the child to the care of God (or society, if you like). As fate would have it Gandhi's plan did not materialize, but that evening's discussion between my parents was enough to make me interested in the Shanti Sena.

Gandhi's idea, I learnt later, had three phases to it. His first phase envisaged an India that had forsaken all arms and with a foreign policy that aimed to create an atmosphere of friendship with the world, beginning with its neighbors. This would minimize the chances of aggression on India's soil. It would also create world sympathy for a disarmed India if she were invaded by some outside country.

The second phase in Gandhi's vision was to have an army of nonviolent soldiers, well trained and disciplined, ready to lay down their lives to prevent the invading army from entering Indian territory in case of an invasion.

Gandhi's third phase was, perhaps, most difficult, but it was also most practical because it had come out of Gandhi's experience of various nonviolent struggles during his life-time. In this phase Gandhi envisaged that in case the invading army overran the "cannon-fodder" and entered Indian territory, the civilian population of India would non-cooperate completely with the invading army, even at the risk of life. They would make it impossible for the invaders to rule over them.

I have given these two examples in order to make a couple of humble suggestions, regarding the topic raised in this book. The first example, though only at the micro-level, has something to teach us. It teaches us that intervention in a conflict situation is part of human nature and no amount of argument about its difficulty will prevent it from happening in spite of recurrent failures. It also teaches us that physical strength is not the only strength that counts. Even a child's intervention can act as a moral influence. The numbers may be of importance in intervention, but they are of secondary importance.

The second episode is not the story of a success. It is only a vision, yet to be tried. Its trial may teach us new lessons regarding nonviolent interventions. The factor where Gandhi's idea differs from all those discussed in this book, including his own articulated before a European audience in 1931, is that it should not be a third party intervening between two warring factions, but that the victims of the aggression themselves should be taking up the means of nonviolent resistance and non-cooperation. Because Gandhi throughout his life had taken sides with the victims of various situations, his nonviolence was based on the idea of making the victims strong nonviolently instead of expecting some other party to intervene to help. Even those who plan to intervene as a third party have often to take sides with the underdogs, as in the case of Nicaragua and Haiti in this book.

Ultimately a nonviolent strategy works more effectively if the people who suffer themselves take up nonviolence as their means of liberation. Activists and peace researchers will have to put their heads together to make nonviolence more acceptable to the sufferers.

When it comes to a case of third party intervention, the intervention has to be nonpartisan. But in many of the cases mentioned in this book, the third party has to act as if it were accepting the status quo as just. We cannot, however, forget the fact that at the root of most of the violence in the world is structural violence, which cannot end without changing the status quo. In such circumstances nonviolence will have to take side with the victims, and try to change the attitude of both the perpetrators of violence as well as the victims of violence.

I am glad the editors and authors of some of the chapters of this book are conscious of the problem of the escorts of today being limited mostly to white-skinned people. The situation is a comment on present day politics and economics, which has divided us into North/South as also White/Colored worlds. This also underlines the need of fundamental change in human structures. Here I would like to emphasize a problem that has been cursorily discussed in one of the chapters of this book. I have observed that most of the white world, particularly the European and North American pacifists, treat nonviolence more or less as a technique and not as a way of life. I submit that this question is not only a subject for ideological debate, but it has much deeper implications. With technique, one changes situations superficially, not necessarily affecting the status quo. When nonviolence is considered as a totally different way of life, it has to deal with fundamental questions like changing the values, attitudes, relationships, institutions and finally the structures of the society. Those looking for permanent solutions to our problems will have to deal not only with current conflict situations, but also with the fundamental changes mentioned above. I hope that consideration of the problems posed during nonviolent intervention will interest researchers and activists in fundamental change which can come only when nonviolence is defined as a way of life.

I congratulate the editors for having done the much needed work of bringing the history of nonviolent intervention in the present century together in one book. They have also analyzed the phenomenon of this recurrent vision in a masterly way. They have dealt with the subject with the sympathy expected of activists and the objectivity of scientific researchers. This enthralling book is certainly going to make both the activist and the researcher think afresh.

Narayan Desai

ACKNOWLEDGMENTS

We dedicate this book to Charles Walker who first gave us the personal inspiration to become involved in a peace team (in the case of Yeshua) or, through his writings, to study the peace team movement (in the case of Tom), and for his work to keep the vision of peace teams alive. George Willoughby is thanked for suggesting to Yeshua that he should collect the histories of these actions when he was told that the peace movement was not learning its lessons in mobilizing peace teams.

We would also like to express our gratitude to all the authors of chapters in this book. Most of them are overworked and unpaid activists who have undertaken the writing as extra burdens that promised no tangible rewards and have shown great patience while waiting for us to get this book into print. Narayan Desai was very generous in writing the foreword at a time when he was not in the best of health.

We are also indebted to the then School of Social Sciences at La Trobe University, in Melbourne, for providing the funds to allow Robert Burrowes to undertake the task of writing the theoretical chapter which provides the framework for this book, and the Outside Studies Program Committee of what is now the Faculty of Humanities and Social Sciences at the university for funding Tom's visit to the Spark M.Matsunaga Institute for Peace at the University of Hawai'i in order to finalize the production of this book.

Finally, we would like to thank Carolyn Stephenson for invaluable help, as well as Ralph Summy and Brien Hallett of the Matsunaga Institute for Peace for not only having enough faith in the work to publish it but for playing the role of editors so skillfully. From the exchanges between us regarding content and style, a far better document emerged than would have been the case if had gone it alone. It is for this sort of productive dialogue that editors should be made.

CONTRIBUTORS

Beth Abbot is North-South Co-ordinator for the Canada-Guatemala Solidarity Network, Project Accompaniment. She is based in Halifax, Nova Scotia.

Dave Bekkering has spent the last five years working with peace and human rights organizations in the former Yugoslavia (including 15 months with the Balkan Peace Team/Otvorene Oci). Since 1996 he has been involved with the Social Reconstruction Project in the divided Bosnian town of Gornji Vakuf.

Robert J.Burrowes is a nonviolent activist. He was a member of the Gulf Peace Team and is author of *The Strategy of Nonviolent Defense: A Gandhian Approach*.

April Carter taught Politics at Somerville College in Oxford and at the University of Queensland, in Brisbane. She was an organizer of the Sahara Protest Team and the San Francisco to Moscow March and is the author of *The Politics of Women's Rights* and *Peace Movements: International Protest and World Politics since 1945*. Her theoretical interests relate to democracy, the state, and militarism.

Narayan Desai is the son of Mahatma Gandhi's personal secretary and grew up on Gandhi's Ashrams. Between 1962 and 1974 he directed the Indian Gandhian peace brigade, the Shanti Sena, and has served as the chairperson of War Resisters' International and as a director of Peace Brigades International. He heads the Institute for Total Revolution, a training center for Gandhian activists, in Vedchhi, India.

Ed Griffin-Nolan has lived a large portion of his adult life in South America working among the poor. From 1985 to 1988 he was on the staff of Witness for Peace in Nicaragua and is the author of *Witness for Peace: A Story of Resistance*. He currently writes and practices massage therapy in Syracuse, NY, where he lives with his wife Ellen and three children.

A.Paul Hare teaches Sociology at Ben Gurion University of the Negev. He was a member of the Cyprus Resettlement Project and with Herbert H.Blumberg was the editor of *Liberation Without Violence: A Third-Party Approach*.

Robin Hayes has been a National Co-Coordinator of IFCO/Pastors for Peace since May 1995, primarily focussing on the organization's work in Chiapas, Mexico. She has helped to organize and lead over a dozen solidarity projects, including several Pastors for Peace caravans to Cuba, Nicaragua and Chiapas and human rights observer delegations to Chiapas.

Kathleen Kern has been a full-time worker with Christian Peacemaker Teams since 1993, serving on project assignments in Haiti, Washington DC, and Hebron. She is the author of *When It Hurts to Live* and *We Are the Pharisees*.

Ed Kinane has provided protective accompaniment with Peace Brigades International in Guatemala, El Salvador and Sri Lanka and has spent two months in Haiti as a Cry for Justice volunteer. He is the former Chair of PBI's Sri Lanka Project. Currently he convenes PBI/USA's Executive Committee and is active in the campaign to close the US Army's School of the Americas, in Fort Benning, Georgia.

Liam Mahony has worked with Peace Brigades International since 1987 in Guatemala, Haiti and in its International office. He is the co-author (with Luis Enrique Eguren) of *Unarmed Bodyguards: International Accompaniment for the Protection of Human Rights*.

Andrew McMillan is a freelance journalist and writer. He was on the *Lusitania Expresso* and is the author of *Death in Dili*.

Yeshua Moser-Puangsuwan is the co-ordinator of Nonviolence International's South-East Asia Office and was an organizer and participant of the Dhammayietra in Thailand and Cambodia. He is the current editor of *Peace Teams/Peace Services Information Networker*.

Christine Schweitzer is a nonviolent activist from Germany. She has worked with different German peace organizations and was the first coordinator of the Balkan Peace Team. She is an editor of the magazine *Fiedensforum* and a member of an alternative research institute.

Thomas Weber teaches Peace Studies and Politics at Melbourne's La Trobe University. He is the author of *Conflict Resolution and Gandhian Ethics* and *Gandhi's Peace Army: The Shanti Sena and Unarmed Peacekeeping*.

INTRODUCTION

1

THE RECURRENT VISION AND THE PEACE BRIGADE MOVEMENT

Yeshua Moser-Puangsuwan and Thomas Weber

The Recurrent Vision
For as long as there have been wars there have also been plans to stop them. There have been saints who have preached nonviolence, leading political figures and academics who have advocated various grandiose schemes to achieve world peace through alliances, world government or international armies, and people who have put their lives on the line, by physically placing their bodies between disputing parties to try to end conflicts, or by taking risks in order to try to end oppression. And while bloody conflicts and injustices exist, even in far away places, there will always be people of goodwill who will cross borders, often at great personal risk, to intervene as peacekeepers, peacemakers or peace-builders.

And now the world is watching. Innumerable wars and armed conflicts rage or simmer in different countries or neighborhoods around the planet, viewable from television sets or doorsteps, depending on one's location. Humanitarian aid agencies, supported by churches, house war-weary people fleeing men with guns. Governments try to intervene in armed conflicts by sending men with guns, sometimes under United Nations auspices, to "help." At times soldiers in these new roles have complained that they feel humiliated because they are prohibited from responding in line with their traditional training. As soldiers and global strategic thinkers show little ability to creatively transform their conflict intervention methods, there are calls for the development of a nonviolent alternative.

However, during this century there have already been many types of nonmilitary interventions that have brought succor to those suffering as a result of violence or natural disaster. Various forms of aid and assistance programs as well as interventions to protect human rights, make up the rich mosaic of humanitarian intervention that can be either governmental or nongovernmental, and either coercive or non-coercive (see Lewer and Ramsbotham, 1993).

The list of nongovernmental and non-coercive interventions is broad. Some of these actions long ago moved from vision to reality and are far better known around the world than the intercession, interposition and accompaniment actions that are the focus of this book. The activities of organizations such as the International Committee of the Red Cross (Nobel Peace Prizes in 1917, 1945 and 1963), Oxfam, Amnesty International (Nobel Peace Prize in 1977) and Greenpeace International, among others, are of particular importance. These organizations intervene directly in international affairs, they do so nonviolently and the bulk of their membership (if not field workers) are grassroots workers and supporters.

The International Committee of the Red Cross (ICRC) is probably the world's best known humanitarian and relief organization. The organization received its mandate from the Geneva Conventions of 1949 and works to ensure the application of international humanitarian law in situations of armed conflict. Most notably it seeks to ensure the safety and medical care of noncombatants and the wounded. It also provides an invaluable tracing service, helping families reunite or receive word about the whereabouts of living family members in areas in which essential services are no longer functioning. Field workers also make visits to military prisons in an attempt to guarantee at least minimum standards of incarceration are maintained (that is, freedom from torture, basic medical treatment and dietary requirements). The ICRC, as distinct from national Red Cross societies, is not a voluntary or totally nongovernmental organization. Over half the ICRC budget is provided by the Swiss Government and its field workers are paid professionals.

The other well-known organizations listed above also deserve mention. Oxfam undertakes long-term development projects in the Third World. The focus of its work is technical assistance rather than peacekeeping in any narrow sense, and its field workers are salaried. Amnesty, sends "paper proxies," rather than volunteers, in extremely effective letter-writing campaigns to secure the release of jailed political prisoners and curtail the use of torture, judicial and extrajudicial executions as well as other human rights crimes. Greenpeace International began as a people's initiative sending a boat to stop nuclear testing in the Aleutian Islands. Since then it has also engaged in nonviolent direct action against commercial whaling, seal culling, and the dumping of radioactive and toxic wastes. Today many of Greenpeace's international activists, such as the crew of the *Rainbow Warrior*, are salaried staff rather than volunteers.

Even the vision of individuals crossing borders and nonviolently placing themselves in conflict situations in intentional efforts to reduce violence or bring about social change has grown far beyond the dream of those, like Maude Royden, who saw large groups of volunteers interposing themselves between warring armies and thus hopefully bringing an end to the carnage. It has been realized that violence can be structural as well as direct, that local activists may be better able to deal with the situation if their safety is ensured, and that changes can be brought through international pressure if enough people are mobilized. The vision, when it became manifest, went on to spawn many variants. And these manifestations of the recurrent vision, from the anti-nuclear weapons actions of the 1950s and 1960s to the present actions in the Balkans and Central America, show increasing vitality and demonstrable success.

A long and rich history of nonviolent humanitarian political interventions, that is, nongovernmental efforts at sending peace missions, known as Peace Brigades, Peace Teams or Peace Armies, already exists. These *ad hoc* citizens' efforts have been sent out since the time of the League of Nations. In total there have been more such citizens' missions than UN Peacekeeping missions. These people's actions, however, are not as well known. They are underfunded and can send few volunteers to the field, leaving them invisible to global media.

The Peace Brigades Movement
The voices for a completely unarmed peacekeeping force have been heard regularly throughout this century. Pacifists who believed in stopping conflicts and protecting victims could hardly have done otherwise but call for such a force if they wished to maintain consistency. But there were practical reasons also. Charles Walker, the American Quaker advocate of a World Peace Guard, suggests that the military may not be the best instrument for securing peace. He criticizes the proposals of some military veterans of UN missions who have been pushing the concept of a military agency which includes peacemaking (conflict resolution) and peacebuilding (socio-economic development and reconstruction) functions (Walker, 1971, p.233). A peace force which has been engaged in military operations will find it difficult to talk to the party it has been shooting at. If violence is used, then a peacekeeping force may, in critical situations, "become a paramilitary force with aspects of an occupying army" in which case community relations programs, even those attempted by dedicated officers, cannot hope to overcome or mitigate the community's

hostility. Perhaps, as Walker notes, it is an inevitable consequence that "the effect of a military force will be estimated in military terms." And finally, following a survey of peacekeeping possibilities, he concludes that "peacekeeping missions by military forces are likely to serve primarily the interests of the superpowers; and threaten to isolate, exploit or dominate smaller and weaker nations, particularly in the Third World." Walker and other advocates of the unarmed alternative see these problems as inherent in military forces, especially those under the control of a supranational authority where the large powers dominate and have rights of veto.

Current popular dissatisfaction with international peacekeeping, as it is now practiced through the United Nations, and peace enforcement as conducted by NATO, is leading to an upsurge of interest in nonmilitary peacekeeping. The governments of Germany, Denmark and Holland have recently stated their intent to develop a new form of international peacekeeping that does not rely solely on armed troops. These governmental initiatives have followed, and at times led to, nongovernmental forums being established to debate the methodology to be used by such unarmed units. The government of Austria has helped in the financing of a center for the study of peacekeeping with a significant focus on unarmed intervention. Two multinational conferences took place in 1994 and 1995 involving participants from 30 countries, and twice as many nongovernmental organizations, seeking to establish large-scale nongovernmental peacekeeping contingents.

One of these conferences, a consultation in Washington, DC, on the concept of peace teams, which was funded by the United States Institute for Peace, was attended by participants from more than 20 countries with experience or interest in nongovernmental and governmental peacekeeping. Several European states (notably Germany, Denmark, Austria and Sweden) are considering or have decided to devote a portion of their defence budget to examining the unarmed option. Denmark, the Society of Friends (Quakers), and groups devoted to UN reform are outlining an unarmed option, sometimes referred to as "White Berets," to operate under the auspices of the UN. Further, partisan efforts (that is those aiming to bring about change by identifying themselves with the oppressed) have become accepted as quite normal over the past few decades.

In short, interest in this type of activism has never been higher. United Nations Volunteers have initiated a new peacemakers program in Burundi modelled, in part, on the work of Peace Brigades International. Nongovernmental groups currently sending volunteers to the field include Witness for Peace, Christian Peacemaker Teams, SIPAZ, Project

Accompaniment, the Balkan Peace Team and Peace Brigades International. Combined, they are currently placing and supporting almost 100 volunteers in conflict zones scattered across a dozen countries. Compared to the mid-1980s when there were only two organizations attempting this work, with a handful of volunteers working in two countries, it is clear that this is an idea that has taken on a life of its own.

It is somewhat surprising, therefore, that there is currently no single publication which collects into one volume the history of past and current actions of what we can term Peace Teams, the contingents that have made ordinary citizens players in situations of conflict in the international political arena. Their history is traced through articles appearing in small circulation journals, or internal newsletters of the groups themselves. It is time that this literature was presented in one volume that was easily accessible to the many peace activists now engaged in peace brigades work, and to those whose interest in the area is more academic, as well as to a public which is seeking more compassionate responses to the world's conflicts than those usually resorted to.

It should be noted that unarmed nonviolent interventions do not only take place in the international arena or in an organized way. Where many of our cities resemble urban war zones there is much to be said for acting locally. Elise Boulding has talked of a "Peace Team" (being a "multi-ethnic/racial, multicultural group of persons under secular or religious nongovernmental sponsorship, national or international in character, who have undergone specific nonviolence training in conflict areas in their home countries") creating social and physical "safe spaces" or "peace zones" in conflict-ridden inner city areas. She gives the Sisters of Loretto Project in Denver, Colorado as an example (Boulding, 1994, p.2). Other examples include the Mennonites' peace monitors at Wounded Knee (Schrag, 1977), the actions of the Christian Peacemaker Team in Washington, and nonviolent community safety and peacekeeping actions (at large festivals, rallies and marches) by the Melbourne volunteer organization Pt'chang (Alderson *et al*, 1997). While this book details the history and activities of citizen-based, *international*, nonviolent crisis intervention initiatives, it is hoped that it will also provide lessons for those wishing to act nearer to home.

Numerous cases of spontaneous interposition that have interrupted conflicts have also been recorded. The most important early account of these examples, of what is now commonly referred to as "people power" is contained in Gene Keyes' 1978 article "Peacekeeping by Unarmed Buffer Forces." In that paper Keyes reports on spontaneous interpositions in Algeria in 1962, in Aden in 1967, and in China in 1968 (Keyes, 1978). Following the French pullout from Algeria, a large-scale civil war seemed inevitable. In towns such as Boghari, "A crowd of war-weary men and women created a human barrier between the opposing forces. When the soldiers pressed forward, the civilians forced them to embrace each other and fraternize." In what was the former federation of Southern Arabia, over 2,000 demonstrators, including women, children and the elderly, "stopped heavy fighting between rival nationalist groups... when they marched through battle-torn streets screaming for a ceasefire." During China's Cultural Revolution a mini-war erupted between two Maoist student factions at Tsinghua University in Bejing. Eventually, a contingent of workers, some 60,000 strong, entered the university shouting the slogan "use reason not violence, use reason not violence, lay down your weapons and form a big alliance." The workers stood their ground in the face of extreme provocation and violence and their action eventually did lead to an alliance of the fighting factions. More recently, in the Philippines, Bangkok, Tiananmen Square in Bejing, Moscow, Belgrade and in Jakarta the efficacy of spontaneous people power has clearly been demonstrated.

These actions are inspiring and historically important, offering insight into the dynamics of what Keyes calls "massive nonviolent buffer actions," however they do not provide adequate guidance for those *planning* interventions in areas where the activists have little or no relationship with the belligerents.

Our focus here is to provide examples of nonviolent nongovernmental international peace intervention initiatives undertaken by grassroots activists, and to attempt to distil the lessons provided by these examples.

Organization of the Book
For those who have bothered to look at the past it is becoming increasingly obvious that alternatives to the mainstream style of peace interventions are not merely theoretical. There have been many attempts to think through a nonviolent approach and many examples of this vision have now been attempted in practice. The main focus of this book is to chronicle the vision of nonviolent cross-border interventions and to look in detail at some of its manifestations.

The chapter in the section headed "Maude Royden and Beyond" introduces the vision of the good-willed people who first advocated nonviolent cross-border intervention and examines early manifestations of this vision by detailing the history of peace brigades that made it into the field.

The chapter in the next section, "Towards a Comprehensive Typology," attempts to bring some order to the terminology used in these interventions and provides a framework for our selection of readings in the more practically oriented part of this book, the sections dealing with different types of recent nonviolent cross-border interventions. This is important because on the rare occasions that such interventions have been recognized in the literature, the terminology used to describe them is generally so imprecise that the issue is merely confused further. A recent example illustrates the point. Some years ago the *Journal of Peace Research* published an article assessing the viability of what were called "interpositionary peace forces" (Weber, 1993). The article was criticized by some members of Peace Brigades International (PBI), one of the groups described, as being "dismissive" of their organization. There seemed to be some concern that the article dealt with the short lived Gulf Peace Team (GPT) experiment in great length and spent far too little space on the 12 years of PBI activity. It is true that out of the article's 19 pages one and a half dealt directly with the GPT, and PBI was covered in just one paragraph. That paragraph pointed out that PBI was attempting to do something entirely different from establishing an unarmed interpositionary peacekeeping force. The conclusion was that the prospect for success (by almost any measure one cares to use) of large-scale interpositionary peace forces was slim. Instead the "most appropriate task for those advocating the establishment of such 'forces' are in the realms of interventionary peacekeeping, limited to escort duties and the like" (Weber, 1993, p.62). That some PBI members felt slighted by not being included at length in a catalog of failures is at first glance puzzling. But on further reflection it becomes clear why this was so.

The problem, to a large degree, seems to be one of definition. The term "nonviolent interposition" was used for actions such as those contemplated by Maude Royden and her "Peace Army," the Indian Gandhians during the border war with China, Non-Violent Action in Vietnam, and lastly the Gulf Peace Team. What PBI was doing was characterized as "nonviolent intervention." In that article, the activities of the World Peace Brigade were cataloged somewhere in between. The article was clearly about the failure of activities that PBI was not engaged in. The basis for the misunderstanding seems to be a lack of agreed definitions for various forms of nonviolent intervention. The terms "nonviolent intervention," "nonviolent interposition" and "nonviolent unarmed peacekeeping" were used, and have been used in the past, without adequate definition, and often interchangeably.

While occasionally efforts have been made to clarify the area, so far none has been accepted as the standard. Hare and Blumberg, in *Liberation Without Violence*, their classic early collection of essays dealing with third-party efforts to bring about nonviolent social change, categorized actions as either partisan (where although the actors identify with the oppressed in a second-party approach they "have enough detachment from their own causes to try in some sense to seek solutions which incorporate the needs of all parties") or nonpartisan (neutral third-party) national cases. They further distinguish between partisan or nonpartisan transnational cases (Hare and Blumberg, 1977, pp.1-2).

More recently the efforts to systematize these initiatives have intensified. For example, in 1993 Lewer and Ramsbotham produced an analysis of what they called "third-party humanitarian intervention." Their typology did not include nonviolent interventions as a category. More recently still, reminiscent of the Hare and Blumberg typology, L'Abate, Schirch and Rigby each have attempted to construct categories that focus on nonviolence. L'Abate provides a simple typology of nonviolent interventions in armed conflicts. He produces a grid with levels of conflict (either large-scale or small-scale) on one axis and types of interventions (external or internal to the country) on the other. Schirch, in her discussion of the most appropriate types of interventions, has provided the most comprehensive typology to date. She distinguishes three categories of intervention: interpositionary peacekeeping (where peacekeepers place themselves physically between groups engaged in violent conflict), intercessionary peacekeeping (which includes accompaniment and presence), and other peacekeeping tasks (a long list that includes activities such as observing, documenting and monitoring, alerting the international community, showing solidarity, facilitating communications, activism, peacemaking and peacebuilding). Rigby attempts something different. He has quite rightly argued that too much attention has been placed on the most extreme form of intervention (that of activists placing their bodies between conflicting parties), and too little on the large range of other nonviolent interventions that can exercise an influence in conflict situations. By using the example of the Israel/Palestinian conflict, he examines how citizens of one country or region can intervene to affect conflict processes and outcomes in other parts of the world.

These efforts, while laudable, are still inadequate for the task we have set ourselves in this book—at one level they do too much, at another not enough. The field they cover can be too great, and overly simple typologies add little to our understanding of the area. In these all-encompassing typologies the focus on nonviolence and cross-border activism can be lost. In short, the time has come to bring some order to a bewildering set of definitions and attempt to formulate a comprehensive typology of cross-border nonviolent interventions in an attempt to offer a broad definition between the confusing terms: intervention, interposition and intercession.

The central part of the book, chapters 4 through 16, provides a detailed chronicle of recent major peace brigade actions and examine the lessons that can be drawn from them. While Robert J.Burrowes' typology provides the format for this part of the book, we are only concerned here with some of his categories. While local nonviolent actions sometimes attempt to influence the outcome of violent struggles across borders, they are not concerned with direct interventions. And because nonviolent invasions are not likely to occur, the following readings focus on the categories Burrowes classifies as mobilization actions, nonviolent humanitarian assistance, nonviolent reconciliation and development, nonviolent witness and accompaniment, nonviolent intercession, nonviolent solidarity, and nonviolent interposition.

As far as possible the papers are original works written by those who took part in the various actions and most of the main readings relate to recent initiatives. For the categories of nonviolent reconciliation and nonviolent intercession, where there has either been no recent initiatives that we are aware of, or we have been unable to secure an article on a recent action, we have included earlier previously published material.

The final section looks to the future of nonviolent intervention and unarmed peacekeeping.

REFERENCES

Alderson, David, Sh'ana Costable and Anthony Kelly. 1997. *The Pt'chang Report: The Story of the Confest Safety Project* (Melbourne: Pt'chang).

Boulding, Elise. 1994. Letter to "Colleagues Concerned with International Nonviolent Peace Services," 4 February.

Hare, A.Paul, and Herbert H.Blumberg (eds.). 1977. *Liberation Without Violence: A Third-Party Approach* (Totowa, NJ: Rowman and Littlefield).

Keyes, Gene. 1978. "Peacekeeping by Unarmed Buffer Forces: Precedents and Proposals," *Peace and Change*, vol.1, nos.2&3, pp.3-11.

L'Abate, Albert. 1995. "Nonviolent Intervention in Armed Conflicts," in Manmohan Choudhuri and Ramjee Singh (eds.). *Mahatma Gandhi 125 Years* (Varanasi: Sarva Seva Sangh/Gandhian Institute of Studies) pp.141-155.

Lewer, Nick, and Oliver Ramsbotham. 1993. *"Something Must be Done": Towards an Ethical Framework for Humanitarian Intervention in International Social Conflict* (Bradford: Department of Peace Studies, University of Bradford).

Rigby, Andrew. 1995. "Unofficial Nonviolent Intervention: Examples from the Israeli-Palestinian Conflict," *Journal of Peace Research*, vol.32, no.4, pp.453-467.

Schirch, Lisa. 1995. *Keeping the Peace: Exploring Civilian Alternatives in Conflict Prevention* (Uppsala: Life & Peace Institute).

Schrag, James L. 1977. "Report from Wounded Knee," in A.Paul Hare and Herbert H.Blumberg (eds.), *Liberation Without Violence: A Third-Party Approach* (Totowa, NJ: Rowman and Littlefield), pp.117-124.

Walker, Charles C. 1971. "Peacekeeping: A Survey and an Evaluation," appendix to Lincoln P.Bloomfield *The Power to Keep the Peace: Today and in a World Without War* (Berkeley: World Without War) pp.228-243.

Weber, Thomas. 1993. "From Maude Royden's Peace Army to the Gulf Peace Team: An Assessment of Unarmed Interpositionary Peace Forces," *Journal of Peace Research*, vol.30, no.1, pp.45-64.

MAUDE ROYDEN AND BEYOND

2

A HISTORY OF NONVIOLENT INTERPOSITION AND ACCOMPANIMENT

Thomas Weber

Introduction—The United Nations and Peacekeeping
Since the end of the Cold War there have been greatly increased deployments of UN peacekeeping forces around the globe, and experiments with far larger, more complex and more lethal versions of peacekeeping (parading under the name of "peace enforcement"). While the UN peacekeeping model has been the product of historical forces, those forces are rapidly disappearing and any consideration of the future role of peacekeepers must be undertaken in light of the new emerging world order and not merely through past UN peacekeeping experiences. Even the argument that, at least in the foreseeable future, non-specialist troops would continue to be called together from disparate small nations to undertake peacekeeping operations in the name of the UN is no longer the case—and any consideration of future peacekeeping operations must take the ending of a bipolar world into consideration.

Because of costs, organizational problems and the troubling philosophical implications of such a development, the prospects for a standing UN army are still very small, however united Security Council actions of the Korean type are again being entertained. The unanimous Security Council decision to blockade Iraq in 1990, following its invasion of neighboring Kuwait, seems to have been the start of a new enforcement role for the Council. During 1992, without the request from a specific host country, United Nations troops were deployed in Somalia and the former Yugoslavia. And, increasingly the original UN version of peace maintenance through the deployment of Article 43 troops (that is those that are drawn from the permanent Security Council members rather than exclusively from small powers) is becoming a possibility. This may mean a far stronger emphasis on peacekeeping and nonconsensual peace enforcement within the UN or by organizations such as NATO.

While prospects for the employment of this type of peacekeeping s seem to be increasing, the model is just as unsuitable for effective conflict resolution as the one generally still employed. Further, since the UN peacekeepers won the Nobel Peace Prize in 1988 countless problems have emerged for UN-style peacekeeping.

Proposals for Implementing an Alternative Vision
However, as this book clearly demonstrates, the story does not end with the United Nations or NATO. There is also a long but little known history of attempted unarmed intervention across borders and especially in the form of interposition (where an attempt is made to physically place a nonviolent "buffer" between two opposing armed forces in order to prevent fighting between those forces). Most of the early major initiatives stalled at the proposal stage primarily because of a lack of money and the absence of international organizational and logistical support. The Gulf Peace Team (GPT) and efforts in the former Yugoslavia are but the latest examples in this enduring tradition and they suffered some of the same problems. The GPT, for example, was hurriedly established and so had the backing of less internationally known personalities than some recent previous attempts and it soon became clear that members had not clearly formulated their strategic objectives and that their projection of the numbers they could mobilize, and the impact they could have, were wildly optimistic. Yet the GPT did manage, for the first time, to place a sizeable group of peace campaigners between belligerents in a time of war. A peace camp was in place on the border between Iraq and Saudi Arabia when the hostilities of Operation Desert Storm commenced.

Tracing the history of these various initiatives from Maude Royden's grand, but doomed, proposal to interpose civilians between warring factions, to the protective accompaniment employed by Peace Brigades International (PBI) shows the development of the ideas and how the recent activities of peace brigades relate to the experiences of earlier efforts.

While some of the peacekeeping attempts within this tradition have shared personnel, often the organizers of later attempts seem not to have adequately learned the lessons of their predecessors. The same problems are grappled with and the same philosophical debates conducted anew. By reviewing this now sizeable historical legacy it should be possible to tease out the major lessons and to make planned international unarmed intervention an effective alternative for stopping hostilities and building peace.

Maude Royden's Peace Army. This proposal dates back to 18-19 September 1931 when Japan accused China of blowing up a Manchurian railway line over which it had treaty rights. This so-called "Mukden Incident" was followed by the Japanese seizure of the city of Mukden and an invasion of Manchuria. Military occupation of the region was completed rapidly and on 18 February 1932 Japan established the puppet state of Manchukno.

In a London sermon, shortly after the Japanese invasion, Dr Maude Royden, a former suffragist and long time peace activist, one of England's first women pastors and an acquaintance of Mahatma Gandhi's since her visit to him in India in 1928, proclaimed: "I would like now to enrol people who would be ready if war should break out to put their bodies unarmed between the contending forces, in whatever way it be found possible—and there are ways that you do not think of now in which it would be possible."

The idea of the Peace Army received little publicity until the last week of February when, following renewed Japanese aggression, Royden met with Anglican Church reformer Rev H.R.L.Sheppard and Scottish minister Dr Herbert Gray and formulated a concrete proposal.

Their now famous letter appeared in the London *Daily Express* on 25 February 1932. It urged that "men and women who believed it to be their duty should volunteer to place themselves between the combatants.... We have written to the League of Nations offering ourselves for service in such a Peace Army." The Army, to be under Sheppard's leadership, was to act as a human barrier between the combatant parties and thus end the fighting. Royden explained that what they wanted was "an army of pacifists who should offer themselves to the League of Nations as the 'shock troops' of peace."

The operation of such an army could only come into being when the circumstances were right and in this case the proposers believed that they were. As Royden explained:

> In modern warfare, the interposition of an unarmed body of civilians of both sexes between two opposing armies will practically always be an impossibility. At that moment it was *not* impossible. China and Japan were fighting across the streets of Shanghai and Shanghai is on the sea. If the League of Nations could have gathered a Peace Army, transported it to Shanghai and landed it on the Bund or quay which was then under international control, we soldiers of peace would have been but a few hundred yards from the battle,

a battle that did not involve guerrilla warfare, airplanes or a vast front of trenches. According to Royden few of the critics of the Peace Army scheme, who charged her with preparing for the last rather than future wars, realized this:

> The flood of correspondence which followed like a spate on the appearance of our letter in the press showed that most of the writers were hypnotized by the ideas of modern warfare that have been generated by the conduct of the last war. Certainly it might well have been believed that the opportunity for intervention of the kind we supposed could never arise. The fact remained that it had arisen. Chinese and Japanese soldiers were facing each other and firing at each other across the streets of Shanghai, and even a few thousand unarmed volunteers would have been seen, would have been effective, and could, by their acceptance of death without resistance, have stirred the conscience of the human race (quoted in Weber, 1988, pp.205-206).

The press reporting generated by the appeal was enormous. Because of the inspirational nature of the call, it gripped the public imagination. Royden claimed that "leading articles appeared in newspapers of countries so widely different as the United States of America and Sierra Leone. Comment, even when skeptical, was friendly. We could not say that the world was ignorant of our offer."

Two days after the publication of the appeal the *Manchester Guardian* summed up feelings about the proposal in a lengthy article entitled "Turning Both Cheeks." The paper noted the practical difficulties involved in bringing the "admittedly extreme" suggestion into reality:

> One has to assume an adequate number of men and women with leisure and means to undertake a journey to the Far East; one has to assume that, arriving in China, they would be able to make their way between the Chinese and Japanese trenches, and that they would be suitably equipped to stay long enough in their precarious situation to make the cessation of hostilities that their presence brought about more than just a temporary lull (quoted in Weber, 1988, p.206).

The paper, however, also endorsed the idea:

> At the same time the suggestion is well worth considering, since it is seriously made by people whose good faith is beyond doubt and who have every intention of attempting to put it to the test of practice. And if on the surface it appears fantastic, is it really any more fantastic than the actual fact of war? Is it really any more fantastic for a number of civilized individuals to bear testimony to their belief in peace by risking their lives than for the same individuals to take up arms and devote themselves to slaughtering other individuals for any of the reasons commonly put forward in justification of war? (quoted in Weber, 1988, p.206).

However, the Peace Army was never put to the test. Royden, Sheppard and Gray sent their letter to Sir Eric Drummond, the Secretary-General of the League of Nations, with the entreaty that he should not regard the plan as "fantastic." Drummond replied that he did not at all consider the idea as fantastic but regretted that it was not in his constitutional power to bring the proposal before the League's Assembly.

By way of consolation he, at least tacitly, encouraged them to try to bring the proposal before the Assembly, which was at that time in session, through the formal demand of one of the member states, and released the letter to the representatives of the world's press, ensuring international publicity.

Meanwhile, volunteers enrolled themselves for service in the Peace Army. However, even with the worldwide publicity, barely one thousand recruits enlisted. The organizers approached Sir John Simon, Secretary of State for Foreign Affairs and head of the British Delegation to the League, and the leaders of several governments represented at the Assembly, with their plan. However, with so small a number of recruits they could not expect the League to take them too seriously, and they received only "courteous refusals or silence."

Royden later lamented that, "Perhaps we should have sought to go alone. Perhaps three pacifists being killed in a manner so much in the spirit of Mahatma Gandhi might have worked a miracle." That, though, was not the initial plan and an operation on the scale they envisaged was impossible to undertake on a voluntary basis. Government support was necessary for ships and finance. Without government help the plan faded. "While we were writing to Prime Ministers and Foreign Secretaries and awaiting replies," Royden recalled, "the opportunity was lost. Fighting spread over a vast front. Our project became impracticable." And she added "It seems in the highest degree unlikely that it will ever be practicable again."

Henry Brinton's Peace Army. Brinton, a pacifist member of the League of Nations Union, who was to become Honorary International Secretary of what remained of Royden's Peace Army, attempted to chart the likely outcomes of intervention by a buffer force between warring troops. For this purpose he published a small book, entitled *The Peace Army*, a few months after the Royden/Sheppard/Gray proposal.

With the hindsight of seventy years, Brinton's book looks extremely naive; yet it reflected the hope and belief of many pacifists in the 1930s. Brinton claimed that as hostilities do not arise in a day "there would be ample time for preparations." Before any hostilities broke out it would be announced that the Peace Army was being sent in as a precautionary measure. If the landing was opposed by force, the ensuing slaughter of unarmed civilians would so affect the conscience of the attackers that it "would probably be the end of the war" (Brinton, 1932, pp.73-74).

Following an unopposed landing "the situation would be more complex and the result a little more difficult to foresee." If the Peace Army could become a buffer force between the protagonists prior to the outbreak of fighting the opposing parties would have to come to some mutual agreement as to what to do with this force. And the resulting "protracted negotiations" would probably prove fatal to the "hawks" in both countries. "Attention would be drawn away from the feelings of righteous hate which had been worked up, once such sentiments are allowed to die down, a war would be impossible" (Brinton, 1932, p.74).

If the war was to start with the Peace Army between the combatants "it would be impossible to carry on an organized war." The problem of what to do with the unarmed force, which the combatants had not been taught to hate would lead to such chaos that "the organization of hostilities would be bound to break down, and again delay would occur, which would probably be final" (Brinton, 1932, pp.74-75).

Brinton's picture of hostilities involving an unarmed buffer force may have mirrored Mahatma Gandhi's vision based on the belief of fundamental human goodness. It was, however, envisaged in a more innocent time, one that preceded extermination camps and the acceptance of the annihilation of civilian populations where such is considered necessary for ruling elite security. This vision was also short on logistical details—Brinton saw the Peace Army as British equipped and organized, but the reception of Royden's proposal demonstrated the lack of willingness on the part of national governments to become involved in such schemes and the practical impossibility of voluntary organizations doing so. His way of accounting for modern weapons of mass destruction is positively utopian. He notes that as deadly as the weapons of land warfare are, they are relatively insignificant when compared to the horrors of the airplane—and a Peace Army can do nothing to prevent air attacks (or counter the parachute dropping of troops for that matter). Brinton was still hoping that international agreements would outlaw the use of air-fleets.

Brinton's efforts notwithstanding, the idea of a Peace Army gradually petered out with the approach of the Second World War. Pacifist concerns in Britain shifted from the prevention and ending of wars by the interposition of a peaceful buffer force, to focus on the Peace Pledge Union organized in the mid 1930s by Sheppard. At its height, a few years later, close to 150,000 Union members had signed the pledge that stated: "We renounce war and never again will we support or sanction another." Thus the pacifist movement entered a reactive phase of opposition and finally, with the rise of Hitler and with a growing suspicion that Gandhi's methods might only be workable against the British, the idea of large-scale nonviolent armies gradually disappeared.

Acland and Bell's Proposals. Following the Second World War a World Pacifist Meeting held in India tentatively suggested the setting up of international "satyagraha units" (that is those following Mahatma Gandhi's technique of nonviolent action), but it was again the British who publicly resurrected the call for peace armies. With the growing tension in the Middle East, on 2 April 1956, British MP and champion of world government, Henry Usborne wrote to the *Manchester Guardian* urging that the UN recruit a volunteer corps of 10,000 unarmed people to patrol and hold a two kilometer-wide demilitarized zone close to the Egyptian/Israeli border. Usborne suggested that this "peace force" should be "equipped only for passive resistance and designed to ensure that the present border is not violated by force. Its tactics would be essentially those of satyagraha."

Nothing came of the proposal and a few months later, with the formation of the UN Emergency Force to keep the peace in the Sinai, much of the thinking of UN protagonists and international dispute settlement theorists turned to the exploration of the possibilities opened up by this first major step in practical international peacekeeping.

Nevertheless, in 1958 former MP Sir Richard Acland suggested that Britain take the initiative in setting up a world police force that would eventually be adopted by the UN. The force, in Acland's proposal, was to be international, consisting of 5,000 to 15,000 members that could be recruited covertly where national restrictions made such action necessary. It was envisaged that an unarmed component of the force would parachute into trouble spots

> without anyone's permission or request. It will be in effect a "U.N. Observer Corps" with at least four advantages over anything the world has seen as yet. It will be always in instant well-trained readiness; it will be sufficiently numerous to do a thorough job; it will be equipped for mobility and self-maintenance anywhere; lastly (and most important...) it will not be under anyone's veto (Acland, 1958, pp.94-95).

The following year the Reverend Ralph Bell advocated an approach to war that he saw as an alternative to the pacifist position (do nothing because of a lack of an agreed practical policy) and the militarist position (want to fight). He called his approach the "Active Non-Violent Resistance Army." The way to build this army, he thought, was to do it gradually through the organization of "small groups of pioneers" in active nonviolent resistance until the numbers were such that a national or international meeting could be called to determine a feasible policy given the number of recruits available, and to appoint the leaders of the movement. Bell's central thesis was that merely to say "No" to war was not enough; what was required was an alternative positive approach.

The de Madariaga/J.P.Narayan Proposals. There was a model such as the one Bell was seeking already in operation. In India the Shanti Sena, or "Peace Army," founded by Gandhi's spiritual heir, Vinoba Bhave, had been active since 1957 (see Weber, 1996). The Sena, however, specifically included peacemaking and peacebuilding functions as of equal importance to the third-party intervention role that had been the main focus of the advocates of interpositionary peacekeeping. In the West, 1957 saw the beginning of anti-bomb campaigns. In the following few years the growth of nonviolent action moved into the international sphere—for example in 1958 the voyage of Quaker Albert Bigelow's ship *The Golden Rule* into the US Pacific hydrogen bomb testing areas, in 1959 the Sahara Protest Team, organized by peace groups to protest French Nuclear weapons testing, various large European peace marches, and the 1960 San Francisco-Moscow peace march.

While all these actions were of an *ad hoc* nature, eventually the strands led to the formation of an international nongovernmental organization that would focus, again in an *ad hoc* fashion, on nonviolent intervention on the world scene, and in turn help to build a world movement based on nonviolence as a political force. However, in 1960, Salvador de Madariaga, Spanish writer, pacifist, former champion of the League of Nations and political critic, and Vinoba Bhave's chief lieutenant and former India Socialist Party leader, Jayaprakash Narayan (known as JP), wrote to United Nations Secretary-General Dag Hammarskjöld with a proposal for the setting up of a Peace Guard organization. Although no reply was received, the suggestion was later published and again, although largely overlooked (and completely overlooked by the UN), it rekindled concrete moves to establish an unarmed interpositionary peacekeeping force.

The Madariaga/Narayan proposal called for the formation of an unarmed international police force that would be an alternative to armed UN forces. They argued that, in a world "split into various political camps," UN forces operate in a way that "the objectives, prejudices or policy of those who have succeeded in putting the UN machinery in motion will be clearly discerned," and consequently conflicts complicated (Madariaga, 1960, p.19).

The authors of the proposal believed that a body of regular "Peace Guards" who intervened without weapons between two forces in combat might have considerable effect. Their legitimacy would flow from a previously negotiated charter binding all United Nations members. This charter would ensure the inviolability of the Guards, their right to go anywhere at any time upon being given an assignment by the United Nations, and their right to intervene in any conflict when asked by one of the parties or by the UN Secretary-General.

These Guards were to be parachutists who

> should be able to stop advancing armies by refusing to move from roads, railways or airfields. They would be empowered to act in any capacity their chiefs might think adequate for the situation, though they would never use force. They should be endowed with a complete system for recording and transmitting facts, such as television cameras and broadcasting material (Madariaga, 1960, p.20).

As could be expected, given the fate of Brinton's plan for a peace army and Royden's attempt to set one up, nothing came of the proposal. Hammarskjöld's understanding of the *realpolitik* of the United Nations precluded him from entertaining the idea of such a force and so the inheritance of this line of peacekeeping came to rest with the nongovernmental world pacifist community.

Proposal for a Northern Ireland Peace Force. In 1971 the Fellowship of Reconciliation put forward a proposal to "explore the need for, and the feasibility of, a fully trained, disciplined and maintained corps for nonviolent action in Northern Ireland"

The aim of the proposed Irish Peace Force was to "attempt to establish its presence at points of violent conflict." The theory behind the proposed action was spelled out as, "Simply by observing, interpreting feelings, tending the injured and calming emotions trained people can be of considerable help, whether or not they are fully accepted by the combatants. Their presence can be seen as a symbol of, and a witness to, more humane action." And further, the leap of faith that usually accompanies such calls:

> Often the interposition of an unarmed team between violent enemies can be a barrier against an irrational clash. Its existence could encourage others to join in. (Relatively limited numbers, and injuries sustained in such action, will often inhibit violence more than a large or armed intermediary force). On the spot conciliation and other determined intervention can be options for a qualified and respected group ("Northern Ireland," 1971).

The proposal was featured prominently in *Peace News* and circulated "as an invitation to others to take interest." The next few issues of the newspaper carried several rejoinders and critiques. The debate in the main centered on the questions about the effectiveness of peacekeeping, as generally attempted by the United Nations and advocated by Royden's original "Army" idea (that is without the inclusion of substantial emphasis on peacemaking and peacebuilding), and the choice of action to be taken where the problem was structural. Several replies stated that as the problem resulted from British imperialism the most efficacious path would be to stay home and work against the British military presence. Another correspondent went further, criticizing the proposal as being "concerned with the point of conflict rather than the source of conflict." The case was made that

> [t]he notion of a neutral peacekeeping force should not be taken seriously by pacifists. If the force really has no objective beyond keeping the peace then it is serving the interests of the status quo and is not neutral. If we presume to interfere with the political design and the moral purpose of men bent on violence then we must reveal a deep understanding of the predicament and a willingness to suggest alternative means of achieving of their goals which are justifiable (Overy, 1971).

Such action is slow and unglamorous with none of the emotional and moral impact that would have followed, say, the slaughter of Sheppard, Gray and Royden's force in Shanghai. The departure of the World Peace Brigade from Africa following the dropping of the proposed Rhodesia march clearly demonstrated how the hard work of peacemaking seems relatively unenticing when the highly visible peacekeeping or nonviolent direct-action element is removed, yet peacekeeping without peacemaking can end up being little more than a stunt. For the defence, Harding of the Fellowship responded that the critics gave no real answers stressing that the problem in Northern Ireland was one of security, the lack of which means an increased reliance on armed force. The alternative to a nonviolent peacekeeping force, he maintained, would be communal or civil war (*Peace News*, 14 October 1971).

The plan to introduce a World Peace Brigade type presence into Northern Ireland continued for half a dozen more years. Although the debates surrounding the proposed brigade brought many important philosophical issues into the open, nothing came of the project. Instead, the next focus of international pacifist action became strife-torn Cyprus with the main emphasis, this time, directly on peacemaking and peacebuilding rather than interpositionary peacekeeping.

A World Peace Guard and Peaceworkers. In September 1971 Jayaprakash Narayan had again sent a letter to the UN Secretary-General. The UN had been unable to play a constructive peacekeeping role during the Bangladesh war and now the Shanti Sena was suggesting that unarmed contingents could be of value in such crises ("Vinoba Urges," 1971, pp.110-112). The letter suggested "certain radical changes in the peacekeeping machinery" of the United Nations. The Narayan proposal, in brief, was "to have an unarmed peacekeeping volunteers' force as part of the machinery for the solution of international conflicts." JP stressed that a new method of peacekeeping was necessary, one that not only contained violence but also had the ability to "create conditions for better relationships between the conflicting parties" (quoted in Walker, 1981, pp.92-94).

While again nothing came of this proposal, the theorists did not stop formulating ever more refined ideas. The experience of Charles Walker in Cyprus enabled him to draw up a detailed model for a World Peace Guard unit that could replace the UN forces on the island. While the Turkish invasion that swept away the Cyprus Resettlement Project made the document obsolete it provided the basis for further developments of the peace brigade idea.

There was one other major visionary statement of the idea—one that has been the inspiration for much thinking about nonviolent intervention by peace teams in areas of conflict. In 1981 Walker published his small booklet *A World Peace Guard: An Unarmed Agency for Peacekeeping*. There he noted that "The basic idea of a World Peace Guard is indeed a resilient one, cropping up particularly in times of crisis. It is then left stranded for lack of money, organizational and political support, or impetus from peacekeeping specialists" (Walker, 1981, p.54).

Charles Walker, a member of the North American Regional Council and Coordinator of the International Secretariat of Peace Brigades International from its inception and the major propagator of the peace brigade idea, clarified his concept further and was determined to keep the impetus going by calling for the need "to record, analyze and publish case histories and accounts of 'intervention episodes' based on a nonviolent approach." Further, he did all he could to help popularize the idea before a consultation on peace brigades, held in Canada in 1981. He urged "those of us who want to work further on this proposal [to] write, talk and meet so that a way opens."

This proposal was for an unarmed nonviolent equivalent of the mooted United Nations ready-for-action standby force. A World Peace Guard (WPG), in Walker's view, was to be a peacekeeping agency composed of trained volunteers from many countries. It was to be committed to a discipline of nonviolent action, prepared to carry out peace missions between belligerents, whether inter- or intra-national, or in situations beyond the control of local authorities. The WPG was to undertake third-party functions and services in conflict control, working in a nonpartisan fashion, to fulfil a mandate given to it by the contending parties and/or others involved (Walker, 1981, p.12).

Although unarmed, Walker saw the WPG as neither defenseless nor powerless. When it arrived at its place of operation, a legitimizing mandate would presumably already have been conferred on the Guard. This would be based on an agreement between some local authority and an outside agency. The mandate "might flow from" the UN, a regional organization, a joint call from two groups on the verge of hostilities, an international conference growing out of an emergency, or, from a call from a beleaguered partisan group. Once a Guard was established with a ready reserve and the capability for rapid mobilization, the mandate could come from negotiations between the WPG and any of the above. Walker saw this mandate for use of the WPG as emerging primarily in situations where military intervention "appears to be impracticable, inappropriate, unlikely or counterproductive" (Walker, 1981, p.13).

Although the sanctioning power of weapons would be absent, Walker noted that it is generally "organizational power that counts rather than firepower; that is, the power to state what a peacekeeping unit is going to do and then do it." Weapons can interfere with the attainment of desirable objectives. Where this means taking casualties (presumably during interposition between belligerents), Walker justified the sacrifice by noting that, firstly, military commanders have had to face such decisions although their troops were untrained for such an eventuality or even aware that it was a possibility; secondly, it may be an option that the hard facts of the situation require on "prudential grounds"; and, thirdly, "an armed group ordered not to fire may be rendered immobile, but a group *known to be unarmed* still have a chance to take initiative" (Walker, 1981, p.21)

During a meeting with the work team of the Cyprus Resettlement Project in 1973, leading peacekeeping expert Michael Harbottle suggested that a WPG could take one of three organizational forms: that of an *ad hoc* project, a specialized agency or a political agency. Walker, in his elaboration (Walker, 1981, pp.33-36), stated that an *ad hoc* group can be formed most easily to meet the challenge of a crisis situation. However, it would not have the advantage of careful planning and a lack of training would leave it with the problems faced by UN soldiers who overnight have to become peacekeepers. Further it would have difficulty in raising funds unless a dramatic situation had already occurred.

A specialized agency would be one that was known to have certain capabilities such as a set of plans and procedures, rosters of available experts, periodic consultations and assessment meetings, established relationships with key individuals and groups in the political arena, as well as the capability to develop a ready reserve. Such an agency would be open to invitations to undertake actions and would be the most appropriate agency to undertake UN mandated missions. The "specialized agency" seemed to have some drawbacks however. It could become "excessively technical" and "nonpolitical" in such a way as to render it incapable of "certain political initiatives that can be critical in a rapidly escalating conflict." Further, if it became excessively costly and reached the point that it had to rely on governments for the necessary funds, it "might run afoul of the same political obstacles endemic in UN operations."

Walker believed that the idea of a political agency could lead to the most optimistic of the possible scenarios for the future shape of the WPG. It would arise "if the forces of nonviolence enter a rapid growth period in several parts of the world." The hope was that there would be a progression in the development of the Guard through three categories: "starting with ad hoc projects, leading onto a specialized agency which would coexist with a later political group and be aided by it" (Walker, 1981, p.33).

In the early 1960s the World Peace Brigade (WPB) had been set up as such a group with the purpose of projecting the idea and practice of nonviolent intervention on the world scene through actions that could "make a difference," and of building a world movement based on nonviolence as a political force. According to Walker, such political versions of the Guard would have "a commitment to combat imperialism, colonialism, oppression of minorities or egregious threats to peace." Somehow such a team would still be "capable of nonpartisan action" and although "tilting emotionally toward one side" would nevertheless be capable "of scrupulous fairness in the service of a peacekeeping mission" (Walker, 1981, p.35).

From the time of the World Peace Brigade onwards, the constructive, peacebuilding side of operations was stressed, Walker noted that even in Cyprus, where both sides welcomed the help of the Cyprus Resettlement Project, a thick UN file of proposals for technical and educational aid remained unimplemented because of the political implications: "Mild UN attempts to help one side were severely criticized by the other, as partisan or not exactly comparable" (Walker, 1981, p.50).

The Walker model of a peace army seems to be saddled with contradictions that had not been clearly thought through. In any case Walker himself admitted that "a World Peace Guard as a political agency could be organized only in a growth period of the forces of nonviolent action." Without this, funds, resources, personnel and energy for such a project would be lacking.

Whatever the nature of the Guard, until the end of the Cold War it was difficult to see how it could operate where either the Great Powers or their interests were involved. The questions of whose peace, and what kind of peace is to be kept, remained.

Walker did see solutions to this dilemma. He claimed that the constructive works question may be resolved by way of parallel action. That is, where the WPG identifies special needs it can "pave the way quietly for initiative by other groups, national or international," becoming directly involved in such work itself only when the need "encompasses areas in both jurisdictions, where the Peace Guard could facilitate a coordinated effort." Further, he believed that people's brigades could be composed from the region itself in such a way as to combine "a force from below with dedicated but nonpartisan peacekeepers who enlist for such a cause." And, finally, he replied to his critics that there is a need to "recognize that to some degree the problem is beyond complete resolution, and that every conflict will have to be adjudged in context" (Walker, 1981, pp.52-53).

As Walker wrote on the topic and others were actively trying to popularize the idea internationally, still others were equally diligent in their efforts to develop a peace force linked to the United Nations. One of these attempts got under way in 1978 when Raymond Magee, one of the originators of the American Peace Corps concept, helped found the organization "Peaceworkers." Peaceworkers tried to convince the UN to develop its own peacekeeping/peacemaking force on the peace team model. The proposed UN Volunteer Peaceworkers Service was to send teams of peaceworkers to conflict areas where they would assist with arbitration and mediation, provide unarmed buffer forces if necessary, undertake reconciliation work, and engage in relief work. In order to press for the resolution of a conflict, the teams could organize nonviolent actions in the form of marches, fasts and civil disobedience.

The Manifestation of the Vision
The earlier part of this history of visionary proposals paved the way for actualization of the peace team idea beginning at the Triennial Conference of the War Resisters' International at Gandhigram in India in December 1960. Radical pacifists from the USA and from Europe, peace organizations from Europe, Africa and the USA and the Shanti Sena combined "to set up the machinery necessary for initiating a founding conference for a world peace brigade" (Olson, 1964, p.34). And the legacy of the World Peace Brigade that resulted from these conferences are the many nonviolent cross-border intervention initiatives that are currently working in the world's trouble spots.

The World Peace Brigade. The founding conference of the World Peace Brigade was held in the town of Brummana, on the outskirts of Beirut in the Lebanon, immediately following Christmas of 1961. Fifty-five delegates "from all major non-aligned groups and constructive program agencies" (Olson, 1964, p.34), representing thirteen countries, gathered in order to "establish a World Peace Brigade for Nonviolent Action, and to plan its initial projects" (Deming, 1971, p.92).

Proposals concerning the work to be undertaken by the Brigade started to emerge before the conference convened. Indian Shanti Sena leader Jayaprakash Narayan saw the WPB reflecting the Shanti Sena's work of providing a nonviolent alternative to the police force as well as a nonviolent alternative to the army. He saw the long term value of such a force as more than what it could actually achieve by way of immediate peacekeeping. For JP the changes in ways of thinking that it could initiate were of equal importance:

> The only existing agency for maintaining world peace, the United Nations, is employing nothing but armed forces to achieve peace; and no one sees any contradiction in that. The very idea that it is possible to achieve peace through a non-violent force is absent from the minds of both the peoples and their governments. The emergence of a World Peace Brigade would give that idea a concrete form. That might become a landmark in the world's quest for peace (*Muste Papers*, Box 39, Folder 28).

An Indian "Preparatory Conference on the World Peace Brigade," held in Varanasi on 31 October and 1 November, concluded that the WPB should not undertake purely relief or service projects like "sending trained volunteers for work in developing countries," and War Resisters' International (WRI) Secretary, Arlo Tatum, stated that the WPB "must become specific if it is to exist in the world;" that already at the founding conference they had to put up "concrete proposals if only for rejection and substitution." He suggested that the international functions of the Brigade should include border patrols in troubled areas, the offer of volunteers to any nation prepared to disarm, the inspection and control of disarmament agreements, the undertaking of fact-finding missions and development of an information network so that pre-emptive measures could be taken before crisis situations develop (Tatum, 1961, pp.3-4).

At the conference itself it was realized that there was a need to emphasize a program which satisfied the strong feelings of both the Cold War actionists and the constructive programists. It was consequently decided that two projects should be planned—one in the area of national liberation in Africa and the other against preparation for war by the superpowers. Some of the 55 delegates were concerned lest the actions of the Brigade be negative, or shallow, or all protest. The importance of reconciliation and service was stressed. Although by the end of the five day meeting neither of the initial projects had taken final form, a statement of principles was issued on New Year's Day, 1962. Those principles stated that "The World Peace Brigade is constituted to band together those who respond to this call and seek to bring the liberating and transforming power of non-violence to bear more effectively on our world." Besides organizing the Brigade for anti-Cold War action, the conference set forth as one of its aims the revolutionizing of "the concept of revolution itself by infusing into the method of resisting injustice the qualities which insure the preservation of human life and dignity and to create the conditions necessary for peace." The idea was to form a disciplined core of people, from many countries, who had already proved themselves in local actions (in order to discourage the recruitment of those simply seeking adventure), who could be brought together in numbers sufficient to be effective "in situations of potential or actual conflict, internal and international" (quoted in Weber, 1993, p.51).

The Brigade was constituted in three regions under co-chairs Jayaprakash Narayan (Asia), the veteran US peace movement leader A.J.Muste (America), and Scottish clergyman and a leading figure in Britain's anti-nuclear weapons Committee of 100, Michael Scott (Europe). The regions recruited volunteers from within their area in order to make up an Emergency Force that was ready to go anywhere in the world on 24 hours' notice. Others held themselves in a Ready Reserve, committed to consider any action call. All Brigade volunteers were to undergo training in local units or in the regional training center.

However, according to an insider, Indian Shanti Sainik (and later Secretary of the WRI) Devi Prasad, the structural foundations and preparations for the Brigade were not adequately put into place at the beginning (Prasad, 1971, p.2). It attempted to operate before it was ready. In its few short years of existence the WPB only managed to conduct three projects—the proposed Northern Rhodesia March, the *Everyman III* voyage and the Delhi to Peking Friendship March—none of them particularly successful.

Following the Beirut conference an Indian delegate of the WPB travelled in eastern and central Africa to determine the work of the Brigade and to offer its services to African leaders to help them "to keep the pace of revolution going and to keep that revolution non-violent" (Olson, 1964, p.36).

At this time a political crisis was brewing in the region as Zambia (Northern Rhodesia) demanded national independence from the white dominated Central African Federation. Prime Minister Sir Roy Welensky was equally adamant in his desire to maintain the *status quo*.

Kenneth Kaunda, leader of the multi-racial Zambian United National Independence Party and then still a firm advocate of nonviolence, was planning a general strike because of Britain's lack of action on promised elections for majority rule in Zambia.

The WPB had meanwhile established a training center in Dar es Salaam, Tanganyika, from where they offered to mobilize thousands of marchers, mainly Africans but also others from around the world, in an international Freedom March that would cross the Tanganyikan border into Northern Rhodesia in the face of Federal Rhodesian troops if progress on the independence question was not made.

The aim of the march was many-faceted. It was to dramatize the Zambian political situation to the world, provide a useful example of the value of nonviolent direct action to militant Africans who were increasingly embracing violence to achieve their desired goals, and to undertake such constructive projects as organizing house construction and sanitation teams to work in the border areas devastated by units under the control of the Federal Government and to maintain essential services during the threatened general strike.

The two-pronged plan of the strike and march was never carried out. The massive boycott of the Federal elections left Welensky with a hollow victory when only 10% of the electorate cast its vote for his party. With Welensky's bargaining power *vis à vis* London weakened and with the prospect of the involvement in the march of a number of government figures from semi-colonial and Commonwealth nations and a prolonged strike, Britain proposed new constitutional provisions which Kaunda accepted (see Walker, 1977).

Here was a success of sorts for the WPB. The impact of the threatened march on the politically favorable outcome for Zambia is widely recognized. However, as Olson notes, to some even this success was seen as something of a failure because the march had not been held and nonviolence had not been demonstrated. Prasad further adds that in any case it would not in fact have been possible to carry out the planned march, citing as evidence the joke about the Brigade which was labelled an "army of generals and not an army of soldiers" (Prasad, 1971, p.3). The pressure of other priorities and the shortage of resources meant that after the solution of the Zambian crisis the Brigade faded out of Africa.

Theodore Olson, the administrative secretary of the North American Regional Council of the WPB at the time, concluded that the Zambian project confirmed the African suspicion that nonviolence was mainly talk and that in the hard realities of political action, nonviolence was largely irrelevant (*Muste Papers*, Box 39, Folder 34).

Prasad added that with the proposed march into Northern Rhodesia the WPB was out of its depth. "It was sheer good luck for the organizers," he claimed, "that the project had to be given up, otherwise it would have proved the greatest flop in the modern history of non-violence" (Prasad, 1964, p.1).

The other projects were perhaps even less immediately successful. The peace protest voyage of *Everyman III* was to be centered on the Soviet Union as the Brigade's counterpart of the non-WPB based *Everyman I* and *II* voyages to the United States Pacific nuclear test zones, and as a follow-up to the 1960-61 San Francisco-Moscow Walk for Peace. The ship was to sail from London to Leningrad "to speak directly to the people of the Soviet Union and personally hand out...50,000 leaflets printed in Russian" (Prasad, 1971, p.3). If permission was obtained, the sailing trip was to continue to Moscow by canal and the protesters were to spend four to six weeks in the Soviet Union to challenge the population to protest against nuclear weapons testing by all nations including their own. If entry was forbidden, the crew planned to enter the USSR by means that were illegal but nonviolent.

The ship was not allowed to berth in Leningrad, and when it was threatened with being towed out to sea the crew tried to jump ashore but were restrained by guards. As towing commenced, an attempt was made to scuttle the boat and three crew members tried to swim ashore. They were prevented from doing so by the authorities.

Olson notes that the "fuzzy symbolism of the vessel's name... was...representative of the unclear thinking in WPB" since it become involved "in a rather standard pacifist anti-nuclear protest voyage" (Olson, 1964, p.39). Even Charles Walker, a founding member of the WPB and chief proponent of the peace brigade idea, had to admit that instead of "putting the European Council in business" the project, which resulted in heated dispute, "left bitter memories and after-effects" (Walker, 1982).

The third and final action of the WPB, the Delhi to Peking Friendship March, occurred largely by default. Following the Sino-Indian border clash of October 1962, Jayaprakash Narayan wanted to personally lead a band of Shanti Sainiks into the battle area "to offer nonviolent resistance to the aggressor and to intervene and appeal to both sides to stop the fighting" (Scarfe and Scarfe, 1975, p.380). When asked whether the Shanti Sainiks should go to the front to meet the Chinese aggression, senior Gandhian Vinoba Bhave replied that it would be foolish to do so.

This plan brought out serious divisions and led to heated arguments in the till-then seemingly united Gandhian movement (Weber, 1990).

Vinoba appeared to many to be supporting the official "patriotic" view of the war by pushing for energies to be put into "a narrowly-conceived constructive program" (Olson, 1964, p.39).

This less than unequivocal opposition to the war policies of the Government caused "keen disappointment among western pacifists" who "have even characterized the peace army [i.e. the Gandhian Shanti Sena]...as a non-violent department of the government" (Tandon, 1965, pp.157-158). Eventually JP "was forced back upon the World Peace Brigade for any attempt at mediation in the border dispute with China" (Scarfe and Scarfe, 1975, p.382).

An international team of 19 marchers, including 11 Indians and five Americans, led by Michael Scott, departed on 1 March 1963 from Rajghat, in New Delhi, the place of Mahatma Gandhi's cremation. The march across northern India was at times met with demonstrations that labelled the exercise as traitorous. Despite media criticism for having a pro-Chinese bias, had unsympathetic questions asked about it by right-wing politicians in both the Uttar Pradesh Legislative Assembly and the Indian Parliament, and criticism from Vinoba, it attracted large and usually supportive crowds.

Although a lengthy letter was sent to the China Peace Committee soon after the commencement of the march, Chinese reactions were hostile from the outset. In part at least this was because of JP's involvement in the march. The Chinese had labelled JP "a notorious ultra anti-Chinese element" and "a notorious reactionary Indian politician brought up in the lap of US imperialism," because of his vigorous condemnation of the Chinese invasion and takeover of Tibet ("Two Statements," 1963, p.3). Being refused permission to enter China, or even Burma, East Pakistan or Hong Kong, eventually this project, too, petered out in the eastern Indian state of Assam.

Olson, in his assessment during the dying phases of the venture, noted that the march "remained a tiny witness project, unable to break out of the pattern of the past. It absorbs all the meager resources of the Brigade. It supplies no picture of the dynamic of non-violence" (Olson, 1964, p.40).

Ed Lazar, veteran of the San Francisco-Moscow march and crew member of *Everyman I*, who was with the march until the end, produced a detailed assessment of it for the Assam Friendship March Conference held in January 1964. He concluded that while his belief was that nonviolent organizations could only be developed through action, he had realized that the action had to be within the "limits of reach" of the organization and that, first, there had to be a solid base to work from:

> The WPB has no such base of support as yet; at present it is an idea with a letterhead. In order to develop from an idea to a real international shanti sena it seems to me that there first must be developed local, regional and national shanti sena. A very short term project is possible with a top heavy international group but weakness at the base becomes increasingly apparent with the passage of time, which makes sustained international shanti sena at this time extremely difficult if not self defeating. As the idea of shanti sena becomes more real in local situations I feel the international idea and organization will command more respect which is in many ways essential for effectiveness (*Muste Papers*, Box 41, Folder 3).

Michael Scott also felt that the "scope and concept" of the Brigade had proved to be different from his original conception becoming "only a kind of launching pad for projects involving small teams of people in conflict areas." He was not enthusiastic about the *Everyman III* voyage and came to believe that his "early misgivings about the march to China were justified." He concluded nevertheless that "There is a future...for a kind of international peace force and...the UN will stand in need of such a force as time goes on and it may be that this should be organized separately from the UN itself" ("Letters and other information," 1963, p.5).

After about two years of "operation," without being formally disbanded, the World Peace Brigade simply faded away. Without the stimulus of dramatic action as an immediate prospect it was not possible for the WPB to recruit and train volunteers for further peacekeeping work (Olson, 1964, p.38). Its base had not been expanded to the stage where it could be self-perpetuating and as the Sino-Indian war was producing a crisis among the large Indian contingent, much of the US leadership turned their attention to the civil rights movement back home. Competition for scarce funds became intense and JP claimed that the underestimation of the costs of international organization and the lack of mechanisms to allow ease of consultation at the international level added to the Brigade's problems in to becoming a viable organization.

In October 1965 the New England Committee for Non-Violent Action organized an extended training program in the USA with the intention of taking the first step towards the re-creation of a WPB style international nonviolent peacekeeping corps. The organizers, Robert Swann and Paul Salstrom, envisaged the corps undertaking actions like the nonviolent "invasion" of South Africa that had earlier been mooted by the Brigade. One of the strategies for organizing the corps was to attract the alumni of the US Peace Corps into a "parallel" nonviolent, nongovernment controlled organization (Swann and Salstrom, 1965). However, the World Peace Brigade was not yet ready for resurrection.

The Shanti Sena and the War with China. The most heated debate on the value of nonviolent interposition followed close on the foundation of the WPB when the Indian Gandhian movement had to decide how to respond to the Chinese invasion in October of 1962 (see Weber, 1990). The Gandhian leadership split over the issue with JP wanting to lead a group of Shanti Sainiks to place themselves between the opposing forces and Vinoba Bhave who quickly admitted that he suspected that China was the aggressor and claimed that the best "defence measure" was Gramdan (his "village gift" movement that sought to create sharing, cooperative villages) rather than direct intervention.

JP was unwilling to criticize Vinoba, then the undisputed leader of the Gandhian movement, and this left him in an untenable position. He went as far as tendering his resignation as chairman of the Shanti Sena and eventually was forced to rely on the World Peace Brigade to initiate a diluted form of nonviolent action, the previously described Delhi to Peking Friendship March.

Vinoba knew that with the numbers available the proposed intervention between the opposing forces would not have proved effective, could not be supported by the government, and that "attempts to organize non-violent resistance by the Shanti Sena would arouse public hostility and react on the movement's other activities." The JP supporters, on the other hand, felt that "unless the movement is prepared to risk offending the government and the chauvinists, it will be discredited as the vanguard of the non-violent revolution" (Ostergaard & Currel, 1971, p.257). At a conference of Gandhian workers in Tamilnadu in May 1963, following the Chinese withdrawal without any peace effort on the part of the Shanti Sainiks, JP added that "the tragedy of the situation is that India is just adopting the same method against which we have been advising others" (Narayan, 1963, p.5).

Vinoba knew that state power rested on military support, and consequently was of the belief that "the citizens of a country which maintains an army have no right to conduct satyagraha in another country" (Tandon, 1965, p.195) and that wars would only cease when a world government came into existence. There were two alternate ways to bring this about. Firstly, the United Nations had to be strengthened so that it could boast an army bigger than that of either the United States or the USSR, or, more practically, it had to raise a large peace army that would interpose itself between warring factions. This was the basis of his periodic offers to raise 100,000 Indian volunteers for a UN peace force. Secondly, the causes of war had to be removed by bringing about mutual goodwill between people through a spiritual revolution that would ultimately make the coercive apparatus of the state, and eventually the state itself, redundant.

Vinoba admitted that one of the most significant questions to be asked was whether a situation could be achieved where satyagrahis could "go to the theater of war and, facing bullets, offer nonviolent resistance" (Shah, 1985, p.76). However, rather than pushing for the creation of an international Shanti Sena, Vinoba preferred that "fellow-pilgrims the world over" create model units of the Shanti Sena in their own countries (Ram, 1962, p.499).

During its active years (prior to Indira Gandhi's "emergency" imposed in 1975) the Shanti Sena regularly undertook peacekeeping work in riot situations in India but it never again attempted to field an interpositionary peacekeeping force in the international arena (although some leading sainiks did serve in the non-partisan reconciliation and development oriented Cyprus Resettlement Project).

Non-Violent Action in Vietnam. With the United Nations peacekeeping forces expected to take care of non-partisan peacekeeping, the focus shifted back to more second-party grassroots approaches. In 1967, at the height of the Vietnam war, an English group planned to place a team of nonviolent volunteers in US target areas in North Vietnam in order to demonstrate "opposition to American aggression and to share the dangers of bombardment with the Vietnamese people" (Arrowsmith, 1972, p.4). Originally some of the members of NVAV (Non-Violent Action in Vietnam) had a grander vision, seeing the aim of such an action as trying to halt the bombing (and hence the war) and saw particular significance in the fact that

> it would be a serious attempt, for the first time in history, by a sizeable body of people to intervene non-violently on the spot in an actual war occurring thousands of miles away from where they lived. Thus it could put active pacifism—non-violent resistance—on the map as a potentially viable way of settling major conflicts to a greater extent than ever before (Arrowsmith, 1972, p.10).

NVAV had difficulty raising funds or capturing public attention. Much time was spent debating not only the merit of the tactics to be employed but often also the strategic aims of the project itself. Although problems were encountered obtaining the required permission from the various governments involved, in January 1968 a team of twenty-six (including the Reverend Michael Scott) left London for Cambodia. They had little prospect of forward passage to Vietnam or even of reaching war-torn areas on the Vietnam/Cambodian border where US bombing was destroying villages.

Revising their goals, the team attempted to gain authorization to undertake constructive village rebuilding work in the most ravaged Cambodian district. However, team members ended up languishing in relative luxury at a government facility in Phnom Penh for almost a month, often squabbling among themselves, with only a brief, escorted tour to the border areas, prior to going their own ways; some engaging in rather standard anti-war protests in South-East Asia before being deported back to London.

While NVAV achieved little in terms of its original aims, it did manage to mobilize a team of nonviolent activists and send them towards a war zone. Perhaps it also helped to cause a shift in thinking away from emphasizing interpositionary peacekeeping (possibly as a result of a realistic assessment of the likelihood of success for such ventures) to focus on non-partisan constructive ventures in conflict areas, the approach to be taken a few years later by the Cyprus Resettlement Project.

The failure of the World Peace Brigade and NVAV, and the non-emergence of Swann and Salstrom's nonviolent peacekeeping corps notwithstanding, the calls for such types of peacekeeping efforts in the world's trouble spots continued. During the "Prague Spring" and Soviet invasion of Czechoslovakia in 1968, War Resisters' International coordinated an *ad hoc* effort of solidarity with the Czechoslovakian people. Four teams, representing seven different nationalities, went to Eastern Bloc capitals to distribute leaflets and to protest by putting into practice the very freedoms which the Czechoslovakian people were attempting to defend.

Peace Brigades International and the Gulf Peace Team. Following several world crises at the end of the 1970s (starting with the taking of American hostages in Iran and the Soviet intervention in Afghanistan) and a call from the ageing Vinoba Bhave for a new World Peace Brigade, Magee and Cyprus Resettlement Project veterans came together at an international conference in Canada in September 1981 to again explore the idea of nonviolent intervention across borders. At the close of the Grindstone Island meeting in Ontario, the founding statement of Peace Brigades International was released.

While the vision held by many for the WPB was not realizable at the time, lessons had been learned and it became clear that projects involving small teams in conflict areas should not be seen as a second best option, but rather as an important way of supporting local organizations. Although PBI ostensibly took the form of "a specialized agency dedicated to unarmed peacekeeping and peace-making" (Dijkstra, 1986, p.402), and aiming to "promote, support, and coordinate local peace brigades, based in communities, states or provinces, and nations," in practice it has not attempted to set up any unarmed interpositionary peacekeeping force. Instead, PBI's peacekeeping ventures have centered around intervention in conflict situations by small numbers of outside escorts who can accompany and thus protect local human rights activists.

Besides PBI, there have been several projects that have monitored conflicts at international borders (for example Witness for Peace), provided international monitors for the safe return of refugees from Central American countries (Refugee Escort Services and Project Accompaniment), placed teams with Palestinians in the territories occupied by Israel (Mideast Witness, Christian Peacemaker Teams), sailed into Indonesian waters to challenge Indonesian sovereignty claims to East Timor (Peace Mission to East Timor), sent teams into conflict areas in the former Soviet Union to provide an outside nonpartisan observer presence (Memorial Human Rights Observer Missions), and provided a nonviolent presence in Haiti (Christian Peacemaker Teams, Cry for Justice) and the former Yugoslavia (Balkan Peace Team).

The Iraqi invasion and annexation of Kuwait in August 1990—with the resulting build-up of United States led and United Nations sanctioned, military forces in neighboring Saudi Arabia—resulted in the formation of the Gulf Peace Team. Following the outbreak of fighting during "Operation Desert Storm" and the subsequent close of the GPT's camp in Iraq, discussion among Team members centered on the establishment of further peace camps (in particular on the Israel/Jordan border to guard against an Israeli invasion) and, in a consideration of interventionary peacekeeping in forms other than interposition, to the provision of nonviolent escorts for humanitarian convoys of food and medical supplies to affected citizens in Iraq and Kuwait. The ending of the war overtook GPT efforts to set up the new camp. However, fifteen activists did leave Amman as escorts for a truck convoy to Baghdad. Although Team members were not granted permission to re-enter Iraq the convoy arrived safely in Baghdad, possibly because of the publicized escort operation. Some Team members subsequently formed another organization called World Peace and Relief Teams which not only continued to send volunteers to safeguard shipments, but collected supplies and shipped them to Iraq in defiance of the UN trade embargo. Since the GPT, the main attempt at direct interposition in a war zone was the less than successful, but lesson-rich, Mir Sada action.

Conclusion

Few people are talking any longer of a Royden style "Peace Army." The current ongoing efforts, particularly by Peace Brigades International and allied organizations, are far less dramatic but probably more practical. Work is being undertaken at the grassroots level while efforts are simultaneously being made to interest the UN in providing unarmed peacekeeping forces and a significant international peace corps style organization. Generally the emphasis has shifted from large-scale interpositionary efforts to more modest and practical accompaniment and witness initiatives and the less glamorous peacebuilding and peacemaking dimensions of conflict resolution.

While in the main the vision may have altered, the Gulf Peace Team has clearly demonstrated that the interpositionary vision is an enduring one. Regardless of the seeming failure of earlier efforts, there are always those who are willing to place their bodies between combatants in times of war. Perhaps it is time for these nonviolent activists to concede that Royden may have been right when she concluded that nonviolent interpositionary peacekeeping by unarmed civilians will practically always be an impossibility. From past experience it appears that, at the present time, there is a greater chance of these would-be peacekeepers making a physical difference in some areas of armed conflict by selectively using the tactic of interventionary peacekeeping in the form of accompaniment and witness, rather than continuing with the dream of strategic interposition on the battlefield.

Most wars do not have clearly defined front lines and Henry Brinton's 1932 concern over airplanes, that could overfly such lines where they do exist, is even more valid today with enormous advances in military technology. And even in a situation where interposition is possible it is hard to envisage the resources and personnel being ready to act proactively. If interposition is reactive, as it would have been in most of the past envisioned attempts if they had proved successful, there may be ethical problems with peace activists protecting aggressors from would-be liberators (a charge that was levelled against the GPT).

It would appear, therefore, that not only the most possible but also the most appropriate nonviolent cross-border interventionary tasks are in the realms of humanitarian assistance, witness, accompaniment and solidarity.

This scaled-down version of the peacekeeping vision seems more capable of providing tangible results, as well as achieving the same symbolic impact, with far smaller numbers than are required for interposition. Ideally such actions should be aides to peacemaking and peacebuilding efforts while they continue in their efforts to encourage the establishment of local peace brigades and perhaps to interest the United Nations in the creation of a truly nonviolent and unarmed peacekeeping force.

REFERENCES

Acland, Richard. 1958. *Waging Peace: The Positive Policy We Could Pursue If We Gave Up the H-Bomb* (London: Frederick Muller).

Arrowsmith, Pat (ed.). 1972. *To Asia in Peace: The Story of a Non-Violent Action Mission to Indo China* (London: Sidgwick and Jackson).

Bell, Ralph. 1959. *Alternative to War* (London: James Clark).

Bigelow, Albert. 1959. *The Voyage of the Golden Rule: An Experiment with Truth* (Garden City, NY: Doubleday).

Brinton, Henry. 1932. *The Peace Army* (London: Williams and Norgate).

Deming, Barbara (ed.). 1971. *Revolution and Equilibrium* (New York: Grossman).

Dijkstra, Piet. 1986. "Peace Brigades International," *Gandhi Marg*, vol.8, no.7, pp.391-406.

"Letters and other information from the Delhi-Peking March," 1963. World Peace Brigade, North American Regional Council. Manuscript.

Madariaga, Salvadore de. 1960. "Towards the Ideal Federation," *The New Leader*, vol.18, no.25, pp.17-20.

Muste Papers. A.J.Muste Collection, Swarthmore College Peace Collection, Swarthmore, Pennsylvania.

Narayan, Jayaprakash. 1963. *Sarvodaya Answer to Chinese Aggression* (Tanjore: Sarvodaya Prachuralaya).

"Northern Ireland: A Proposal for Nonviolent Intervention," 1971. *Peace News*, 10 September.

Olson, Theodore, 1964. "The World Peace Brigade: Vision and Failure" *Our Generation Against Nuclear War*, vol.3, no.1, pp.34-41.

Ostergaard, Geoffrey, and Melville Currel. 1971. *The Gentle Anarchists: A Study of the Leaders of the Sarvodaya Movement for Non-Violent Revolution in India* (Oxford: Clarendon Press).

Overy, Bob. 1971. "Letter," *Peace News*, 17 September.

Prasad, Devi. 1964. "Some Thoughts on the World Peace Brigade," mimeographed report, War Resisters' International.

———. 1971. "The World Peace Brigade," *Peace News*, 6 August, pp.2-3.

Ram, Suresh. 1962. *Vinoba and his Mission (Being an Account of the Rise and Growth of the Bhoodan Yajna Movement)* (Varanasi: Akhil Bharat Sarva Seva Sangh).

Scarfe, Allan, and Wendy Scarfe. 1975. *J.P.: His Biography* (New Delhi: Orient Longman).

Shah, Kanti (ed.). 1985. *Vinoba on Gandhi* (Varanasi: Sarva Seva Sangh).

Swann, Robert, and Paul Salstrom. 1965. "Towards a Non-Violent Peacekeeping Corps," *Peace News,* 8 October, pp.6-7.

Tandon, Vishwanath. 1965. *The Social and Political Philosophy of Sarvodaya After Gandhiji* (Varanasi: Sarva Seva Sangh).

Tatum, Arlo. 1961. "The World Peace Brigade: Some Specific Proposals," *The War Resister,* vol.9, no.3, pp.3-6.

The World Peace Brigade...for non-violent action (n.d.) Pamphlet, *Muste Papers,* Box 40, Folder 7.

"Two Statements from China," 1963. *Peace News,* 19 April, p.3.

Walker, Charles C. 1977. "Nonviolence in Eastern Africa 1962-4: The World Peace Brigade and Zambian Independence," in A.Paul Hare and Herbert H.Blumberg (eds.), *Liberation Without Violence: A Third-Party Approach* (Totowa, NJ: Rowman and Littlefield) pp.157-177.

———. 1981. *A World Peace Guard: An Unarmed Agency for Peacekeeping* (Hyderabad, AP: Academy of Gandhian Studies).

———. 1982. "The World Peace Brigade: A Look at Some of its Problems," mimeographed report, Peace Brigades International.

Weber, Thomas. 1988. "Gandhi's 'Living Wall' and Maude Royden's 'Peace Army'," *Gandhi Marg,* vol.10, no.4, pp.199-212.

———. 1990. "Peacekeeping, the Shanti Sena and Divisions in the Gandhian Movement During the Border War With China," *South Asia,* vol.13, no.2, pp.65-78.

———. 1993. "From Maude Royden's Peace Army to the Gulf Peace Team: An Assessment of Unarmed Interpositionary Peace Forces," *Journal of Peace Research,* vol.30, no. 1, pp.45-64.

———. 1996. *Gandhi's Peace Army: The Shanti Sena and Unarmed Peacekeeping* (Syracuse: Syracuse University Press).

TOWARDS A COMPREHENSIVE TYPOLOGY

3

CROSS-BORDER NONVIOLENT INTERVENTION: A TYPOLOGY*

Robert J. Burrowes

Introduction
As the world becomes more integrated because of advances in communications and transportation technologies, the number of actors who are willing and able to intervene across national borders—as well as the motives and methods for doing so—continues to multiply. Interventions across national borders by governments, multinational corporations, nongovernment organizations and violent groups have been studied extensively. But, with the exception of those few scholars (most notably Weber, 1988; 1993; and 1996) doing systematic research into this phenomenon, there is at least one category of cross-border interventions that is often either not identified or else it is divided among other categories: those types carried out by nonviolent activists to prevent or halt violence, or as part of a campaign to bring about social change that is contrary to elite interests.

For example, in a report published in 1993, Nick Lewer and Oliver Ramsbotham discussed that category of interventions known as "third-party humanitarian intervention." These interventions, according to Lewer and Ramsbotham, are undertaken in the name of the international community to remedy the denial or violation of human rights. In their report, Lewer and Ramsbotham offered a typology of interventions in this category. According to this typology, interventions are primarily "non-official" (non-governmental, including informal intervention by individuals) or "official" (governmental and intergovernmental) although there are some that are "semi-official" (such as those carried out by organizations like the Red Cross). The inter-ventions themselves may be either non-coercive or coercive, and any coercion may be non-military or military. According to this typology then, humanitarian interventions may be classified as being non-official, non-coercive (for example, Quaker mediation), official non-coercive (for example, diplomatic representations), official coercive non-military (for example, UN sanctions) and official coercive military (for example, the US intervention in Somalia). Their list of possible activities for those who undertake humanitarian intervention includes: mediation, counselling, diplomatic activity, the support of anti-war and human rights groups, fact-finding missions, the provision of economic or humanitarian aid, human rights monitoring, media reporting, military intervention, the provision of peacekeeping forces, the conduct of problem-solving workshops, religious dialogue, research, and education in nonviolent action and conflict resolution (Lewer and Ramsbotham, 1993, pp.25-28, 32, 38). Notably, their list does not include nonviolent intervention itself. For the sake of clarity, and given its rapidly increasing importance, nonviolent intervention should be accorded a separate category.

But even among authors who have written about this category of intervention, there is no consensus regarding the terms or definitions used. In fact, terms such as "nonviolent intervention," "nonviolent interposition" and "unarmed peacekeeping" have often been used interchangeably. This has made it difficult to distinguish, for example, between what Peace Brigades International does and what the Gulf Peace Team did.

As a form of political and strategic activity, nonviolence can be classified in many ways: one way is to distinguish three *contexts* for its use. First, nonviolent *action* can be used to compel reform in a national context (as it was during the civil rights movement in the United States). Second, nonviolent *defense* can be used to conduct a national liberation struggle (as it was in India), to resist and overthrow a repressive dictatorship (as it was in the Philippines during 1986 and in the "velvet" revolutions of Eastern Europe during 1989), or to defend against military intervention (as it was for eight months in Czechoslovakia during 1968-69). And third, nonviolent *intervention* can be used to precipitate changes across national borders or in neutral territory on the oceans. Historically, intervention of this nature has taken many forms and the principal purpose of this chapter is to illustrate the diversity and importance of these types.

The chapter begins by identifying a set of criteria that can be used to differentiate and evaluate the major categories of cross-border intervention; it also briefly illustrates these categories. The chapter then examines those types of intervention that are undertaken by groups with an explicit commitment to nonviolence; that is, by groups that believe that grassroots nonviolent action is the most ethical and/or effective form of political practice for preventing or halting violence, or for bringing about desirable social change.

Criteria for Distinguishing the Types of Cross-Border Intervention
Within the limited context of those forms of intervention that take place across national borders, there are many categories. For the purpose of this chapter, three other criteria are used to distinguish these categories: Who conducts the intervention? Why? And how?

1. *Who?* The intervention can be classified by the nature of the party that carries it out. There are four primary classes of actors: organizations controlled by, and for the benefit of, national elites (such as the United Nations and its agencies, governments and multinational corporations); violent organizations that act on behalf of national elites (including state-organized death squads) or those with a grievance (including some national liberation movements); nongovernment organizations (NGOs) such as those that perform humanitarian services; and grassroots organizations committed to preventing or halting violence, or to facilitating nonviolent social change.

2. *Why?* The intervention can be classified by the nature of its political impact. At one end of the spectrum, the intervention might reinforce the dominant social cosmology; at the other end, it might facilitate structural change and the creation of social cosmologies that satisfy human needs (Burrowes, 1996). To classify an intervention according to this criterion, it is pertinent to ask two further questions: Who gains? And what do they gain?

A party might intervene to reinforce the dominant social cosmology, thus, for example, preserving or improving its capacity to derive benefits from the existing pattern of exploitative economic relationships. This occurs, for example, when governments' use of "foreign aid" stifles demands for a restructuring of the dominant capitalist world order to make it more equitable. In this type of intervention, elites gain by preserving their privileged access to economic resources.

A party might intervene without having significant impact on the nature of the dominant social cosmology. This occurs, for example, when an international aid agency provides humanitarian relief in response to a natural disaster. In this type of intervention, many parties gain (including the disaster survivors who receive some relief and the aid organizations whose work is legitimized) but any structural factors that contributed to the natural disaster (like those that allow corporate logging of the Himalayan forests despite the massive flooding it causes) are left unaddressed.

Or a party might intervene to prevent or halt violence, or to facilitate social change that might be structural in nature. This type of change is facilitated, for example, when foreign activists (such as those working with Peace Brigades International) escort local activists who have been threatened with violence by elites. In this type of intervention, ordinary people gain because the grassroots activists working for social justice are afforded some protection to continue their work.

3. *How*? The intervention can be classified by the means used to conduct it. For the purpose of this chapter, intervention might be military, economic, ideological or nonviolent, although these means are not mutually exclusive.

A party might intervene militarily to defend its own vested interests. This occurs, for example, when the United States invades another country, as it has done repeatedly throughout the South during the past two centuries ("Instances of Use of U.S. Armed Forces," 1969). A party might also intervene militarily to "enforce peace." This occurs, for example, when the United Nations sends troops (as it did to Cambodia and Somalia) to prevent fighting. And a party might intervene militarily to defend or promote a political cause. This occurs, for example, when foreign governments supply military weapons to local terrorist groups (such as death squads composed of police), or when a revolutionary organization uses guerilla warfare.

A party might intervene economically to secure benefits or to provide development assistance. This occurs, for example, when multinational corporations invest in the economies of the South to secure access to indigenous resources (such as cheap labor, minerals or rainforests), or when development organizations (such as Oxfam) provide resources to impoverished people to facilitate community development.

A party might intervene ideologically to win converts to a political system or a way of life. This occurs, for example, when Christian missionaries seek to convert people from indigenous forms of spirituality, or when Western culture (including styles of speaking, behaving, dressing and entertaining) is exported to non-Western countries.

Or a party might intervene nonviolently to prevent or halt violence, or to facilitate social (and perhaps structural) change. This occurs, for example, when nonviolent activists interpose themselves between two parties to prevent or halt violence, or when they sail vessels into test zones to prevent or halt nuclear testing.

What is Nonviolent Intervention?
A study of the historical literature reveals that people who practice nonviolence do so in a variety of contexts, for a variety of reasons and in a variety of ways. Some authors have attempted to illustrate this

diversity by developing comprehensive typologies of nonviolence. These include the well-known typology presented by Gene Sharp (Sharp, 1967) and some that are less well-known (Summy, 1985; Bond, 1988; Burrowes, 1996). Separately from these typologies of nonviolence, there have been several attempts to classify the types of action used by nonviolent activists. These have included the classification produced by Sharp (1973) and the feminist classification developed by Berenice Carroll (1989).

According to Sharp, there are three classes of methods of nonviolent action: protest and persuasion, noncooperation and nonviolent intervention. Nonviolent intervention is a class of methods involving the disruption or destruction of established behavioral patterns, policies, relationships or institutions that are considered unacceptable; or the creation of preferred alternatives. The *disruptive* class of methods includes nonviolent blockades and occupations, fasting, seeking imprisonment and overloading facilities (such as courts and prisons). The *creative* class of methods involves establishing alternative political, economic and social institutions such as non-hierarchical cooperatives, organically-grown food markets, ethical investment groups, alternative schools, energy exchange cooperatives as well as parallel media, communications and transport networks or even parallel "governments" (Sharp, 1973, pp.357-445). The creative class of methods is what the Gandhian literature refers to as the "constructive program."

In Sharp's classification system, the category of nonviolent intervention is further subdivided into five types: psychological, physical, social, economic and political. Physical intervention, for example, occurs when the actual physical presence of the activists disrupts normal operations (Sharp, 1973, p.371); this happens, for instance, when activists blockade the entrance to a military base. Political intervention occurs when activists adopt a practice that disrupts normal operations (Sharp, 1973, p.416) as, for example, when they overload an administrative system by submitting an excessive number of documents. In most contexts, as illustrated below, an act of physical intervention also causes political disruption because the nature and/or location of the intervention is symbolically important and delegitimizes normal operations, or because it can be used to inspire or generate grassroots political activity elsewhere.

Using the above classification system, one major subset of the category of nonviolent intervention is those forms that occur, or have impact, across national borders. While the origin of this idea can be traced to World War I, since the 1950s interest in this category of nonviolent action has grown steadily. The many attempts, successful and otherwise, that illustrate the diversity of forms this category of nonviolent intervention can take include the following: the nonviolent invasion of Goa in 1955 when Indian activists crossed the border in support of local nationalists; the attempt by the Sahara Protest Team in 1960 to prevent a French atomic test by travelling by car from Ghana into the Algerian test zone; the humanitarian aid convoys run by Operation Omega into Bangladesh following the invasion by (West) Pakistan in 1971; the efforts by the Cyprus Resettlement Project in 1972-1974 to help restore communal harmony in Cyprus and to assist in the resettlement of refugees; the attempts by Greenpeace and Sea Shepherd vessels to disrupt whaling since the 1970s; the personal escorts provided by Peace Brigades International for threatened activists working in Central America and elsewhere beginning in 1983; the participation of 1,300 activists from all over Europe in the "1990: Time for Peace" actions in Jerusalem during 1989; and the intervention by the Gulf Peace Team (by placing itself on the Iraqi/Saudi Arabian border) before and during the outbreak of the Gulf War in 1991.

As the above examples illustrate, these types of intervention go beyond those that are usually discussed in existing classifications of nonviolent action; they are also different from those types of intervention undertaken by governments, the United Nations, multinational corporations, NGOs and organizations that are explicitly violent. Cross-border nonviolent intervention, then, is action that is avowedly political, but nonviolent: it is generally contrary to elite interests and often carries within it the seeds of profound social change. It is sometimes illegal—that is, an act of "civil disobedience"—and is often carried out in life-threatening circumstances.

For the purpose of this chapter then, and in accordance with the four interrelated criteria (context? who? why? how?) that were outlined earlier, nonviolent intervention is action that is 1. carried out, or has impact, across a national border, 2. by grassroots activists, 3. with the aim of preventing or halting violence, or facilitating social change for the benefit of ordinary people or the environment, 4. by applying the principles of nonviolence. Because nonviolent intervention is a very common but diversely applied phenomenon, I have devised a set of types to highlight its variety. In the discussion below, nine types are identified, and each is distinguished by the intention that guides actions within the type. A brief outline of the origin of each type is also provided.

Before proceeding, two points should be noted. First, although the types of nonviolent intervention that are described below are treated as distinct, there are some actions that do not fit neatly into a single type.

A Typology 51

The purpose of this chapter is not to define a set of mutually exclusive types of nonviolent intervention and to insist that they be used to categorize all actions of this nature. The purpose is to present a simple typology that offers a clearer picture of the nature and extent of nonviolent intervention and, by doing so, to make it more visible. This, in turn, might help activists and scholars to better understand the phenomenon, to analyze it, and to devise more effective ways of doing it.

Second, there are many questions that could be considered in any evaluation of the following acts of nonviolent intervention. Was the tactic of nonviolent intervention part of a complete strategy that guided the intervention itself? To what extent did this tactic complement a strategy for social change being implemented by nonviolent activists working at the scene of the intervention? What was the nature of the political and strategic assessments that guided the decision to intervene? What were the political objective(s) and strategic goal(s) of the intervention? How were they decided? Were they achieved? Which principles of nonviolence (if any) were specifically chosen to guide the formulation of strategy, the development of organizational structures and processes, and the tactic of intervention itself? What strategic considerations led to the selection of nonviolent intervention as the appropriate tactic? To what extent did the act of nonviolent intervention grow out of, and draw participants from, local nonviolence networks (including faith-based communities) that can build on any achievements? Although both better strategy and more effort to develop and utilize local nonviolence networks would substantially improve the effectiveness of acts of nonviolent intervention, it is not the purpose of this chapter to discuss how these might be done.

1. Local Nonviolent Actions and Campaigns
Intention: to take nonviolent action locally in support of a struggle in another country.

The idea of taking action locally in support of a struggle overseas has a long history. It is one outcome of the recognition by many nonviolent activists that governments and corporations by their nature, and because they are the principle beneficiaries of direct and structural violence, will never respond willingly to calls by people (especially those from the South) that military repression or social and economic injustices be ended. Nonviolent activists who take action of this type try to either prevent or halt the violence or injustice directly, or, less effectively, to exert pressure on elites to reverse policies that support it. This type of cross-border nonviolent intervention, which occurs without any activists physically crossing a national border, is undoubtedly the most common, as the following examples illustrate.

From the 1950s to the 1990s, nonviolent activists throughout the world conducted local action campaigns designed to put pressure on the South African government to end apartheid. These campaigns were critically important because, despite rhetoric to the contrary, it was never a priority of Western elites to end apartheid; too many governments and corporations benefitted from black exploitation in South Africa and from the terrorism of the apartheid regime (Herman, 1982, pp.73-76). These campaigns included organized consumer boycotts of South African exports, campaigns to exclude South Africa from international cultural and sporting events, and campaigns to persuade governments and corporations to stop supplying finance, oil and weapons to the South African government. The combined impact of these campaigns was ultimately instrumental in assisting black South Africans to end apartheid.

Since the 1960s, local nonviolent action campaigns have been an important factor in the struggle to end exploitative practices by multinational corporations throughout the South. These campaigns have taken many forms and have often been economic in impact. For example, in contrast to the efforts of mainstream conservation groups that spent the years 1988-1991 lobbying the Australian government to ban the import of rainforest timbers, the Melbourne Rainforest Action Group (MRAG) implemented a grassroots nonviolent action campaign that included much respectful dialogue with involved parties, a public education program, and many nonviolent actions (including twenty river blockades, by swimmers and surfers, of ships carrying imported rainforest timber). The campaign was designed to persuade consumers, trade unions, plywood manufacturers, hardware store owners, merchants, timber importers and others to withdraw from the rainforest timber trade and thus slow corporate destruction of Southeast Asian rainforests. By the time the government had completed its official inquiry and announced that it would not ban imports of rainforest timber, the MRAG campaign had been instrumental in cutting Australian imports by a quarter.

Sometimes, local action can have immediate and direct impact in preventing or halting elite violence overseas. For example, following the Beijing massacre in 1989, the Chinese government set up telephone numbers so that people could inform on pro-democracy activists. Solidarity activists from around the world jammed the lines to stop this ("Protest Calls Ring Up a Win," 1989).

In some circumstances it has been possible to organize local action that has directly impeded a foreign elite's capacity to use military violence. This has occurred when key groups of workers have intervened; for example, when dock workers have acted to prevent warships or military supplies from leaving port. This happened in 1920 when London dockers refused to load the *Jolly George* with ammunition and other supplies for use by the Polish government in its military aggression against the Soviet Union (Graubard, 1956, p.92). It also happened between 1945 and 1949 when thirty-one Australian trade unions refused to repair, load, or service 559 Dutch vessels—including warships, merchant ships, oil tankers, and barges—that were intended to assist Dutch military operations to restore colonial rule in Indonesia after World War II. This action (which immobilized or delayed Dutch ships, soldiers, and munitions in Australian ports) temporarily incapacitated the Dutch war machine and inspired bans of a similar nature in several other countries (Lockwood, 1982). Similar action took place in 1971 when the International Longshoremen's Association in the United States banned the loading of military cargo onto Pakistani ships following the West Pakistani regime's genocidal assault on East Pakistan (which subsequently became Bangladesh). This ban followed an approach by activists involved in a nonviolent action campaign to halt US military and economic aid to West Pakistan (Taylor, 1977).

2. Mobilization Actions
Intention: to draw attention to a grievance of international concern and to mobilize people to act in response to that concern.

The idea of international mobilization actions dates from the 1950s when nonviolent activists recognized the need to mobilize people all over the world to respond to an emerging set of threats that were being generated by governments and multinational corporations and that, unlike earlier issues, were perceived to be global in scope. In the beginning, activists were particularly concerned to mobilize opposition to the nuclear weapons race. Since then, actions have been organized to mobilize people to respond to a wide range of peace, social justice and environmental issues, that have ranged from regional to global in scope. There have been many international actions of this type as the examples below illustrate.

On 1 December 1960, 11 nonviolent activists left San Francisco on a walk across the United States and Europe to mobilize people to work for nuclear disarmament. On 3 October 1961, after covering 5,700 miles, the walk concluded with about 30 activists from nine countries demonstrating for peace and disarmament in Moscow (Lyttle, 1966).

On 1 March 1963, an international team of 19 marchers, inspired by the Gandhian leader Jayaprakash Narayan, left Delhi for Beijing to protest against the violence of both governments in the India-China border war and "to establish friendly relations between the people of India and China" (Scarfe and Scarfe, 1975, pp.380-385).

In December 1989, 1,300 peace activists from all over Europe travelled to Jerusalem to participate in the "1990: Time for Peace" actions. These actions, primarily organized by the Italian Peace Association, were designed to bring Europeans, Israelis and Palestinians together to pressure the Israeli government to negotiate for peace with the Palestinians. They were also intended to mobilize European activists to get more involved in the Palestinian struggle. The actions included "a pageant of human solidarity" by 5,000 women on 29 December and a human chain of 30,000 people around the walls of the Old City on 30 December. More than 100 activists were arrested. Another 60 were hospitalized as a result of police brutality (Clark, 1990).

There have been many other mobilization actions of this nature including the 1962 voyage to Moscow of the *Everyman III* to urge a halt to nuclear tests, the 1963 Quebec-Washington-Guantanamo Walk for Peace to protest the US naval base at Guantanamo in Cuba (Cooney and Michalowski, 1987), the 1982 voyage to Leningrad of the Greenpeace vessel *Sirius* to protest Soviet nuclear weapons testing, the 1983 flight over the Berlin Wall of the Greenpeace hot-air balloon *Trinity* carrying pleas for peace and disarmament (Brown and May, 1991), the proposed 1988 *al-Awda* "boat of return" trip (which was aborted after the Israeli government blew up the ship) from Athens to Israel to protest Israeli deportations of Palestinians and to generate support for the Intifada (Rigby, 1988), the 1991 Walk for Peace and Justice in the Middle East, the 1992 voyage of the *Lusitania Expresso* from Darwin to Dili to lay wreaths at the scene of the 1991 Dili massacre and to mobilize support for East Timorese independence (Mackinolty and Metherell, 1992), and the 1992 Walk for a Peaceful Future in the Middle East (Lyttle, 1993b). The continuing popularity of international actions of this nature is highlighted by the recent conduct of several others. For example, in December 1994 an international team of people from the major religious traditions left Auschwitz to walk across 15 countries on the eight-month Interfaith Pilgrimage for Peace and Life to Hiroshima (Deats, 1995).

3. Nonviolent Humanitarian Assistance
Intention: to provide humanitarian assistance despite the danger and in defiance of the legal, political, economic and/or military constraints imposed by elites.

The idea of providing nonviolent humanitarian assistance had occurred to some nonviolent activists by the early 1970s (and perhaps earlier) when it became clear that there are some contexts in which humanitarian assistance is required but governments or even humanitarian agencies will not act. This failure to act is usually justified in terms of the danger of providing assistance or the "need" to respect the national sovereignty of another elite. Nonviolent humanitarian assistance is a relatively undeveloped type of nonviolent intervention but, as the examples below illustrate, it has considerable potential to make humanitarian assistance a vehicle for nonviolent social change.

From August 1971 to 1973, British activists involved in Operation Omega distributed food and clothing to victims of the West Pakistani invasion of (what became) Bangladesh. Declaring their intention to enter Bangladesh without Pakistani permission, the first mission was detained and expelled before it could complete its work. The second mission, in September 1971, consisted of two teams: one team entered the border where the Pakistan Army was no longer in control and distributed food as planned—the first relief of its kind distributed in Bangladesh by any organization since the invasion on 25 March. The other team entered Bangladesh at a location where it was immediately detained by the Pakistan Army. Subsequent teams continued to deliver relief supplies throughout the next two years (*Peace News*, 1977).

In 1976, the international action group Operation Namibia organized the voyage of the *Golden Harvest*. The vessel, with a crew representing eight nationalities, travelled from England down the west coast of Africa to deliver a cargo of nearly 5,000 books (on topics such as economics, African history and politics, and alternative technology) to the people of Namibia. These books were specifically banned by the South African government which illegally occupied Namibia at the time. The books were collected by people from all over the world in response to a request by, and as a gift for, the Namibians. Apart from meeting a humanitarian need, the trip drew attention to the illegal occupation of Namibia and the active support of many governments for the apartheid regime in South Africa (Woodward, 1978).

Since 1988, the US organization Pastors for Peace has organized more than 20 humanitarian aid caravans to Nicaragua, Cuba, Guatemala, El Salvador and Mexico in support of communities and NGOs that are working for peace with justice and dignity, and in defiance of US foreign policy in the region. In the August 1993 caravan, 14 women and men arrived in Havana aboard a yellow school bus carrying 100 tons of "Friendshipment" aid—school supplies, computers, powdered milk, rice, vitamins, medicines, bicycles, clothing, bibles, and other supplies—from the United States. Pastors for Peace organized this caravan as part of its ongoing campaign to end the US embargo of Cuba. The bus was impounded by US customs officials for 23 days before a fast and barrage of solidarity appeals compelled US authorities to release it. Pastors for Peace—who refuse on principle to apply for a US export license—thus completed their trip in defiance of the US embargo: "a policy that causes a great deal of suffering for 11 million Cubans" (Peace Media Service, 1993). The sixth caravan to Cuba was attacked by US police and customs agents on 31 January 1996, leading to several injuries and 18 arrests ("US Embargo Against Cuba Challenged," 1996).

4. Nonviolent Reconciliation and Development
Intention: to facilitate conflict resolution, community reconciliation and/or community development by participating in projects that encourage conflicting parties to work together to achieve shared aims in defiance of the legal, political, economic and/or military constraints imposed by elites.

The ideas that community security can exist despite conflicts among national elites, and that nonviolent action might be a key feature of efforts by people to resolve community differences, evolved out of the work undertaken by Gandhian Sarvodaya activists in India during the 1930s and 1940s; they stem from the recognition that much conflict is structural in nature and that cleavages within and between communities are often deliberately generated or aggravated by national elites. Consequently, efforts to resolve conflict often require political action and not merely conflict resolution processes that ignore structural causes and elite pressures. By helping one or more local parties to confront injustice by developing a nonviolent response that explicitly incorporates a "constructive program" or community development component, a local community can be united and empowered to engage a more powerful opponent and to seek an outcome that allows a return to genuine harmony. Although this type of work is very common, especially among communities in the South, there have been only the first tentative steps to undertake this type of nonviolent action internationally.

For more than 35 years, the small Puerto Rican island of Culebra was used by the US Navy as a bombing and gunnery range. After years of fruitless official complaints, in 1970 pro-Independence Puerto Ricans decided that the best way to halt this increasingly intrusive and destructive practice was to use nonviolent action; their initial response was to organize a three-day encampment (that involved more than 600 of the island's 725 inhabitants) at the impact area, thus forcing the cancellation of a planned bombardment. Subsequent developments led to the idea of rebuilding a chapel, originally destroyed by the US government in 1941, in the target area with the assistance of a US nonviolent action group called A Quaker Action Group (AQAG). In January 1971, two local pro-Independence groups and AQAG spent three days building the chapel before several activists were arrested and the building was demolished. In response, even more Culebrans turned out to rebuild the chapel. On 8 February, the US Navy tore it down for the third time. At the subsequent trial of all those who had been arrested, local and AQAG activists were imprisoned for three months. This, however, only inspired greater resistance which ultimately led to the cessation of US Navy bombardment in 1975. Many ordinary Culebrans, refusing to be excluded from the celebrations organized by local political leaders—who were keen to stifle the independence aspirations of the people involved in building the chapel—rebuilt the chapel one more time as a symbol of the people's resistance to foreign and local domination (Walker, 1977a).

The Cyprus Resettlement Project (CRP) took place over a two year period from 1972 to 1974. The project involved visits by several international teams (totalling about 25 volunteers) to Cyprus to assist local people within the majority Greek and minority Turkish communities to work together planning and implementing a resettlement program for Turkish villagers that included repairing and building houses. These villagers had left, or been forced to leave, their homes during the intercommunal conflict in 1963 and had "barricaded" themselves in the Turkish quarter of Nicosia. The project was working very modestly but effectively in one village, and thus helping to reunite the communities, when it was brought to a halt by the Turkish invasion of Cyprus on 20 July 1974. Although it was too early for the project to claim any credit for it, there was plenty of evidence to show, in this village anyway, that many Greek Cypriots were determined to protect the lives and property of Turkish Cypriots whatever the respective national governments and armies of Greece and Turkey were intent on doing (Hare, 1984; Hare and Wilkinson, 1977). At the very least, the CRP was reinforcing this predisposition to build local communal unity and to "immunize" this unity against possible future calls, by ethnic elites, to defend "ethnic identity" by fighting other ethnic groups. As events in the former Yugoslavia illustrated yet again, such calls are usually issued by elites intent on mobilizing local communities to help secure objectives that are unrelated to ethnicity or the interests of ordinary people.

5. Nonviolent Witness and Accompaniment

Intention: to create a safe, localized political space so that activists can engage in nonviolent activity.

The idea of providing nonviolent witnesses and accompaniment arose in the early 1980s in response to the recognition by nonviolent activists that one important weapon used by imperial elites to suppress nonviolent struggles for justice in the South is to "disappear" or kill its activists. By providing witnesses who can document and publicize human rights abuses, and by providing nonviolent escorts and safe meeting places so that threatened activists can continue their work, nonviolent intervention of this nature is able to expand the political space available for social change activism. Moreover, nonviolent accompaniment provides the opportunity for nonviolent activists to create structures, organizations and processes that model the new society (Coy, 1993, p.240). Nonviolent accompaniment is a steadily growing field of nonviolent intervention as more organizations undertake this type of work. Some of these organizations are discussed briefly below.

Peace Brigades International (PBI) was set up at an international meeting of nonviolent activists in Canada in September 1981. Inspired by the experience of the World Peace Brigade (Walker, 1981) and the Cyprus Resettlement Project (Hare, 1984), PBI was established as "a specialized agency dedicated to unarmed peace-keeping and peace-making" (Dijkstra, 1986, p.402). Although its founding statement was quite ambitious, its main functions have been to develop political contacts, to report human rights abuses, to provide nonviolent escorts for threatened activists, and to activate its Emergency Response Network (ERN) in a crisis. An ERN alert, for example, might ask PBI supporters around the world to immediately contact nominated officials requesting the release of an arrested activist. PBI has been active in Guatemala beginning in 1983, El Salvador beginning in 1987, Sri Lanka beginning in 1989 (Coy, 1993) and Colombia beginning in 1994.

Christian Peacemaker Teams (CPT), an organization set up by Mennonite and Brethren churches in the United States during the mid-1980s, organizes short-term delegations to act in conflict situations by undertaking nonviolent witness (as a deterrent to violence) and human rights monitoring (Christian Peacemaker Teams, 1994). CPT sent its first five-person team to the Gaza Strip for two months in 1993 (Christian Peacemaker Teams, 1993) and has sent several delegations to Haiti since 1993, originally as part of the "Cry for Justice: Nonviolent Presence in Haiti" project.

The Balkan Peace Team (BPT) was established by a coalition of European-based peace organizations in 1993 to support the initiatives of indigenous peace organizations in the former Yugoslavia. The BPT sends international teams of long-term volunteers to the region to witness and report human rights violations and to provide escorts for peace and human rights activists who have been threatened as a result of their nonviolent activities (Bjorken, 1994; Balkan Peace Team, 1994).

This type of work is also undertaken by other groups. Most importantly, this includes Witness for Peace (an organization that has undertaken another type of nonviolent intervention as discussed below) which has provided personal escorts for activists in Nicaragua since 1983 (Griffin-Nolan, 1991) and, in one development of the original idea, for refugees returning from Southern Mexico to Guatemala since 1993 (Davis and Hines, 1993).

6. Nonviolent Intercession
Intention: to be present in a zone of political, social, economic or ecological violence; to highlight the suffering the violence is causing; to generate solidarity action (sometimes limited to lobbying elites) by grassroots activists and networks in other parts of the world; and, if possible, to stop the violence directly.

The idea of nonviolent intercession arose in the late 1950s because some nonviolent activists recognized that orthodox channels were unlikely to lead to an early end to certain evil practices, even if those practices were highly violent. In practices of this type, elite and official interests usually coincide, rendering the likelihood of strong interventionary action by the responsible authorities negligible. Nonviolent activists who use nonviolent intercession try to either prevent or halt the practice directly, or to publicize the practice as a means of generating political pressure for institutional reform. Nonviolent intercession is a popular and well-known type of nonviolent intervention as the following examples illustrate.

There have been many attempts to prevent or halt nuclear weapons testing in the Pacific Ocean. Although several of these have been organized by US nationals against US testing, many have been undertaken by international teams attempting to halt either US or French testing. In May and June 1958, the US ketch *Golden Rule* attempted to sail into the Eniwetok test site to halt US testing. On both occasions, the US Coast Guard intercepted the vessel and arrested the crew who were subsequently jailed (Bigelow, 1959). Later that same year, the fifty foot ketch *Phoenix* attempted to enter the same area before its captain was arrested

(Reynolds, 1962). In 1962, the *Everyman I* intended to disrupt US nuclear weapons testing by sailing into the Christmas Island test zone, and the *Everyman II* managed to reach the Johnson Island test zone before being boarded by the US Coast Guard (Cooney and Michalowski, 1987, pp.145-147). In September 1971, an international crew of 12 sailed the Greenpeace vessel *Phyllis Cormack* towards the US nuclear weapons test zone at Amchitka Island off Alaska. In 1972 and 1973, the Greenpeace ketch *Vega* sailed into the French nuclear weapons test zone at Mururoa Island. In 1972, the ketch was rammed by a French warship before being towed away; in 1973, members of the crew were savagely beaten by French navy commandos. From that time onward, protest voyages of various types were made irregularly. In 1985, the Greenpeace vessel *Rainbow Warrior* was due to lead a flotilla to Mururoa Island once again. To prevent it from doing so, on 10 July 1985 French Secret Service agents sank the *Rainbow Warrior* in Auckland harbor, killing one of its crew (Brown and May, 1991). And in August and September 1995, a flotilla of vessels from several countries sailed around or into the French test zone at Mururoa Island, as most national elites were finally yielding to forty years of unrelenting grassroots pressure to halt nuclear testing.

Between December 1959 and January 1960, the Sahara Protest Team attempted to prevent a French atomic test by travelling by car from Ghana, through Upper Volta (Burkina Faso) and the French Sudan (Mali) into the Algerian test zone. The team originally consisted of 21-nonviolent activists from Basutoland (Swaziland), Britain, France, Ghana, Nigeria and the United States. Despite three attempts by teams of different numbers and composition, each time they crossed the border into Upper Volta, the activists were turned back by French troops. The French test went ahead on 13 February 1960 (Carter, 1977).

On 27 June 1975, the Greenpeace vessel *Phyllis Cormack* initiated a new phase in the struggle to save the world's whales. The crew sailed the vessel into a Pacific whaling area where they dropped activists into three inflatable zodiacs between a Soviet whaler and its target whales. Despite the obvious danger, a Soviet gunner fired a harpoon over the heads of the Greenpeace activists killing a whale. Film of their courageous intervention secured worldwide media coverage. Subsequent campaigns of this type, conducted by Greenpeace in 1976 and 1977, saved many whales and put increasing political pressure on whaling nations. Since the mid-1970s, several Greenpeace and Sea Shepherd vessels have prevented or halted whaling operations by many national and pirate whalers. Apart from subjecting themselves to great physical risk, activists have been arrested and imprisoned, zodiacs have been seized, and vessels have been illegally impounded by the navies of whaling nations (Brown and May, 1991; Day, 1992). Greenpeace and Sea Shepherd vessels continue to impede the operations of the last few whaling fleets.

There have been many other acts of nonviolent intercession. These include the actions to halt the annual slaughter of harp seal pups in Newfoundland by Greenpeace activists who positioned themselves between the (Norwegian and Canadian) hunters and their intended victims in 1976, and who sprayed the seals' fur with dye in 1981; the Greenpeace actions, since 1978, to disrupt the dumping of highly toxic radioactive wastes at sea and, since 1983, to disrupt driftnet fishing; and the 1989 obstruction by Greenpeace activists of French construction of an airstrip in Antarctica (Brown and May, 1991; Cooney and Michalowski, 1987).

7. Nonviolent Solidarity
Intention: to be present in a zone of military violence to share the danger with local people; to highlight the suffering the violence is causing; to generate awareness of, and support for, grassroots initiatives to halt the war; and to generate solidarity action by grassroots activists and networks in other parts of the world.

The idea of being present in nonviolent solidarity with the victims of war is an old one but it was not until the early 1990s that the idea was put into practice on an organized basis. Despite its recent introduction, this type of intervention actually derives from the oldest type: that of nonviolent interposition. It arose out of the desire to demonstrate that foreign activists shared the concern of local activists in ending a particular war. By travelling into the war zone, solidarity activists also highlight the role played by local grassroots networks in working to end the war and demonstrate the commitment of activists in foreign networks to support them in this struggle. When undertaken by foreign activists who are well connected to their domestic grassroots networks, this type of nonviolent intervention might also inspire increased resistance to the war back home. Nonviolent intervention of this type is based on the recognition that it is local activists who usually know how to most effectively resist the military violence that is occurring and that it is their initiatives that should guide solidarity activity by grassroots networks elsewhere. There are several recent examples of this type of nonviolent intervention.

In April-May 1992, a team of international activists joined hundreds of Cambodians, including many Buddhist clergy, as they walked through the war-ravaged countryside between the Thai border and Phnom Penh in the first Dhammayietra to promote peace and reconciliation in Cambodia (Bernstein and Moser, 1992). International participation in these cross-country walks, again through areas in which there was fighting between Cambodian government troops and the Khmer Rouge, was also a feature of the Dhammayietras held in 1993 and 1994. A monk and a nun were killed in crossfire, and several people were injured, during the 1994 walk (Bernstein, 1994). The 1995 Dhammayietra was timed to accompany the Interfaith Pilgrimage for Peace and Life as it crossed Cambodia on its way to Hiroshima.

On 11 December 1992, an international contingent of 500 people calling themselves Solidarity for Peace in Sarajevo, travelled into Sarajevo (in the former Yugoslavia), spent the night there, and then distributed food, medicines and toys to the four major religious groups who lived in the besieged city (Lyttle, 1993a).

In August 1993, about 2,000 people from many countries arrived in Split, on Croatia's Adriatic coast, to join the project Mir Sada/We Share One Peace which hoped to establish peace camps in three cities in Bosnia that were under the control of different parties in the war: Sarajevo, under Muslim control, Kisseljak, under Croatian control, and Ilidza, under Serbian control. After much fruitless discussion and despite the debilitating impact of inadequate leadership, poor organization and, incredibly, the withdrawal of the two organizations that generated the project, Mir Sada survived in skeletal form to accomplish a much more modest objective. On 11 August 1993, an international "peace caravan" of about 65 people arrived in Sarajevo and spent the next two days, under occasional sniper fire, delivering messages of solidarity and participating in cultural activities (Gulcher, 1993; Lyttle, 1994).

From 1 to 20 December 1993, Sjeme Mira (Seeds of Peace)—a group of 20 experienced activists from six countries—conducted a series of actions in Croatia and Bosnia. The actions included an interfaith prayer service each day, visits to refugee camps, the distribution of a leaflet advocating nonviolent resistance, walking between towns and cities carrying signs and banners, a visit to West Mostar and, for five of the group, a visit to East Mostar. During the visit to each of these war-ravaged cities, members visited a hospital, a school and other important locations; they also left gifts of food and medical supplies (Lyttle, 1994).

8. Nonviolent Interposition
Intention: to position nonviolent activists between conflicting parties to help prevent or halt war.

The oldest form of nonviolent intervention of the type discussed in this chapter is nonviolent interposition. Interposition is usually defined as "the physical act of placing a 'buffer' force between two opposing armed forces in order to prevent an outbreak or renewed fighting among those forces" (International Peace Academy, 1978, p.V/20). For the purpose of this chapter, an interpositionary group might also locate itself between a military force and its civilian target. While the origin of this type of nonviolent intervention can be traced to the initiative of Guildhouse members in England who recruited a small band of people "willing to put their bodies between the opposing forces" during World War I (Weber, 1988, p.204), it was not until Maude Royden issued a call to enrol people willing "to put their bodies unarmed between the contending forces" following the Japanese invasion of China in 1931 (Royden, 1931, p.7) and Gandhi's discussion of the idea in a different context a few weeks later (Gandhi, 1958-84, vol.48, pp.420-421), that the idea attracted its first round of substantial discussion (Weber, 1988). It has gradually gathered momentum since that time.

There have been three major proposals and three attempts at nonviolent interposition. Two of the attempts were successful in the limited sense that the interpositionary team located itself between the conflicting parties.

On 25 February 1932, a famous letter by Dr Maude Royden, the Rev. H.R.L.Sheppard and Dr Herbert Gray appeared in the London *Daily Express* calling for volunteers for a "Peace Army" that would place itself between the warring Chinese and Japanese forces in the city of Shanghai. The force was offered to an unresponsive League of Nations but as fighting spread over a vast front, the project became impracticable (Weber, 1988). Although attempts were made over the next few years to resurrect the Peace Army (in slightly less ambitious forms), and a book was published (Brinton, 1932), the idea eventually faded.

In 1962, the World Peace Brigade offered to mobilize thousands of people to march from Tanganyika (Tanzania) into Northern Rhodesia (Zambia) if progress on the latter's independence was not made. The march proved unnecessary when, following heavily boycotted elections, Britain proposed new constitutional provisions that were accepted (Walker, 1977b).

In 1962, prominent Gandhian leader Jayaprakash Narayan proposed to lead a contingent of the Shanti Sena (Gandhian peace army volunteers) between the warring armies of China and India. This provoked heated debate within Gandhian circles and the Chinese declared a ceasefire before the pro-interposition members of the Shanti Sena could act (Scarfe and Scarfe, 1975, p.380; Weber, 1990, pp.70-72).

In 1968, at the height of the Vietnam War, 26 people calling themselves Non-Violent Action in Vietnam (NVAV) planned to place themselves in US target areas in North Vietnam to demonstrate "opposition to American aggression and to share the dangers of bombardment with the Vietnamese people." Despite their requests before and after arriving in Cambodia, Hanoi refused to issue visas to the group (Arrowsmith, 1972).

In 1983, Witness for Peace (WFP) was established by Christian activists in the United States. Its original mission was to send teams of volunteers to Nicaragua to deter attacks on the Nicaraguan people by the US-sponsored Contras. They did this by living in villages located in the war zones throughout Nicaragua and by documenting and publicizing military attacks on civilians. During the 1980s, some 4,000 North Americans participated in this program. As a result of their trips to Nicaragua and subsequent speaking tours in the United States, these activists were able to educate the US public about the US government's active role in the war, to generate significant media coverage of this involvement, and to inspire much grassroots nonviolent action and political lobbying designed to deny US funding to the Contras and to prevent a full-scale US invasion of Nicaragua. There is considerable evidence to suggest that the work of WFP (both in Nicaragua and the US) was a significant factor in achieving both of these outcomes (Griffin-Nolan, 1991; Sider, 1988, pp.41-54).

In January 1991, 73 people from 15 countries camped on the Iraqi/Saudi Arabian border as part of the international effort to prevent war in the Persian Gulf following the Iraqi invasion of Kuwait. As it turned out, the Gulf Peace Team (GPT) was on this border during the outbreak of the Gulf War. The GPT spent another ten days on the border and then four days in Baghdad before leaving Iraq, where their presence had inspired nonviolent resistance to the war by activists in many countries. After flying home from Jordan, many GPT members spent time informing local populations about the bombing and suffering they had witnessed and in taking further nonviolent action to halt the war (Burrowes, this volume).

9. Nonviolent Invasion
Intention: to invade, and perhaps occupy, a violent (or potentially violent) space to lower the risk or level of violence, or to expedite social change.

The idea of nonviolent invasion probably stems from various practices undertaken by satyagrahis (nonviolent activists) during the Indian independence struggle and particularly the attempts to enter various salt works during the 1930-31 Salt Satyagraha. Although nonviolent invasion might take place for a number of reasons, it could be a direct response to the recognition that elite interests will prevent decisive action by governments to recognize or restore historical sovereignty. And while this happens frequently enough in a national context, which is why many indigenous peoples have acted to reoccupy their land, there has been at least one case of nonviolent invasion across a national border for the same reason.

For several months in 1955, groups of Indian satyagrahis nonviolently invaded Portuguese Goa on many occasions in support of the Goan nationalist movement. These orderly and disciplined invasions led to police detentions, beatings and the killing of several activists. The invasions climaxed on 15 August 1955 when over 3,000 satyagrahis, organized into groups of between 12 and 50, crossed the border from India into the Portuguese colonial enclaves of Goa, Daman and Diu. At least 15 of these activists were killed and 225 injured when the Portuguese police opened fire without warning (*Keesing's Contemporary Archives*, 3-10 September 1955, 14401-2).

Conclusion

Although the physical presence of those who engage in nonviolent intervention is important, their intervention is more than merely physical. As mentioned earlier, apart from any physical disruption, an act of nonviolent intervention might cause political disruption because the nature and/or location of the intervention is symbolically important and delegitimizes normal operations; this occurs when Greenpeace disrupts the slaughter of whales. Or, nonviolent intervention might cause political disruption because it can be used to inspire or generate grassroots political activity; this occurs when PBI mobilizes its supporters to request the release of an arrested activist. In all of these cases, but for different reasons, grassroots activists exercise their power to prevent or halt violence, or to facilitate social change that leads to greater justice.

Nonviolence is an ancient and worldwide practice; nevertheless, new ways of applying it continue to be invented. Consequently, activists will undoubtedly generate new types of cross-border nonviolent intervention that go beyond the nine identified above. And within those types, they will invent new ways of practicing nonviolence.

NOTE

* This work forms part of larger research projects on nonviolent intervention in which Thomas Weber and I are engaged, and I thank Tom for his inspiration and support for this research. I also thank the School of Social Sciences at La Trobe University for funding the research and writing of this chapter. I am indebted to Brian Martin, Anita McKone, Ralph Summy and Thomas Weber for their comments on drafts.

REFERENCES

Arrowsmith, Pat (ed.). 1972. *To Asia in Peace: The Story of a Non-Violent Action Mission to Indo China* (London: Sidgwick and Jackson).

Balkan Peace Team. 1994. *Newsletter*, no.5, November-December, p.4.

Bernstein, Elizabeth. 1994. "Walking for Peace and Reconciliation in Cambodia: The Third Dhammayietra," *Nonviolence Today*, no.40, September-October, pp.11-13.

Bernstein, Elizabeth, and Yeshua Moser. 1992. "Washing away the Blood," *Nonviolence Today* no.29, November-December, pp.5-7.

Bigelow, Albert. 1959. *The Voyage of the Golden Rule: An Experiment with Truth* (Garden City, N.Y.: Doubleday).

Bjorken, Johanna. 1994. "Balkan Peace Team soon to start in Croatia," posted on the PeaceNet conference *yugo.antiwar*.

Bond, Douglas G. 1988. "The Nature and Meanings of Nonviolent Direct Action: An Exploratory Study," *Journal of Peace Research*, vol.25, no.1, pp.81-89.

Brinton, Henry. 1932. *The Peace Army* (London: Williams and Norgate).

Brown, Michael, and John May. 1991. *The Greenpeace Story* (London/New York: Dorling Kindersley).

Burrowes, Robert J. "The Persian Gulf War and the Gulf Peace Team," (this volume).

———. 1996. *The Strategy of Nonviolent Defense: A Gandhian Approach* (Albany, N.Y.: State University of New York Press).

Carroll, Berenice A. 1989. "'Women Take Action!' Women's Direct Action and Social Change," *Women's Studies International Forum*, vol.12, no.1, pp.3-24.

Carter, April. 1977. "The Sahara Protest Team," in A.Paul Hare and Herbert H.Blumberg (eds.), *Liberation without Violence: A Third-Party Approach* (Totowa, NJ: Rowman and Littlefield) pp.126-156.

Christian Peacemaker Teams. 1993. "CPT to Gaza," *Signs of the Times,* Summer, pp.1-2.
——. 1994. "Haiti Team Stays Amidst Violence," *Signs of the Times,* July, pp.1-2.
Clark, Howard. 1990. "Peace around Jerusalem," *War Resisters' International Newsletter,* no.228, January-February, p.5.
Cooney, Robert, and Helen Michalowski (eds.). 1987. *The Power of the People: Active Nonviolence in the United States* (Philadelphia: New Society Publishers).
Coy, Patrick G. 1993. "Protective Accompaniment: How Peace Brigades International Secures Political Space and Human Rights Nonviolently," in V.K.Kool (ed.), *Nonviolence: Social and Psychological Issues* (Lanham, Md: University Press of America) pp.235-245.
Davis, Andy, and Laurie Hines. 1993. "Strength to think of the Future: Accompaniment for the Long Haul in Southern Mexico and Guatemala," *Witness for Peace Newsletter,* vol.10, no.3, pp.9-11, 15.
Day, David. 1992. *The Whale War* (London: Grafton).
Deats, Richard. 1995. "On Pilgrimage in 1995," *Fellowship,* vol.61, no.1-2, p.3.
Dijkstra, Piet. 1986. "Peace Brigades International," *Gandhi Marg,* vol.8, no.7, pp.391-406.
Gandhi, M.K. 1958-84. *The Collected Works of Mahatma Gandhi,* 90 vols. (New Delhi: Government of India, Publications Division).
Graubard, Stephen R. 1956. *British Labour and the Russian Revolution 1917-1924* (Cambridge: Harvard University Press).
Griffin-Nolan, Ed. 1991. *Witness for Peace: A Story of Resistance* (Louisville: Westminster/John Knox Press).
Gulcher, Ernst. 1993. "Sarajevo 1993: If you do not come back I will come and get you," posted on the PeaceNet conference *yugo.antiwar.*
Hare, Paul (ed.). 1984. *Cyprus Resettlement Project: An Instance of International Peacemaking* (Beer Sheva: Ben-Gurion University)
Hare, A.Paul, and Ellen Wilkinson. 1977. "Cyprus—Conflict and its Resolution," in A.Paul Hare and Herbert H.Blumberg (eds.), *Liberation without Violence: A Third-Party Approach* (Totowa, NJ: Rowman and Littlefield) pp.239-247.
Herman, Edward S. 1982. *The Real Terror Network: Terrorism in Fact and Propaganda* (Boston: South End Press).
"Instances of Use of U.S. Armed Forces Abroad, 1798-1945," 1969. *Congressional Record—Senate,* 23 June, pp.16839-44.
International Peace Academy. 1978. *The Peacekeeper's Handbook* (New York: International Peace Academy).
Keesing's Contemporary Archives.

Lewer, Nick, and Oliver Ramsbotham. 1993. *"Something Must be Done": Towards an Ethical Framework for Humanitarian Intervention in International Social Conflict* (Bradford: Department of Peace Studies, University of Bradford).

Lockwood, Rupert. 1982. *Black Armada: Australia and the Struggle for Indonesian Independence 1942-49* (Sydney: Hale and Iremonger).

Lyttle, Bradford. 1966. *You Come with Naked Hands: The Story of the San Francisco to Moscow March for Peace* (Raymond, NH: Greenleaf Books).

——Lyttle, Bradford. 1993a. "Solidarity for Peace in Sarajevo," *Midwest Pacifist Commentator*, vol.8, no.1, pp.1-8.

——. 1993b. "Walk for a Peaceful Future in the Middle East," *Midwest Pacifist Commentator*, vol.8, no.2, pp.1-20.

——. 1994. "Sjeme Mira," posted on the PeaceNet conference *nonviolent.action*.

Mackinolty, Chips, and Mark Metherell. 1992. "Indon warships ready," *Age* (Melbourne), 10 March.

Peace News. 1977. "Operation Omega," in A.Paul Hare and Herbert H.Blumberg (eds.), *Liberation without Violence: A Third-Party Approach* (Totowa, NJ: Rowman and Littlefield) pp.196-206.

Peace Media Service. 1993. "Yellow Bus to Cuba," posted on the PeaceNet conference *peacemedia.new*.

"Protest Calls Ring Up a Win," 1989. *Sun* (Melbourne), 13 June.

Reynolds, Earle. 1962. *The Forbidden Voyage* (London: Cassell).

Rigby, Andrew. 1988. "Alawda: The PLO Boat of Return that Never Sailed," *War Resisters' International Newsletter*, no.219, February-March, p.3.

Royden, A.Maude. 1931. "Reminder to Youth," *The New World*, November, p.7.

Scarfe, Allan and Wendy Scarfe. 1975. *J.P.: His Biography* (New Delhi: Orient Longman).

Sharp, Gene. 1967. "A Study of the Meaning of Nonviolence," in G.Ramachandran and T.K.Mahadevan (eds.), *Gandhi: His Relevance for our Times* Second ed. (New Delhi: Gandhi Peace Foundation) pp.21-66.

——. 1973. *The Politics of Nonviolent Action* (Boston: Porter Sargent).

Sider, Ronald J. 1988. *Exploring the Limits of Non-violence: A call for action* (London: Spire).

Summy, Ralph. 1985. "Typology of Nonviolent Politics," *Australian Journal of Politics and History*, vol.31, no.2, pp.230-242.

Taylor, Richard K. 1977. *Blockade: A Guide to Non-violent Intervention* (New York: Orbis Books).

"US Embargo Against Cuba Challenged," 1996. *Reconciliation International*, April, p.10.

Walker, Charles C. 1977a. "Culebra: Nonviolent Action and the US Navy," in A.Paul Hare and Herbert H.Blumberg (eds.), *Liberation without Violence: A Third-Party Approach* (Totowa, NJ: Rowman and Littlefield) pp.178-195.

——. 1977b. "Nonviolence in Eastern Africa 1962-4: The World Peace Brigade and Zambian Independence," in A.Paul Hare and Herbert H.Blumberg (eds.), *Liberation without Violence: A Third-Party Approach* (Totowa, NJ: Rowman and Littlefield) pp.157-177.

——. 1981. *A World Peace Guard: An Unarmed Agency for Peacekeeping* (Hyderabad, India: Academy of Gandhian Studies).

Weber, Thomas. 1988. "Gandhi's 'Living Wall' and Maude Royden's 'Peace Army'," *Gandhi Marg*, vol.10, no.4, pp.199-212.

——. 1990. "Peacekeeping, the Shanti Sena and Divisions in the Gandhian Movement During the Border War with China," *South Asia*, vol.13, no.2, pp.65-78.

——. 1993. "From Maude Royden's Peace Army to the Gulf Peace Team: An Assessment of Unarmed Interpositionary Peace Forces," *Journal of Peace Research*, vol.30, no.1, pp.45-64.

——. 1996. *Gandhi's Peace Army: The Shanti Sena and Unarmed Peacekeeping* (Syracuse, N.Y.: Syracuse University Press).

Woodward, Beverly (ed.). 1978. *The 1978 WRL Peace Calendar: Nonviolent Struggle Around the World* (New York: War Resisters League).

MOBILIZATION ACTIONS

Intention: to draw attention to a grievance of international concern and to mobilize people to act in response to that concern.

4

THE VOYAGE OF THE LUSITANIA EXPRESSO*

Andrew McMillan

Introduction
> Indonesia has come under strong international criticism over its role in East Timor since the massacre in the provincial capital Dili.... A special investigation found at least 50 people were killed when troops fired on a crowd of civilians attending a funeral.... Meanwhile, the Indonesian military commander in East Timor, Brigadier General Theo Syafei, has established a special task force to deal with a peace ship due in the province within a week.... General Syafei said the task force, comprising soldiers, police and immigration officers, would drive the ship away from East Timor if it tried to enter Indonesian territory illegally.
> *N.T. News*, 18 February 1992

Some bunch of crazies was planning to sail a boat from Darwin to Dili to lay a wreath in Santa Cruz cemetery as a mark of respect for the people who'd been killed on 12 November 1991. And they thought they could get away with it.

According to the press releases, *Missao Paz Em Timor* (Mission For Peace In Timor) was coordinated by students from *Forum Estudante* magazine in Portugal. Galvanized into action by the 12 November massacre, they'd set up a Support Commission to "collaborate in the definition of strategies and practical aspects such as logistics, financing, diplomatic and international law issues, media etc." They set about raising money, came up with a million bucks, and chartered a ship to sail half way around the world to Australia. The ship, the *Lusitania Expresso*, sailed from Lisbon in January with just half a dozen crew on board.

Forum Estudante editor Rui Marques was still flinging faxes around the world in mid February, hunting for support. Student organizations around the globe were hit with literature promoting Peace In Timor as

> an international students' mission that is organizing a boat trip to Timor at the beginning of March 1992. The Mission will also include journalists from every kind of Media, mainly from TV networks. In a symbolic gesture,

this mission will lay a wreath of flowers at the Santa Cruz cemetery, a land which has been stained with the blood of the students of Timor. This will remind the world of the human rights violation in East Timor, the urgency of dialogue, and the need for international action.

The invitation to join this exercise said, "Although the risk is minimal, the students' participation is voluntary and of their own responsibility. All expenses including return trip from their country of origin, board and lodging, will be paid by the organization."

The invitation went on to brighter aspects of the voyage, suggesting the trip would be of two to five days duration in a warm and humid climate and that participants would need light but warm clothing, a sleeping bag and raincoat. A five to ten day stay was anticipated.

Hell, what could be sweeter than a tropical cruise into the old Spice Islands with a bunch of crazy journos and a boatload of nubile young students with delightful accents? I signed on and got the Wild Turkey and Chivas duty free.

In the last week of February, as he concludes his international tour to shore up support in the wake of the massacre, Indonesian Foreign Minister Ali Alatas brands the proposed peace mission as "political and not at all humanitarian." In The Hague, he announces that a decision to ban the peace ship from entering Indonesian waters has been taken to avert "new provocations" in East Timor. The statements are backed up by an immediate blanket ban on all foreign journalists intending to enter East Timor by land, sea or air.

A day or so later, ensuring maximum publicity for the exercise, the Indonesian House of Representatives' Home Affairs Commission recommends that the navy sink the peace ship if it tries to dock in East Timor.

Hard core action on that scale is perfect fodder for the international media and within days journalists are taking up residence in Darwin to check out the scene.

Missao Paz Em Timor is fast gathering steam. Around 70 students have signed on from universities and colleges in France, Japan, Cape Verde, Guinea, the US, the UK, Australia, Germany, Canada, Denmark, Sweden, Brazil, Italy, Spain, Portugal, The Netherlands, China and Czechoslovakia and the major media networks are taking an interest in proceedings.

1 March 1992
The Portuguese have chartered a Boeing 737 to fly the Europeans from Lisbon to Darwin. Its passengers include students, journalists, a Portuguese medical team and a handful of guests led by former Portuguese president General Antonio Ramalho Eanes. At the eleventh hour, on 1 March, their

adversaries pull a swifty. When the crew lodge their flight plan, the Indonesian authorities refuse permission to fly through Indonesian airspace. The flight is aborted and confusion reigns. To get the participants into Darwin on normal commercial flights is going to cost another $A480,000.

After talks with Portuguese President Mario Soares, organizer Rui Marques cancels the gig. Hours later, *Missao Paz Em Timor* is back in business. "Fortunately," Rui Marques tells a Lisbon press conference, "it has all been resolved, with the help of anonymous donors." Half-a-million dollars worth of anonymous donors.

"The strength of our mission," says Marques, "is our fragility. We are just students with a wreath of flowers and a few television cameras as our only weapons."

Delayed by a day, the entourage flies out of Madrid on Sunday 2 March. They're due to enter Australia via Sydney on a regular Thai Airways flight, arriving at 10:55am Tuesday and transferring to Darwin a day later. Portuguese President Mario Soares gives the mission his blessing. "Personally, I can only admire the efforts of those who have undertaken this initiative," he says.

3 March 1992
Darwin swelters in the cling-wrap heat, a slow town of 70,000 on Australia's far north coast, isolated from the rest of the continent by crocodile-infested coasts and endless deserts and hideous air-fares.

It's not the ideal destination for a holiday, but it is the nearest foreign port to Dili, center of operations for the oil rigs in the Timor Sea, and the logical departure point for a voyage to Timor.

The Mission's Portuguese advance team moves into the Mirambeena Resort, a block from the post office, and sets up the HQ. They work quickly, installing banks of phones and fax machines and establishing communications.

There's no shortage of money around here. The mission has virtually taken over both the Mirambeena Resort and an apartment block up the road. The press center is open 18 hours a day and they've annexed the adjoining conference room.

In the early hours of the morning of Tuesday 3 March 1992, standing around the press center at the Mirambeena, half a dozen Portuguese-speaking journalists are playing "spot the spy."

Flanked by fax machines and telephones and a photocopier that's out of toner, surrounded by walls plastered with news reports and letters of support from around the world, standing over tables littered with coffee cups and ashtrays and typewriters and beer cans, the journalists talk furtively, a bare whisper above the hum of the air-conditioning unit and the wheezing of the fax machines.

Earlier in the evening, Reuters correspondent Wilson da Silva, a Brazilian-born west Sydney boy, booked a taxi from the phone in the foyer. The driver was exceptionally quick. He took da Silva to be Portuguese and quizzed him about the peace boat and its mission. How many journalists were joining this proposed excursion into Indonesian waters? How many students? Paranoia reigns. The cabbie's working for intelligence. But whose?

During the afternoon, Portuguese media liaison officer for *Missao Paz Em Timor*, Paulo Veiga, discovered that in his brief absence, a technician had entered his room at the Mirambeena to repair an appliance. Was his room now bugged? And if so, by whom? By the Indonesians who are known to be running a string of agents in Darwin? Or perhaps by the Australians, who are known to be uncomfortable about the nature of the mission.

Like a good spy I tune in and out of their conspiracies and scan the latest press release.

> The United Nations and most Western countries do not recognize Indonesia's takeover of East Timor; the UN still regards Portugal as the governing authority.... The 60 students from 21 countries will therefore not seek Indonesian authority to visit Dili.... They will seek to apply international law by defying Indonesia's right to stop the mission from reaching East Timor, something the Indonesian authorities have promised to do.... The students, accompanied by some 60 journalists, do not seek to challenge or provoke the Indonesian military vessels now massing around East Timor to block the *Lusitania Expresso*, but to carry out their mission of peace according to international law.

According to reports from Jakarta spewing through the fax machines, the Indonesian naval vessels exercising off the coast of East Timor include a frigate, a patrol boat and a landing craft. An Indonesian naval commander, Admiral Tanto Kuswanto, says of his forces, "I have urged them to keep control of themselves. Nobody is allowed to shoot without orders from the commander."

In Canberra, during question time in the Senate, Foreign Minister Gareth Evans urges Australians not to join the peace mission. "I would certainly urge all Australians to think very carefully before participating in this exercise. One can't exclude the possibility that something, no matter what the intentions of the Indonesian authorities may now be about handling such an incident, may go wrong, resulting in risk to passengers."

The Indonesians, he said, were expected to respond to the vessel's presence in accordance with standard international maritime procedures.

4 March 1992
Shirley Shackleton, the wife of an Australian television journalist who was killed along with his film crew by Indonesian troops while reporting the invasion, now 60 years old, grey as steel, widowed for 16 years, has left her books and her dogs and the coldest darkest corners of her grey weatherboard house in Melbourne and signed on to the peace ship.

"I think the Indonesians are perfectly capable of blowing the boat out of the water if it's only students who are on board," she says on arrival in Darwin. "One of the reasons I'm going is to provide a bit of insurance for those kids.... I think there's a huge danger involved in this mission...the Indonesian navy may be just as out of control as the army.... All I'm thinking is that I'll make myself walk on the ship and then it's in the lap of the gods."

In Jakarta, Indonesian Foreign Minister Ali Alatas says he has approached Australia to do something about the peace boat "but we have to understand that Australia could not bar any foreign boats with all necessary documents. What we do now is to watch out for any development on the matter."

Armed Forces Chief of Staff, General Try Sutrismo, warns that passengers on the peace ship will be arrested and deported. "We have already told them not to come. Our waters are closed to them.... We are doing this to safeguard our integrity and sovereignty."

In the broiling heat of the afternoon, the overseas entourage of 86 mission participants fly into Darwin. A couple of hundred local Timorese, refugees from 1975 mostly, give them an emotional welcome. "The group of 86," said one press report, "received pop idol treatment from local Timorese, some of whom roared approval, while others wept as the group arrived."

At an ensuing press conference, Mission spokesman Antonio Ravara rejects the Australian Foreign Minister's suggestion that the mission is provocative, saying "I can't see how it is provocative to have 120 students from all over the world in the boat trying to show solidarity to young people like us who have been killed." Of the threats to blockade the ship, he says, "If they blockade it, we can do nothing. We must wait there, but we are going to ask the world what they think about the blockade."

Victorian Labor MP Jean McLean argues that "There is no reason why a group of people shouldn't go to East Timor to lay a wreath at the scene of the massacre. My government says we're part of Asia, and if we believe that, we have to support the people of this region, not the dictatorships."

5 March 1992

There's a media briefing in the conference room of the Mirambeena at 1400 hours. Flanked by a panel of students' representatives—Nick Woods from the UK, Ian Whitchurch from Australia, Genevieve Appleton from Canada, Marco Antonio from Cape Verde, the wonderfully named Lorne Rider from the US, Yoko Furiyama from Japan and Reza Muharam from Indonesia—Mission spokesman Antonio Ravara tries to explain what's going on.

> The whole initiative started after the massacre when we feel we have the possibility to really do something that could touch all over the world and catch the attention of the media.
> The main goal of this initiative, it is to make one more step to solve the problem of East Timor. We feel the most important thing to do is to show the world the problem, to make sure that everyone knows what is happening. When people know, they will make pressure on the politicians. And we want to make the most pressure that we could to stop the violation of human rights. That is also a key issue here. We all are very concerned with the violation of human rights in East Timor. We are concerned with the violation of human rights anywhere, but the main purpose of this mission is to denounce the violation of human rights and to stop the violation of human rights. Also we think that to solve this question of the violation of human rights, you cannot put it apart from the self-determination of the territory. It is very difficult to solve this question within a dictatorship like the Jakarta regime without giving the possibility to the people of East Timor to self-determination, to get their independence. That is the political background and that is what we all stand for.

In his singsong Portuguese accent he says:

> This mission is a very complicated one to organize. It cost $1.5 million. All these funds were raised by donations. Those donations were given in several countries, mainly Portugal, donations by anonymous people, students, student organizations, mayors, city councils, and businessmen in Portugal, Australia, South Africa, Macau and other communities all over the world.
> We have a ship of 700 tonnes with the capacity for 600 people. It is a big ship. For us it is very important, the safety of this mission, to make a trip that does not put any risks on the people that are on the ship or to the ship itself. We are going to act strictly on the rules, strictly respecting the maritime international law and the master of the ship is the one who will always have the final word on the actions we are going to make.

When he's asked what the Mission will have achieved if it's turned back, Ravara says:

> Well, we have achieved the attention of the world. Since last month, the Indonesian Foreign Affairs Minister Ali Alatas has spoken almost every day about this. You are all here. And I think that is the most important thing. We are achieving the attention of the world. We think that if the people of East Timor is not a forgotten people, if their struggle is not a forgotten struggle, that if there is the attention of the media and all the

citizens on the situation, it will be much more stable and a big step will have been made to solve their problems. At this moment, the territory is closed to the media. Through this mission we want to oblige the Indonesians to open the territory to the media and the nongovernment organizations. With public pressure we are going to achieve that. It is the only way to guarantee the safety of the Timorese.

There's already a conflict of interest emerging here. When asked what he sees as the ultimate solution for the people of East Timor, Ravara replies, "We feel that the ultimate solution is self-determination. They have for 16 years shown clearly that they want that."

Nick Woods of the UK, a sharp young spokesman for the student element on the mission, butts in saying, "Can I make it quite clear that the main purpose of this mission is to highlight the human rights abuses in East Timor. The political solution isn't really our responsibility."

When asked about the dangers, Woods says:

We don't have any concrete idea of what Indonesia is going to do. There are a number of varied scenarios. The thing to remember is that we're not going out there to create a deliberate confrontation with the Indonesians. We're staying very strictly within international law. Another important point is that we have a contract with the shipping company through which the captain can cancel the mission if he feels that we're going to endanger the boat. We're going to be very clear about that. We're not going to want the boat filled full of holes, so if it comes to a point where things are getting very risky we're going to have to turn back.

Rob Wesley Smith, a Darwin scientist who's devoted much of his time and money to the East Timorese cause in the last 16 years, poses a question, saying, "The local Federal member of Parliament, Warren Snowdon, who's been a supporter of East Timor's independence for some time, has refused to support the mission because it will only be short-term and he is saying the consequences in the long term which might be visited on the Timorese people will be on your heads."

"For 16 years," argues Ravara, "they have been killed. They will keep on being killed if we are not going to do something. We have decided to do a clear action trying to stop that situation. And I say again, the only way to guarantee the safety of the Timorese after we leave, if we arrive in Dili, is the world attention, it's to have the territory open to the media."

The argument is fundamentally flawed, given that severe restrictions have again been introduced because of the mission. The flip-side of the coin though is Nick Woods' observation that "if there's been a quarter of a million deaths already, I'd say the situation is already out of hand."

Yesterday, the Indonesian armed forces (ABRI), whose representatives make up 20 per cent of the Indonesian Parliament, introduced a bill that bars Indonesian citizens who displease their government while abroad from returning home.

Perhaps influenced by that move, a decision has been taken by the organizers of the peace mission to bar two Indonesian anthropologists, Reza Muharam and Juhaeri Harapan, who've volunteered to sail on the peace ship. Says Nick Woods, "We had a long discussion about this and arrived at the conclusion that we could take no responsibility for bringing the Indonesians with us, because the threat to their lives is considerably more significant than to the rest of us, who at least nominally have the protection of our governments, however illusory that might turn out to be."

Somewhere out on the Indian Ocean, a 538 tonne Portuguese car ferry, the *Lusitania Expresso*, is still steaming towards Darwin. It's taking a circuitous route, sailing via Christmas Island so as to avoid Indonesian waters.

Under charter to the Peace Mission, the *Lusitania Expresso* and her crew left Lisbon on 22 January under the Portuguese flag. The ship was due in Darwin a month later for a 27 February departure. But she ran into "weather" around the Middle East and progress was particularly slow. Now four weeks look like stretching into six and people are getting impatient, some suspecting that the delays are deliberate, a stage-managed heightening of the tension, time out to focus the international spotlight the organizers are so sure is going to beam down upon them.

One of the mission's star guests, Ramalho Eanes, calls on Australian Foreign Minister Evans to "press the Indonesian authorities to ensure a peaceful conclusion to the peace mission." The retired general says Evans should do "everything in his power" to stop Indonesia from carrying out its threats against the boat.

If the Indonesians really want to pull the plug on this gig before it gets out of control, they could do it tonight, out off the Ashmore Reef or wherever the ship finds itself in the hours before dawn.

Mission intelligence, drawn from dodgy press reports and suspect communications with the resistance, suggests that the Indonesians have deployed a military task force consisting of a frigate, a patrol boat and a landing barge. They've also brought in a team of immigration officials. The frigate, patrol boat and landing barge are exercising off the coast of East Timor, developing strategies to block the protest ship. The landing barge, I assume, is to be used to transport prisoners from the *Lusitania Expresso* to whatever reception area they might be setting up.

The Indonesian Government has already tried to quietly disrupt the mission by shutting down air space for the chartered plane out of Lisbon. And Ali Alatas has obviously been applying diplomatic pressure around the world.

Each of the students (bar the Portuguese who've enlisted the support of their President, Prime Minister and Parliament) reports pressure from their government not to participate. Nick Woods reports, "We haven't received any encouragement from our own governments. In fact I think anybody who's had contact with their own government has been discouraged quite actively. Certainly the contact we had with the British Foreign Office was fairly negative, and I don't expect that they're very happy about British involvement."

In the US, State Department officials told Lorne Rider that there was no point in going on the mission "since the human rights situation in East Timor has been generally on an upward trend."

Given that those measures obviously aren't working, and nor are the overt threats—if anything, they're strengthening resolve—one has to look at the scenarios. The most likely are that the ship leaves Darwin and is stopped on the high seas as it prepares to enter Indo-nesia's Exclusive Economic Zone. Alternatively, it may be allowed to proceed as far as the 12 mile limit, there to be turned back within sight of the mountains of Timor.

They're the most comfortable scenarios, the ones a person could live with. The worst case scenarios are just that. As I see them, through the dark veil of twisting nerves and that slow surge of adrenalin that kicks through the system every time I contemplate this gig, they line up as follows:

1. Incapacitate the *Lusitania Expresso* in international waters on its way to Darwin, thereby averting media coverage of a delayed confrontation.

2. Sabotage the vessel in Darwin, thereby placing the onus and the stigma on the Australian authorities, or at least leaving a measure of doubt.

3. Interfere with satellite and other electronic transmissions, incapacitate the vessel, board it on suspicion of harboring weapons or drugs, "find" something, place everyone under arrest, and transfer passengers to the landing craft for shipping to an island like Atauro for processing and deportation. And in a scenario like that, there's a helluva lot of room for tragic mistakes.

4. Use serious force, provoking international outrage and ensuing that no other vessel would attempt to transgress. (From the popular Roma Bar to the Mirambeena, discussion of this scenario goes off onto wild tangents,

fabulous conspiracy theories involving Suharto's presidency and the question of succession, the macabre possibility that sections of the military could use such an incident to undermine the government...terrific theories from some of the best minds of our generations.)

And through it all there's little comfort in the knowledge that France—a supposedly civilized nation—was prepared to resort to sabotage and murder in New Zealand by sinking the Greenpeace flagship *Rainbow Warrior*.

6 March 1992

As the *Lusitania Expresso* ploughs through the Indian Ocean en route to Darwin, keeping its communications to a minimum, the mission's strategists hunker down behind closed doors at the Mirambeena, evaluating the potential scenarios.

Two days sailing from Darwin, Captain Luys dos Santos reports by radio telephone that an Indonesian military aircraft has "buzzed" the *Lusitania Expresso*. "I estimate that it flew about 500 feet over sea level. We saw the Indonesian flag on it." The plane overflew the ship four times. "I think they are trying to estimate our position, course and speed."

Rattling the Sabres

> It is understood that the Coast Watch service which regularly patrols the northern coastline has been briefed by the defence forces to monitor the confrontation. If needed, Australian naval vessels will go to the rescue of survivors.
> The head of the Territory's emergency services unit was called to a briefing yesterday by defence chiefs.
> <div align="right">Robert Macklin, <i>Canberra Times</i>, 7 March 1992.</div>

> JAKARTA: Indonesia was last night preparing to confront the Portuguese peace ship when it tries to enter Indonesian waters.... Speculation in Jakarta suggests the ship...will be chased by several warships in international waters.... Students from East Timor University have issued a statement rejecting the planned visit as harmful to East Timorese interests and called on the organizers to abandon their mission.
> <div align="right"><i>Weekend Australian</i>, 7-8 March 1992.</div>

> In the Indonesian capital of Jakarta, academics say under the laws of hot pursuit, Indonesia may have the right to chase the "peace ship" into international waters if it broke or tried to break Indonesian law.
> AFP, AAP

> We are not a Kamikaze mission and we don't want to get killed, so we have to consider seriously the issue of security. If they say they are going to open fire, we will stop in that place for two or three days...to create publicity about the mission.
> Mission control statement

7 March 1992
Eight hundred kilometers away in Dili, the Batik curtain's coming down. Deprived of the monsoons, the streets are dusty, the sweltering heat lifted only by the slightest of breezes off the harbor, not even strong enough to tickle the bougainvillea around the Turismo nor the frangipani on Jalan Merdeka.

In stifling houses behind shuttered windows, students are again at work on their banners. A big demonstration is being planned to greet the arrival of the peace ship. "This time the *Bapaks* [lit. "fathers"] won't dare to shoot us, not with all those foreigners looking on." Today, four people, including the village head of the area near Santa Cruz cemetery, have been arrested in Dili and accused of preparing a demonstration of support for the boat. Outside, squads of soldiers step up their patrols of the crumbling streets.

In preparation for the peace mission, the military are cracking down. An extra battalion of troops has been shipped in, bringing the total number around Dili to 5,000. Travel restrictions on people entering and leaving the town have been reintroduced. Cars are being stopped and searched. Strict curfews are back in force. Says Brigadier General Theo Syafei, the new hard-line head of the East Timor command, "This is to prevent people from coming to the city to hold a gathering."

Down at the Mirambeena, things have been moving as swiftly as they ever do in Darwin's steaming tropical heat. The three Greek participants, from the Hellenic Youth National Council, have withdrawn from the Mission, having been advised that it's too dangerous to proceed.

Around the bar, there's talk of running the blockade, of seeing how far you can push it. Cooler heads urge mission organizers not to cross Indonesia's 12 mile limit and to lay the wreathes at sea. "Or, if Indonesia agreed," suggests West Australian guest Gordon McIntosh, "we could send a small delegation to shore."

"We are a peaceful mission," says the former senator, "and I, like the others, do feel deeply, strongly, about human rights in East Timor. But we have to be levelheaded and careful not to provoke the Indonesian navy."

There's a meeting of all peace mission participants in the conference room set for 2100 hours. At 2125, seeing no vigorous signs of activity, I discuss scenarios with a friend by the pool. When we get back to the press center, the meeting's in progress. There's a tap on the shoulder and a Portuguese voice in the ear. "Excuse me, you must leave. No media is allowed."

In the adjoining press room, a pitched battle erupts as the evicted media contingent clusters around the mission controllers, jostling for an explanation. (What the hell are those kids cooking up in there? Bombs? Boats? Bazookas?)

Dave Stewart, the Canadian who'll be coordinating the press room aboard the boat, is struggling for air beneath a rabid pack of newshounds who want to know the meaning of this outrage. Flustered by the onslaught, he tries to explain that it's a closed meeting for the students to discuss the consequences of the mission and to take, perhaps, the opportunity to withdraw quietly, without feeling bullied by the media glare.

In voices that bring a wind of "shooshes" from the conference room next door, the journos argue that since we're on the boat too—if it goes down, we go down—we have a right to participate in the discussion on matters of safety, a right to know what's going on. One of the Portuguese walks in. The pack plunges and he disappears in the scrum.

Ian Hislop from Channel 7, who'll be feeding to CNN in America, threatens to pull all media off the vessel, thereby nullifying the whole raison d'etre of the mission *vis à vis* gaining international media exposure. After heated discussion in the press room and a vote in the conference room, the media is allowed back in to monitor and contribute to the meeting.

The meeting is being convened by Canadian John Millard, a stocky fellow whose awareness of East Timor was negligible prior to the massacre of 12 November. He handles the job well, keeps the dialogue flowing, but after the excitement in the press room it's a pretty dull way to spend a Saturday night.

Notes should suffice:

> Scenarios discussed. Primary "trap" envisaged by scenarios committee is Indon authorities will allow peace boat into Dili to be met by a pro-gov't anti-Port demo: turn tables on internat media.
> Warnings issued regarding potential for arrest, detention, physical abuse & deportation.... Recognize risks: "There's no shame in pulling out now. You've already made a contribution by coming to Darwin."

Each person is given a form to sign absolving the organizers of any liability:

> I hereby declare I take full responsibility for my participation in the East Timor Peace Mission and I will not press any charges against the Mission Organization.... I also declare that I am aware and accept the Mission Organization as the only valid authority during the mission, and I agree to follow its instructions.

8 March 1992

About five o'clock Sunday, this grey ominous afternoon crammed with swollen charcoal clouds, I'm standing on the wharf, feeling very much alone, when the fabled *Lusitania Expresso* finally heaves into view. For a time, way out there in the harbor, it looked quite grand, this big bright yellow, blue and white ship.

Its arrival is greeted by ferries and motor boats and the lonesome sound of horns on the harbor. There are 500 people on the wharf, all milling around; a lot of Timorese, familiar faces from support networks around Darwin, the overseas students and the media. Camera crews hang out of helicopters, homing pigeons flutter out of cages, and the renowned Elcho Island Dancers strut their stuff. The Elcho Island Dancers are *Yolngu* tribesmen from the wilds of north-east Arnhem Land who recall contact with the Timorese dating back centuries.

As the ship gets closer, it seems to get smaller. And as it shrinks, my fear grows. Okay, so the boat is um, kinda small. Let's take a look at this rust-bucket.

According to the official spec's, the *Lusitania Expresso* is a 538 tonne Portuguese car-ferry capable of carrying 600 passengers and 90 European cars or seven trucks. It's an old workhorse from the Lisbon-Madeira run, a veteran of that 700 mile Atlantic Ocean run from Portugal to the provinces off northern Africa. It was built in 1964 and rebuilt in 1973 when 12.81 meters was added to its length. It now had an overall length of 72.97 meters, and a breadth of 13.27 meters. There are nine watertight compartments, but no bulkhead amidships, and it's said she could sink like a stone.

The Australian Council of Trade Unions has called on the Government to "facilitate and expedite the visit of the ship to Darwin," and urged them "to provide any support and protection of those involved in the peace mission." For their part, Darwin's Waterside Workers have voted to work through the night, providing security for the vessel and guaranteeing a quick turnaround in a slow port. She'll be ready to sail by midday. Overnight, they load enough supplies to last 140 people for ten days.

Upon stepping ashore at Stokes Hill, Captain Luys dos Santos looked keenly at the cameras and, when asked what he'd do in the event of a confrontation, frowned and said, "I will have to take that decision on the spot. I can't speculate on that here. I will deal with that problem as it arrives. My main concern will be with the people on board, their property and the safety of the ship.... If I am told to turn around I think I will. I do not know if I will get to Dili, but I will try."

9 March 1992

The organizers say, "We think that there is some probability of the Indonesians trying to jam our telecommunications; it is confirmed they have the technical capacity to do such a thing. Where this would stop all our contacts with the exterior, such behavior would be immediately apparent to the outside world and the total absence of information would attract even more attention."

The statement goes on to reiterate the purpose of the mission:

> Peace is possible in East Timor. The support of the European Community, the United States, Japan and Australia would be enough to grant the East Timorese their freedom. For this support to happen, it is necessary that the world learns the truth about the brutal repression of the Timorese people. We cannot stress enough that this is the main aim of our mission. This aim has already been achieved to a considerable degree. The *Lusitania Expresso* has brought about more debate about East Timor than ever before. This is a major step towards the essential dialogue that must take place if peace is to have a chance.... On 22 January the *Lusitania* left Lisbon. In the face of considerable difficulties it has arrived in Darwin and is now ready to leave for Timor. We strongly believe that we are making a major contribution to the defence of human rights in East Timor. We are counting on your goodwill and support and believe firmly in the prospect of peace in East Timor.

We haven't even left yet and already this mission's stirring the possum from Jakarta to Washington and beyond, with a little prodding from the Portuguese. In Lisbon, President Mario Soares warns that "If things go wrong we must take appropriate diplomatic and political steps to protest and express solidarity with those who have been running a risk."

The US says the mission

> could raise tensions rather than relax them." The US Government says "There is always a chance that someone or something could trigger a confrontation, in spite of the best intentions of both sides. Such confrontations are, by their very nature, unpredictable. The US hopes that the people concerned with the East Timor issue will use non-confrontational means to make their interests known.

Customs officers guard the gangplank as we haul our gear aboard, squeezing through the crush of tears and cheers of well-wishers on the wharf. I stash my kit in the press room and then join the madding crowd, shuffling down long hot lines to the immigration desk in the saloon. Passports are stamped and it's all heave-ho...but no.

There seems to be a degree of confusion here. Channel 7 reporter Ian Hislop, chief head-kicker for the media contingent in earlier battles with organizers, has gone missing. They're sure he's on the boat somewhere but efforts to find him prove fruitless. Departure is delayed for an hour and then two. And still his name echoes through the intercom from the bridge.

A few hundred supporters crowd the wharf; not throwing streamers or confetti, but waving flags and banners, singing, praying and blessing our journey. There's a lot of emotion in that gathering. The people are mostly East Timorese in exile; people of all ages who've lost their families and those who still have family back there, people who have lived with, grown up with the horrors of the last 16 years, people who do not give up hope for their homeland, people who appreciate the importance of this mission, embrace the people from all nations who have volunteered, who've committed themselves to challenge the Indonesians under the banner of peace.

Fatima Gusmao, who lost three children after the invasion, says, "Day by day this boat has given us hope. It's a big chance for our people back home. It is a good sign, a first step for our country. I hope it will get there safely, but if it doesn't, maybe the next one will.... I try not to worry about what might happen to my family in Dili. The boat going won't make any difference to people in Dili; they have been in trouble with the Indonesians since 1975."

Eventually, the missing journalist is located and escorted off the boat by immigration officials. The passport he's presented is out of date. As Hislop leaves the vessel at 7:15pm, the diesels throb and we pull away from the wharf.

Ship of Fools
>What happened in Dili, East Timor's capital, on 12 November last year, was unpardonable. But compounding that criminal tragedy by engaging in mass seaborne thumbing of noses at Indonesian sovereignty is dangerous, crass adventurism.... The Indonesians are adamant that the *Lusitania Expresso* will not violate their territory. The ship's captain says he will not risk the ship or its passengers. Jakarta appears determined to avoid an incident. Australian and American warships on exercise in the area will reinforce that caution. Let commonsense prevail—in the Timor Sea over the next two days, and over East Timor's whole future.
>Editorial, *Courier Mail*, Brisbane, 10 March 1992.

As we push through the night, the twinkling amber lights of Darwin falling away behind us, the press room heats up.

We haven't been in here more than a few hours and already the press room—this bizarre nerve center jammed with radio telephones, computers, word processors, tape recorders, typewriters, swags, ashtrays, beer cans, water bottles, cigarette packets, short wave radio transceivers, hats, caps and all manner of cameras—is rancid. The air is stale and dense with smoke and the hiss and belch of radio interference, ship-to-shore distortion, voices twisting through the ether like sheets of galvanized iron in a cyclone as reporters hunker down over microphones, trying to get a clear line. There are only two satellite telephone lines available for the 40 radio, television and print journalists, and the competition's getting fierce....

The former Portuguese president, General Eanes stops by and looks around. "Is everything alright?" asks the General.

"No," replies media coordinator David Stewart. "Everything will be alright when we are arrested and interned."

They both smile.

Late into the night, students band together, passing cartons heavy with foodstuffs from hand to hand up steep runged flights of steps, down walkways, through saloons, past bars, along decks and into the galley on the top deck, swinging lines of kids heaving boxes along the decks as slices of Dylanesque folk songs drift down the lines.

Here's Lorne Rider from Brown University in the US of A. Lorne's pure American, long curly hair, glasses and a goofy grin. He's been involved in an East Timor information network in the States for about four years. This is his first step through the wire.

"I've come on this mission," says Lorne,

> out of a tremendous sense of frustration with the American people and the American press at not really caring about an issue that the US has an incredible and obvious complicity in.
>
> We turned our backs in '75 when the Indonesians invaded and we continued to supply a tremendous amount of military and economic aid to Indonesia, and some of our leaders do their best to lobby others to generally ignore this question in its entirety.
>
> It's embarrassing to watch our leaders squirm in a mire of hypocrisy and have nobody care about it. That's why I'm here. I've known about it for several years and I just got increasingly enraged. Especially with the November massacre, I really couldn't stand to be inactive any more....

Further along the chain is Genevieve Appleton, a veil of perspiration clinging to the rosy cheeks of Toronto. She wasn't even aware of East Timor six months ago, the name wouldn't have registered. But then she heard about the massacre of 12 November. Shocked and angered and helpless, she sought to learn more about this troubled place. And then she heard about the East Timor Peace Mission.

> My father got very upset. He said "I hope you've thought about this very seriously." I said "I've already made up my mind."
>
> It's hard to explain why you'd want to do something like that, because it does seem like a suicide mission to parents, but it's not of course. I feel the risk is worth it. So many people have died already.

10 March 1992

Through the night, the omens looked bad. The voyage to Timor is a journey of 42 hours, time enough for things to get out of hand.

Newspaper readers in Australia, Portugal and Indonesia awake to front page stories reporting that nine Indonesian warships and patrol boats are preparing a sea blockade to prevent the *Lusitania Expresso* from entering Indonesian waters. The exercise is believed to be one of the biggest since the Malaysia confrontations in the 1960s.

One hundred nautical miles out of Darwin, the ship cuts back to a speed of five knots as, according to the skipper, a "precautionary" move. The media applaud the move: it suggests a confrontation will be delayed 'til dawn when there's enough light for the television cameras to capture the drama.

On the other side of the Timor Sea, Brigadier General Theo Syafei says,

> If ABRI is threatened, I have ordered: "shoot." If there is another incident (at sea or on land) like 12 November under my command, the number of victims may be greater. We will not use violence. But if they endanger (Indonesian forces) and shoot, we will shoot back. If they shoot once, we will shoot twice.

Fretilin's Darwin spokesman, Alfredo Fereira, tells AAP that his sources report nine ships waiting near Indonesian's 12 mile limit with another three forming a secondary cordon near Dili. "It's a show of power more to impress and scare the East Timorese people than the peace boat," he says. An immigration center has been set up on Atauro Island, 32 kilometers from Dili, to process detainees before deportation.

An unnamed diplomatic naval attache in Jakarta is quoted by Western press as saying, "It is a show of force far exceeding what is needed to stop an unarmed ship." A spokesman for the Royal Australian Navy says the position of the peace ship is being monitored "as a matter of operational routine." In Dili, Admiral Tanto Kuswanto, commander of the Eastern Fleet, challenges the peace ship to break the blockade. "Let's see if they can find a way in," he says.

Australian Defence Department spokesmen, Lieutenant Colonel John Weiland, says the Australian military isn't worried about the ship. "The Australian Defence Forces cannot take part in operations against another country without the express consent of the Government. If there was an incident, it would require a diplomatic, not a military, resolution."

In Melbourne, Australian Prime Minister Paul Keating says, "People have got to weigh their right to protest against the consequences of them doing it. And I'm not sure that anything they may be involved with can materially alter what has happened or the response by Indonesia."

I guess it's too late to get off the boat.

The sea is smooth as glass, the surface broken only by the occasional sighting of a sea snake and schools of flying fish skittering away. For a couple of minutes, Captain dos Santos takes leave of his post and entertains a press conference on the rear deck. "Good morning, ladies, gentlemens, sailors and bums. We are at sea. We are navigating toward the island of Timor, the weather is fine as you can see. I am expecting to arrive at seven o'clock tomorrow morning, at about dawn tomorrow morning."

"That'll be at the 12 mile limit outside of Dili?" asks one of the Aussies.

"Yes, ah not Dili. On eastern side of the island of Timor. From Dili I think that is about 125 miles."

"How far are we from Timor now?"

"Well, let me put it this way. I would rather say to you that we will arrive within sight of the island tomorrow morning, okay."

The Captain returns to his post and the journos, pondering his reluctance to divulge our position, race for the phones.

At 12:35pm, a Royal Australian Air Force P-3 Orion flies over the ship. It's a maritime surveillance aircraft with enough gadgetry on board to keep tracking us past the horizon. There is no communication between aircraft and ship. Yee hah! The Aussies are keeping an eye on us. But all they can see is this yellow and blue margarine tub on a laminated sea, a fluttering stream of flags and a whole bunch of people flicking peace signs at the sun.

Somewhere back there, relegated to a shredder in Canberra no doubt, was a statement issued four days earlier by Australian Democrats spokesman on defence, Senator Syd Spindler:

> Senator Spindler said he was concerned that the Australian Government could be tempted to pass intelligence on the ship's movements to the Indonesian regime.... "This would allow rapid apprehension of the peace ship and would certainly reduce embarrassment to both Governments, but would clearly be contrary to Australia's professed concern for international human rights and political freedom of expression.... Intelligence sharing is totally unacceptable in these circumstances and should be ruled out."

On the day of the ship's arrival we'd all noticed a hulking black submarine lurking in Darwin harbor. When we departed, it wasn't there any more and there was much idle talk around the decks about whether perhaps it was following us, keeping a periscopic eye on the back of the ferry. A couple of students lobbed beer cans overboard to see if they could lure it out. But the cans just bobbed in our wake.

There's a sense of gallows humor at work here. One of the Australian fringe journalists, John Tomlinson, has brought his fishing gear on board, figuring that if we're going to end up sitting out in the middle of the ocean for a few days, he might as well do a spot of angling. Such a scenario could well have deepened the conflict. The idea of getting busted for illegally fishing in Indonesian waters wasn't worth contemplating. Standard procedure for the Australians catching Indonesian fishermen is to arrest the vessel and all aboard, impound the boat and burn it, and either jail or deport the offending crew members. It happens about 30 times a year, and I suspect the Indonesian authorities would love to even the score. And what a catch! A 600 ton car ferry impounded and torched because this red bearded maniac's sitting out on the deck with a fishing rod dangling over the side.

Up on the bridge, Captain Luys dos Santos monitors the radar screen. Dos Santos is in his fifties, a Portuguese mariner who took his holidays and volunteered to lead this mission. He's already stated that he'll turn around if ordered to do so. "They have guns, you know, so I just turn around and go back to Darwin. I have no other choice. I am not a hero. This is a merchant ship. It is not a man-o'war."

A couple of the more twisted Australian students wanted to pump him full of hallucinogenic drugs and paint warships on his windshield. Just to test his reactions to stress, you understand. But I didn't think it was such a good idea at the time.

At 3:40pm, an Indonesian Nomad flies over the ship, passing four times at a height of 60-90 meters. "It was taking our speed and course," says radio officer Amadtu Barreira. The aircraft is a Nomad Searchmaster, a short takeoff and landing twin-engined job designed and built in Australia. It's fitted with ground and sea surveillance radar and is one of 12 such aircraft donated to Indonesia during the 70s, the last six having been given in June 1978.

The Nomad's crew note, no doubt, that we're travelling at nine knots, 200 nautical miles from Timor, 170 nautical miles north west of Darwin.

At 4:05pm, another grey aircraft passes in the distance.

The Captain orders an emergency drill. Everybody's passports have been numbered, but still confusion reigns. Trying to sort out which lifeboat you're on from the charts pinned up in the saloons only complicates the problem. There's a meeting in the forward saloon, a demonstration of lifejacket procedures, a shifting of the deck chairs....

We're advised to expect a confrontation at dawn. Says the Captain, "I estimate we will arrive at the 12-mile limit on the far eastern side of the island at 7:00am tomorrow."

Back in the press room, someone's got hold of renewed threats from an Indonesian commander. He's vowing to sink the ship. A bunch of Australian journalists, figuring this mightn't be the picnic they'd been hoping for, tell the captain they'd like him to turn back if ordered to do so. The implicit dangers of this voyage are obvious to everyone involved.

Ask the students why they're here and the universal answer is, "We're laying our lives on the line to voice concerns that our governments are too gutless to address." Like sure, we might end up dead, but if we do then the international pressure will be so great that Indonesia will have to leave the Timorese alone....

But I don't think it works that way.

> The mood on the ship is reported to have changed dramatically after passengers were told that an Indonesian admiral had threatened to blow the ship out of the water, says an Australian press report.
> However, there was no confirmation last night that such a threat had been made.

At around 8:30, as we slip through flat black seas beneath a quarter moon, the Captain reports radar sightings of two vessels within 24 miles of the *Lusitania Expresso*.

I stand on deck scanning the horizon for lights, wondering why anyone would join the navy or go to war. There's a degree of apprehension here that I've been trying not to think about, a simmering of adrenalin that could turn within the hour, or perhaps the minute, to abject paralysing fear. The fear, I guess, was greatest the afternoon the boat came in and I realized just how small it was. Maybe I was expecting the *Titanic*, or the *Queen Mary* at least, but this wasn't much bigger than a coastal barge.

At around 10:30pm, 27 hours out of Darwin, a jaundiced light appears on the northwest horizon and passes by, a pair of lights now, a couple of miles off to port. It's heading south and those of us keeping the watch on deck are satisfied that it's a merchant vessel heading for Darwin. People start to relax, drifting away from the deck to their sleeping bags on the floors of the lounges. But then the other vessel's twin lights suddenly forge to one as it turns and gathers speed.

Down in the press room, someone yells "It's on!" and there's a scramble for the hardware and a rush for the deck. It's closing in fast, three white lights and a red one to port, looming up behind us as people gather on the deck and flashbulbs explode into the darkness.

Jean McLean, grey hair billowing across her face, says "I'm not doing much until he does. If he stays, I stay, I'm not going to sleep. I'll watch that light all night. I think I'll go and get myself a drink and come back and stare at it."

Ian Whitchurch, a politically active 22 year old from Sydney University emerges from the melee. "Should we get some sleep?" he asks, "Or wait 'til his friends arrive?"

"No sleep 'til Hammersmith," I grunt.

"At least we're not being ignored," he says.

In a corner of the solarium off the deck, portable satellite dishes like delicate umbrellas are trained through the perspex walls. Half a dozen kids sleep on the benches, snoozing through the bleating of the satellite telephone and the jagged aggressive jabbering as Portuguese journalists bark through the stratosphere.

11 March 1992

Elsewhere, the mood on board is subdued. A couple of dozen students are asleep on benches on the deck. Among the others, there's a degree of apprehension, a tensing of nerves. We're well out in international waters, a lifetime away from home, praying the Indonesians won't pull any stunts under the velveteen cover of night. Up on the bridge, the skipper tries to make contact with the trailing vessel, to no avail. The Indonesians are maintaining radio silence.

By 12:30am we're 64 miles from the 12 mile limit, expecting to hit the danger zone at 7:05.

I climb up onto the top deck, up by the funnel and the satellite dishes, above the murmur of the crowd, away from the spark of flashguns, savoring the darkness and the roll of the ship, watching the lights of the frigate jerking up and down about two kilometers off to starboard and 800 meters back. I watch those lights for a long time. Such visions are not compatible with sleep.

There are a couple of Portuguese doctors and a psychiatrist on board, quietly taking care of those for whom the situation is becoming too much. In the chaos of the press room, a tired Australian journo phones his copy through. "Many laughed nervously in unnaturally high voices," he dictates. "Others sat quietly behind steel bulkheads—just in case."

Of Cameras and Guns

At 6:40am on Wednesday 11 March I'm shunted from a fitful sleep on the floor of the saloon. We're 14 nautical miles off the coast. Dawn peels away the darkness, revealing the rugged spinal blue mountains of East Timor ahead. Off to starboard, the smoldering jaundiced lights of the

Indonesian frigate that's been trailing us through the night emerge from the gathering pallor. Off to port, another frigate closes in at speed.

The game is on. The Indonesians have been rehearsing their part in this drama for weeks, and they too have a couple of press cameras aboard. The players on the peace boat haven't actually rehearsed their parts, but a lot of deep thought has gone into their roles.

The warships close in like brothers at a shotgun wedding.

"Maybe if we waved them past," says Whitchurch dryly, "waved them through the course."

"I wonder what they're thinking right now."

"Same as what we're thinking, probably."

"No, they've got the guns."

"There's no turning back now, guys," comes a female American voice.

Lorne Rider appears. Lorne's feeling rested, he slept up top waiting for some action. Studying the frigate off to port, he says, "They got a heli on the back there."

"Yep," says Whitchurch. "I think it's an antisubmarine ship."

"You think it's a what?"

"Antisubmarine. Which doesn't mean a helluva lot 'cos we're not a submarine...yet."

As yet, there's been no contact with the other vessels. On the bridge, the radios chatter, picking up fishing boats and ferries and merchant shipping through the islands...but not a word from the Indonesian navy. Soon, when we hit the 12 mile limit, they'll be obliged to respond.

There's a time when the nerve ends fuse and the intense brooding high of adrenalin collapses into abject fear. I stand there in silence, just watching these grey slabs of metal manoeuvering around us. They look truly ugly, menacing, bristling with guns and antennae.

Everybody's on deck, mostly standing in silence and watching, just watching and waiting. Jako Island and Timor, this rugged blue knuckle of mountains that's been thrust from the sea, loom closer, reaching out into the early morning sun.

At 7:25am there's a burst of activity on the decks of the frigate about 400 meters off to starboard. It picks up speed and slips past. Behind us, the vessel off to port also picks up speed.

On the rear deck, amidst the squabble of microphones, cameras and satellite dishes, a Canberra journalist catches my eye, winks, and mutters into his tape recorder: "Bend over and kiss your arse goodbye."

Up on the bridge, Captain Luys dos Santos stands by the radio, peering through binoculars, waiting for contact. "Good morning sir. This is Portuguese *Lusitania Expresso*, Portuguese vessel from Darwin, bound for Dili, over." Captain Luys dos Santos is a bespectacled man with receding hair and an open necked white shirt. The sweat rolls from his brow as the Indonesian commander barks through the ether.

"This is Papa Kilo Alpha India, Indonesian warship. You are now in Indonesian territoriality. I tell you, directly to leave this area, and proceed your sailing without delay to the high seas ... Over."

"Roger sir. Sir I believe I don't have any permission to continue my voyage to Dili. Is that correct?"

"This is Papa Kilo Alpha India, Indonesian warship. That is correct. I warn you that you are not allowed to stop, anchoring, lowering boats, entering the harbor or the Indonesian territoriality or in the Indonesian waters."

"Roger...Indonesian warship. I just stop my engines now and I will start to, in a short while, turn around on my port side, okay?"

"This is Papa Kilo Alpha India. Roger, you will soon alter, standing by."

"Standing by."

It's 7:30 in the morning. The sun beats down on the crowded deck as the frigates move in beside us, riding on either side of the *Lusitania Expresso* at a distance of 200 meters, so close you can see the officers on deck, the guns on board. They present wonderful photo opportunities for those so inclined.

"Papa Kilo Alpha India, this is *Lusitania Expresso*. Ah, I stop my engines."

"This is Papa Kilo Alpha India. Roger. You will stop your engines."

"Roger sir. I believe I am talking with the commanding officer of the vessel, is that correct?"

"Yes, this is commanding officer speaking."

"Thank you sir. Sir, I have the spokesmen and sponsors of this mission, and ah, they ask me if you could be so kind as to have a word with them. Is that possible?"

"I say again. You are now in the Indonesian territoriality. I tell you, directly to leave this area and proceed your sailing without delay to the high seas...through the normal avenues of international navigation. Over."

"Roger sir, that is well understood, and we will act according to your orders."

"This is Papa Kilo Alpha India, standing by."

"Standing by."

These guys are acting like we're a bunch of Jehovah's Witnesses knocking on the front door of a Saturday morning. The Indonesian commander sounds kinda cranky and certainly doesn't wish to entertain whatever kind of subversive thoughts these troublemakers want to jam into his ears.

"*Lusitania Expresso*! *Lusitania Expresso*! This is Papa Kilo Alpha India! Over!"

"Roger sir, this is *Lusitania Expresso*. Go ahead, Papa Kilo Alpha India."

"This is Papa Kilo Alpha India. I tell you again, directly to leave this area. If you still continue your intentions, I will do something to force you away from this area. Over."

"Papa Kilo Alpha India, I am manoeuvering my ship to turn around, now."

"Roger, you will turn to port. Standing Channel One-Six."

"Standing by ah...sorry sir, did you say standing by Channel Six?"

"I am standing Channel One-Six."

"Standing by One-Six, thank you."

Someone's singing the chorus from *All Tomorrow's Parties* as the ship starts to turn.

"*Lusitania Expresso*, this is Papa Kilo Alpha India, over."

"This is *Lusitania Expresso*, Papa Kilo Alpha India. Go ahead."

"This is Papa Kilo Alpha India, Indonesian warship. I tell you again, directly to leave this area. I tell you again. Directly to leave this area. If you still continue your intentions, I will do something to force you away from this area. Over."

"Yes, yes. Well understood sir. I am manoeuvering, turning my ship, as you can well see, and proceeding to high seas as I have been told by you."

"This is Papa Kilo Alpha India, roger. Standing by, One-Six."

"Standing by One-Six."

Ahead, between the *Lusitania Expresso* and the coast of East Timor, a Soviet-built Indonesian destroyer ploughs through the placid waters of *Laut Timor*. A frigate is on the starboard side, staying with us as we turn and head back into international waters.

There are sound recordists and camera operator and reporters jammed around the door to the bridge listening into the communications as a faint dot appears in the northern sky and grows larger. "Chopper incoming!" An American-built Iroquois comes in fast and circles the ship.

"Everyone to the rear please," says one of the Portuguese.

As the skipper turns the ship to port he says, "In this situation, you must not underestimate the Indonesians. They mean business." With a helicopter hovering above the ship, he says "That's good. The US loves this Rambo stuff." The chopper returns, swinging in from the sun and passing overhead.

"We move to the back now please to throw the flowers," says one of the Portuguese on the bridge. The chopper's circling again.

"Two helicopters! Here comes another."

Ian Whitchurch raises an arm to the sky, flashing a peace sign at the chopper's crew.

"Excuse me," says a cameraman. "Can you do me a favor and point at the ship? Lower your hand, right down, right down, right down, just bring it over this way, lower it, further, bring it up, over this way, drop it, okay go, wait for the chopper, bring it up now..." and the red light flashes on the camera as Whitchurch figures his fingers into a peaceful V and tracks from frigate to helicopter for the news bulletins.

Choppers close in like dragonflies, hovering overhead. The frigates and the destroyer manoeuvre like sharks. One of the choppers is a Bell Sioux, a light observation helicopter similar to the 12 given to Indonesia by Australia in March 1978. It's comforting to know our gifts have lasted so long.

On the rear deck, a Portuguese priest conducts a memorial service for those killed at Santa Cruz. Sweltering in his vestments, he says "We will put the flowers in the sea. The sea will take them to the shores of Timor."

The service is translated in English, barely audible under the clattering ceiling of helicopters. They're coming in low, sweeping around us, filming and being filmed, a flashback to *Apocalypse Now*, loaches hovering and weaving in the morning sun.

As representatives of each of the twenty-one countries aboard cast wreaths into the sea, this bobbing wake of blood red flowers trailing back toward the silent mountains of Timor, they say a few words in their own languages, each person aware that this is their only chance, the closest they'll get to their destination. A tear-streaked Shirley Shackleton flings a tribute of eucalypt leaves and wattle flowers off the stern, saying "Go with our hearts to Timor by an invisible thread. Go with the tide to Timor, join us to the land of the dead."

There's disappointment and frustration, the crushing of naive hopes and the wash of tears on a sun-beaten deck, a scene that would be desperately solemn were it not for the thrusting cameras and microphones and the throb of helicopters above.

Word comes down from the bridge that the Indonesians don't want any more litter chucked into the sea. No more flowers or wreaths or beer cans or anything else. And suddenly it's so quiet, just the rumble of the diesels as Timor falls away behind us and our escorts keep pace in the distance.

Down in the press room, the radio telephones are working overtime as the scenario is relayed around the world. "I reckon we should've waited for the first shot," John Tomlinson says to Gordon McIntosh. Gordon's reply is completely unintelligible, even allowing for the depths of his Scottish accent.

All is quiet for a while. Throughout the ship people look stunned. Mission instigator Rui Marques says a few quiet words into a nest of microphones. "(We have faced) Indonesians who by force take actions against peaceful people, and against solidarity acts, and we feel that we have already achieved our main goal. We have put again on the international agenda, the question of East Timor."

"Red" Harrison from the BBC London, in one of the thickest accents asks, "Can you describe for me the mood among your people now?"

"I think it is everyone calm, reflective, not wanting to say too many words. We too feel sad at not having the boat arrive in Dili, but happy to have achieved the objective of this mission."

"I see many of them are crying," says Red.

"That's an emotional thing, that's a normal thing, but anyway, speaking for everyone, we feel we have achieved our act...we threw our flowers into the sea of East Timor and they will go up in the rivers to the mountain tops again."

Even the press room's strangely quiet now. Just the whirring of tape players, slow playbacks, editors finding the grabs, building stories from something intense but strangely anticlimactic.

"We are stopping ship because we have problems with refrigerator. Thank you."

Beneath us the engines die and the ship's adrift on a painted sea. Behind us, three Indonesian naval vessels—two frigates and a destroyer—cut back on the throttle and slip around us, circling their prey.

What the hell are those crazies doing in there? Refrigeration problems? What kinda bullshit's that? Are the troublemakers staging a coup, effecting a mutiny on the bridge? What the hell's going on over there? Maybe they're gonna make a run for it, swing around and take another crack at getting through. Crazy Balanda [foreigner] might try anything.

We're loitering 35 kilometers from the coast of Timor, well out in international waters, our engines dead, while the Captain and the mission controllers play a waiting game. As the Indonesian warships bristle around us, a conference is called in the saloon. Antonio Ravara explains what's going on:

We have told the Secretary-General of the UN of our situation as we have come here. He has said he hoped nothing bad would happen. We will try to phone him now to ask what else he can do.

We are saying to the Indonesians that we have refrigeration problems and it will take one-and-a-half hours to fix. We are now 10 miles from territorial waters. They said it was okay.

Shirley Shackleton, in a ship-to-shore interview with the Melbourne *Age* says "We have achieved enormous press around the world. We have made people aware of the plight of the Timorese. To go in now on a suicide mission would just be ridiculous."

After the excitement of the showdown and the emotional release of the service on the deck, the tension seems to have melted away and exhaustion's setting in. We've been dead in the water for 90 minutes when Ravara returns to the saloon, announcing that "We will wait some more. We have not received a response from the UN."

Standing off the bow, the Indonesian commander's getting agitated. So too are the Australian television crews who've got their pictures and are keen to get them out.

The original intention of the Mission, to "stop in that place for two or three days...to create publicity about the mission" simply wasn't going to work. While radio and press stories were going out by radio telephone and satellite dish, the television crews couldn't beam their pictures out. They understood that even if the *Lusitania* left immediately, it'd be another 18 hours before she was close enough to Australia to get a speed boat out to collect the film. There was even talk in the press room of chartering some daredevil fixed-wing pilot to come out and somehow scoop the tapes off the deck, but that was soon abandoned.

So when Ravara and colleagues talk of hanging out here for a while, waiting for a response from the UN Secretary-General, the television boys see red, putting the case in no uncertain terms. "Head back now and you keep the story alive for another day. Sit here and it dies immediately." This isn't what the Portuguese had in mind. Cocked Indonesian cannon they could withstand, but with news crews holding blank televisions at their heads, there wasn't much they could do but comply.

Conclusion

I joined the voyage because I needed to complete a journey. A naive tourist's jaunt into East Timor two years earlier had been irreversibly disrupted by events witnessed in Dili: a peaceful student demonstration before the visiting US Ambassador brutally crushed by a riot police riot.

In the end I don't think the peace mission achieved much at all. It concentrated the minds of those involved for a few days, fed the maw of the disposable media all too briefly but did nothing to enhance the lives of the victims, the East Timorese themselves.

A point it brought home was the opposing desires of activists and the needs of the media. Without the media coverage the mission would have been a non-event. But the media feeds on the next story, not the last one. It takes something of greater magnitude, a disaster preferably, to hold the attention longer than an ad break. Yeah, the media are doing their jobs. And their job is not to change the world but to entertain and perhaps inform, but how much information can you expect from a 12 second grab on the news? so once the ship was turned back the story was over, the leaders of the pack tuning into short-wave radios eager to tear at the flesh of the next event wherever it may be happening.

The media want to get in, get the pictures and get out again to file. They run to serious deadlines—the evening news doesn't wait around for a story—so crews don't have time to sit around discussing dialectics. That being the case, given that activists and media are stuck together on a boat in the middle of the Timor sea, the media ends up running the show rather than simply covering it, governing not just what we see but what happens where and when. This time the power of the media could dictate the length of the story, not just as it went to air but as it happened. The pictures from the circus had to get out.

To my mind the bottom line is that Max Stahl of Yorkshire Television achieved more on a tourist visa with a hand-held video camera on the bloody streets of Santa Cruz than all the high-tech gadgetry on board the *Lusitania Expresso*. He showed the world the problem, not the diversion. By showing the problem he sparked the diversion but the students would have learned more and been able to contribute more in the outside world had they been on the ground as tourists with open eyes. Tourists, even the bona fide ones, carry cameras and Walkmans, notebooks, journals or sketchpads. Tourists carry medicines and talk to people.

NOTE

*   The preceding material, with the exception of the conclusion, has been adapted from the latter part of the book, *Death in Dili* (Sydney: Sceptre, 1992). Some of the earlier sections of the book originally appeared in *Rolling Stone* (Australia), and provided the credentials I needed to board the ship.

NONVIOLENT HUMANITARIAN ASSISTANCE

Intention: to provide humanitarian assistance despite the danger and in defiance of the legal, political, economic and/or military constraints imposed by elites.

5

"WAVE AFTER WAVE THEY WENT CROSSING THE BORDER": FRIENDSHIPMENTS BY PASTORS FOR PEACE

Robin Hayes

Introduction
Since its founding in 1988, the organization known as Pastors for Peace has been at the forefront of the solidarity movement in the United States. By organizing national humanitarian aid caravans, first around the issue of US support of the Contras in Nicaragua and most recently to challenge the US embargo of Cuba, Pastors for Peace has demonstrated what its supporters define as a "people's foreign policy"—an alternative, respectful manner of relating to the peoples and governments in Central America and the Caribbean. Using powerful religious symbolism, operating in the tradition of nonviolent civil disobedience and providing a platform where many sectors of the progressive community could unite in action, Pastors for Peace has brought solidarity activism out of the obscure realm of the conventional left and into the mainstream.

Reverend Lucius Walker Jr., an African-American Baptist minister, announced the beginning of Pastors for Peace after being shot during a Contra attack on a civilian ferry boat on the Rio Escondido in Nicaragua in August 1988. Rev. Walker, as the executive director of the Interreligious Foundation for Community Organization (IFCO), was leading a fact-finding mission of clergy that was investigating the effects of US intervention in Nicaragua. Although IFCO had organized solidarity projects with liberation movements in Africa, Central America and the Caribbean, a consistent program of high-profile, cross-border actions had not been established. Rev. Walker has stated that as he lay in a hospital in Managua, contemplating that he had been seriously wounded by a bullet paid for by US tax dollars,

> The inspiration which God gave me was the formation of Pastors for Peace: a means by which pastors and lay people from throughout the United States might respond in a more...religious manner—ecumenically speaking—to the aggression of our own government against the Third World (Walker, 1992, pp.1-2).

Initially, Pastors for Peace was conceived as a project of IFCO that would organize one humanitarian aid caravan to Nicaragua, which arrived in Managua on Christmas Day, 1988. That caravan led to others, and in six years Pastors for Peace delivered 129 vehicles and more than ten million dollars in material aid to Nicaragua, Guatemala and El Salvador (Walker, 1992, p.2).

Unlike most charity efforts, the humanitarian aid caravans were overtly political in nature. Through demonstrating that Central American basic needs (for example for medicines and agricultural supplies) were being denied, and that the problems were created and exacerbated by US foreign policy, and directly addressing those needs by collecting and delivering material aid, the caravans made a strong public statement against US domination of Latin America. Pastors for Peace also specifically collected aid items such as agricultural implements, computers and sewing material, that served as tools of empowerment and which facilitated grassroots community-based projects in Central America. "Pastors for Peace makes a powerful statement," said Yuri Guerra, former Co-Coordinator of Pastors for Peace. "We say to the US government, if you send bombs then we'll send medicine." These acts of giving also provided an unassailable moral position from which solidarity activists could introduce political dissent into the mainstream discourse. While legislators and media outlets may have felt comfortable ignoring left-wing organizations, it was a public relations debacle to attack the motives of a Christian aid-giving organization.

The Pastors for Peace caravans were organized on a national level, and offered churches and activists a concrete manner of supporting their brothers and sisters in Latin America. Pastors for Peace coordinators built a grassroots network out of contacts made through IFCO's "Central America Week" campaign in the mid-1980s. IFCO would target one state or region and organize hundreds of public educational events cosponsored by churches, university campuses, unions and solidarity groups. The Central America Week campaign raised consciousness within many communities about the US government's support and facilitation of state-sponsored violence in Guatemala, El Salvador and Nicaragua. The Pastors for Peace caravans provided an outlet for this consciousness by creating a focal point for action against US foreign policy in Central America.

In just three years after its first caravan to Nicaragua, Pastors for Peace had gained an unsullied reputation among nongovernmental organizations and community-based projects in Central America. As its grassroots network continued to expand in the US and Canada, Pastors for Peace began to look for ways to expand its program. In 1991, while in Nicaragua on an election observer delegation, Rev. Walker met Rev. Raul Suarez of the Ebenezer Baptist Church in Havana, Cuba. Rev. Suarez suggested that Pastors for Peace investigate the possibility of bringing humanitarian aid caravans to Cuba, which was in the throes of an economic depression due to the dismantling of the USSR. During several fact-finding missions to Cuba in the following year, Rev. Walker, members of the IFCO Board of Directors and some Pastors for Peace supporters witnessed how the US embargo of Cuba was directly limiting the access that Cuban people had to basic needs such as food and medicine. It was clear to Rev. Walker and the IFCO Board that in Cuba, as during the Contra War in Nicaragua, the US government was waging war on the most innocent—but in this case using hunger and disease as its primary weapons of intimidation (Walker, 1993, p.62).

Pastors for Peace announced its plans for a humanitarian aid caravan to Cuba, or US-Cuba Friendshipment, for November 1992. Unlike previous caravans to Central America, this was a direct violation of US law. Under the US trade embargo of Cuba established in 1963, any form of trade or travel to Cuba is prohibited, unless licensed by the US government. Pastors for Peace decided that applying for a license to send aid to people in need in Cuba would be an act of complicity with an "inhumane and genocidal" policy that "violated God's law" (Walker, 1992, p.3). Thus, the Friendshipment became more than an act of solidarity with the Cuban people. It was an overt and confrontational statement against US foreign policy.

The first US-Cuba Friendshipment was announced at a pivotal moment for US-Cuba relations. Although the justification for the embargo most often evoked by US officials—the relationship between Cuba and the Soviet Union—crumbled with the disintegration of the socialist Soviet bloc, in 1992 US legislatures passed the *Cuban Democracy Act* which further curtailed Cuba's access to food, medicine and medical supplies. The law, better known as the "Torricelli Bill," reinstituted the prohibition on US subsidiaries trading with Cuba and also prohibited any ship from entering a US port within six months of docking in Cuba. It also called for sanctions against Latin American countries trading with Cuba. The law was internationally unprecedented in its infringement on the economic sovereignty of other countries in regards to trade with Cuba (Garfield *et al*, 1996).

The first US-Cuba Friendshipment united different sectors of the conventional Cuba solidarity community with mainline denominational churches and progressive activists on domestic issues. Using the model of the Central America caravans, Pastors for Peace created a broad-based coalition effort to mount an unprecedented challenge to the US embargo of Cuba. A steering committee of over 23 national organizations and churches was established to organize the collection of aid and vehicles, recruitment of participants and preparation of public events throughout the US. Among the steering committee members were Catholic and Episcopalian bishops, members of the Progressive National American Baptist Conventions, representatives of the National Network on Cuba, International Peace for Cuba Appeal, and Cuba Information Project, as well as renowned scholars and artists. The committee was able to help establish a firm foundation for Friendshipment organization that encompassed historical Cuba solidarity organizations and the ecumenical base of IFCO/Pastors for Peace.

The political strategy behind the US-Cuba Friendshipment fully capitalized on the moral authority of Pastors for Peace. In various press interviews prior to the caravan's arrival at the US-Mexico border in Laredo, Texas, caravan participants and organizers stressed the "immoral" and "inhumane" nature of the embargo and its negative effects on the people of Cuba. This challenge to US law, Pastors for Peace asserted, was an issue of faith and conscience, not of politics. Rev. Walker inferred that the embargo was a restriction of religious freedom because it required a license to carry out the "dictates of the Gospel" (Krane, 1992, p.16A). Organizers and participants often pointed out the "insanity" of the US government for prohibiting the shipment of bibles, powdered milk and medicine to "our brothers and sisters" in Cuba. In addition, Friendshipment organizers stated that Pastors for Peace did not "oppose or support Castro" (Krane, 1992, p.16A).

This redefinition of the US embargo as an issue of humanity and faith versus politics was essential to the organization's ability to defray hostile criticism from US government officials and the right-wing Cuban-American community. As the date of the caravan's border crossing neared, US Treasury Department officials continually asserted that the caravan would not be allowed out of the country without obtaining a license. One week before arriving in Laredo, a US customs spokeswoman asserted, "If they don't want to get a license and they try and ship the goods we have to detain them or arrest them" (Krane, 1992, p.16A). Leaders of the right wing Cuban exile community, which enthusiastically endorsed the embargo as an effective tool in undermining Castro's government, accused the caravan of "propping up Castro's regime."

In order to increase public support for the Friendshipment and an end to the embargo, Pastors for Peace organized educational events in more than 100 cities along nine routes throughout the US on the way to the showdown at Laredo. Speakers who were well versed on the history of US-Cuba relations and the embargo's detrimental effects on the Cuban people travelled to churches, university campuses and community meetings to raise consciousness about US foreign policy toward Cuba and support for the Friendshipment's mission. In a country where accurate information about Cuba is rarely disseminated, the Friendshipment representatives provided many people with their first critical view of the embargo and a concrete way of stating their opposition to it.

The Pastors for Peace caravans had an imagery that was filled with Biblical metaphors. Most of the caravan vehicles were old school buses and trucks, which were brightly decorated with the slogans "End the US Embargo" and "Let Cuba Live" as well as portraits of Rev. Martin Luther King Jr. and Jose Marti, the father of Cuban independence. The peace convoy's organizers often stated that they were "breaking down the walls of Jericho" by crossing the border with aid for Cuba (see Pastors for Peace, 1993). The grassroots caravan effort seemed a modern day David and Goliath story, as a small group of people in old vehicles confronted the most powerful government in the world. This imagery was another aspect of the political strategy of Pastors for Peace. Demonstrating that the innocuous act of donating medicine and powdered milk to another country could evoke the wrath of the US government was a compelling method of illustrating the immorality of the US embargo of Cuba.

In November 1992, over 100 people from diverse racial, geographical and religious backgrounds gathered in Laredo to prepare to challenge the blockade. Among them were ministers, doctors, teachers, students, seasoned political activists and people new to nonviolent action. Each caravan participant, or caravanista, risked receiving a prison sentence of up to 10 years and up to $250,000 in fines for attempting to take humanitarian aid to Cuba under the *Trading with the Enemy Act* of 1917. After participating in a three-day orientation, consisting of strategy sessions, nonviolence training and meditations, the participants attempted to cross the border into Mexico with 12 tons of aid for Cuba.

Since no organization had ever attempted such a challenge to the US embargo, and US Treasury Department officials maintained until the day of the border crossing that the aid would not be permitted to leave the country, caravan participants braced themselves for the worst. Forty-eight vehicles lined up at the Laredo border and when they were stopped by US Customs officers, caravan participants attempted to cross the bridge over the Rio Grande to Mexico on foot with bibles and boxes of medicines. Many caravan participants were placed in choke holds or wrestled to the ground by several heavily armed officers and the aid they carried was violently wrested from their hands. The caravanistas, refusing to be intimidated, continued marching toward the bridge and some were eventually able to carry aid into Mexico. Drivers of caravan vehicles that were lined up at the Customs inspection point stopped Customs officials from seizing material aid.

After several hours of confrontation, the Laredo Customs officials seemed bewildered. Much of the Cuba-bound aid was brought into Mexico despite their efforts to stop it. Dozens of journalists from local and national media outlets had photographed and videotaped the violent arrests of caravan participants, among them clergy and elderly people, by US Customs officials. After several more hours of negotiations with Pastors for Peace, the US Treasury Department decided to allow the entire caravan to pass through to Mexico. The arrestees were promptly released and the caravan continued to Cuba. As a justification for their decision to allow the Friendshipment through, Customs official announced that Pastors for Peace had received a license to take the humanitarian aid to Cuba. However, no Pastors for Peace representative had applied for a license and Rev. Walker summarily refused to accept it:

> Our position has been that we could not accept the license explicitly saying that those who give the license have the right to tell us when and how and how much aid we could bring to our sisters and brothers in Cuba. So we have taken a principled stand...for faith teaches us not to be in complicity with evil powers (Walker, 1992, p.4).

In early 1993, after the success of its first effort, Pastors for Peace announced a second US-Cuba Friendshipment that would arrive in Laredo in July. Having gained national attention for its previous challenge to the US embargo, the second caravan was significantly larger in size and even more diverse in terms of support. Once again the Friendshipment travelled to over 100 cities across the US and Canada participating in public educational events, collecting humanitarian aid and attending press conferences. Over 200 caravanistas arrived in Laredo with over 100 tons of supplies for Cuba in 95 vehicles.

Laredo Customs officials attempted to diffuse the confrontation in the press by asserting that Pastors for Peace would only need a license for medicines, computers and vehicles. The US Treasury Department asserted that the old 286 PC compatible computers and 10 year old school buses could be used for military purposes by the Cuban government. Pastors for Peace remained steadfast that the organization would not seek or accept a license for the caravan. A few days before the Friendshipment arrived at the border, Audrey Adams, District Director of the US Customs Service in Laredo, asserted that she was merely "concerned that the exportation takes place with as little disruption as possible" (Department of the Treasury, 1993). Customs officials asked Pastors for Peace to have their Cuba-bound cargo pre-inspected for clearance. Pastors for Peace refused their request.

On July 29, the imposing US-Cuba Friendshipment lined up at the Port of Laredo to challenge the embargo. Less than a year after the first Friendshipment, during which Customs officers attempted to seize all Pastors for Peace headed for Cuba, the US Treasury Department allowed all foodstuffs, bibles and school supplies to pass through the border. However, officers did attempt to seize all vehicles, medicines and computers on the caravan. Once again, caravanistas attempted to carry humanitarian aid across the border on foot and, for the large part, were successful in bypassing Customs officers with dozens of boxes of sophisticated medicines and computer equipment. Although over 100 caravanistas were photographed and videotaped by dozens of journalists crossing the border with boxes clearly labelled "computer," and "medicine," Laredo Customs officials maintained in the press that none of these items were leaving the country.

After several hours of confrontation, most of the Pastors for Peace cargo was safely in Mexico. Nearly all of the vehicles, including a school bus destined for Cuba, were waiting for further instructions in Nuevo Laredo, Mexico. Toward the end of the day, Rev. Lucius Walker along with 13 other caravanistas boarded another Cuba-bound school bus intending to use the bus as transportation back into Laredo. As Rev. Walker attempted to drive the bus away from the border, Laredo officials informed the bus passengers that it would not be allowed to leave the lot because it was seized. At that time, the caravanistas announced to the officials that they would not leave the bus. The bus was then towed into the US Customs impound lot. After a thorough discussion, the passengers on the bus decided to go on a hunger strike until the bus was released.

The majority of the caravan continued on to Cuba while a small group of supporters stayed behind to organize political and logistical support for the hunger strikers. Pastors for Peace immediately activated its emergency response network and asked thousands of people across the country to contact the White House, Treasury Department and their legislators to express their support and concern for the hunger strikers. Demonstrations were held at US Federal buildings in over 40 cities throughout the US. There were also solidarity hunger strikes in San Francisco and New York. Treasury Department officials and the White House received thousands of phone calls and faxes daily which demanded the release of the school bus. Pastors for Peace also rallied a number of progressive Members of Congress, including Rep. Ronald Dellums and Rep. Charles Rangel, to put pressure on the Treasury Department to resolve the situation. A "Dear Colleague" letter, which implored other Representatives and Senators to urge the Treasury Department to resolve the situation in Laredo, circulated the halls of Congress with over a dozen signatures. The combination of grassroots pressure from the outside with internal political negotiation proved to be a successful means of persuading the US Treasury Department.

Laredo Customs officials would not allow the hunger strikers to return to the lot if they left for any reason. Thus, the hunger strikers settled into their new home, perching lawn chairs on the searing hot asphalt of the Customs impound lot. As a result, the hunger strikers braved daily temperatures of over 100 degrees, a surplus of toxic diesel fumes emanating from the hundreds of commercial trucks that passed through the border and, at first, a complete lack of sanitation facilities A support team of Pastors for Peace volunteers was charged with supplying Gatorade, water and other basic needs to the strikers by handing items over a fence. At the insistence of a few Congressmen, after a few days Customs officers supplied a portable toilet and an informal shower facility to the bus passengers. The gruelling conditions in which the strikers lived accentuated the morality behind their actions. While the 13 bus occupants, whose backgrounds reflected the diverse support base of IFCO/Pastors for Peace, were closer and closer to sacrificing their own lives to secure the school bus' passage to Cuba, the US government's actions remained unsympathetic.

The "Little Yellow School Bus," as the impounded vehicle came to be called, was a powerful organizing tool in itself. Expanding on the David versus Goliath theme of the US-Cuba Friendshipments, the school bus and its passengers were compelling symbols of the ludicrous nature of the US embargo. While Customs officials maintained that the school bus could be used for military purposes by the Cuban government; even conservative journalists found it difficult to dispute the credibility of Pastors for Peace. Rev. Walker stated in a press interview, "We ask ourselves, is the most powerful government in the world truly afraid of a little yellow school bus?" (Pastors for Peace, 1993). Hundreds of media outlets published photographs of the school bus with its hand painted "End the US Embargo of Cuba" and peace symbols behind the chain link fence in the Customs impound lot. As word spread throughout the country about the school bus, the hunger strikers received thousands of encouraging postcards and letters, as well as solidarity messages from Rev. Jesse Jackson and Nobel Peace Prize winner Rigoberta Menchú.

After the hunger strike entered its 18th day, and US officials had received tens of thousands of phone calls, faxes and letters demanding the release of the "Little Yellow School Bus," Rev. Lucius Walker travelled to Washington, D.C. for a series of meetings with the US Treasury Department. Pastors for Peace agreed to allow the World Council of Churches, a nonprofit ecumenical agency, to officially bring the school bus to Cuba on the condition that the Council would not apply for nor accept a license and that Laredo Customs officials would repair the damage done to the bus during the seizure. On the 23rd day of the hunger strike, Pastors for Peace received word that the "Little Yellow School Bus" was free to go to Cuba. In a face-saving gesture, US Treasury officials stated to the press that Pastors for Peace had simply received a license for the bus—though Pastors for Peace had never applied for one.

The triumph of the "Little Yellow School Bus" and the continued successes of the Pastors for Peace US-Cuba Friendshipments in challenging the US embargo of Cuba demonstrate that broad-based grassroots organizing and cross-border actions are powerful tools in protesting the foreign policy of a government. The specific political strategy, unassailable credibility, and extensive outreach efforts of Pastors for Peace have helped build and expand a far-reaching network throughout the US that supports an end to the US embargo of Cuba. Through combining left-wing radical tactics with mainstream Christian values, Pastors for Peace has helped push the national debate over the US embargo to the forefront. The US-Cuba Friendshipments have taken the debate out of the exclusive grip of right-wing Cuban-Americans and conservative pundits and, as a result, redefined the essence of the discourse on the embargo. In addition, Pastors for Peace has forced the US government to reevaluate its procedures of licensing humanitarian aid bound for Cuba.

Pastors for Peace continues to organize humanitarian aid caravans to Cuba despite increased pressures from the US government.

REFERENCES

Department of the Treasury, US Customs Service. 1993. "Customs Moving to Head off Run-In With Pastors," Press Release, 26 July.
Garfield, Richard, Ellen Schmidt and William Whitney. 1996. *US Embargo: Cuba's Affliction* (Oslo: Let Cuba Live).
Krane, Jim. 1992. "Activists Will Try to Send Medicine and Food for Cuba, Defying Embargo," *Minneapolis Star Tribune*, 15 November.

Pastors for Peace. 1993. "Who's Afraid of a Little Yellow School Bus?," video produced by Cathy Scott and May Ying Welsh.

Walker, Rev. Lucius. 1992. "Speech by Rev. Lucius Walker at the Dr Martin Luther King, Jr. Memorial Center, November 27," in Ana R. Gort (ed.), *Wave After Wave They Went, Crossing the Border* (Havana: Editora Politica).

——. 1993. "Speech by Rev. Lucius Walker at the Welcoming Ceremony for the Pastors for Peace, August 25, 1993," in Maria Cristina Zamora (ed.), *Missionaries of Dignity* (Havana: Editora Politica).

NONVIOLENT RECONCILIATION AND DEVELOPMENT

Intention: to facilitate conflict resolution, community reconciliation and/or community development by participating in projects that encourage conflicting parties to work together to achieve shared aims in defiance of the legal, political, economic and/or military constraints imposed by elites.

6

CYPRUS RESETTLEMENT PROJECT:
AN INSTANCE OF INTERNATIONAL PEACEMAKING*

A.Paul Hare

Events Leading up to the Visit of the First Team on Cyprus
Narayan Desai and Charles Walker, both part of the first team to visit Cyprus in 1972, were founding members of the World Peace Brigade (1962), however, there had been no activity involving members of the Brigade since the intervention on behalf of Zambian independence in 1962-1964, the Delhi-Peking March in 1963, and the third party group monitoring the cease fire in Nagaland in 1964-1966. There had been no meetings by members of the World Peace Brigade since its last action and no plans had been made to pass on the responsibility for initiating new projects to any particular set of persons. However, the traditions of the WPB was still very much alive in the memories of those who knew about the work and in plans of others who thought that civilian groups might be formed to act along the lines of the United Nations Forces, but without weapons. Thus it happened that in 1971 discussions were held in India by members of the Shanti Sena (Gandhian Peace Brigade) and in the United States by the staff of the International Peace Academy (IPA) concerning the possibility of placing "International Peace Contingents" in troubled areas of the world.

In March 1972, Hare and Walker of the Haverford College Center for Nonviolent Conflict Resolution prepared a memorandum on "Peace Contingents on Cyprus" at the request of the IPA. The memorandum outlined the purposes, possible tasks, personnel, cost, phases of development, exploration, organization and mobilization, training, launching and operation, and evaluation for a team composed of 12 to 15 persons plus directors to work on Cyprus. The mission would be to provide third party services consistent with the United Nations mandate and to gain experience in non-military peacekeeping and related tasks.

A budget for $130,000 was projected to cover the cost of placing 17 volunteers in Cyprus for one year, plus the costs of seeding and predevelopment, training, supervision and travel, and research and evaluation. The next steps, it was agreed, were for General Indarjit Rikhye, chairman of the IPA, to check the feasibility of the project with persons at the United Nations and persons involved with the UN mission on Cyprus. Hare and Walker were to explore the possibilities that the American Friends Service Committee and the Shanti Sena might sponsor the project.

Although some preliminary discussions were held with members of the American Friends Service Committee staff, it was evident that more detail was needed, in particular about the kind of work that was to be done on Cyprus. Since Hare, Walker, and Narayan Desai (who was then Secretary of the Shanti Sena) were all planning to attend the triennial meeting of the War Resisters' International to be held in England in July, a first visit to Cyprus was planned for August.

The First Team

A team of five persons visited Cyprus during the first two weeks of August. Interviews were held with representatives of the United Nations, and Greek and Turkish officials. Mr Osorio-Tafal, United Nations Representative in Cyprus, suggested that we work on psychological problems that divide people rather than on problems requiring only technical assistance. In particular he suggested that the resettlement of Turkish displaced persons who had left their homes at the "time of troubles in 1963" was a humanitarian problem that might provide a focus for the work. Officials on the Greek side were already committed to the principal of resettlement of Turkish displaced persons. On the Turkish side officials recalled warmly the work of a group of British volunteers who had rebuilt some houses in a village several years before. However, at this time no progress had been made toward resettlement for some years and persons on the Greek and Turkish sides gave different reasons as to why the Turkish villagers had not returned.

At the beginning of November, a proposal was prepared for the American Friends Service Committee providing details of the history of the project, the visit of the first team to Cyprus, and the details of work to be done in several villages to initiate the resettlement process. The budget for one year had now risen to $158,000 with the inclusion of a provision for training in India or elsewhere, for five Cypriots to become members of the team, expenses for construction in three villages, and a special International Peace Academy Institute with a focus on the problems on Cyprus. However, Cyprus did not appear on the list of priorities of the American Friends Service Committee and the project was left without any immediate prospect of funding and other support.

Also it appeared that it might be difficult to secure support from any funding organization without more formal indications, in writing, that officials on the Greek and Turkish sides approved of the project.

During a brief visit to Cyprus in March 1973, Hare drew up the following one page proposal addressed to the Government of Cyprus concerning the resettlement of displaced persons in Cypriot villages:

> An estimated 5,000 Greek and 15 to 20,000 Turkish villagers remain to be resettled from those who moved from their villages at the "time of troubles" now 10 years ago. A number of sensitive issues including the form of local government, security, and land-ownership remain to be resolved before further rehabilitation can take place.
>
> To renew the effort toward resettlement, it is proposed that a working party be formed to collect current information concerning the status of the displaced persons and the conditions in the villages, to work out solutions to the problems which will be acceptable to both sides, and to implement these solutions using the resources of the working party or by calling for additional technical or volunteer help where it may be necessary. The working party would bring a "third party" view to the problem searching for solutions in which all sides can gain. They would combine experience in nonviolent conflict resolution with an understanding of the history of Cypriot problems as they have been viewed by both sides.
>
> The working party would consist of nine persons with experience in work with displaced persons, village rehabilitation, and non-violent conflict resolution. Five of the working party members would be Cypriots, three nominated by the Greek side and two by the Turkish side. Four would be from other countries; one from the Gandhian Shanti Sena (Peace Brigade) in India, one with experience with the British Friends (Quaker) Service Committee, one with experience with the American Friends (Quaker) Service Committee, and I would be the fourth. I am also a Quaker, was Deputy Representative for the U.S. Peace Corps in the Philippines, and have had experience in projects involving non-violent conflict resolution in other parts of the world.
>
> We would expect the working party to spend up to one year working out possible solutions and another two years implementing solutions that may be found. Funds would be obtained from sources outside Cyprus to finance the work of the four persons from India, the United Kingdom, and the United States, and to provide support for the working party. It would be desirable to have the Cypriot Government underwrite as much of the project as possible.
>
> If representatives of the Greek and Turkish sides will approve the project in principle at this time, I will undertake to recruit the non-Cypriot members of the working party and to raise the necessary funds. This may take several months, however, it would be desirable to begin the work as soon as possible.

The proposal was endorsed on the same day by a letter from Mr Rauf Denktash, Vice-President of the Republic of Cyprus, on the Turkish side and by a letter from Mr C.Veniamin, Director-General of the Ministry of Foreign Affairs, on the Greek side on 2 April 1973.

The proposal and the two endorsements were sent to the Lilly Endowment with a request for funds to support the project. A grant of

$25,000 was made by the Executive Committee of the Lilly Endowment and the project was underway.

Since we had given a copy of the Turkish endorsement to the Greek side, we sent along a copy of the Greek response to the Turkish side. In a letter dated 1 June 1973, that we probably received in mid-June, Mr Denktash noted that the Greek side had suggested that rather than have a joint committee, our volunteers might do better acting as third parties. If this was to be the case, the Turkish side said that they would not be able to participate in the project. We apparently did not take this letter as a definite "no" from the Turkish side and proceeded with the next team visit to Cyprus.

The Second Team

During July, a second team of five persons worked on Cyprus. Initially they gathered more detailed information about conditions on Cyprus and the history of the resettlement problem. Reports were written giving the position of the Greek side, the Turkish side, and the United Nations. These reports were given to each party to check the accuracy of the team's understanding of the problems. Copies of the final versions were then sent to all three parties.

Throughout the month, team members met with representatives of each side separately, since the two sides had not yet agreed to meet together face-to-face, to discuss the resettlement process.

As a result of the discussions with both sides, a memorandum giving our understanding of the "Next steps toward the resettlement of displaced persons" was prepared. Four villages were to be selected from the original list of 21 villages in which the Greek side had agreed to rebuild houses. As soon as the Turkish side would be able to prepare lists of villagers who had made a commitment to return, the Greek side would carry out any necessary surveys and provide funds so that reconstruction of houses could begin. We proposed to bring another team to Cyprus during the months of November, December, and January when the surveys of villagers would be complete and the resettlement process would be ready to begin.

The proposal was endorsed by the Greek side on 31 July and by the Turkish side on 1 August.

In August a second request for funds was sent to the Lilly Endowment for the continuation of the project on a larger scale than the remaining funds would allow. A second grant was made of $25,000.

The Third Team

In November, the third and largest team of 18 volunteers arrived to work on Cyprus. This was the period of the most extensive work on the project. There were teams of three or four volunteers living in each of the villages of Dhiorios, Peristerona, Nisou, and Pan Lefkara. Each team collected information related to resettlement from villages in its area and tried to find ways to increase involvement of the villagers in the resettlement process. Some members helped with negotiations between the Ministry of Foreign Affairs, on the Greek side, and the Turkish Cypriot Leadership.

With the arrival of the first two volunteers from India it was now evident to all that we had an international team. When a small group of volunteers, including two men in Indian dress, paid a visit to Vice-President Denktash, he remarked: "Oh, what a lovely sight." He was indicating that he was pleased that people had come from all over the world to show an interest in the problems of the Turkish Cypriots.

At about the same time the Greek side told us that they felt that the report on conditions in Dhiorios, prepared by the second team, was irresponsible and was biased in favor of the Turkish side. This was one of several occasions when our attention was called directly to the sensitivity of each side.

As part of the orientation period, Brigadier Michael Harbottle, former Chief of Staff for the UN forces on Cyprus, briefed the team recalling lessons learned during his service on Cyprus. Harbottle had also been helpful in advising the first team before its arrival on Cyprus and providing names of some of the initial contacts.

A suggestion was made to the Greek side to publicly designate a sum of money from the government budget for the resettlement of displaced persons. This would give some visible evidence to the Turkish side that the resettlement process was moving forward. We also suggested that houses be reconstructed in each village in a two-phase process. Although it was not publicly stated, this was a move to avoid having any Turkish villagers labelled as "trouble makers."

On 12 December 1973, a front page story in the *Cyprus Mail* about "Further aid to displaced Turks" announced the fact that the Government of Cyprus would repair houses of Turkish Cypriots who had left their homes and villages ten years before during the "time of troubles." The next day the paper quoted Mr Osorio-Tafal, as saying that this step by the Government "would contribute to more understanding and would create better conditions for furtherance of a solution" to the Cyprus problem. In press releases, both the Greek and Turkish sides noted the contribution of the Cyprus Resettlement Project in helping to facilitate the process of resettlement.

On 17 January 1974, after many consultations on both sides of the Green Line, officials from the Greek and Turkish sides meet face-to-face with members of the CRP and a representative of the Untied Nations to discuss the next steps in the resettlement process. There is no written statement describing the purpose of the meeting since we were unable to find a wording for a statement that was acceptable to both sides.

The Fourth Team

In mid-April a team of five persons arrived to review the progress towards resettlement and to decide whether or not any further service by the project seemed desirable. They found that a new political development had brought the Intercommunal Talks to a halt and that the Government had not yet voted the money to begin the reconstruction in the four villages. However, it appeared that the political situation might be "clarified" by the end of May, allowing the work to proceed.

As an interim project, to assure some movement towards resettlement and as a sign of the goodwill of the citizens of both sides, the team proposed that a four-week work camp be held in one of the villages, beginning the second week of July.

As a final phase of the Cyprus Resettlement Project the team also proposed that after the Greek side had completed building the first set of houses, four volunteers would return to Cyprus for six months. They would live in one or two of the villages and be concerned with all of the villages to which Turkish families were returning. Where necessary the volunteers would act as third-parties on any issues arising from the resettlement process. The Greek side approved both plans for the work-camp and for the final phase of the project on 17 May 1974.

The work-team began in the village of Peristerona in early July. Team member, Ellen Wilkinson, an American Quaker, described some of the details of the work-camp:

> When Paul Hare, three other CRP members, and I returned to Cyprus in April to check on the progress of our work, we found that nothing could be done until money was passed by the Government to begin the reconstruction. As an interim project a work camp was suggested. The Turkish side agreed to the participation of their youth in a mixed project. We considered it to be one way to achieve our previous goal of resettlement and contact between the communities on a private, non-political level. It was the latter area which came to be the workcamp's most important aspect as Cypriots not only arranged the details of the camp but began visualizing how the experience might be expanded or adapted in the future.
>
> To undertake the project we needed the approval of the officials and leaders from both communities. To this extent we were depending on political support.

The officials on the Greek side seemed to have trusted us as neutral and reliable workers. If they felt that as a whole the workcamp was innocuous, at least one of them felt strongly that any association between Cypriot youth would be valuable and should be encouraged.

The Turkish side's interest came from the hope that houses would actually be completed. They also saw the scheme as a way to find money in the future from sources outside the island and thus not have to depend on the Greek Cypriots if large governmental funds were never allocated.

While waiting for verbal support from our political sources, we went to representative of various private business and social groups for an idea of the kind of interest we could expect if we were to undertake the project. Several people from the private sector responded favorably, and eventually representatives of both communities gave us verbal approval. Paul Hare and the other CRP members left Cyprus, as they had planned, in the first days of May. I stayed to organize the workcamp with the one guideline that I should find what assistance I could by the end of May and proceed only if our support looked adequate at that time. This was primarily a Turkish concern as they wanted to guard against the work turning into a show of intercommunal harmony accomplishing nothing substantive. Neither side wanted any publicity about the camp for we would have no control over its coverage by the press.

We chose the second week in July as a target starting date. This gave me just over two months to organize the camp. I had to find assurances of monetary support before proceeding, yet many of the organizational details, such as recruiting the students, had to be begun by mid-May. To compound the problems the site of the workcamp was changed in late May because a large construction project was about to begin in the village we had originally chosen. Peristerona, the second workcamp site we chose, was in many ways a better site but the switch meant a time-consuming duplication of work as we had already chosen the houses to be repaired and had listed the materials we would have needed.

By the end of May enough support had been promised to make our randomly-chosen goal of 5,000 Cypriot pounds, about $15,000, seem realizable. There was, however, no formal review of the project and no one asked to see any exact figures. I was frequently in touch, however, with the people who were concerned with the job, primarily the District Officer and a man from the Turkish side's social service.

Dan Sipe, an American not previously involved with the CRP, arrived on Cyprus on 2 June to help co-ordinate the project. By 8 July, when the workcamp began, we had arranged a technical committee to plan for the supplies and oversee the construction, had found students from technical schools and various youth organizations, and we had raised approximately $1,300 in cash and over $3,000 worth of supplies and equipment from private individuals, clubs, and companies. In addition, we received $6,000 from the Cyprus government which would go directly to building costs and would have been enough to finish any work not completed during the camp. We also put $1,500 of our CRP grant directly into the workcamp fund.

We would not have been able to find such support had we remained alone, approaching individuals as two Americans with another do-good project for the residents of Cyprus. During the first month I made contact with as many clubs and business organizations as possible. Interested members from these groups plus people from social and technical agencies formed a loose committee to raise money and oversee construction details. Most of these volunteers were found through people who had come to know one or more members of the CRP when the group was on Cyprus in the winter. As groups lent their support their individual members were contacted easily and not necessarily by us.

When Dan Sipe arrived, he took over many of the technical and all the financial matters. He also organized the details of the co-ordinating work so that our Cypriot helpers each had a reasonable amount of responsibility and so that our own job stayed as much in the background as possible.

The Cypriots who helped did so for varied reasons. Some felt that the project was cosmetic in its fundamental nature but also felt they must participate to appear to maintain the hope that eventually the communities could live in concord. We two were the first to admit that it would not be through scattered projects such as the workcamp that a situation of trust and mutual confidence between the two sides would be created. The workcamp's appeal was first, that it could be seen as a symbol of these possibilities, and secondly, that it touched a feeling in many of the older generation that their children's separations was sowing the seeds for future hatred and strife.

The camp itself started on schedule on 8 July, with all the confusion of last-minute details one might expect but can't anticipate. We were using dishware borrowed from the Ministry of Education, beds and bedding from the United Nations, and tables and chairs from a Turkish boarding home. We hired a cook from the village, used the two village schools for sleeping, and were addressed the first night by the head of the village who spoke out in favor of better relations between the two communities. We would have held a party for our supporters and the villagers the night of 15 July if there hadn't been a coup d'etat.

We could have reasonably expected three more weeks of "gratifying social interaction" but the fact that the students could get along perfectly well socially might now be judged against the fact that their communities can not get along politically. Though the workcamp was totally different in nature and backing than the early CRP work, they both, in the end, failed because of political reasons.

As a project, the two-and-one-half months preparation for the workcamp was beneficial in that it:

a. Gave Cypriots a means of making a small step towards reconciliation and in a way that they could, in the future, initiate their own follow-up work.
b. Provided a way to bring to a large number of private citizens details on a political matter, in this case resettlement. For example, some members of the clubs we contacted were also active in politics and did not have up to date information on the resettlement issue.
c. Raised some peoples' interest in the possible usefulness of international groups such as the CRP. If given the chance, several of our contacts would have liked to do similar work in other countries.

The material benefits of the workcamp, the number of houses to be built (six) and the number of students to be involved (40 in all), were significant. The fact that so many Cypriots helped, wanting to see it work and eventually lead to something more substantial, was what can be counted as the workcamp's success.

The workcamp did not end quickly on the day of the coup. During the first two days of the coup I was stranded in Nicosia under curfew and without a car. On Wednesday, 17 July, I returned to Peristerona to find six of the students and the foreman, a Greek Cypriot hired with the government's grant money, still working on the houses. Three students had been in Nicosia and returned to their families the first day of the coup. The others had left by private means to their homes in neighboring villages. Dan Sipe had left Cyprus for America two hours before the coup broke out.

After finding transportation home for the remaining students I set about reorganizing the workcamp. I probably would have ended the project at that point if the foreman and one of the most technically qualified students, both Greek Cypriots, had not urged me to continue. They laid the plans for a scaled down but feasible continuation and I looked for and received local governmental approval and promises for continued delivery of materials. We would have resumed work on Monday 22 July.

The Turkish invasions of Saturday 20 July, again brought a halt to our plans. The Turks of Peristerona were confined, by their Greek neighbors, in the village mosque, perhaps ten yards from the house the students had nearly finished. One of the boys who had helped the project was among the 80 or so Turks in the mosque. The student who had helped re-organize the work stayed in the village though he was one of the few Greek Cypriots of his age who did not carry a gun.

I was allowed to visit the mosque whenever I wished. In the village, I was given hospitality by various Greek Cypriot families in Peristerona, many of whom showed concern over their neighbors in the mosque. The Turks who were being held saw me as a possible guarantor of their well-being and the Greeks perhaps viewed me as someone who would tell the outside world how they treated the Turks. Under the conditions, I felt the Greek Cypriots made every effort to respect the lives and properties of the Turks. This was especially due to the vigilance of several older Greeks who knew the village Turks well.

I stayed in Peristerona for about a week until all the Turks, except the fighting age males, were released from the mosque. At that particular time most people on the island felt a peace agreement would be forthcoming and, indeed, a ceasefire was soon put into effect. I left the remaining workcamp funds with the person who had been the main organizer of the camp, a Greek Cypriot from Nicosia. The money was to be used to finish one of the houses, provide a donation to the village, and any remaining funds be given to island relief agencies.

I do not know what has become of the villagers. As of 16 September, Peristerona was still in Greek hands. It seems to me, however, that the security of the Turkish Cypriots held in Peristerona depended a good deal upon the relations which had been built over years of living and working alongside their Greek neighbors.

The fact that the Greek villagers made every effort to accommodate the Turks and protect their lives and property from outsiders was an indication to me that the security which the Turkish Cypriots have so long been seeking did not finally lie in the hands of the politicians or armies. The goals and ideals behind the Cyprus Resettlement Project affirm the principle that security comes from good neighbors more than from good politics or armies.

Termination of Mission

On 28 March 1975, in response to a letter about the possibility of further work on Cyprus, Denktash, now President of the Turkish Federated State of Cyprus, indicated that there was no further need to continue the Cyprus Resettlement Project. There were similar indications from the Greek side.

A week later, at the end of a one week visit to Cyprus, Hare issued a "Termination of Mission Report" after interviewing persons on each side to see if there is a possibility of further work involving resettlement. The text of the report was as follows:

> The principle mission of the Cyprus Resettlement Project, as agreed by both sides in March 1973, was to help with the resettlement of approximately 7,000 Turkish Cypriots who had left their villages during the time of troubles in 1963. Acting as a third party we helped develop a plan for resettlement, beginning with four mixed villages, which included supplying names of families who wished to return, assessment of the cost of repairs to houses, and a vote of funds by the Administration. Final details of the plan were considered at a meeting of technical personnel from both sides with a UN Officer as an observer. The final vote of funds was delayed pending clarification of the political situation. Before that could happen, the Coup occurred in July 1974.
>
> Before the Coup there were also approximately 6,000 Turkish Cypriots who had left urban areas, primarily the suburbs of Nicosia. We were not involved in their resettlement since this depended upon the outcome of the Intercommunal Talks. Nor had we any responsibility for the approximately 3,000 Greek Cypriot displaced persons, mostly from urban areas, whose housing problems were being handled directly by the Administration.
>
> As a result of the military and political events since July, which created a population displacement of some 200,000 persons (mostly Greek Cypriots as of September 1974), who were either refugees or displaced, or in villages which were cut-off, all proposals specifically designed for the displaced persons of the earlier period have been terminated. Thus the principle work of the Cyprus Resettlement Project has also been terminated.
>
> We also tried to promote collaboration and reconciliation between the Greek Cypriots and the Turkish Cypriots at the unofficial level. Our most visible effort in this area was the workcamp in Peristerona where 14 Greek and Turkish Cypriot students had spent a week repairing six houses for Turkish Cypriots students who had left the village in 1963. When the Coup occurred on 15 July 1974, Ellen Wilkinson, who had organized the camp, continued the work with a few students until the arrival of the Turkish Army on July 20 which brought all work to a halt. Any further collaboration of an unofficial nature between Greek and Turkish Cypriot does not seem possible at this time.
>
> A third function of our project was to provide an unofficial channel of communication for the discussion of humanitarian problems. This function is now performed by several agencies: the United Nations High Commissioner for Refugees, the International Committee of the Red Cross, the Red Crescent, the recently created Humanitarian and Economics Branch of the United Nations forces in Cyprus, and a special committee with four representatives from each community and the participation of UN officials and the International Committee of the Red Cross which is concerned with humanitarian issues.
>
> Although the number of Cypriot displaced persons is now over 10 times as great as it was in 1963, it seems best to terminate the Cyprus Resettlement Project since it was formed to meet a specific set of conditions which no longer exist. Future work on humanitarian problems should begin with a current appraisal of the situation so that new projects can be designed and personnel recruited to meet the needs of Cyprus at this time.

We know that the British Quakers have a team on Cyprus which is currently making an appraisal of the situation. Should they, or any other group committed to the principles of nonviolent conflict resolution, find that the experience or the personnel of the Cyprus Resettlement Project could be useful in the future, we are again ready to take up the work on behalf of the people of Cyprus.

Evaluation by Project Member Kate Kemp

Limitations of the CRP. Perhaps the main limitation was one imposed by the project itself: time. I felt that three months was hardly sufficient time to achieve the task, and it was certainly much too short a time to try to move into the field of community action/social change. Another fundamental limitation was the lack of Greek or Turkish language speakers. The difference made by having a fluent Turkish speaker in Dhiorios was very considerable. As a thought for future such actions, a number of project members who speak the indigenous languages should be a priority in selection. The nature of the project itself, a transnational team, posed some problems. Thus we lacked basic consensus over our aims, approach, roles, etc. This could have been overcome had we all arrived at the same time so that initial orientation could have involved discussion of these points. We might well never have reached agreement, but we could have saved a lot of time (and perhaps confusion) later on in the project. (The staggered arrivals, though unavoidable in this phase of the project, were not, I felt, a particularly good thing). The lack of a real common language within the project also proved to be a minor problem (and it might have assumed greater importance had the English speakers been fully aware from the beginning of the lack of general comprehension). Translation was possible, but it was a cumbersome process and often did not make for ease of communication. The project was based on the idea of consensus, and although I am sympathetic to the idea and the concept of non-organization, I feel that a little structuring and organization often helps considerably in the day to day running of such a project. We had a certain amount of both, but could occasionally have done with more.

Communications within the group could I think have been improved; they were adequate, but a central (telephone) message desk, or something similar, might have been useful. Finally, one limitation that particularly affected village work was the time lag between our work and the negotiations. Work in the villages was dependent on the stage of negotiations to a large extent; therefore we were sometimes held back by the negotiations. For example we had nothing concrete on which to base our work until mid-December when the Government made their public announcement about resettlement; I personally was very concerned not to simply "raise hopes" until I could be sure that the process of resettlement was indeed on the move. Ideally, negotiating should have been ahead of the village work, rather than running concurrently with it. (This is more of a thought for future actions, rather than a criticism of the CRP, because the situation was not as it had been expected or planned for).

Successes: The primary successes were at the negotiating level, since they really allowed the other work to continue and to become more concrete. Thus negotiation resulted in the Greek Government's public announcement on resettlement, committing their interest and financial support. Secondly, priority lists (of villages to be resettled) were established, facilitating the actual process. The UN civilian section agreed to "monitor" the resettlement process after the withdrawal of CRP in January. Finally, an informal meeting between members of the Government and the Turkish leadership interested in resettlement, was arranged with CRP acting as a third party.

At the village level we were able to achieve a certain amount of data collection, information on potential returnees, the surveying of Turkish houses (with both the Greek and Turkish engineers separately) and a general airing of the issue of resettlement and its problems. Many of the successes in the villages may seem rather nebulous, but I felt that we had some minor breakthroughs, and that the whole process of resettlement at the village level was getting off the ground. For example, perhaps partly as a result of the work we did in Dhiorios and Lapithos towards resettlement, rebuilding houses and resolutions of fears about personal security, 15 and six additional families respectively, decided to return. In one Turkish refugee village, there had been little enthusiasm to return, or trust that this would be possible, but after we had talked to men in the village from various mixed villages, they themselves arranged a meeting for us to gather the necessary information and organized applications for their return.

In other villages, they were successful in similar and other ways, both concerning resettlement and more generally in the field of community action. For example, three of the Shanti Sainiks went on a "padyatra" (walking tour) which they felt had been a success.

Evaluation by Project Member Zena Lutrin
The CRP was made up of people from four nations, of all ages. They had very different world views, interests and reasons for being in Cyprus. They were called upon to work in concert on a problem and obviously there were difficulties and tensions. Most of the people had in common a commitment to nonviolence. However, I do not believe that this was a big factor in giving the group a common ideology. Not all members subscribed

to nonviolence in the same way. There were differing interpretations of what nonviolence meant to the individual from those who were prepared to lay down their lives in Cyprus to those who believed that nonviolence is justified under certain circumstances.

Added to this were differing political attitudes and beliefs and different views on the problems of Cyprus itself. About the only common ground held by the group on an ideological level was the belief that Turkish and Greek Cypriots should live together in peace and that resettlement of Turkish refuges was a good thing. (Although for different reasons.)

Added to the different perspectives of members were differing emphases, interests, and skills. This obviously led to a great deal of frustration of individuals and a certain lack of satisfaction with the project.

The Indian members of the team had specific skills. They were village organizers in India and were used to working with people. They believed that action by the people was essential in any political system. They were committed to changing society by people action and were involved in this in India. Village work and actions was their reason for being in Cyprus. Fundamental to this was encouraging good relations between villagers i.e. Greeks and Turks. As soon as the Turkish Administration heard of the first effort to organize a meeting between Greeks and Turks they blackballed it. Their given reasons were twofold: a. The Government would publicize events like this and take political capital for themselves, b. High level communications and co-ordination of resettlement was necessary before any lower level meetings took place. Thus, a portion of the group were frustrated from doing what they considered vitally important work, the work for which they were most qualified.

Other members of the group were also committed, as a basic principle, to radical social change. They felt the CRP should be organizing on a "people" level. Others felt that this would jeopardize the resettlement work. As with the issue of mixed meetings it was decided by the group to water down this and go as far as was thought possible without antagonizing the Government or Administration. This was obviously not very far.

Other members of the group had qualms about working with the power holders in the society. This applied particularly to the Administration. Group members had doubts about their sincerity as peace in Cyprus would mean appreciable loss of power. The Administration appeared to exert much more direct control over their people than the Government. Added to this was the fact that the Turks had not had an election since 1960. (The new Turkish leader Mr Denktash had been unopposed when "elected" in 1971.)

Considering these factors and the divergent cultures and interests of members of the CRP it is not surprising that there was little group cohesion. What is surprising is that they were able to work together as well as they did.

The group constantly discussed their role in Cyprus. Most of these discussion came out of the problems discussed above. Discussion centered around questioning whether the CRP should be confining its activities to facilitating the resettlement process at the official level. No absolute decisions were ever taken, but the implicit decision was that action on other levels should be curbed so as not to jeopardize the other work, thus the compromises were made. These issues constantly simmered throughout the project.

The CRP was run on the Quaker principle of consensus. The group subscribed to total equality among members and it was important to members that decisions were made by all.

In view of the nature of their work the negotiating/co-ordinating team made on the spot decisions which affected the whole group. The fact that all village teams and most views were represented there caused most of the decisions to be in keeping with the views of the group as a whole, and major policy was always discussed by the full group.

A problem arose because one member of the group took more of the burden than others. Of the whole team there in November and December he was the only one who had been in the project from its inception and on all previous trips to Cyprus. It was the first visit to Cyprus for the rest of the group. Parsons (a sociologist) postulates that systems high in information will control those high in energy. In this case the group member was high on both. Although other members did become *au fait* with the project and especially the negotiation, many felt that he, having had much more experience both of negotiating and the project, was more qualified to act.

This member of the team believed that the group *per se* and each member equally should be responsible for the project. Transferring this responsibility and spreading it around the group caused many strains. I think that the group emerged stronger for the pains and there was much more harmony among members.

On a "housekeeping" level there were problems within the group with language. English, being the mother tongue of the majority, was used, but some of the Hindi speakers were not fluent in English and this meant that group members could not communicate fully with each other. This problem was not very difficult to overcome.

Communication between villager teams was a problem not as easily overcome. None of the houses had phones. Meetings had to be prearranged and emergencies dealt with by the people on the spot. Otherwise communication involved driving many miles and perhaps finding the people sought away. This factor was not crucial but it was a limitation on the optimal functioning of the group.

NOTE

*   Reprinted with permission from A.Paul Hare (ed.), *Cyprus Resettlement Project: An Instance of International Peacemaking* (Beer Sheva: Department of Behavioral Sciences, Ben-Gurion University of the Negev, 1991), pp.1-21, 60-66.

NONVIOLENT WITNESS AND ACCOMPANIMENT

Intention: to create a safe, localized political space so that activists can engage in nonviolent activity.

7

PEACE BRIGADES INTERNATIONAL: NONVIOLENCE IN ACTION*

Liam Mahony

Introduction

In late 1981 an international nonviolence conference was convened at Grindstone Island, Canada, to found Peace Brigades International (PBI). From Europe, Asia and the Americas, the participants brought together decades of experience working in a variety of conflicts and organizations: Quakers, Indian activists in the Gandhian tradition, other seeking models to prompt future large-scale initiatives in the United Nations, and many more. What they had in common was an idea, reflected in their founding statement:

> We are forming an organization with the capacity to mobilize and provide trained units of volunteers in areas of high tension, to avert violent outbreaks. Peace brigades, fashioned to respond to specific needs and appeals, will undertake nonpartisan missions which may include peacemaking initiatives, peacekeeping under a discipline of nonviolence, and humanitarian service. [A] brigade may establish and monitor a ceasefire, offer mediatory services, or carry on works of reconstruction and reconciliation. Those who undertake these tasks will face risks and hardships.
> We are building on a rich and extensive heritage of nonviolent action. We are convinced that this commitment of mind, heart, and dedicated will can make a significant difference in human affairs.

The Grindstone island conference was certainly not the first time that international nonviolence activists had gotten together with ambitious dreams. But PBI succeeded in putting these dreams into action. A decade and a half later PBI is managing simultaneous projects in six different conflicts. Hundreds of volunteers have worked in its projects, and tens of thousands more have supported the organization from their homes in over 15 countries.

Guatemala: The Birth of Protective Accompaniment

The growth and reputation of PBI was initially the result of its work in the mid-1980s in Guatemala, where the first team of volunteers arrived in 1983. Guatemalans were paralyzed, facing an efficient system of state terror. Tens of thousands had been killed or disappeared, millions had fled their homes. State forces had murdered hundreds of university professors, union leaders, church workers and anyone else involved in democratic organizing. In 1981 they even went so far as to firebomb the Spanish embassy when poor farmers staged a sit-in.

The PBI team in its first year could barely find anyone willing to consider nonviolent political action. What they did find were victims. Family members of the disappeared regularly appeared on PBI's doorstep asking for help. Seeing their pain and hopelessness, PBI volunteer Edith Cole took a radical step: in April 1984 she travelled to El Salvador and asked the COMADRES, a seven-year-old organization of mothers of victims of war, if they would record a taped message of hope for Guatemala family members.

A few weeks later, several Guatemalan women asked Edith if she would go with them to ask the Guatemalan Archbishop to say a special mass for the disappeared. While they sat in the waiting room, Edith played them the tape. The effect was electric. The Salvadoran woman on the tape shared her grief and loss, striking an emotion chord among the Guatemalans. She urged the Guatemalans to organize themselves, emphasizing the importance of direct action and outlined a list of organizing tactics. Finally, she suggested that the effort was survivable but not without losses and not without external support. The COMADRES had sought allies in two of the only spheres relatively independent of state control: the church and the international community. Charged by the tape's message, the Guatemalan women asked the Archbishop to host an organization of families of the disappeared under the protection of the church. He refused—it was too dangerous.

As they walked out of his office, Edith offered them the PBI house for their meetings. "It isn't the church," she said, "but at least its something." The women placed ads in the Guatemala City daily papers inviting the public to the special mass which the Archbishop had agreed to offer. With just three days notice, a large crowd turned out for the event. The women left the mass and came over to the PBI house to establish a new organization: the *Grupo de Apoyo Mutuo*, or GAM (Mutual Support Group). Their founding statement carefully avoided any hint of political affiliation or even protest:

> We are not in opposition to anyone, nor are we accusing anyone in particular. What brings us together is our profound love for our lost ones and our need to give each other moral and spiritual support. We are asking

all mothers, wives and family members in general who have suffered the same situation to join us. Together we will succeed in bringing our loved ones home. They are the center of our lives.

Every Saturday the GAM met at the PBI house. Soon hundreds of people were showing up. Not surprisingly, though, many viewed PBI with suspicion. Ester de Herrarte recalls: "At first I was frightened to come. It might be a trap. I didn't know who these Brigades were."[1] Some feared they might be the CIA. But the family members kept coming.

There was nowhere else to go. Mixed in with the mistrust was a feeling of safety. Ester de Herrarte remembers:

All of us have fond memories of how PBI opened their arms to us. The simple fact of being located in a house with foreigners committed to nonviolence was a big support in the beginning. It's thanks to that support that we were able to organize ourselves, because those were really difficult times.

Hundreds of Guatemalans had lost their loved ones and met in the morgues before, without forming an organization. What was different in the spring of 1984? The GAM's founders had all lost a loved one in 1984. In fact, due to a rash of kidnappings at the University of San Carlos, more than half had lost someone in the two weeks immediately prior to the founding. They may have been desperate, but they had not yet given up. They were still looking. Most of all, they were looking for hope. But hope was not enough—they needed a plan. The social function of terror is not simply to destroy hope. It also serves to isolate people and convince them that there is nothing that can be done, even if they have the motivation to try something. Confusion, inaction and frustration can quickly snuff out a spontaneous flame of hope.

The COMADRES tape moved these frightened family members from confusion to decisiveness. But they still needed security. They had families, other loved ones vulnerable to disappearance. They had to have some minimal assurance that their struggle to find their loved ones would not simply compound the tragedy. The COMADRES had formed in 1977 with the powerful figure of Archbishop Romero to protect them; the Salvadoran Catholic Church was still a credible deterrent. The GAM members, denied church protection, turned to PBI, an unknown international NGO. It was a desperate recourse to keep the momentum going.

For the first several months the organization grew rapidly, holding regular vigils and masses. They met twice with the de facto president General Mejía Victores, who agreed to set up a special commission to investigate disappearances. But nothing happened. By late 1984, GAM members were frustrated, and they began to call publicly for cutoffs in international aid to Guatemala. The GAM's president, Nineth de García, describes what happened next:

> In December [1984] we began to receive the first threats. We didn't want to take them seriously at first, so we wouldn't lose our morale. They want to break one's morale. In January we all started getting anonymous threats. In February, Hector Gomez, our public relations secretary, told us he was being followed and closely watched. He had even discovered that his identity papers had been removed from the local municipal offices. We were very worried.

On 14 March 1985, General Mejía publicly accused the GAM of being manipulated by the forces of subversion. On 15 March, police searched the home of GAM member Angel Reyes. PBI and other human rights organizations in the US, Canada, and Europe began an international pressure campaign to safeguard the GAM. Various GAM members reported that their houses were being watched and they were receiving telephone threats. The GAM was beginning to feel besieged. On Saturday, 30 March, Hector Gomez left a GAM meeting at the PBI house. He was found dead the next day with his hands tied behind his back, no tongue, and signs of beating and burns. At Gomez's funeral on Monday, unknown men in civilian dress took photos of the mourners. PBI volunteer Alain Richard described an emergency GAM meeting at the PBI house a few days later:

> The GAM members were completely discouraged. There were only a few people. I shouldn't say only a few, there were 60-80 people, but compared to having hundreds and hundreds at previous meetings. During that meeting, they had a phone call announcing that some US Congresspeople would come for the GAM demonstration scheduled for April 13. At that moment the group got more courage.
> After that meeting, I took Nineth and Isabel and María Rosario aside and told them, "You know, they will do everything to kill you this weekend. Please promise me not to leave your home this weekend for any reason."

It was the last GAM meeting for María Rosario Godoy de Cuevas, a founder and secretary of the group. The next morning she drove to the pharmacy with her brother and two-year old son, who was ill. Their bodies were found that evening in their car in a ravine. The police report declared it an automobile accident, but Western diplomats said all three were slain before the car plunged into the ravine. Archbishop Penados angrily told the press that he had information that the cause of death was strangulation. Mourners at the funeral noted that the baby's fingernails were missing.

Nineth de García recalls:

> It was a terrible time for us. There was a recomposition of the GAM at that moment. A lot of people fled into exile, and others left the GAM for good. The rest of us decided that we had a historical responsibility, from that moment until the last day of our lives. We were weak, just human beings, but we knew we had a great love for Guatemala. We decided, OK. Fine. We're brave, we're strong, and we're decided, but if we don't have the support of foreigners here we will not survive. After that we were accompanied for 24 hours a day by Peace Brigade members.

PBI was then very shorthanded. In fact, when Hector Gomez was killed, Alain Richard was alone in Guatemala, and had to leave the country soon to renew his visa. Just before María Rosario's death two more volunteers arrived. But the idea of personal accompaniment, according to Alain, did not arise until after her death.

> The night before I had to leave, a close diplomatic contact visited me, along with Jean-Marie Simon of Americas Watch, and they told me "Listen, you've started to be with these women. That has to continue. How can you make sure you have enough people to do that?" I got on the phone right away, and I kept calling even from Mexico while renewing my visa, to round up more people.

This was the beginning of PBI "escorting": providing the surviving GAM leadership with round-the-clock unarmed bodyguards. At the time, such a commitment was utterly beyond PBI's capacity. Yet this service would come to define its role in Guatemala.

Peace Brigades recognized it was doing something new in the field of human rights protection. But no one knew if it would work. Why would a death squad which had pulled out the fingernails of an infant exercise restraint in the presence of an unarmed foreigner? Later Alain Richard learned from a confidential diplomatic source that the entire GAM directorate was on a death list.

> I had to report that to the team. It was quite scary for one guy who was escorting. He broke down, and we had to try to encourage him during the night. I said to him, "We can discontinue your escort. One of us can do it. If you think it is not fair to your wife, we understand that you might not want to." I had to be pretty calm, even cold. This was not a time to give someone a false sense of security. He said, "So do I understand that the person I am to escort might be killed?" I replied, "That is correct." "And does it mean that I might also be killed?" "That is correct." And I added, "Isn't this why you came?" "Well, yes, I wrote my will before I came, but now that its closer...." I said, "I think they will try to avoid killing you. But nevertheless you never know if someone who is not experienced might hurt you by mistake." The following morning I asked him if someone should go in his place. He said, "No, I'll go." In fact, he stayed with us for quite a time. No other GAM leaders were killed.

The following year US journalists Allan Nairn and Jean-Marie Simon, citing military sources, reported that Jaime Martinez Jiminez had carried out the two killings. Martinez, chief of the homicide division of the Department of Technical Investigation, was operating under orders of a G-2[2] military intelligence commander named Colonel Carlos Dorantes Marroquín. No one, however, was ever prosecuted. Surviving GAM members were certain they were going to die. First they had lost family members. Then in the previous year they had built an organization for mutual support and grown to depend on each other like family. They were living through the trauma of loss all over again. The *New York Times* reported:

> The two remaining directors, Nineth de García and Isabel de Castañon, said this week they hope to keep the group alive. But the two young women are clearly terrified. After months of emotional agony in their search for their husbands who have disappeared, they now confront a barrage of death threats that diplomats say are chillingly credible. At least three nations have quietly offered asylum. But the GAMs leaders stayed and fought, risking all (Kinzer, 1985).

Nineth de García credits PBI for her survival: "Thanks to their presence I am alive. That is an indisputable truth. If it had not been for them, I would not be here telling you this today."

The Guatemalan military may have ignored international opinion in its decision to murder the GAM's leaders in 1985. But with ongoing protective accompaniment from PBI, high-profile killings ceased. The military looked for other ways to intimidate and control the GAM.

A bare six months after accompaniment began, the GAM made a bold move, taking over the National Cathedral during the presidential elections of October 1985. PBI volunteers held vigil outside, 24 hours a day. The five day occupation gained headlines, embarrassed the government and angered General Mejía Victores, who wanted to avoid a similar disruption of the runoff elections scheduled for December.

This time the attack on the GAM was more subtle: Mejía used the immigration department to cut off the visas for ten PBI volunteers. When PBI and the volunteers' embassies protested, the immigration chief explained that PBI's work was illegal meddling in internal politics. But then he made a telling offer: perhaps the visas could be renewed if PBI could guarantee that GAM would not disrupt the runoff elections. PBI dismissed this attempt at manipulation. Then, rather than protest further, the organization accepted the expulsions and rapidly recruited a half-dozen new volunteers to replace those who had to leave. The GAM was never without accompaniment.

The survival of the GAM opened the door for a gradual rebirth of democratic activism in Guatemala. PBI accompanied GAM leaders around-the-clock for over four years. When the organization moved into its own office, PBI continued a regular presence well into the 1990s.

Developing the Accompaniment Tool

The modern notion of a nongovernmental, international protective presence can be traced at least back to the formation of the International Committee for the Red Cross (ICRC) in 1863. The ICRC was the first NGO to successfully convince warring nations to honor the moral and symbolic force of an outside neutral party. The bulk of international human rights and humanitarian law, subsequently developed, presupposes a deterring effect of international moral pressure. The formation and growth of nongovernmental organizations like Amnesty International in the 1960s and 70s broadened this concept by involving everyday citizens in direct pressure campaigns. By building a network of letter writers, Amnesty proved that even unknown prisoners in relatively obscure parts of the world could be protected by the power of international opinion. Where Amnesty protected the rights of a political prisoner by projecting pressure with a mass of letters, PBI accompaniment manifested similar pressure much more immediately, with volunteers risking their lives to stand beside human rights activists to prevent arrest or attack.

Implementing this ambitious accompaniment program forced PBI to build a stronger organization. It needed more fundraising, more volunteer recruitment, better volunteer training and selection. Networks had to be built to back up the volunteers' symbolic presence with international clout.

It is doubtful that the fledgling PBI could have met this challenge were it not for the confluence of political factors provided by the Central American conflicts of the 1980s. PBI drew from the loosely knit nonviolence movement, including activists from around the world, some tracing their commitment back to Gandhi, others to resistance to military conscription, struggles against the Vietnam war, or the more recent antinuclear efforts. Accompaniment also attracted people from the rapidly growing human rights movement. But by far the biggest quantitative impulse came from the Central American solidarity movement. This movement provided a base of financial support, interested and politically educated volunteers and a broad network of political pressure to protect PBI in the field.

Over the next few years hundreds of volunteers went to Guatemala, and experienced something completely unexpected and inspiring. Canadian volunteer Sel Burroughs wrote later:

> Escorting [GAM President] Nineth de García for five days was one of the most dynamic experiences of my life. Nothing happened. But I had time while I followed and waited, to observe and support a brave, dedicated, caring and vulnerable woman.... Escorting is difficult. It involves being ready to move at someone else's schedule, hours of waiting and intermittent exclusion and inclusion in the lives of the person you are responsible for.

To meet accompaniment demands in Guatemala, PBI set up a two-tiered system of long-term team members and short-term escorts. Long-term team members maintained political contacts, analyzed the political situation, and determined the team's work priorities. They provided orientation and support for hundreds of two week or one month escorts. The accompaniment relationship was by no means easy. Nineth de García, for instance, lived with accompaniment constantly for over four years, all the while receiving threats against both herself and her daughter:

> I have to tell you that I am very grateful for it, but it was also very hard. I felt I had no space. I don't know how to explain. I was watched in the streets, the press always wanted to know what I thought and did, my life was hanging from a thread, and I needed these foreign volunteers. But they are from different cultures and different ways of thinking, and in one's home things are totally different. There were moments of happiness, but also difficulties, like in any human relationship. First of all, its pretty hard for a foreigner to understand all the pain that you are carrying around with you. I've seen many friends fall. Sometimes you feel so hopeless and desperate, and all you want is a space where you can yell and scream. And you get home, and there's still this foreigner with you, and there's nothing you can do. You're stuck.

Volunteers and GAM members alike wondered just what the accompaniment should do if a death squad actually arrived to abduct them. Should they try to interfere and risk getting abducted as well? Or get away to communicate the news and start a rapid international alert?

There were no simple formulas or easy answers to all the "what ifs?" But in the course of day-in day-out accompaniment and endless discussion, PBI was developing a new protective tool. Formal orientation manuals were created for short-term escorts. Regular discussions amongst volunteers analyzed the political situation and potential risks. Logs were kept noting any threats, surveillance, or suspicious coincidences to maintain continuity and organizational memory amidst rapid volunteer turnover. These logs helped volunteers recognize the risks around them, even if their own brief visit was uneventful.

Outside Guatemala, the organization built links with human rights and Central America solidarity organizations and developed an extensive rapid-response network to mobilize international pressure in response to emergencies. This Emergency Response Network became a major feature of PBI's operations. Over the years the organization built up a telephone tree of thousands of people around the world. If someone being accompanied was attacked or threatened, the team would contact the project staff in Canada, who would quickly alert key callers around the world, who would in turn activate their branches of the telephone tree. Within a few hours, Network members would send hundreds of telexes to the Guatemalan government or military, protesting the attack. The goal of the response network was to multiply the protective power of the accompaniment, while giving thousands of citizens around the world a way to learn about Guatemala and take effective action.

Accompaniment and the Democratic Image

The Guatemalan government in the late 80s was trying to create a new image for itself. After years of terror, a new constitution was written, and in 1986, civilian president Vinicio Cerezo took office. Human rights abuse continued, but this abuse contradicted the government's desire for a clean image. This dynamic actually helped accompaniment function: the state wanted to avoid bad press, and was less likely to attack activists in the presence of foreigners. When asked later whether international accompaniment successfully protected people during his presidency, ex-President Cerezo responded, "Definitely!", and even cited examples.

Likewise, Cerezo's defense minister Hector Gramajo is quick to explain how carefully they tried to analyze the international consequences of each decision, taking into account the political costs of upsetting the international human rights community:

> The problem is, military men always view with suspicion anything that looks like social organization, especially when they are facing subversives. It's a logical suspicion. What are we going to do? So the effort of trying to reconcile the needs of security and development, through the process of reconstruction, was really forcing the army to come to grips with a new concept: internationalism.

When Gramajo and Cerezo were in power in the late 80s, they were constantly besieged by international human rights campaigns. But Gramajo took it in stride:

> Really, they were literally volcanoes of letters of protest. But if you look into it you find they're really just chain letters. The signers don't even know what they're signing. Or maybe they're from student associations or something. So you have to figure out how to measure the difference between an unimportant chain letter, and a real clamor that's going to affect the international conscience. And that's very difficult to distinguish. You have to figure out how to evaluate it. You have to watch for when it reaches the level of an intergovernmental problem. When it moves from the opinion of an organization to the opinion of a state. If Amnesty International puts out a report, well, that's just Amnesty International. But if the Organization of American States, informed by Amnesty International, puts out a report against us, then we're fucked! If they can penetrate the OAS we're screwed, because we're signers of all these covenants and treaties.

This process of calculating the impact of international human rights campaigns confirms the logic of accompaniment. Gramajo and Cerezo were probably much less likely to blunder into international scandal than their predecessors. They wouldn't order assassinations in front of international witnesses. In fact, under their regime death squads consistently targeted unknown rank-and-file members of civilian organizations, avoiding the more high-profile leaders whose death would create scandals. But Gramajo was still a soldier at heart, committed to the counterinsurgency strategies whose heavy human rights toll increased steadily throughout his regime. He and Cerezo endeavored to undermine the credibility of both domestic and international human rights organizations. They won broad support in the diplomatic corps, garnering increased aid from the US and Europe. Meanwhile, though, Cerezo's minimal efforts at reform alienated and angered the extreme right. When right-wing attacks increased against the civilian movement and human rights groups, the government's rhetoric deflected the resulting human rights pressure. Groups like the GAM, the Council of Ethnic Communities or PBI were thus more vulnerable to attack from the more extreme right-wing factions. While human rights groups worked to strengthen their international shield, Cerezo and Gramajo worked to weaken it.

The Movement Grows
The GAM's courage proved that overt political action was survivable. This survival, with accompaniment, was in turn a broad advertisement for the value of PBI's protection, and in the late 80s and early 90s, many new civilian organization came knocking on PBI's door when they faced threats. This included dozens and dozens of different unions, high-profile exiled Guatemalans such as Rigoberta Menchú who returned to visit, and a historic new movement of indigenous Mayans fighting for their rights.

In June 1987, workers at the Lunafil thread factory went on strike and occupied the factory grounds in Amatitlan, outside of Guatemala City. Facing death threats, and knowing that union activists had already been murdered at other factories belonging to the same owner, the workers asked PBI to stay with them. PBI volunteers could not actually occupy the factory, as this would contradict the nonpartisan stance of the organization—not to mention call down the wrath of immigration officials again. So, for the next 13 months, PBI volunteers camped out at the factory entrance on the side of the highway. Twenty-four hours a day, rain or shine, one or two PBI volunteers were always there. Gangs of thugs would come and harass and threaten, or drive by firing shots in the air, but no one in the union was abducted or killed. The Lunafil strike drew international support, and inspired a spurt in union organizing activity throughout Guatemala. After PBI's steadfast presence at

Lunafil, dozens of unions asked PBI for protection when they felt threatened.

According to labor organizer Sergio Guzman:

> It's not that the threats necessarily stop when you have accompaniment. Accompaniment questions the threat. It confronts it. I once got a threat on the telephone and the voice said, "Even while you have accompaniment you're going to be the victim!" That says a lot in itself: that they're paying attention to the accompaniment. For them it is something that matters. During the times when we've had accompaniment personally it has helped to have more freedom in our activities. Its enabled us not to leave off of those activities which were committed to.
>
> You call off the accompaniment when you feel you've reached a politically different situation. It doesn't mean the systematic violence is over, because that's a question of roots. It's more subjective when the accompaniment has fulfilled its task of calling the violence into question.

Meanwhile, up in the highlands of El Quiché, schoolteacher Amilcar Mendez had been trying to build a movement for human rights among Mayan farmers. Throughout the mid-80s, Mendez spoke out, but found no support. Highland residents were too frightened, and Mendez himself had to flee El Quiché three times. The third time, with PBI's help, he and his family found refuge in Canada. But Mendez couldn't stand it in Canada, and in less than two months he was back in Guatemala with a new plan of action: to build an organization in El Quiché which would resist the army's oppressive system of civilian patrols. The civil patrols were a cornerstone of the army's counterinsurgency system in the highlands: every adult male was forced to spend one day a week on patrol. Patrolling could mean just that: searching for guerrillas or spying on your own village, but it also meant hard labor, working on the army's construction projects with no pay.

One unique aspect of Mendez's plan was his conscious use of international support. His hope was that the rural farmers' fears could be overcome if they saw that the movement had international support. So he constantly brought foreigners up to El Quiché to talk with victims of the patrol system's abuses. In 1988, he asked PBI to begin regular accompaniment in El Quiché. That same year small groups of men in rural villages began to refuse patrol service. Mendez, with PBI accompaniment, travelled from village to village encouraging this resistance, and teaching villagers the Guatemalan constitution, which prohibits forced servitude. In July, 1988, he brought together representatives of dozens of towns at his home, where they formed the Council of Ethnic Communities, or CERJ, its Spanish/Mayan abbreviation. Over the next six years, PBI maintained a regular presence in El Quiché with CERJ activists. The CERJ did for the civil patrol issue what the GAM had done with disappearances. Through sheer courage and perseverance, they took a taboo subject and put it on the national agenda. Amilcar Mendez declares unequivocally that he would not be alive were it not for international accompaniment. Even then-President Vinicio Cerezo agrees with him:

> This foreign presence diminished the possibility of threats and human rights violations. Take Amilcar Mendez as an example. Now of course we never thought to do anything against him. But there were definitely people and groups who were out to get him. The fact that he had these international connections, right up to the US Congress, protected him even from attacks that might have come without high-level authorization.

PBI accompanied CERJ members and events throughout the Guatemalan highlands, where local Mayan activists faced murderous patrol leaders who seemed at first not to care much about a foreign presence. Gradually, though, as international pressure built against the patrol system, accompaniment became more and more effective. In December 1995, Amilcar Mendez was elected to the Guatemalan Congress. In 1996, after eight years of CERJ pressure, the Guatemalan government began to dismantle the patrols.

The CERJ was only the beginning of the flowering of a new Mayan movement in Guatemala. After 1988, dozens of new Mayan groups formed. PBI was asked to accompany the Mayan widows organization CONAVIGUA, the Committee for Campesino Unity (CUC), the Council of Displaced Guatemalans (CONDEG) and many others. These new organizations changed the political landscape of Guatemala, pushing for structural social, economic and political changes to combat the oppression and poverty they were living.

In 1989, PBI decided that the continual stream of short-term volunteers was too problematic. The stresses and pressures were too great, and required deeper orientation and preparation. The minimum length of stay was increased to six months and the two-level team structure was eliminated. This shift curtailed one of the key sources of institutional growth: the publicity and support work of volunteers returning home, since the flow of over a 100 volunteers per year was reduced to a trickle. But PBI was more concerned about maintaining trusting relationships in the field, a high-level of discretion and analysis, and a strong sense of team continuity and affinity, all of which were suffering.

Accompaniment Under Attack

On 19 January 1989, during an army press conference, self-professed guerrilla deserter Angel Reyes described to reporters how he had worked together with the GAM and the guerrilla movement to discredit Guatemala, and accused PBI of relaying messages between guerrilla contacts in Guatemala and Europe.

In May of the same year, Rigoberta Menchú and several exiled colleagues returned to Guatemala for a visit. During their stay, hard-line right-wing forces attempted a coup d'etat. The coup was quickly subdued by General Gramajo, but the same afternoon PBI began to receive threatening telephone calls: volunteers were instructed to tell Menchú and Amilcar Mendez to leave the country within 48 hours or they would be killed, and the PBI house would be bombed.

PBI volunteer Patty Mutchnick was accompanying Rigoberta Menchú:

> The day was a waiting game. After the fifth threatening call of the day, I heard Rigoberta jokingly say, "I wish they'd get this straight. Do I have twenty-four hours from the 8am call or from the 10am call?" Rigoberta knew as well as I that when I went out to scan the street for snipers and dangerous men behind tinted windows, the actual physical protection I offered her was absurd, and to myself in that moment, laughable. I was absolutely vulnerable, and so were they.

Menchú cut off her stay and flew back to Mexico. A few months later, threats were replaced by attacks. On 15 August, PBI volunteers Jennie Roitman and Laura Hernandez were at the offices of the GAM. They were up on the second floor, getting ready to spend the night with 20 GAM members, mostly children, who were staying there. A little before 8pm they heard the shots, and someone banged on the door. Jennie was on her way down the stairway to investigate the noise when a bomb exploded, destroying the room at the bottom of the stairway. Singed but uninjured, she went back up the stairs.

A mile away at the Peace Brigades house, as the rest of the team was just sitting down to dinner, two grenades were thrown over the garden wall. The explosions jolted the house, filling the air with smoke and glass. Everyone instinctively jumped under the dinner table. The force of the blast shattered most of the windows in the house, but luckily the dinner table was protected from the flying glass by a dividing wall. No one was injured. PBI volunteer María Serra told the press, "If we'd been in the other room, we wouldn't be here to tell you about it." Police who inspected the damage later stated that if the second grenade had been a few inches closer to the tanks of cooking gas, half the block would have gone up.

Shocked by the attack, yet grateful for their survival, PBI volunteers took turns spending the night watching for intruders and guarding the gaping holes that had once been windows. The next few days were spent frantically scheduling meetings with the diplomatic corps and government officials. Meanwhile, PBI's Emergency Response Network barraged President Cerezo with international telexes demanding that he investigate the attacks and ensure the safety of both PBI and the GAM.

Unlike previous PBI alerts, this time it was European and North American citizens who had been victimized. The resulting response was much greater. European and North American elected officials contacted Cerezo demanding that their constituents be protected. When the house was repaired, PBI held a reception for the diplomatic corps and the press to announce it had no intention of leaving Guatemala.

But the attacks didn't stop. On 20 December 1989, volunteers Meredith Larson, Rusa Jeremic and Mitchell Goldberg were walking home in the early evening when two men ran from the shadows and knifed all three. The men vanished as quickly as they had appeared, stealing nothing. The injured volunteers got home intact, and were quickly sent off to the hospital. Jeremic and Goldberg had flesh wounds; Larson had to return to the US for treatment of a damaged nerve. According to Spanish PBI volunteer María Serra, "After that I think they had to realize: if you knife them and they still don't leave well, you either have to kill them, or accept that they're staying."

A US Department of Defense intelligence report, written shortly after the August bombings but classified secret until 1996, stated that the "Special Operations" section of the D-2 (Guatemalan Army Directorate of Intelligence) was responsible. It went on to suggest that the D-2 has used the recent disturbances as a cover to intimidate leftist opposition organizations (Intelligence Oversight Board, 1996).

The bombing and knifing actually gave PBI increased credibility and visibility in Guatemala. According to María Serra,

> From the moment of the bombing, we achieved a legitimacy with the authorities that we'd never had before. When you have government ministers and ambassadors coming to your house, that's sending a clear message to the death squads. They'd better take care, because this is who they're messing with.

Meredith Larson wrote after the attack, "It is some sick measure of our success that some people have been trying very hard to frighten us into leaving, with the death threats, bombing and this attack."

This "sick measure of success" argument was echoed by many of PBI's contacts in the civilian movement. They would point to their own history and say, "When you start to be really effective, they attack you." But of course for PBI the argument was self-contradictory: the whole notion of accompaniment as a protection is that you are effective because they won't attack you. Prior to these attacks, PBI was seen as the organization that had protected the rise of the GAM and the CERJ. Now it was the international group that had gotten bombed and knifed. Its success rate was slightly tarnished: the GAM, after all, had been bombed with PBI volunteers inside. Guatemalans made jokes about "Who is protecting whom?" But they respected PBI's steadfastness, and kept asking for PBI accompaniment. If the bombing and knifing temporarily reduced the sense of protection that PBI's accompaniment offered, this was more than countered by the long-term increase in confidence in the organization.

The Institutionalization of Accompaniment

The Guatemalan civilian movement continued to expand in the 1990s. PBI could not possibly meet all the accompaniment demands it received, but its accompaniment work became a model which many copied. In 1989, when PBI had to reduce its presence with the GAM, the GAM recruited independent volunteers with no organizational ties to live in their office and accompany them. After 1991, Amilcar Mendez also recruited accompaniment volunteers from other sources in the solidarity movement. These experiments saw mixed success, depending on the organizational support the volunteers brought with them. For instance, the GAM could not maintain consistency or training with its new volunteers, and the effort was short-lived. Mendez and the CERJ sometimes had the same problem, but later they were able to benefit from a long-term presence of volunteers associated with the US-based Human Rights Watch.

PBI eventually had enough diplomatic support to force some level of institutionalized recognition from the government. After 1991 volunteers were granted special long-term visas sponsored by the Guatemalan Congressional Human Rights Commission. But the biggest step in the institutionalization of accompaniment was the return of Guatemalan refugees from Mexico. Over 100,000 had fled north across the border during the violence of the early 80s, and had been living in UN-supported refugee camps. In January 1993, after several years of negotiations with the government, the refugees began an organized return. The negotiation itself changed the legal context for accompaniment, since the refugees insisted that the government sign an agreement approving their right to international accompaniment of their own choosing throughout their return and integration.

Beyond this new legal stability, the refugee return attracted vast international support. A score of new organizations were formed around the world to accompany them, based on the PBI model. Veteran PBI volunteers offered consulting and training to these new organizations in the United States, Canada, Spain, Germany, England, Switzerland, Sweden, and the Netherlands. Between 1993 and 1997, hundreds of volunteers came to live with returned refugees. The refugees themselves assert that they would not have returned without the of accompaniment. Their successful return helped inspire rapid developments in the Guatemalan peace process, contributing to the eventual signing of peace accords in 1996.

Accompaniment in El Salvador, 1987-1991

In El Salvador, the PBI experience was significantly different from Guatemala. El Salvador was implementing state terror policies similar to Guatemala, but with much less subtlety. In addition to mass murders and disappearances of Salvadoran activists, the government carried out systematic campaigns of harassment, detention, and expulsion against foreigners. El Salvador's military leaders hated foreigners, made no secret of it, and showed very little capacity for avoiding scandalous incidents.

PBI arrived in El Salvador in June, 1987, on the invitation of Bishop Gomez and several other Salvadoran organizations. In contrast to Guatemala, the civilian movement was vibrant and busy, and within a few months, volunteers were overwhelmed with protective accompaniment requests. Much of the time was spent maintaining a visible presence in key offices, in particular with the COMADRES (Mothers of the disappeared and detained), CRIPDES (Christian Committee for the Displaced of El Salvador), and the UNTS (National Unity of Salvadoran Workers). The UNTS was an umbrella federation of dozens of unions, church, student and campesino groups, and through this association PBI received new requests regularly.

Over the next two years the war heated up, and with it the repression against the civilian movement skyrocketed. PBI volunteers were eyewitnesses to detentions of union leaders. They were inside movement offices while the army surrounded them, or invaded arresting everyone inside. At other offices, death squads set off bombs at night while accompaniment was inside. On 14 different occasions, PBI volunteers were detained, interrogated, and invited to leave the country. In hundreds of other instances they were stopped by soldiers on the street, interrogated and intimidated. Yet the more the government harassed foreign volunteers, the more the Salvadoran civilian movement valued the accompaniment. Lutheran Bishop Medardo Gomez, who himself was extensively accompanied, explained this apparent contradiction to a PBI delegation:

> Hope can only be kindled where there is solidarity. It is much easier to throw yourself into any commitment when you have someone with you, protecting you.... I can throw myself from a high place, if I know that there is someone there to make sure I am not destroyed by the fall. You give us the force to be able to throw ourselves into our work. You have been expelled. You have suffered some of the same problems as those whom you have helped. When you look back on this work, do not forget that it is precisely because you have suffered with the people that you have been able to support them in building their resistance.

One of those PBI accompanied was Humberto Centeno, the most visible leader of the UNTS. Centeno had been jailed and tortured several times, and was once violently detained right in front of two PBI volunteers. Nevertheless, he continued to trust in PBI accompaniment:

> The way I lived it was this: if Humberto Centeno, condemned to death since 1985, so to speak, had gone around with a police escort, if I asked the state to protect me, I wouldn't have lived 30 days.... If Humberto Centeno had only depended on the accompaniment of fellow unionists or church workers, I also have no doubt that we'd all have turned up dead in some alley.... But, when Humberto Centeno goes around with someone from the United States, Canada or Spain, well, to kill us together would bring the state a heavy political cost. I'm certain that the fact that I went around with foreigners is one of the reasons I am still alive.

It was difficult to measure the protective impact of accompaniment when the government was so clearly harassing foreigners. As attacks increased, the increasing demand for accompaniment was a statement of faith and hope. Alicia de García of the COMADRES summed it up simply: "Look at what they did while you were there, and just imagine what they might have done if you weren't!"

The repression reached a climax in November of 1989, when the FMLN launched a full-scale offensive against the city San Salvador. Backs against the wall, the Salvadoran army declared a state of siege and launched aerial bombings against the poorest civilian neighborhoods, where they believed the FMLN to have established a base of support. During the fighting in the street and the bombing, PBI volunteers continued to accompany civilian movement leaders, who were now all in hiding. In addition, volunteers maintained a presence in several sanctuaries set up by the churches. After a week of fighting, the Army entered the Jesuit University and murdered six Jesuit priests and two church workers.

During the next several days, despite a massive international outcry, soldiers stormed each of the different church sanctuaries—where thousands of Salvadoran families had gone to flee the bombing—and arrested all the foreign volunteers inside. Five PBI volunteers were arrested, interrogated by Treasury Police, and told to leave the country. It took PBI five months of pressure and diplomacy before it could install a new team into El Salvador.

After the 1989 offensive all parties seemed to recognize that the war was a hopeless stalemate, and pressure for a negotiated peace settlement mounted rapidly. Nevertheless, human rights abuse continued, as well as harassment of foreigners. Three more PBI volunteers were arrested in 1991. With each arrest of a volunteer, PBI activated its international emergency response network, and in several cases evidence shows that this external pressure helped bring about the release, not only of the PBI volunteer, but sometimes also the Salvadorans arrested with them.

When US PBI volunteer Phil Pardi was arrested together with Salvadoran activists Gloria and Ernesto Zamora, within a few hours he got a visit from a staff member of the US Embassy. According to Phil,

> Actually the first thing he said to me was "Well, Phil, you're very popular, you ever think of running for mayor of Cambridge, Massachusetts? I think half the town of Cambridge has probably called me." He was also asking me why the people who were calling him knew Ernesto and Gloria. That told me that the phone calls and the faxes were also about Ernesto and Gloria. This embassy guy just wanted to get me out of there. He kept saying "Well, Phil, you're just in the wrong place at the wrong time." And I kept saying "No, I was in the right place at the right time." But he just didn't get it.

Phil and Gloria were released that same afternoon. Ernesto was freed the next day, with no charges.

In 1990 and 1991 the Salvadoran government and the FMLN signed a series of peace accords, prompting the July 1991 arrival of 150 UN observers (ONUSAL), and, in January 1992, a final ceasefire. The political opening, ceasefire and UN presence brought by the negotiating process resulted in a virtual termination of protective accompaniment requests. The war was over, and while violence and inequality continued in many forms, protective accompaniment was no longer the service Salvadorans wanted from foreign NGOs. After holding on for five precarious years, PBI closed its project in El Salvador.

Accompaniment in Sri Lanka

The island nation of Sri Lanka lies 25 kilometers off the southeast coast of India, on the other side of the world from Central America, geographically and politically. After two millennia of relatively peaceful coexistence between its Tamil and Sinhala population, and a calm transition from civilized British colonialism to successful parliamentary democracy, this beautiful island became a hellhole: rival armies were killing civilians by the thousands, throwing them in the ocean, leaving them in the street, or sticking their victim's heads on poles to teach a lesson to others. In late 1989, when PBI's accompaniment model was being most sorely tested in both Guatemala and El Salvador, the request came to try it in this far more complex conflict, with utterly different political and cultural underpinnings.

Sri Lanka was suffering through two simultaneous but different civil wars in the late 1980s. The Tamil Tigers had been fighting in the north for a separate Tamil state since the early 80s. Meanwhile, the Maoist Sinhalese-based JVP (Peoples Revolutionary Front) was waging a vicious terrorist rebellion in the south. It was in response to this second confrontation that the government carried out its worst human rights abuses, murdering and disappearing thousands of young Sri Lankans.

The first request to PBI came from the Sri Lankan Bar Association, whose lawyers were assassinated whenever they attempted to file habeas corpus cases inquiring after detained persons. PBI arrived in Sri Lanka in October, 1989, and shortly thereafter began accompanying one of the only lawyers left who dared to work on habeas corpus cases.

In February 1990, renowned Sri Lankan journalist Richard De Zoysa was abducted from his mother's home and murdered. His mother, Dr Manorani Saravanamuttu, recognized one of his abductors as the chief of police. Saravanamuttu and her lawyer Batty Weerakoon took the bold step of prosecuting the police. PBI began accompanying Weerakoon and Saravanamuttu in their homes and when they went to court. In May, 1990, both Saravanamuttu and Weerakoon were threatened, anonymously, for pursuing the case. Weerakoon was certain that the threats came from the police, acting on high-level orders. He immediately sent a letter to President Premadasa, demanding that steps be taken to ensure both his own and Dr Saravanamuttu's safety. As a result, Weerakoon was assigned two plainclothes police escorts. Weerakoon accepted the bodyguards, but wanted PBI as well:

> These two young policeman were genuinely wanting to offer protection, but I just can't see how the police can protect me from the police. [If] anybody wanted to do something, they could be put out of the way, or even if something did happen, even with the best of intentions, no evidence would be forthcoming from them. But PBI was different. They could act independently, and say what they saw, both here and abroad. A man could trust on that.

PBI's policy had generally been to accompany only those who chose nonviolent means of protection, but the team made an exception in this case. According to PBI volunteer Yeshua Moser:

> Batty said to us, "If I refuse a police guard it makes it easier for the government to excuse themselves when I get bumped off, by saying that they tried to protect me but I refused." Shortly after he said this to me, his wife cornered me in another part of the house. After hearing that we may refuse to accompany him, she exclaimed with great emotion, "Guns can't protect him, but your presence is a power that must be reckoned with."

Dr Saravanamuttu pointed out a similar distinction: "The armed protection is there to protect you against an armed force, but PBI is there to protect you against the order to use armed force."

PBI continued to accompany Saravanamuttu as she pursued the case through the courts into 1992. The case was cut short in early 1993 when President Premadasa was assassinated in a bombing: Among the dead was a member of the Presidential guard, Ronnie Wijesinghe, the same police official accused by Dr Saravanamuttu of kidnapping her son.

"When they kill me..." That's how Buddhist monk Baddegama Samitha[3] casually began a sentence, talking with a PBI volunteer in early 1991. A monk and political activist, the Venerable Samitha had worked to hide and protect young men who were fleeing the search-and-destroy missions of the government forces in 1989. "I felt that I had a kind of obligation to protect these youth. I am a monk, and I feel that life is more important than anything else. When someone is on the run, you just protect them."

In some cases Samitha found them hiding places. Other times he intervened after they had been detained, using his status as a Buddhist monk to gain access. Buddhist monks have an especially revered position in Sri Lanka. But his protection of others put his own life in danger. At the end of 1989, while Samitha was travelling again in Europe, an unidentified gunman came looking for him at his temple. Learning of this threat, his friends in Europe urged him not to return to Sri Lanka.

> I said, no, no, no, I am not going to avoid this, I am not going to hide. I must go back. My presence in Sri Lanka isn't worse than my living like a refugee here. I said, Let's take some action and try to protect me, but I must go. Some friends there then suggested that I should not be alone, that I should ask for the protection of PBI.

Two PBI volunteers met Samitha at the airport when he arrived in Colombo. He was accompanied off and on for the next several months, usually when he came to the capital, and at times at his monastery in the south. Having foreign accompaniment in a small Sinhalese village was a bit of an oddity, but Samitha felt that the other villagers understood and appreciated his need for protection. For safety, he had to limit his movements and avoid certain locations. He made PBI's presence as visible as possible, taking them at times on visits to the local police station or army base.

While this went on, European embassies interested in Samitha's welfare demanded that the government protect him. Samitha took PBI volunteers to a meeting with Presidential Assistant Bradman Weerakoon (not to be confused with the lawyer Batty Weerakoon) When interviewed four years later, Presidential Assistant Weerakoon remembered the case very well. Responding to European embassy pressure, Sri Lankan President Premadasa had asked Weerakoon to investigate Samitha's situation. It had not been easy at first, since Weerakoon didn't really know who was doing the threatening. So he contacted all the different security forces, and made sure they knew of the President's concern. "PBI really protected Samitha, saved his life," declared Weerakoon, confirming that international pressure had been the determining factor in moving President Premadasa to take action.

PBI went on to accompany many other activists and organizations in Sri Lanka. In addition to a regular presence in the capital city of Colombo, in 1992 and again in 1996 the organization stationed volunteers in the eastern city of Batticaloa, where Sinhala, Tamil and Muslim villages were all victimized by the warring parties.

The successful maintenance of a project in Sri Lanka was an important step in PBI's growth. Unlike Central America, in Sri Lanka PBI could not depend on the support of a broad-based international solidarity movement to provide money, volunteers and political education. The project was constantly short on funds and volunteers.

Most volunteers had no prior knowledge of Sri Lanka when they first came to PBI. These difficulties weakened the project's implementation, but they had to be faced if PBI hoped to show that its model of nonviolent intervention could be applied in a variety of conflicts—and not just those which were globally popular.

The project also effected an important internal change in the organization. PBI was founded on a broad commitment to global nonviolence, and in the 80s it had carried out explorations for potential projects in Israel/Palestine, Northern Ireland and South Africa. But in practical terms PBI had become nearly indistinguishable from a Central American solidarity organization in the course of its first decade. The Sri Lanka experience helped expand the focus again, opening the doors to considering other possibilities.

Seeing both the difficulties and the opportunities, PBI held a General Assembly in 1992 which confirmed its interest in expansion to other conflicts. Over the next few years, new projects were started in Colombia and Haiti. Additional exploratory work was carried out in Chad, and the former Soviet Republics. PBI also got involved in joint coalition projects, including the Balkan Peace Team, the SIPAZ (International Service for Peace) in Chiapas, and the Cry for Justice coalition which sent volunteers to Haiti in 1993. As this chapter is being written, the organization is considering new project proposals in several African nations, the Philippines, Burma/Myanmar, and Turkey, among others.

Accompaniment, the simple idea of just being there with people, is now becoming broadly accepted as a powerful means of protecting human rights. The model developed by PBI over the course of a decade will likely be copied and improved upon in more and more conflicts around the world, by many new organizations, and may even be implemented on a large scale by, for instance, by the United Nations. What began as an ad-hoc, heartfelt nonviolent response to the murders of GAM members in

1985 has become an institution transcending PBI. It is a legacy PBI can be proud of.

State Terror in the 90s: Colombia
Perhaps the most impressive testament to the growing credibility of protective accompaniment was demonstrated by the breakneck pace of PBI's expansion in Colombia, and the manner in which the Colombian civilian movement absorbed it into their toolbox of strategies for confronting state violence. Responding to several requests from Colombian human rights groups in the early 1990s, PBI installed teams in two different cities in late 1994, fielding 12 volunteers. By 1998 the project had more than doubled, expanding to a third city and fielding a total of 24 volunteers. Its funding more than tripled in the same period, as international humanitarian NGO agencies, and especially churches, recognized both the power of PBI's work and the dire need for it in Colombia.

The Colombian human rights situation was the worst in the hemisphere, and the majority of those violations were carried out by paramilitary organizations unofficially aligned with the military. This reality is often obscured by the focus of media attention on Colombia's role in international narcotics trade. This focus is encouraged by both the Colombian and US governments, who use the "drug war" to mask a much broader campaign of state terror aimed at controlling civilian initiatives critical of the state or the military. Colombian and international human rights organizations had to develop a major campaign to educate the international community as to this reality. For PBI protection to function, it needed to be backed up by an effective network of political pressure. When PBI started its work, this network was still in its infancy, but through the mid- to late-90s it gathered steam, bringing together the small Colombian international solidarity movement with larger organizational efforts such as Amnesty International, whose work both complemented and protected PBI's on-the-ground presence with outside pressure.

The Colombian government denies responsibility for paramilitary and death squad violence. As if to prove its innocence, in 1994 it offered threatened human rights groups the protection of armed agents of the Department of Administrative Security (DAS). The Association of Families of the Disappeared (ASFADDES) accepted the armed DAS protection for a brief period, but when PBI arrived they quickly changed over, assuring the government that independent nonviolent protection was much more in keeping with their humanitarian mission, but insisting that they nevertheless would continue to hold the government responsible for their safety. Another group, the Regional Committee for Human

Rights, or CREDHOS, similarly opted for nonviolent accompaniment over armed protection.

A dramatic example of an accompaniment intervention came in late 1997, when PBI began accompanying Mario Calixto, president of the Sabana de Torres human rights organization. Calixto had received death threats demanding he leave the country by December. On 23 December, two masked and armed men broke into the Calixto family home, held the family at gunpoint, and demanded Mario leave with them. Two PBI volunteers stepped between the guns and the family and calmly explained their role as international witnesses to whatever transpired. Whether the men were just confused by the intervention or had specific orders not to attack in the presence of foreigners is unknown, but they left that night without Mario Calixto, an extraordinary conclusion to an otherwise ordinary death squad disappearance. A year later Calixto received the Robert F.Kennedy human rights prize for his work. With no end to the violence in sight, the demand for PBI's services in Colombia keeps growing.

Beyond Accompaniment: Education and Reconciliation
PBI's attempt to meet the overwhelming demand for accompaniment in the 1980s in Central America pushed most other types of work to the sidelines. But PBI was never originally conceived of as a human rights organization focused on protection. Its mandate was much broader, encompassing a variety of different strategies for encouraging nonviolent action and seeking nonviolent solutions, including active education, mediation, negotiation and resource sharing.

In the early years, some PBI volunteers offered advice and workshops on nonviolence to members of the GAM in Guatemala. In 1987, the PBI team took the first steps towards institutionalizing "Peace Education" as an ongoing part of its work. Volunteers collaborated with the Guatemalan Human Rights Commission in exile to design a series of "human rights workshops." PBI was concerned that it not fulfil a "teaching" capacity that could better be done by Guatemalans, but the Guatemalans in exile insisted that such workshops would be far too dangerous for Guatemalans to facilitate themselves. PBI members gave these workshops to various organizations, especially union groups and farmers. In 1988, when Amilcar Mendez and several Guatemalan organizations did begin offering similar workshops, PBI discontinued its program.

Also in 1988, PBI carried out a short-term project in Nicaragua, sending several international experts in conflict resolution and civilian-based defense to dialogue with Nicaraguan government and civilian leaders about alternatives methods of defense.

In 1989 PBI's teams in both El Salvador and Guatemala initiated a much broader range of workshops, including conflict resolution, negotiation methods, group process, political analysis, as well as specialized topics such as "community responses to fear and torture." These workshops, based on popular education techniques developed by Paolo Friere and others, focused on sharing techniques and methods and on developing the participants' abilities to address their own problems. Thereafter, peace education workshops became a regular feature of the teams' work, although accompaniment remained the dominant task.

When PBI was asked in 1993 to work in Haiti, the country was living under a military dictatorship and activists wanted accompaniment. By the time PBI actually fielded a long-term team in 1995, both the situation and the demand had completely changed. President Aristide had been reinstalled as the popularly-elected President, and UN forces controlled the country. Haitian activists no longer felt a need for accompaniment. What they did want were workshops and training in nonviolent conflict resolution. The country faced a mammoth task of complete construction of democratic institutions, and had no functional system, legal or otherwise, for resolving disputes. Within its first year PBI had built a project almost entirely devoted to workshops in nonviolent conflict resolution, working in collaboration with Haitian activists interested in the same objective. The team was asked to work with rural communities where local land disputes threatened to lead to bloodshed. In direct collaboration with the United Nations human rights monitoring mission, PBI also facilitated workshops with Haitian judges. Numerous other workshops in nonviolence were organization through the Catholic Church's commission for Justice and Peace.

Reconciliation with Native People: The North America Project
In 1989 violent confrontations erupted on the Akwesasne (Mohawk) reservation on the border between New York state and Canada. The struggle pitted competing tribal factions against each other in a battle for control over the reservation and its economic development. Several former PBI volunteers got involved in an ad-hoc nonviolent monitoring presence at barricades set up on the highways entering the reservation. The following year, after the Quebec government allowed a private enterprise to begin construction of a golf course on sacred Mohawk land near Montreal, armed Mohawk warriors took over and shut down one of the major commuter bridges into Montreal. The prolonged armed standoff led to another *ad hoc* monitoring presence, and woke up the nation to the deep tensions that existed between native people and the Quebec and Canadian governments.

PBI then began deliberating opening a new kind of project to support and encourage nonviolence in conflicts involving native people. Initially, PBI thought to provide a pacifying presence based on the models it had developed in other conflicts. But the geographic and cultural context demanded something quite different. Native people were not facing death squads or terror states. They were embroiled in extremely complicated conflicts as much among native groups as against the white power structure around them. They faced a type of structural violence built into the legal and economic system within which they had to operate to survive. And they were struggling with widely differing philosophies and strategies as to how to go about this survival.

PBI's North America Project started with training sessions aimed at building up a core of volunteers who would be "on-call" to respond to requests for a PBI presence. The preparation was focused on cultural sensitivity, learning how to understand and work with native people, and studying the interwoven forces of the conflicts. At the same time, PBI built up a network of contacts in native communities throughout North America. PBI offered nonviolent support for native groups struggling against injustice or internal conflict, and simultaneously worked to educate nonnative people about racism and structural violence.

One of the longer-term programs the project carried out was among Innu communities in Northern Quebec who were struggling over the proposed construction of hydropower projects: the communities were divided since the projects would be a potential source of employment, but they would flood native land. In a series of visits over several years, PBI volunteers played a role which might be called "passive reconciliation." They simply listened, giving all the different opinions in the conflict a willing and open ear. As they earned trust, they were later informed that PBI was the first group to ever come in with a nonpartisan stance and listen to everyone, and that fact alone helped to calm the tension.

In numerous other instances, PBI volunteers visited communities where violence had occurred or was feared, provided a monitoring presence, an open ear, and attempted to offer unbiased analysis to the outside world. Conflicts involved anything from fishing rights to logging to concerns over racist judges.

The North America Project saw reconciliation on a much broader level than individual communities' conflicts. The structural injustices they were learning about evolved from a historic clash between different world views. One objective of the project became that of education of the majority white community—and of PBI's own membership—about the world vision of native people and how the European-based economic and legal systems inherently tend to destroy native culture and traditions, sparking disillusionment, anger and hopelessness and giving rise to a host of related social problems, from alcoholism to crime. Year after year, project volunteers carried out interviews with native community leaders, government officials and others, and wrote articles to analyze the conflicts and educate the broader world community.

Like the Sri Lanka project before it, the North America Project expanded PBI's mission and its membership, attracting people interested in native concerns, and people more interested in struggling with the structural injustice and racism going on within first world countries than in travelling to the third world.

Modelling International Decision-Making
As PBI grew from an idea to an international organization, one of its major challenges was working out a way to implement its nonviolent principles internally as well as externally, while at the same time building an efficient bureaucracy that could make and implement effective and informed decisions about complex conflict situations. The organization began with a small directorate made up of veteran nonviolence activists. As the Guatemala project developed the organization went through numerous transitions: some organic and some tumultuous.

One of the key issues was the difficulty in determining where "expertise" lay for different types of decisions. The team in the field had first hand information and an immersion in complex and delicate political situations, while the outside committees were sometimes quite removed from it. Team members, on the other hand, often stayed a relatively short time, and could not easily take into account the long-term history and continuity of the organization; nor did they always have the longer nonviolence experience of the activists on the project's steering committee or international directorate. The result was constant struggle over which type of experience was most relevant to a decision. As PBI developed multiple projects, the only workable solution was for the international directorate to delegate most of the project-related decisions to semi-autonomous project steering committees. These committees, in turn, held intense week-long meetings with the team in the field several times a year to hash out policy and program strategies. The meetings had to be sufficiently thorough to enable the project committees to absorb as much as possible of the current field reality from the team, and for team members in turn to clearly understand the long-term concerns of the more experienced project committee members.

One of the reasons so much delegation and meeting was necessary was because from the start PBI committed itself to working internally with a consensus decision-making process. Consensus strives to be a non-hierarchical process in which participants have an equal voice in a decision.

Its strength is that when it works it can build stronger organizations in which participants feel valued and are highly invested in decisions they have molded. Creative decisions can arise from involving more people. In order to function well, though, consensus requires trust among participants, and takes considerable time. It works best among participants who know each other and are together for enough time to work out good decisions. It is quite difficult to implement when participants are relative strangers and are geographically dispersed. So it was impossible for the project committees or international directorate to participate effectively in decisions that needed to be made quickly by the team in response to an emergency, even though these decisions could have a profound impact on the organization.

As more and more volunteers passed through teams, PBI faced a new challenge: how to involve these returned volunteers and build the organization. Volunteers returned from the field inspired and brimming with ideas, and often found no place to go with them. Gradually, PBI built up a system of membership organizations called "country groups" throughout North America and Europe. Country groups were charged with fundraising, recruitment, training and building political support for the organization. In some countries, this process succeeded in establishing firm organizations, sometimes with permanent offices and full-time staff. In other cases, they remained a loosely-knit association of volunteers who joined together for sporadic campaigns to support the global organization.

Representatives of this expanding network of activists supporting the organization around the world came together in General Assemblies in 1989 and 1992 and revamped PBI's international structure. Instead of an international directorate of experienced nonviolence experts, PBI instituted a representative International Council. Each field project had a representative on the Council. Country groups were represented by region: one representative for North America, one for Europe and one for the Pacific. Each representative had the responsibility of involving their constituent base in a rather complex series of feedback loops by which a broad-based international consensus was sought on major international policy questions.

This new system would never have functioned but for the technological changes with which it coincided. In 1989 PBI began to operate globally with fax machines, and by the early 1990s nearly the entire organization was functioning via electronic mail. This enabled rapid and inexpensive global communication, without which the objective of democratic participation from the base groups would have been prohibitively expensive. But it still did not overcome two of the basic challenges of consensus process: trust and time. Electronics allowed for an increase in the quantity of information and correspondence, but the nature of that sort of interchange can never achieve the same trust-building effect as face-to-face contact over time. And without trust, consensus inevitably breaks down.

The deeper involvement of base groups in decisions called for a far more time-consuming process of multiparty negotiation. This not only sapped the energy which these grassroots activists might have put into fundraising or otherwise building support for the organization, it also stretched out decision-making timelines. The new system is roundly criticized as bulky and inordinately slow, but it has nevertheless achieved one of its key objectives: any PBI activist from the grassroots can have an ongoing voice in the organization's key decisions (as long as they have access to electronic mail—the implicit exclusiveness of this new technology has not yet been confronted by the organization). The challenge ahead is to clarify again a certain level of delegation in order to authorize smaller and more efficient bodies to make those decisions which must be made more quickly.

Conclusion
There are many challenges ahead for Peace Brigades International, and many unanswered questions. How might PBI-style accompaniment protect an activist against threats from an attacker who is not controlled by the state (such as the Tamil Tigers), and thus perhaps untouchable by international pressure? How might PBI intervene in ethnic or communal conflicts? How can an organization like PBI attract more participation and involvement by volunteers from third world nations? How can an effective peace intervention be carried out in places like Turkey or the former Soviet Republics where it is very difficult to find volunteers who speak the language? Can PBI continue to expand, while still conserving its commitment to grassroots democratic participation in decision-making?

Activists PBI once protected are now major political players in their countries, crediting PBI with their survival. New requests continue to arrive from around the world. In the fields of peace education and reconciliation PBI is developing new models, bridging the gap between the international desire for effective intervention against violence and importance of trusting and empowering local activists to come up with solutions to their own problems within the appropriate cultural context. Whatever its future, PBI has clearly left its mark on the history of nonviolent intervention and human rights protection.

NOTES

* Most of the material for this chapter comes from Liam Mahony and Luis Enrique Eguren, *Unarmed Bodyguards: International Accompaniment for the Protection of Human Rights* (West Hartford: Kumarian Press, 1997). The research was generously funded by the John D. and Catherine T.MacArthur Foundation.

1   Directly quoted material comes from interviews with, or letters from Gam members Ester de Herrarte, Nineth Montenegro de García, Alain Richard, and also from Sel Burroughs, General Hector Gramajo, Sergio Guzman, President Vinicio Cerezo Arevalo, Patty Mutchnick, María Gabriela Serra, Meredith Larson, Bishop Medardo Gomez, Humberto Centeno, Alicia de Garíma, Phil Pardi, Batty Weerakoon, Yeshua Moser, Dr Manorani Saravanamuttu, Ed Kinane, Venerable Baddegama Samitha, and Bradman Weerakoon.

2   The G-2 is the bureaucratic label, and the popular name of the most notorious of the army's agencies. With as many as 2,000 employees collecting and computerizing information on subversives, the G-2 directed official death squads to carry out assassinations and disappearances. General Benedicto Lucas García explained, "If the G-2 wants to kill you, they kill you. They send out a squad and that's the end of it" (Nairn, 1986).

3   Venerable is the accepted respectful manner of referring to a Buddhist monk in Sri Lanka. While this will often be shortened to simply Samitha in the text, no disrespect is intended.

REFERENCES

Intelligence Oversight Board (IOB), 1996 *Report on the Guatemala Review*, US State Department, June 28.

Kinzer, Stephen, 1985, "Killings Chill Rights Group" *New York Times*, April 19.

Nairn, Allan, and Jean-Marie Simon, 1986, "Bureaucracy of Death" *The New Republic*, June 30.

8

PROJECT ACCOMPANIMENT: A CANADIAN RESPONSE

Beth Abbott

International accompaniment is important ... without international accompaniment, the people are like worms the army can just step on...
Guatemalan refugee in Mexico awaiting return to the Peten

Guatemala—A Political Background

Numbers can sometimes be misleading, but in Guatemala the figures that speak to that country's modern history cannot be more clear. One hundred and fifty thousand people have died since the military coup of 1954. Another 40,000 have disappeared and are presumed murdered. At least one million people have been displaced. Over 85% of the population lives in poverty. Seventy-three percent of Guatemalan children are malnourished.

Guatemala is a country characterized by an increasing concentration of wealth amid pervasive poverty. It has one of the most regressive tax systems in the world, and the highest rate of infant mortality, illiteracy and malnutrition in the region (Project Accompaniment, 1993, p.9).

The antecedents of this ongoing pain and injustice can be traced all the way back to the Spanish Conquest in the 1500s. The Mayan people suffered greatly under 300 years of Spanish colonial rule, beginning with the invasion by Pedro de Alvarado in 1524. In 1821, Guatemala won independence from Spain, but conditions did not improve for most people.

Today, the majority of people living in Guatemala are indigenous. They have been systematically excluded from Guatemala's political and economic mainstream. The areas of the country with the highest levels of political violence have been those with the highest concentration of indigenous people.

Most of the Mayan people are farmers and yet the land ownership in Guatemala is one of the most unbalanced in all of Latin America. Two percent of the population owns 65% of the land. Most Guatemalans live on plots of land that are too small to support them. As a result, many people have been forced to leave their own lands to find part-time work as laborers on large plantations owned by Guatemala's elite. Wages have been low, generally much lower than the basic minimum wage. Working and living conditions are subhuman, and services virtually non-existent. Attempts to bring about change and to improve the social and economic conditions of the poor have been (and continue to be) met with brutal repression.

The present political situation has its origins in the coup of 1954, when a combined United States and Guatemalan military operation overthrew the democratically elected government of Jacobo Arbenz and replaced it with a military dictatorship. (Arbenz had introduced a program of modest land reform that redistributed 400,000 uncultivated acres to landless peasants. The program offended both Guatemalan and United States landowners.) In the aftermath of the coup, thousands of people were killed and the expropriated lands returned to their former owners.

The coup destroyed democratic institutions in Guatemala and ended a ten year period of social and economic reform. From 1954 to 1986, the country was ruled by a series of military governments supported by the traditional landed oligarchy. Their response to opposition has given the country its reputation as the worst human rights violator in the western hemisphere.

Armed opposition to the generals began early in the 1960s when a number of small guerrilla armies began operating, mostly in the north of the country. The Guatemalan government's counter-insurgency campaign, supported by the American Green Berets, killed 3,000 people. In the 1970s, the popular movement grew enormously in strength and visibility. During this time, many died as the result of direct army attack and others were killed by "death squads" associated with the military. Among the victims were community, church, student and labor leaders who had begun to organize and educate the people. By early 1979, the military and death squads were killing 100 to 200 persons per week.

But the worst was yet to come. Under the direction of General Romeo Lucas Garcia and General Efrain Rios Montt, "blood flowed like water" (Falla, 1994, p.8), as the army stepped up its counter-insurgency war. Its target was not only the armed insurgents but also the indigenous communities in the north that were considered sympathetic to the insurgents' cause. The military pursued a "scorched earth" policy of destroying more than 400 villages. The words "massacre" and "slaughter" describe the Guatemalan peoples' experience of the early 1980s.

Taking Refuge

> *It started in Cuarto Pueblo...the army opened fire on those in the marketplace. They killed many there and burned their bodies with gasoline. Many women were in the church. They separated the young ones from the old and for three days they raped them. Then they put them back in the church and burned the church down. It was after that we decided to leave.*
>
> Project Accompaniment, 1993, p.5

Many of those who witnessed and escaped this horror became refugees in Mexico. Some crossed the border within days of the army's scorched earth rampage; others waited some months before moving on to Mexico, their hopes that the violence was over shattered as they learned of more killings. They took with them the clothes on their backs and their terrifying memories of the rape, torture and assassination of their families and neighbors.

The first part of the refugees' exile in Mexico was one of great hardship. Most were ill, malnourished, frightened, and emotionally drained. Temporary camps were set up on the Mexican side of the border. Few refugees moved further north than the Mexican state of Chiapas because they wanted to be as close as possible to their homeland. They hoped that their time as refugees would be short (Manz in Falla, 1994, p.194). This was not to be.

The "official" population of Guatemalan refugees in Mexico grew to 46,000. These were the refugees who were recognized and supported, at least minimally, by the Mexican government and the United Nations High Commissioner for Refugees (UNHCR). A number much greater than this also fled to Mexico, but were left to fend for themselves by integrating as best they could into Mexican society.

The Desire to Return Home

> *We don't forget our land in Guatemala. We want our land back. We're tired of being here...we have no land here.*
>
> Project Accompaniment, 1993, p.5

In 1984, the Mexican government forcibly relocated many refugees to the more distant states of Campeche and Quintana Roo; others were moved deeper into Chiapas, away from the border. Living conditions in the camps varied greatly as the years passed, with some camps featuring larger, more permanent homes, potable water and sufficient land to cultivate. Others, mostly in the state of Chiapas, lacked material resources, but still developed into particularly well-organized communities with strong refugee leadership. Many "dispersed" refugees —those not living in official refugee camps—also came together to organize a collective return home. They are represented by their own association, ARDIGUA.

The Guatemalan refugee population is not a homogenous group. The refugees come from different ethnic backgrounds, practice different religions, and speak 23 different languages. But they share one binding experience: that of flight from the violence of their own country's army (Manz in Falla, 1994, p.196). Despite the peace negotiations which were taking place around the time of the first collective returns, the refugees in Mexico were aware that the human rights situation in their homeland was not an encouraging one. Yet, the majority who originally expressed interest did not abandon their dreams to return home. The refugees said that they were "Guatemalans not Mexicans" and that their lives had been in a state of suspension since their arrival in Mexico. Many had children who had never seen Guatemala, and they did not want their children to "lose a sense of who they are and where they belong" (Project Accompaniment, 1993, p.19). Those refugees who owned land in Guatemala wanted to reclaim that land for their children.

There were also many pragmatic reasons for wanting to return. As long as the refugees remained in Mexico, they had few economic prospects. Many worked as farm laborers on Mexican plantations during short harvest seasons. Wages are low. Other opportunities were limited by the restriction of movement placed on the refugees by the Mexican authorities.

As well, the refugees had been under pressure from several fronts to return home. Neither the Mexican government nor the UNHCR were prepared to support the Guatemalan refugees in Mexico indefinitely. The Mexican authorities made it clear that they wanted the refugees out of Chiapas, and encouraged them to move to the less populated states of Campeche and Quintana Roo. If Chiapas was to become a center for industry under the North American Free Trade Agreement (NAFTA), as some anticipated (Project Accompaniment, 1993, p.19), the Mexican government may have felt it necessary to clear up the "refugee problem" first.

At the same time, the UNHCR had been reducing its support to the Guatemalan refugees. With world-wide demands on its resources and services increasing, this situation was certain not to improve.

The Accords
The process which would facilitate the refugees' return home began in earnest in 1987, with the formation of the Permanent Commissions of Guatemalan Refugees in Mexico (CCPP). The Permanent Commissions were mandated by the refugees to negotiate with the Guatemalan

government the conditions for a safe return. After much consultation, the CCPP listed seven conditions that must be met for a "collective, voluntary, and organized" return to their homeland. Among these conditions were the right to return to their original lands, to be free from military harassment, and to be accompanied as they returned home and resettled. After lengthy negotiations, the Accords between the CCPP and the Guatemalan government were signed on 8 October 1992, with all seven conditions accepted.

The third section of the final agreement specified that the refugees had the right to international accompaniment "during the period of transfer, resettlement and reintegration." Furthermore, the agreement required the government to "facilitate the stay of members of international organizations and foreign individuals."

Project Accompaniment: A Canadian Response
Canadians had been working in solidarity with the refugees for several years before the Permanent Commissions were formed. The work of Project Accompaniment ("Project A") in the 1990s grew out of the relationships built between Canadian individuals and groups and the Guatemalan refugee community in Mexico throughout the 1980s. The Christian Task Force on Central America in British Columbia, for example, started organizing tours to the refugee camps soon after the refugees arrived.

In May 1988, the Permanent Commissions made a formal request to Canadian and other overseas organizations for support and accompaniment in their efforts to coordinate a collective return of the refugees.

In 1989, an *ad hoc* group known as the Guatemalan Network Coordinating Committee obtained funding from several Canadian non-governmental organizations and churches for what was then called "Project Acompanante." The first objective of the project was "to raise the consciousness of Canadian people about the situation in Guatemala and to design action strategies for the support in Canada of Guatemala and Guatemalan refugees and displaced people in their plans for their 'return'." It was increasingly recognized, however, that the actual return home would not be soon, and that "accompaniment" referred to offering support, including a physical presence, to the refugees before, during, and after they returned home. "It means walking together, working together; it is more than US accompanying THEM from place A to place B. Accompaniment must be part of a long-term plan involving education, network-building in Canada, and action" (White, 1989).

The Guatemalan Network organized a national consultation for groups working on Guatemala in 1989, and the following year coordinated a tour of Canadians from three regions to the refugee camps. A second tour took place in 1991. Prior to and following each tour, groups across Canada organized educational activities centered on the refugees. These efforts included: letter writing campaigns, information sessions, lobbying at church conference meetings and with politicians, and newsletter articles (Project Accompaniment, 1992, p.2). The delegations' experiences with the refugees greatly deepened our understanding of accompaniment, and we were able to focus on offering a presence with the refugees *now*, while they worked toward "the return" when the time was right.

In December 1991, Project Accompaniment was represented in Chiapas at an international seminar on the return organized by the Permanent Commissions. The project's goals were presented as twofold:

> (1) Within an international context of solidarity, to augment the capacity for solidarity, church and NGO partners to better network, and to animate awareness and action amongst Canadians in support of the Guatemalan struggles;
> (2) From this growing community base, to select and train persons for physical accompaniment of the Guatemalan refugees back to Guatemala and in their resettlement process (Project Accompaniment, 1992, p.3).

In 1992, a consortium of NGOs, churches, and solidarity groups under the auspices of the Central America Monitoring Group formed a committee with Project Accompaniment to seek funding from the Canadian government for a comprehensive support program, including the work of Project A. The group's application to the Canadian International Development Agency's Rehabilitation and Reconstruction Fund was successful.

Staff were hired in both Canada and Mexico, and the first national Project A Steering Committee meeting was held in September of that year. The first training program took place, and the first Project A accompanier arrived in Mexico in November. Several more began their assignments in the next few months, and were in place for the first return of 2,500 refugees on 20 January 1993.

The First Journey Home
The sun is coming out as we return to our land.
Guatemala News, January 1993

The first refugees to return under the terms of the October 1992 Accords arrived at their final destination after nine days of trekking through the country by bus, cattle truck and on foot. Their new home was a stretch of jungle in a highly militarized zone in Ixcan, the northernmost municipality of the Quiche region. The refugees were returning home— home to one of the areas most hard-hit by the army's scorched earth campaign over a decade earlier.

The journey itself was not without difficulty. In fact, there was conflict with the government every step of the way. CEAR, the government's agency responsible for refugees and returnees, contested the refugees' preferred route; failed to provide adequate food and shelter en route; failed to prepare the infrastructure promised for the new community; allowed a powerful military presence on the journey; and refused the assistance of NGOs and churches which had made arrangements to welcome the refugees. Nevertheless, the fact that nearly 2,500 Guatemalan refugees were finally making the trek home after ten years in exile was very powerful. The media in Guatemala City reported

> ...when they finally entered the city, and the 66 buses slowly wound around the central park, the air was filled with noise: bells ringing, fireworks going off, noisemakers, the motors of the vehicles, marimba music, bicycle bells and the bells of the ice cream vendors, the applause and shouts of "viva!" It was into this atmosphere that the first baby (a girl) of the return was born (National Coordination Office, 1993).

Learning to "Accompany"

The first return, and each subsequent one, as well as all the support and physical presence we offered in between, taught us a tremendous amount about how to "accompany." We learned from each and every accompanier's experience.

Many Canadians are well-accustomed to the traditional notion that as "northerners" we have much to offer our neighbors in the south—like money, material aid and technical "know-how." Instead, the most important thing we were being asked to provide was merely our presence, our visibility as foreigners, in the hopes that this would protect the refugees/returnees from their own government's military.

We were asked to accompany the refugees in many capacities. We accompanied land delegations to various parts of Guatemala to investigate potential land for resettlement. We accompanied returnee women to the nearby river while they washed their families' clothes. We made our presence known when military helicopters flew over the community or army patrols passed through the cornfields. The role of the accompanier was actually a passive one (contrary to the Guatemalan military's allegations!). We were not organizing, initiating, instigating; we were supporting, observing, and mostly, just "being there."

It is fair to say that the job of accompanier is not for everyone. We recruited people who had the personal and emotional qualities needed to work in a unique situation. While the daily pace of accompaniment may be quite slow, the underlying context (living in a highly militarized zone in a highly militarized country) is very demanding and often stressful. Volunteers must be committed to nonviolent action, have a good understanding of cross-cultural issues and be security-conscious. The ability to speak Spanish well (and not to lose that ability in tense situations!) is also very important. Accompaniers must be willing to live simply and they must be flexible. (Our first list of personal criteria for accompaniers did not mention flexibility but constant changing of plans and needs in the south made it obvious that this was a *very* desirable trait for accompaniers, and the word was added and emphasized on the final application form.)

Over 1400 Canadians have now accompanied in Guatemala with Project A between 1993 and 1999. Their ages range from those in their early twenties to those well into their sixties. They have included nurses, a doctor, a ferry worker, adult educators, film makers, social workers, students, journalists, geologists, tree planters and civil servants.

Clearly, accompaniers must be well-prepared to cope with military confrontation. However, our experience shows that the majority of every accompanier's time is actually spent carrying out the day-to-day tasks of living in a very isolated rural community. The returnee community's ability to engage in the mundane activities of life in a relative climate of tranquillity is a sign that the accompanier's presence is "working." To be effective, our training program therefore had to evaluate participants on their ability to cope with situations ranging from the frustration and boredom of constant delays, to the fear and anger brought on by a confrontation with the military.

A Project Accompaniment experience did not finish when the volunteer hopped on a plane for home. All accompaniers were sponsored by a community group or organization, and made a commitment to continue their "accompaniment" upon returning home through education, outreach, and media work.

Against All Odds

In January of 1999, the government of Guatemala and the representatives of the refugee organizations signed an agreement affirming the official end of the collective returns. Most of the Guatemalan refugees still living in Mexico at the time opted to remain in their adopted country. A small number are expected to repatriate as individuals or families in the near future. A process which was originally thought to take a few years actually stretched out for more than six years. The main impediment throughout was the Guatemalan governments's lack of will.

The government was required by the agreement to provide credit to purchase land for those returnees who did not already own land. Yet the refugees' requests for credit were frequently met with delays, excuses and outright resistance by the government. Guatemalans who settled on land left behind by the refugees in the early 1980s had been illegally granted titles by the government and were encouraged to refuse to allow the rightful owners to return home.

The military has engaged in a major public relations effort in neighboring communities to portray the returning refugees as "subversives" and capitalized on any divisions they are able to create or enhance within or between communities. Instead of "facilitating" the work of accompaniment groups as the Accords required, a systematic campaign to discredit those accompanying the refugees was launched by the government.

Project A accompaniers witnessed, on more than one occasion, members of the Guatemalan army threatening returned refugees (and indirectly speaking to the important role of international accompaniment). In the Ixcan, soldiers on patrol called out to the returnees saying "the foreigners are here for a few years, but we, the army, will remain long after they are gone" (Project Accompaniment, 1996, p.4).

The returning refugees' safety, a key condition of their return, was often not ensured. Military intervention in the return communities varied from harassment (with frequent army patrols passing through) to outright atrocities (attacks against communities resulting in the death of children and adult returnees). Military violence was unleashed against returned refugees, Permanent Commission representatives and their families, and the staff of international human rights bodies. Yet despite all this, over 32,000 refugees made their way home through the collective return process.

Living Up To the "Peace"
On 29 December 1996, the Guatemalan government and the armed opposition (URNG) signed the Accord for a Firm and Lasting Peace, which officially ended the war and activated a series of thematic accords signed in the previous few years. The implementation of many of these promises is yet to take place. Some much needed transitions from military to a civilian society have been more cosmetic than real. A well entrenched and widespread atmosphere of impunity prevents justice for many victims of the war years. The trial of those responsible for the 1995 massacre of 11 people in the return community of Xaman, for example, is mired in political corruption and military intimidation. (This case is of particular interest to those involved in accompaniment, as the community had been temporarily without their usual international accompaniers when the massacre took place.) Likewise, the investigation into the 1998 murder of Monsignor Juan Gerardi—immediately following his release of a highly participatory and thorough report coordinated by the Human

Rights Office of the Archbishop of Guatemala—is fraught with bias, evidence tampering, and gross government interference. The Guatemalan government's clear unwillingness to address the cloak of impunity covering the country raises serious doubts about the potential fulfillment of the Peace Accords.

Conclusion
The physical accompaniment program offered by Project A came to a natural close as the refugees completed the return process in early 1999. However, the support offered by Canadians for those who are struggling to build peace in Guatemala continues in a variety of forms, including through a new national solidary network with Guatemala. The human rights situation for all Guatemalans must be seen in the context of a country where impunity reigns, despite a signed peace agreement and the relatively successful return process. For returned refugees in Guatemala, and others working for peace and justice, international accompaniment—in every sense of the word—will continue to make a small but important contribution. Our ability to act in solidarity has been greatly strengthened by the voices and experiences of 140 accompaniers and the Canadian communities with which they work.

A Personal Recollection by Team Member Randy Kohan
In late August, 1993, a delegation of nine Guatemalan refugees and two members of Project A, including myself, made a ten-day visit to Guatemala. This delegation represented a larger block of refugees living in southern Mexico who shared a desire to return home. Their objective was to seek the assistance of the national and international governments, the Catholic Church and NGOs as a means of obtaining land to which they could return.

As the visit drew to a close, Joaquin wanted to visit his home town to obtain his baptismal and birth certificates. Joaquin was representing ARDIGUA, an organization of the dispersed refugees living in southern Mexico. For six hours, Joaquin and I rode in the back of a small pickup truck as it wound its way up the rocky, windy road to Todos Santos in the department of Huehuetenango. With us were two men from the Catholic Church—one, a lawyer; the other, a driver.

After obtaining Joaquin's papers, we were detained by members of the civil patrol. (Civil patrols were created during the time of the military's "scorched earth policy" of the early 1980s. Today, they number over half a million civilians, armed and trained by the Guatemalan military. The UN consistently refers to them as the number one abusers of human rights in Guatemala.) Joaquin was asked to get out of the truck and then led to the civil patrol's one-room building for questioning. For several hours, he was accused of having committed crimes against the community as a member of the armed resistance during the early 1980s. He was beaten and threatened with death.

Ultimately, with the help of the UN and the office of the Human Rights Ombudsman, Joaquin was released back to Mexico where he continues to work for ARDIGUA. What impact did my presence, through Project A, have on the outcome? It is difficult to answer this question with any certainty. However, other refugees on the delegation expressed the view that the civil patrol may well have taken Joaquin's life had an international accompanier not been present. The fact that I was called upon more than once to identify myself and Joaquin to the hostile crowd may have dampened the desires of those eager to take drastic action. In other words, an international presence provided a deterrent to yet another serious human rights violation in Guatemala.

There is no doubt that the civil patrols are capable of killing. In July of that year, another civil patrol massacred three members of CONAVIGUA (a Guatemalan women's organization). A protest the following month against the July massacre led to another civil patrol attack in which one person was killed and three others wounded.

Project A's presence in this case also precipitated the involvement of the Canadian Embassy in Guatemala. Project A collaborates with the Embassy, both as part of the orientation process for new accompaniers and also as an integral participant in security plans for accompaniers once they are placed in the field. Since the Embassy is also a member of GRICAR (an international monitoring body in the return process), they necessarily joined international condemnation of the civil patrols and the violation of the 1992 Accords signed between the Guatemalan Government and the leadership of the refugees in the Mexican camps.

The involvement of a member of Project A in this instance also activated the Urgent Action Network across Canada. Thus, the plight of the refugees was forcefully brought to the attention of many Canadians who responded with letters of protest to Canadian and Guatemalan government officials.

Finally, regarding the importance of international accompaniment, I am reminded of our last meeting with members of Guatemalan NGOs in Mexico City just prior to our return to Canada. While pessimistic that significant change would take place in their homeland in the near future, they expressed excitement and gratitude about the role that an international presence was playing in Guatemala. Simply by working openly, they credited us with helping to create the small spaces needed by Guatemalans working for change—the same spaces that had been closed for so many years by violence and repression directed against the popular movement.

Perhaps, then, the greatest impact made by international accompaniment is our contribution to the breathing space we provide Guatemalans who struggle to bring about justice in their own country. Perhaps that role is the most concrete example of true solidarity in action.

REFERENCES

Falla, Ricardo. 1994. *Massacres in the Jungle: Ixcan, Guatemala 1975-1982* (Boulder, Co.: Westview Press).

Guatemala News, January 1993, translated and edited by Toby Mailman from El Diario/La Prensa, New York.

Manz, Beatriz. 1994. "Epilogue," to Ricardo Falla, *Massacres in the Jungle* (Boulder, Co.: Westview Press) pp.191-211.

National Coordination Office on Refugees and the Displaced of Guatemala (NCOORD). 1993. *Refugee Update*, January 25.

Project Accompaniment. 1992. "Proposal," submitted to the Central America Monitoring Group, February.

——. 1993. "Is Corn Subversive?," Project Accompaniment, Atlantic Delegation Report: Mexico and Guatemala, 18 November—1 December, p.9.

Project Accompaniment of Canada. 1996, application to the Democratic Development Fund, January.

White, M. 1989. letter from Atlantic Guatemala Accompaniment Team to solidarity groups, NGOs, church groups and others involved in Guatemalan solidarity work, Halifax, N.S., 1 September.

9

CHRISTIAN PEACEMAKER TEAMS

Kathleen Kern

Introduction

In 1984, Ron Sider gave the keynote address at Mennonite World Conference, calling for the Christians of the world to band together and form a Christian peacemaking army that woul intervene nonviolently in situations of conflict. "I believe the Lord of history wants to use the small family of Anabaptists scattered across the globe to help shape history in the next two decades," he wrote. But to do that,

> we must not only abandon mistaken ideas and embrace the full biblical conception of shalom. One more thing is needed. We must take up our cross and follow him to Golgotha. We must prepare to die by the thousands. Those who have believed in peace through the sword have not hesitated to die. Proudly, courageously, they gave their lives. Again and again, they sacrificed bright futures to the tragic illusion that one more righteous crusade would bring peace in their time. For their loved ones, for justice and for peace, they have laid down their lives by the millions. Why do we pacifists think that our way—Jesus's way—to peace will be less costly? Unless we Mennonites and [Anabaptist] Brethren in Christ are ready to start to die by the thousands in dramatic, vigorous new exploits for peace and justice, we should sadly confess that we really never meant what we said. Unless comfortable North American and European Mennonites and Brethren in Christ are prepared to risk injury and death in nonviolent opposition to the injustice our societies foster and assist in Central America, the Philippines and South Africa, we dare never whisper another word about pacifism to our sisters and brothers in those desperate lands. Unless we are ready to die developing new nonviolent attempts to reduce international conflict, we should confess that we never really meant the cross was an alternative to the sword. Making peace is as costly as waging war. Unless we are prepared to pay the cost of peacemaking, we have no right to claim the label or preach the message.
>
> Our world is at an impasse. The way of violence has led us to the brink of global annihilation. Desperately, our contemporaries look for alternatives. But they will never find Jesus's way to peace credible unless those of us who have proudly preached it are willing to die for it.

Holding up Witness for Peace as an example, Sider then proposed that the Anabaptist churches multiply such a nonviolent witness exponentially. He proposed that the church develop a peacekeeping force of 100,000 persons ready to move into violent conflicts and between warring parties. He suggested that the historic peace churches decide to spend 25 million dollars over a three year period to develop such a force.

"The most sophisticated expertise in diplomacy, history, international politics and logistics would be essential, so would a radical dependence on the Holy Spirit," Sider wrote.

> Such a peacekeeping task force of committed Christians would immerse every action in intercessory prayer: There would be prayer chains in all our congregations as a few thousand of our best youth walked into the face of death, inviting all parties to end the violence and work together for justice.

Using Sider's speech as a springboard, a group of Mennonite Church leaders founded Christian Peacemaker Teams (CPT) in 1986. In a letter to the author (18 January 1995), director Gene Stoltzfus writes, "CPT came into being fundamentally because none of the existing [Mennonite] agencies felt called or able to engage in active peacemaking—meaning direct support of nonviolent forms of struggle, activism and public witness." In 1993 it put out the following brochure:

> Christian Peacemaker Teams (CPT) is a unique initiative in peacemaking among cooperating Mennonite and Brethren churches. Our ministry emphasizes the skills of negotiation, public witness and nonviolent direct action. This church based ministry is a timely gift that our denominations bring to the late 20th century world.
> Our churches have been involved in nonviolent activities since the 16th century Anabaptist movement. Through the years, objections to militarism have been expressed in tax resistance, refusal to purchase warbonds, alternatives to military conscription and challenges to military industrialization. In more recent years, our people have called for nuclear disarmament, and end to covert warfare by wealthy nations and for justice for the poor.
>
> *Focus.* Our peacemaking ministry is based on Christ's example. Our primary resources are our faith, our mutual support, our tradition of sustained witness and our sense of urgency. We have learned that justice in all relationships is vital. But even when justice is not practiced, we strive to take practical steps toward loving the enemy as suggested in scripture. CPT's work has focussed on issues of violence and militarism within US and Canadian communities as well as Iraq, Palestine, Israel and Haiti.
>
> *The CPT Mandate.* 1. We believe the mandate to proclaim the Gospel of repentance, salvation and reconciliation includes a strengthened Biblical peace witness.
> 2. We believe that faithfulness to what Jesus taught and modelled calls us to more active peacemaking.
> 3. We believe a renewed commitment to the gospel of peace calls us to new forms of public witness which may include nonviolent direct action.

4. We believe the establishment of Christian Peacemaker Teams is an important new dimension for our ongoing peace and justice ministries. ...To be authentic, such peacemaking should be rooted in and supported by congregations and churchwide agencies. Let us begin.

In 1990, CPT sent its first delegations to Iraq in an effort to help prevent the Gulf War and to the Oka Indian reservation in Quebec to intervene in the standoff between the Mohawks and Quebec provincial police. As a part of the witness in Iraq, CPT also sponsored Oil Free Sunday in an attempt to connect the churches' faith to the imminent war over oil. Approximately 40 percent of Mennonite and Church of the Brethren congregations participated in some way.

In April, 1992, as the sentencing for the Rodney King trial approached, Mennonite Churches in the Los Angeles area called CPT and requested that it send a delegation to south Los Angeles, because the situation there was about to "explode." Gene Stoltzfus, director and founder of CPT, explained that it took nearly two months to put a delegation together. After the Los Angeles riots, members of the CPT Steering Committee felt that CPT needed to have a full-time Christian Peacemaker Corps ready to move immediately into a conflict situation.

Since its founding in October 1993, the Christian Peacemaker Corps has responded to invitations in Haiti, the West Bank City of Hebron, and the Columbia Heights neighborhood of Washington, DC.

Haiti

In 1990, in closely monitored elections, an overwhelming majority of the Haitian people chose Jean-Bertrand Aristide to be their president. After serving in office for seven months, he was overthrown in a coup d'etat led by the man he appointed to head the Haitian military, Raoul Cédras. In July 1993, the US-brokered Governors Island accords signed by both Aristide and Cédras specified that Cédras would step down at the end of October 1993. In return, Aristide agreed to refrain from criticizing US policy and to encourage Haitians not to flee the country.

When the date neared for Aristide to return, US President Bill Clinton ordered the warship *Harlan County* to prepare the way. On 25 October, hundreds of armed paramilitary thugs greeted the *Harlan County* at the dock, and Clinton ordered the ship to pull away—to the astonishment of almost everyone.

In the period between July and October, CPT joined with a coalition of organizations (including Pax Christi, Peace Brigades International, Witness for Peace, and the Washington Office on Haiti) that operated under the title of Cry for Justice. The stated purpose of Cry for Justice was to send teams to different areas of Haiti in order to provide a violence-deterring/human rights-monitoring presence. In September 1993, when Dante Caputo pulled out the OAS human rights monitors from Haiti because he deemed the situation too dangerous for them, the need for international teams became even more desperate.

Thirty October came and Aristide didn't. It seemed as though the US had lost interest in restoring Aristide to power. Cry for Justice disbanded. At the invitation of Father Samedi and the parish of St Helene, in the western seaport town of Jérémie, CPT stayed on.

Daily Routine
Initially, the team in St Helene began every morning with devotions and a meeting, although at times this morning meeting was more or less abandoned (depending on the makeup of the team.) The team would then separate and go visiting throughout the community of St Helene. CPTers accumulated a great deal of information about military and paramilitary activity this way and would make a point of visiting the areas in which this activity occurred.

When Haitians in Jérémie told the team about significant human rights abuses, they wrote reports and sent them to contacts in Port-au Prince, who in turn disseminated them to various human rights agencies. Eventually people began coming to the team with stories of human rights abuses they wanted documented.

Following afternoons spent on language study and naps, the members of the team would again make rounds in the early evening. Meetings with the Democratic underground or friends in hiding generally took place at night.

Highlights
Dramatic episodes in Jérémie happened infrequently. As the US belatedly tightened the embargo on Haiti, CPTers saw instead the long slow starvation of the people they worked among. However, two highlights of the CPT experience in Jérémie in which the author participated were the *bat teneb* and the demonstration after the US military arrived in Haiti in September 1994.

Bat Teneb. At noon on 7 February 1994, the bells of the downtown cathedral in Jérémie began to chime as usual, but they were soon drowned out by the noise of dozens of people banging on pots, pans and the tin roofs of their houses. That morning, CPT's interpreter had told the team that people would be participating in a *bat teneb*—or "beating away the shadows"—all across Haiti that day.

Bat teneb has a long tradition in Haiti as a sign of social protest. On this particular day, the people of Haiti wanted to call for President Jean-Bertrand Aristide's return. This 7 February marked the third anniversary of Aristide's inauguration. Because of the September 1991 coup d'etat, he had spent the last two Februaries in exile.

The team walked through the neighborhood at noon to see how many people would pick up their pots. The entire action lasted for a minute or less and members of the team assumed it would not make much of an impression. Two hours later ten heavily armed soldiers gathered outside the rectory compound. Haitians living in the rectory encouraged the four team members to go down to the heavy metal gate and talk to the soldiers. As they did so, a soldier with grenades hanging from his belt dashed to the side, SWAT-Team style, and covered the three women and one man, all unarmed, with his automatic rifle. The soldier who seemed to be in charge said that someone had reported that several Haitians had been standing on the roof of the rectory, banging drums and generally disturbing the peace.

"What is the purpose of the people who were making that noise," the interrogating soldier asked. "Are you satisfied with what they did?"

"It is not for us to be satisfied or dissatisfied with what they did," replied Joel Klassen, the member of the team most fluent in Creole. Joel further responded by saying that no one in the neighborhood seemed disturbed by the noise. After further dialogue, the military person said, "Give a message to the people who made this noise. If they do this again, they will be arrested, and you will be arrested, too."

Demonstration, 30 September. On 30 September 1994, Haitians organized nationwide demonstrations to commemorate the 5,000 people murdered for political reasons since the 1991 coup. Patrols of soldiers from the US Special Forces began to come up to the rectory several times a day, asking for Father Samedi, who was living in Archbishop Romelus' house at the time because of death threats. When CPT finally learned that the patrol wanted to talk to Fr Samedi about the demonstration, they told the Special Forces patrol that he was not in charge of organizing it, but they could introduce them to the people who were.

Someone from the rectory ran to fetch the demonstration's organizers from St Helene. Obviously expecting to meet resistance, the officer in charge began the conversation by explaining why it was important for everyone to work together. The St Helene organizers assured the Special Forces men that they had things under control.

Not satisfied, the commander began to explain the things that could happen if the St Helene people were not more forthcoming about certain details, such as the route of the demonstration....

"Oh," said one of the leaders of the parish. "You want to know the route. We're going to start in the church, make a right go down the road until we reach....." Everyone visibly relaxed. The organizers began describing how they were going to monitor the parade to ensure that no violence would occur.

The Americans, for their part, began telling the St Helene people that the Haitian military had informed them that the people of St Helene were going to engage in indiscriminate killing and looting during the demonstration.

Everyone laughed. Then the church choir director said, "Well, we wanted to dump the [cement slab upon which the army and paramilitary units had performed ritual sacrifices] into the ocean. Is that looting? And we wanted to do the same to the one in the FRAPH compound." (FRAPH is the Front for Advancement and Progress of Haiti. Ostensibly, it was the political wing of the military, however, most of the violent attacks we witnessed or heard about in Jérémie were perpetrated by FRAPH members.)

Thus began a twenty minute discussion over whether dumping the slab on the wharf into the sea and destroying the slab in the FRAPH compound constituted looting. The Americans were about evenly divided in their thinking. Finally, the organizers from St Helene and the Special Forces patrol agreed that the one on the wharf was fair game and the one in the FRAPH compound was not.

Of all the major population centers in Haiti, Jérémie alone had a demonstration on 30 September in which no one got hurt. The project in Jérémie did not represent the totality of CPT's Haitian experience. Its contacts in Port au Prince forwarded CPT reports to the press and connected these reports to the larger picture of what was happening in Haiti. CPT also sent short term delegations to Haiti to learn about the situation there, do public witnesses and report back to their congregations about what they had seen. In the United States, CPT staff spent hours getting out articles, and alerting churches to prayer action campaigns.

Since the Jérémie project closed in the winter of 1995, CPT has kept a two or three person team in Haiti that has travelled around the country monitoring election campaigns and investigating residual paramilitary violence. Members of the team served as election monitors in the December 1995 elections.

Hebron

Hebron is a city of about 120,000 Palestinians in the midst of which live 450 Israeli settlers. It is also home to the Il-Ibrahimi mosque, where legend has it that Abraham, Sarah, Rebekah, Isaac, Jacob and Leah are buried. The Israeli settlers in town call it the Cave of Macpeleh (See *Genesis* 23). Muslims, Jews and the Christian crusaders have all identified it as a holy site for the last millennium. As is true in other cases, one's terminology defines one's political stance.

In 1929, an Arab mob, with the encouragement of the British colonial occupiers, attacked the Jewish Quarter which had been established in the 16th century by Jews fleeing the inquisition in Spain. At least 67 men, women and children were hacked to death and many more wounded. An equal number were saved by their Muslim neighbors, but the massacre still looms large in the collective memories of both Jews and Muslims in Hebron and affects current interactions between the two groups.

Because the patriarchs and matriarchs are purportedly buried in Hebron and because there had once been a thriving Jewish Quarter there, when Israel's settlement policy began to take root in the 70s, the Hebron area became a special target for the right-wing religious adherents of Gush Emunim (Bloc of the Faithful).

Kiryat Arba—the oldest settlement in the West Bank—was founded in 1970 by Rabbi Moshe Levinger. He and a band of armed supporters took over the only hotel in Hebron and refused to leave. To appease them, the army gave them an old soldiers' camp on the outskirts of Hebron. Gradually, settlements moved inside the city center under the protection of the Israeli military and despite the protest of the local Palestinian inhabitants. In 1980, six yeshiva students in Hebron were killed by a militant offshoot of the PLO. Israeli military response was swift and two more settlements appeared in the center city.

Relations between the settlers and Palestinians continued to deteriorate throughout the period of the intifada and reached their logical culmination in the February 1994 massacre in the Il-Ibrahimi mosque.

Official reports of the massacre stated that the settler Baruch Goldstein, a medical doctor from Brooklyn, NY, began spraying Muslim men and boys with bullets at 5:30am. At least 39 worshippers (the official figure) died in the mosque. The Israel Defense Forces (IDF) shot an equal number in the demonstrations that followed. The army put all Palestinians in Hebron under curfew for two months, while allowing the settlers to roam the streets freely. By the time Christian Peacemaker Team arrived there a year later, people expressed as much bitterness about the collective punishment imposed upon them as they did about the massacre.

Daily Routine

The days in Hebron had a way of becoming very full. The team began every morning with devotions in the park in front of the mosque. When it finished with formal prayers and singing, members of the team would pick up trash, fix broken benches in the park or play with local children. Afterward, we would separate and visit people. Usually some members of the team stopped in to see some journalist friends to pick up the news, others would visit friends or families living near settlements in the city. Twice a week, two members of the team taught English classes to Palestinian high school students. These classes had a way of turning into discussions on the theory and practice of nonviolence. When possible, the team snatched moments to do writing in the afternoons, go visiting late afternoon and early evening and write more in the evening. Every Saturday, it spent the afternoon and early evening on Dubboya Street (which connects the settlements of Tel Rumeida and Beit Hadassah and has often been the scene of violent encounters between settlers and Palestinian residents and shopkeepers) to serve as a violence deterring presence as hundreds of settlers from all over the West Bank converged on Hebron.

Highlights

As mentioned above, the team in Hebron kept very active. The following three anecdotes from the Hebron experience were selected because of the international attention they received and because they enhanced CPT's credibility with their Palestinian hosts and with Israeli peace and human rights groups.

The Water Truck Incident. One of the families to whom the CPTers became closest was the Abu Haikel family. Their property lies between the settlement of Tel Rumeida and an Israeli soldier camp, both of which have in effect, put them under a sort of siege for the last decade. One day, the team stopped to see Hani Abu Haikel in the tea shop he runs and he told them that his cistern had run dry and that he had been unable to take a shower for over a week.

In the summer, the settlements between Bethlehem and Hebron consume most of the water supply. Consequently, people in Hebron who live on the high ground do not get running water because there is not enough pressure in the pipes. They must buy their water from the municipality or from private sources.

However, Hani said, the municipality had decided to stop delivering water to people who lived near settlements because it had had one too many windshields broken by settlers throwing rocks. The team contacted the municipality and told the people there that we would accompany any water trucks it might send out.

As it happened, Wendy Lehman and the author were out of town when Cliff Kindy and Jeff Heie got the call that a water truck was ready to go immediately. They dropped everything and walked with the water truck through the settlement of Tel Rumeida. Soldiers at the checkpoints detained them both. Cliff tried to explain to the officer interrogating him that Hani had been without water for over a week.

The officer said, "But why do you care? Why are you doing this?" Cliff told the officer that if he had been in Germany during the time of the Third Reich, he would have done the same thing on behalf of the Jews.

"Are you calling me a Nazi?" the officer asked.

Cliff and Jeff were later told that they were being held on charges of entering a closed military zone and calling soldiers Nazis. (Israeli friends from the Hebron Solidarity Committee subsequently called the team to say that they, too, had been arrested for making statements nearly identical with Cliff's.)

The IDF spokesperson said that Cliff and Jeff had called the soldiers Nazis and "cursed them in every known language." In the following weeks, if settlers saw the team having friendly conversations with soldiers, they would draw them aside and the team would hear them telling the soldiers that those were the people who had called soldiers "Nazis." Three positive things happened as a result of the water truck incident: 1) Linda Brayer, a lawyer for the Society of St Yves volunteered to represent Cliff and Jeff. She and her legal staff also eventually provided free legal help to several of the families in Hebron. 2) A *Washington Post* reporter came to spend the day with the team (Jeff was from Washington and the reporter's editor told him to work the local angle). While talking to a settler in Tel Rumeida, he dispelled some rumors that had been circulating about Cliff being a Hamas activist and the sporadic death threats that the team had been receiving stopped. 3) The subsequent publicity drew both Israeli and international attention to the water shortage in Hebron. The mainstream Israeli public expressed outrage when they saw footage of the settlements in the West Bank with swimming pools and well-watered lawns and then learned that Palestinians in Hebron did not have enough water for drinking and washing. Prime Minister Rabin sent a fact-finding mission to Hebron to determine the extent of the water shortage—even though the West Bank cities had been complaining for years of water shortages.

Opening the Gates of Hebron University. On 22 July 1995, CPT and members of the Jerusalem-based Hebron Solidarity Committee (HSC) responded to an invitation to open the gates of Hebron University. The military had kept them closed since the beginning of the intifada, even though the University does not stand near a settlement, checkpoint or road that the military frequently uses. Students either had to climb the front gate or walk nearly ten minutes out of their way to come in through the service entrance.

Using sledgehammers, CPT and members of the Hebron Solidarity Committee began to attack the gates to the applause of students and faculty. After about an hour, the Israeli military appeared and arrested CPT members Cliff Kindy, Kathleen Kamphoefner, Wendy Lehman and HSC member Maxine Kaufmann Nunn for refusing to leave a closed military zone.

The group spent the night in jail. The police took the women to Abu Kabeer prison and Cliff to the Russian Compound, where he spent the night in a cell next to some Hebron settler youth who had been arrested for assaulting a police officer the day before.

An Israeli friend posted bond and the authorities dropped the matter. Students and faculty gave the team a reception at the University and two members of the team later went in to talk to Captain Eyal Ziv who had been in charge of the arrests. They told him what CPT had done in Haiti and why the team had come to Hebron. They asked why the army wanted the gate closed and he smiled tolerantly and said essentially that it was for security reasons that they could not understand. He also told the team that representatives of the University had been in dialogue with the Israeli Civil Administration and CPT had ruined negotiations. (This was a lie, according to sources the team consulted at the University. Administrators had never come to the Civil Administration to ask for the doors to be opened. "It is not for them to give permission. It is our right," a friend said.)

The two team members explained that they were pacifists and would stand between him and an assailant to protect him, which seemed to impress him. When they told him they would stand between a soldier and the person at whom he was pointing a gun, they frowned, and said, "You understand I will have to arrest you if you do this." They said they understood.

The Attack. The following incident is written in first person, because it involved a personal attack on the author: On 30 September, just hours before I was scheduled to leave the country, Wendy and I arrived early for our Saturday afternoon presence on Dubboya Street. The streets outside the settlement of Beit Hadassah seemed to be swarming with settlers. Wendy heard noises and shouting coming from around the corner and went to investigate. She called to me to follow her. Some settler teenagers were throwing bottles at people in the marketplace. As I turned to walk in her direction, I heard people further up the street calling, "Kathy. Don't go. They are coming."

I looked behind me and saw about twenty men ranging in age from the mid-twenties to early forties walking purposefully up the street. I turned and continued walking toward the lower Tel Rumeida checkpoint. Suddenly, a sort of battle cry went up behind me and I heard them running. Someone yanked at the red checked keffiyeh* I had tied to my backpack. I kept walking. Someone yanked harder, pulling me over onto my back. Several of the men spat on me as I laid on the ground.

The men ran past and began breaking the windows on all the cars standing in the street. I got up and began taking pictures. A very large man turned around and shouted, "No. No pictures."

I am not sure in what sequence the following events took place. Five or six men ran back toward me and tried to grab my camera way from me. One of the men punched me in the ear and knocked me to the ground, but I maintained my grip on the camera. As the men dragged me around on the ground by my camera strap, I noticed that the checkpoint at Beit Hadassah had no soldiers in it. I decided to begin screaming in order to attract attention.

By the time Wendy came back, I was on my feet again and told her they were trying to take my camera. She had the presence of mind to snap a picture and then joined me in trying to retain the camera. We both went down on the ground again. Eventually, the same man who had hit me stomped on Wendy's hand and we lost the camera.

The man ran toward the settlement of Beit Hadassah holding the camera high above his head. As his friends ran with him, laughing and cheering, the scene reminded me of high school athletes running with the football after making a touchdown.

As a result of the attack, Israelis and internationals from the Jerusalem and Tel Aviv area came down and participated with the team in the Saturday afternoon Dubboya Street presence. Increased contact with the police in Hebron also helped increase the level of respect and understanding between us and the officers.

On 4 November, Diane Roe, who had come to join the team after I left, was knocked to the ground by young Israeli men, and the Palestinian teenage girl to whom she had been speaking was dragged along the ground by her hair braid. The young men kicked her as she screamed. The

New York Times later conflated the two attacks in article about Yigal Amir, Prime Minister Rabin's assassin:

> Such trips to Hebron were one of the brothers' frequent activities. Several weeks ago, witnesses say, the two swaggered in the lead of such a group, some of whom broke ranks and attacked a line of Christian women peace activists who regularly placed themselves between the Jews and Palestinians, knocking two of them down and dragging them by their hair (Kifner, 1995).

The team in Hebron thinks the boys who attacked Dianne were too young to have been the Amir brothers. It is possible that the brothers were a part of the 30 September attack on Wendy and me.

Washington
Between May and July, 1994, three members of CPT investigated the possibility of setting up a project in Washington, DC. CPT subsequently received an invitation from the Sojourners Neighborhood center to establish a "violence-free zone," embracing a single neighborhood in which all residents were invited to help eliminate violence.

The Crackhouse. In September 1994, the DC project officially began. The first team, consisted of CPT members Cole Arendt and John Reuwer and two members of the Brethren Voluntary service, Tammy Krause and Jeff Heie. The team began by instituting a listening project in the Columbia Heights Neighborhood. Talks with neighbors soon identified a local crackhouse owned by Mr Kingsley Anyanwutahu as the locus for much of the violence in the neighborhood. In fact, more than 40 of Kingsley's properties in the DC area were home to drugs, prostitution and violence. His tenants live in dangerous and unsanitary conditions.

The team's main strategy thus became closing down the crackhouse. They found that many of the neighbors had attempted to do so over the years and that many of them were unaware of the efforts of their fellow neighbors. CPT invited all the neighbors to the Sojourner's neighborhood center and began strategizing with them.

One of the obstacles the neighbors had faced was the Washington, DC bureaucracy. Since many of them held down jobs or had small children at home, they simply did not have the time to jump through all the hoops that the DC bureaucracy put in front of citizens trying to make changes. CPT members thus spent a large part of their time running from office to office (sometimes going the full circle after the fifth or sixth person to whom they had been referred, referred them back to the original office from which they had sought help). In the course of their research, they were able to collect the numerous building code violations that Mr Kingsley, as he was known, had committed.

At one of the neighborhood meetings, CPT members suggested that the residents of Columbia Heights talk to the residents of the crackhouse. While the neighbors initially were suspicious of the prostitutes and drug users who lived there, when they found out that the residents of the crackhouse were as upset with Mr Kingsley as the neighbors were, they got together over pizza and began strategizing together. The Columbia Heights neighbors subsequently helped the crackhouse residents by looking for housing for them and storing the belongings of those people who wanted to look for their own housing. In one case, they helped a woman return to her home community in Georgia.

In December 1994, the Columbia Heights held a candlelight vigil in front of the crackhouse. Initially planned to call the city's attention to its negligence in allowing the house to remain open, the vigil turned into a celebration. The day before the DC city government had sent two people to brick up the house.

In October 1995, a District of Columbia court sentenced Mr Kingsley Anyanwutahu to six years in prison for operating slum houses in violation of building codes, tax codes and permit regulations. In one of the most unusual events in this case, the judge offered to allow the mass of letters he had received on Kingsley's properties from "ordinary citizens" to be used as evidence of the "will of the people." These voices were compelling, said the judge. CPT workers who helped encourage citizens to contact the judge prior to sentencing feel that these letters may have made a critical difference in the outcome of the case.

Originally charged for violations in 28 of his properties, Kingsley could have faced 13 years in prison and almost $239,000 in fines. Kingsley and his attorney, a former District of Columbia legal counsel, entered a plea bargain with the city's lawyers. Eventually Kingsley was charged for violations in 11 houses. Chief Judge Hamilton chose to ignore this plea bargain and sentenced Mr Kingsley to a stiff six year jail term on 19 September. Twenty-two days into his sentence, he was to reappear before the judge, and there was apprehension that Mr Kingsley would be deemed no danger to the community and released as called for in the original plea bargain. Instead the judge indicated that he was unwilling to hear any further pleas or appeals on behalf of Mr Kingsley until he has dispossessed himself of all his properties and paid the over $110,000 fine. (Even while the sentencing was pending, Kingsley continued to advertise his properties, transfer deeds, and try to collect rent on court-seized units.)

Halloween. In October 1994, CPT helped facilitate a safe Halloween for Columbia Heights children after listening to neighbors lament that their children had not been able to participate in trick-or-treating for the last ten years. They handed out florescent green signs for neighbors to put in windows to indicate that their houses were safe places for children to come and ask for treats.

The October 1994 Halloween was such a success the area for the October 1995 Halloween was doubled. Over 25 orange hat citizen patrollers in four squads kept watch on every block and helped trick-or-treaters cross dangerous intersections.

On Halloween night 1995, over 350 children enjoyed safe trick-or-treating throughout the South Columbia Heights neighborhood thanks to the combined efforts of area residents and Christian Peacemaker Teams. While some residents patrolled the streets with flashlights and whistles to ensure a violence-free environment, families sat on their porches to greet the excited children dressed in colorful costumes.

The event also spread to other communities. Bernice Taylor of Sojourners Neighborhood Center got her own community in Northeast Columbia Heights to put out flyers as well. By encouraging people to come out for Halloween, her neighbors enjoyed the largest trick-or-treating in years. "We stole your idea," she said, "and we are glad we did!"

Currently, the people involved with the CPT Washington project operate out of the Warner apartments, a focus of violence in another part of the Columbia Heights neighborhood for the last several years. The decision to move into the public housing project came in response to many requests from Columbia Heights neighbors. The 44 unit complex is a center of drug activity and prostitution. Police statistics from 1992 through 1994 show that over half of the police runs in the block around the building were to this single address. They hope to continue working with the local Orange Hat patrols and neighborhood groups to target the violence in the building.

Other Projects

In addition to the three major projects run in Haiti, Hebron and Washington, DC, CPT has continued to send short-term delegations to these areas in order to assist the teams with special projects and to report back to home congregations about the situations in these places.

For the past three years, CPT has initiated a campaign against violent toys. These campaigns have involved sending hundreds of resource packets to congregations in the United States and Canada to help families in the congregation identify toys that perpetuate a culture of violence and to make suggestions for nonviolent toys and video games. Also as part of these campaigns CPT has helped post-Christmas demonstrations at toy stores that carry violent toys and games. CPT has also participated in efforts to close down Project ELF in northern Wisconsin for the last several years and has had several of its members arrested for trespassing on this defense facility. (ELF stands for Extremely Low Frequency waves which are transmitted to Trident submarines in order to ensure first-strike capability.) CPT publishes a bimonthly newsletter entitled *Signs of the Times* and organizes prayer campaigns among Mennonite, Church of the Brethren, and Quaker congregations to support CPT workers and their local hosts.

Conclusion

Although CPT borrows from decades of experiences of Mennonite volunteer workers around the world and from the experiences of activists from many religious backgrounds, it is still a relatively new phenomenon.

Traditionally people from Anabaptist backgrounds have been "the quiet in the land" and the idea of committing civil disobedience—even to the point of undergoing arrest—is a concept with which many members of Mennonite and Church of the Brethren congregations are not comfortable.

Because of its relative newness, there are many dilemmas that Christian Peacemaker Teams have not fully sorted out. We have a policy against giving monetary or material aid, which places us in difficult situations when our hosts live in deep poverty. We are still working to develop appropriate relationships with the military and paramilitary people we encounter in the course of our work. How can we treat them with the love and respect that Jesus would have showed them without alienating our hosts? Most of the people who have invited us to come serve as a violence-deterring presence are not pacifists and we will continue to struggle with the issue of what it means to stand in solidarity with people and remain true to our own pacifist convictions.

In spite of these struggles, CPT is establishing a unique niche in the annals of peacemaking. Because it is rooted in the congregations of the Mennonite and Brethren churches, it offers a venue for conservative evangelical Christians to participate in significant peacemaking ventures. CPT's religious base has also helped it communicate more effectively with the devout Catholics of St Helene and the devout Muslims and Jews in Hebron. We understand what it means to act out of religious conviction, which provides an opening to dialogue with religious peoples involved in conflict.

We are not yet close to Ronald Sider's vision of a 100,000 member nonviolent army, but we dare to hope outrageously. What choice do we have? We have chosen to follow Jesus—who performed history's most outrageous act of nonviolent resistance by rising from the dead.

NOTE

* We wore the keffiyehs (checked head coverings that some Palestinian men wear) on our backpacks so that Palestinians would not mistake us for settlers. Many of the settlers had strong reactions to them. One woman said it was the equivalent of wearing gang colors. Even one of our Israeli peace activist friends told us he felt uncomfortable with us when we displayed them. He told us it showed we had definitely "sided" with the Palestinians.

REFERENCES

Kifner, J. 1995. "The Zeal of Rabin's Assassin springs from Rabbis of Religious Right," *New York Times* (International Edition), 12 November, p.12.

10

BALKAN PEACE TEAM INTERNATIONAL IN CROATIA:
OTVORENE OCI (Open Eyes)

Dave Bekkering

Introduction

At the end of February 1994, Johanna Bjorken and Vic Ullom from the US, James Derieg from England and Øystein Kleven from Norway arrived in Zagreb to explore the necessity of and possibilities for a permanent presence of the international peace and human rights movement in Croatia. They were sent to Croatia by representatives of a joint project established by nine well-known international peace and human rights organizations as Balkan Peace Team-International (BPT-I). After their initial three months' assessment the four volunteers decided that a presence was definitely required and that it was necessary to have a second office in Split. After May 1994, the Zagreb office had three volunteers and the Split office two.

Most of these early volunteers have now left the "field" but are still engaged in BPT-I work in different ways. One is currently a member of the Coordinating Committee, another takes care of the BPT newsletter, a third engages in propaganda and fund-raising activities in the German speaking countries, and a fourth is in contact with the teams in her capacity as representative of Amnesty International.

After three months, a name, *Otvorene Oci* ("Open Eyes") was chosen, and after having been in the field for six months the teams determined their own mandate. This resulted in the following information sheet containing the principles and goals of Otvorene Oci as well as its main fields of work:

> Otvorene Oci (Open Eyes) is the Croatian branch of Balkan Peace Team-International. Balkan Peace Team-International is a cooperative initiative taken by several international nongovernmental organizations experienced in nonviolent conflict resolution. The aim is to promote

peaceful resolution of the conflicts in the territories of the former Yugoslavia.

Otvorene Oci is a team of international volunteers committed to nonviolent conflict resolution and human rights. In the Spring of 1994 we established a permanent team of long-term volunteers in Croatia. Otvorene Oci has representatives in Zagreb and Split. Whereas the Split representatives consider Dalmatia as their operational field, the Zagreb office covers the rest of Croatia and functions as the central office.

We are independent observers and supporters of positive efforts in Croatia to promote peace and human rights and to build democracy. As an international presence Otvorene Oci is committed to respond to the needs of domestic organizations and individuals.

Otvorene Oci engages in activities in the following fields:

Civil Society Development. Cooperation with groups which advocate peaceful resolution of conflicts and human rights. We offer developing NGOs practical information on setting up and running an NGO, identify possibilities of cooperation and create links between them.

Nonviolent Conflict Resolution. Otvorene Oci is available to mobilize domestic and international resources for workshops and trainings in nonviolent conflict resolution and mediation. We also encourage and assist grassroots projects for community conflict resolution.

Human Rights Advocacy. Otvorene Oci supports and empowers local activists who are working to improve the human rights situation. We give people appropriate referrals to those who can give assistance in case of human rights violations. We provide an impartial international presence at meetings, demonstrations, trials and at the scene of possible human rights violations when requested or deemed useful. We are also prepared to accompany human rights activists in their work when requested.

In addition to these activities, information dissemination is an important part of our work. Otvorene Oci is an independent source of information into and out of the region.

Otvorene Oci is working in the spirit of the internationally recognized Universal Declaration of Human Rights, which charges every individual with the responsibility to protect and promote human rights. We are committed to this responsibility in an entirely nonviolent and impartial manner, cooperating with all initiatives committed to nonviolent conflict resolution, regardless of nationality, religion, gender, ethnicity or political viewpoint.

At the forth Helsinki Citizens' Assembly in Tuzla, on 21 October 1995, Otvorene Oci presented its activities to the interested public. The presentation clarified how the principles, goals and mandate described in the above information sheet lead to the day-to-day nonviolent interventions in the conflicts in the Republic of Croatia.

To understand the work of Otvorene Oci it is important to place its activities against the background of major developments in Croatian society itself and NGO development in Croatia.

The Context of the Mandate I: Democracy and Civil Society

Transition. Not only has Croatia been trying to cope with the transition from the Yugoslav-style "communist" political and economic system to a pluralist democracy and a market economy, which has left the social systems of many other East European countries in a shambles, it has been trying to do so under very difficult circumstances. During this process, the country was at war and people are still inclined see their country as being at war. At the same time the country has to deal with roughly 400,000 refugees and displaced persons. This has to be kept in mind when assessing the development of democracy and efforts towards reconciliation and human rights protection.

Centralization. Building a pluralist democracy is not proceeding smoothly. The HDZ (Croatian Democratic Union) was democratically chosen but, according to observers and the parliamentary opposition, it rules as though it is running a one-party state. The vice-president of one of the biggest opposition parties, HSLS, Mr Kovacevic, stated in an article in the independent daily *Novi List* that "the authorities are preparing the public for dictatorship."

Centralization tendencies also came to the surface in the way central state bodies dealt with a regional counterpart. In February 1995, the Constitutional Court overruled the decision of the Istrian County Court to provide the Italian population with clearly defined minority rights. In addition to this, Istria has been publicly denounced as the "second Krajina" of Croatia because of its attempts to strive for more autonomy.

The problems Croatia has with creating an independent judiciary came out into the open when, in the beginning of March, the Croatian Minister of Justice, Mr Crnic, handed in his resignation out of protest against what he described as dictatorial tendencies within the judicial system. In Mr Crnic's opinion, the problem is that the Council of Judges, which plays the main role in the restructuring of Croatia's judicial system and appointing new judges, has itself apparently been chosen in a non-constitutional way. Croatia's Upper House of Representatives was supposed to nominate the judges. Instead, a commission nominated by president Tudjman and headed by his friend Mr Pasalic, named the members of this council and subsequently the Parliament confirmed this choice at a time when no members of the political opposition were present. As a result, well known and competent judges were left out, and judges who were unknown, but politically acceptable to the HDZ, were appointed. Mr Crnic's resignation came after his appeals against the nomination of 25 higher court judges were not heeded.

Recent developments, however, show a crack in HDZ's power monopoly as it did not win the November 1995 elections in major towns like Zagreb, Split and Rijeka. In Zagreb the president of the City Council is a member of the former communist party (SDP) and the mayor of Zagreb is a member of the HSLS. In addition, the HDZ did not get the two-thirds majority it needed to change the constitution.

The World of NGOs. However, this tendency towards centralization does not prevent civil society from flourishing. The number of NGOs is steadily increasing and existing NGOs are expanding their activities. The Coordination of Human Rights Groups established to coordinate the activities of all the NGOs in Croatia is steadily taking on a more solid form. In Zupanja, a Center for Peace, Nonviolence, Psychological and Social Help and Human Rights ("Peace and Good") was established. As a follow-up to initiatives within Croatia's Anti-War Campaign, a conscientious objectors' NGO ("Union 47"), the Center for Peace, Culture and Nonviolence ("Mali Korak"), and the Center for Direct Protection of Human Rights were established in Zagreb. An organization called "MIRamid" was set up to provide training in conflict resolution and human rights monitoring.

A doubling of the "Citizen's Committees for Human Rights" occurred as a result of a rift between two sections within it, causing a new "Committee for Human Rights" to emerge. In Split, the International Rescue Committee and the Croatian League for Peace opened new branches. Following the signing of the Erdut Agreement between Croatia and Serbia concerning United Nations Protected Area sector East, efforts to establish human rights monitoring offices and social and physical reconstruction projects are being initiated.

In Split, a group for the "affirmation of women" was formed, as well as two women's groups within the Dalmatian Committee of Solidarity (in Split and Knin). As far as networking is concerned, the Zagreb women's group, "Be Active, Be Emancipated," has presented a plan for the establishment of a women's network group.

In general, more support for Croatian NGOs is gradually coming from international funders and organizations, with the mainstream media slowly starting to publish some of their appeals or statements, indicating a slowly growing recognition of their efforts.

The Context of the Mandate II: Human Rights
To quote a voice from the field, a Split human rights activist from the Dalmatian Committee for Human Rights defines government activities in the field of human rights as a "system of human rights abuse designed

for ethnic cleansing." However, on 27 February 1994, the former Special Rapporteur to the UN, Tadeusz Mazowiecki, in his speech at the 51st session of the Commission on Human Rights in Geneva, signalled an improvement in the overall human rights situation in Croatia.

A Deteriorating Situation. The circumstances have changed since then and the human rights situation is no longer improving. The two Croatian army operations, "Flash" and "Storm," resulted in many grave human rights violations—violations which are still occurring at the time of writing. The killing of elderly Serb civilians, the systematic looting and burning of Krajina Serb property, the preventing of the return of those Serbs that fled, the holding prisoners without charge and denying them sufficient legal representation, and the failure to protect citizens from danger are ongoing problems. Cases of job dismissal related to ethnicity have been reported, as well as illegal confiscation of property. Krajina Serbs have also suddenly found birth and death certificates invalid as well as marriage documents.

Just before the 1995 elections in Croatia, certain parts of the *Law on Minorities* were suspended by the HDZ, decreasing the number of seats in parliament for the Serb minority from 13 to three.

Housing. On the housing issue, Mr Mazowiecki voiced concern about judicial procedures aimed at legalizing forced evictions from apartments but also noted a cessation of illegal forced evictions from former JNA (Yugoslav People's Army) apartments and a Constitutional Court decision declaring administrative evictions illegal.

The battle for apartments has clearly moved into the courts. Of special concern is a law which has been used increasingly to take away people's apartment rights. Law "102a" defines "enemy activity" as a reason for losing these rights.

Since the amendments to the Croatian *Law on Apartments Under Tenancy Right* came into effect on 17 August 1994, allowing tenants of former JNA apartments only 60 days to collect all their documents for their application to buy their own apartment, a new wave of violent and illegal evictions has descended on towns like Zagreb and Split. An indirect effect of the Croatian army operations has been the growing power and status of the army and also the growing liberties the Military Police, the Military Housing Commission and the soldiers themselves take in their efforts to "liberate" apartments from their tenants. Civilian and military police do little to prevent these evictions.

Refugees and Displaced Persons. Another disquieting development is the Croatian government's desire to strip Bosnian refugees and Croatian displaced persons of their status before the conditions for their return meet with UN conventions. The relocation of Bosnian Muslims to Bihac, and Croats from the Banja Luka area to the former Krajina, to places where they do not choose to live, is not a positive sign for Croatia's human rights record.

The situation of the 25,000 Muslim refugees from the Bosnian Bihac area in the Kupljensko refugee camp in former UNPA sector North is of special concern to the human rights movement in Croatia. The refugees live on a roadside in UNHCR tents and other makeshift shelters and are not allowed to build more permanent dwellings. They have no access to medical care and await their fate to be settled at the negotiating table, or by the force of the Croatian Special Police.

Media. The report written by Mr Mazowiecki in January 1995 about the media in Croatia states that the Republic of Croatia has considerable potential to promote and guarantee freedom of the media. Nevertheless, the Government, by different methods (economic, administrative and even force) has succeeded in controlling most of the media outlets. Moreover, only one new independent newspaper has been established in recent times (*Dan*); *ARKzin, Feral Tribune, Boomerang, Erasmus, Start* and *Nove Generacije* remain the current independent periodicals and *Novi List* is the only really independent daily newspaper.

Nine months after the special tax on *Feral Tribune* had been imposed, the government decided to repeal its decision. In another positive development, the government announced a law concerning the acquisition of broadcasting frequencies, thus opening new possibilities for private and independent broadcasters. Unfortunately, an independent and very popular Istrian radio station (*Radio Labin*) was deprived of its frequency.

The World of NGOs. Human rights NGOs are present all over Croatia: in Zagreb, Osijek, Zupanija, Karlovac, Split, Rijeka, Porec and Dubrovnik. Croatian human rights NGOs are setting up new offices in Knin (former sector South), Vrhovina (former sector North) and Vojnic (former sector North) and trying to maintain the office in Gavrinica (former sector West).

With the help of Oxfam, cooperation has commenced between NGOs from Croatia and Serbia. Since the signing of the Erdut Agreement and the Dayton Peace Agreement, Croatian and Serbian NGOs have been engaged in starting up human rights monitoring offices in the former United Nations Protected Area sector East.

The Context of the Mandate III: Peace and Reconciliation

Although the Croatian government has repeatedly stated that it intends to reintegrate the occupied territories peacefully, the Croatian army has done the opposite. Former sectors West, North and South have been militarily integrated with the loss of hundreds of lives, causing ongoing human rights violations which include the continued killing of Krajina Serb civilians.

The leaders of Bosnia, Croatia and Rump Yugoslavia signed the Dayton Peace Agreement on 14 December 1995, and people's hopes were raised that a peaceful solution could be found. As far as the United Nations Protected Area sector East is concerned, the Croatian government and the authorities of the sector have been negotiating the gradual and peaceful integration of the territory into the Republic of Croatia, leading to the signing of the Erdut Agreement in December 1995. The Croatian government, however, does stress that it reserves the right to take the area by force if the implementation is not carried out in a satisfactory manner.

The World of NGOs. Although in 1995 Croatia still perceived itself as a country at war, and the striving for reconciliation with the other side was regarded by many as an act of treason, the general atmosphere in Croatia appears to be offering more possibilities for working in the area of peace. New centers for peace were established during the year and existing centers have increased their efforts. A good sign is the fact that centers for peace are inclined to be more open about their ideas. Not long ago public tribunals or meetings were unheard of. Croatia's Anti-War Campaign has organized a few public meetings on how to work for peace and so have the centers in Osijek and Rijeka. Croatia's network of peace groups also decided to increase their activities and to use the means of advertisements in national newspapers to spread their ideas.

More activities in the field of peace education are being undertaken, including education at primary and secondary schools (Mali Korak in Zagreb, Center in Osijek, Sunflower in Rijeka, Peace and Good in Zupanja and in Pakrac).

Meetings that discussed the possibilities of a peaceful solution to the remaining territorial conflicts in sector East were held in Osijek between several NGOs. Meetings are being arranged in Mohács, Hungary between displaced persons from sector East currently living in Osijek, Vukovar and Vojvodina. The Erdut Agreement and the Dayton Peace

Agreement prompted NGOs from Croatia and Serbia to initiate the establishment of social reconstruction projects and community building projects.

Otvorene Oci: Work in the Field
Otvorene Oci's main goal in the field is to support domestic NGOs working for human rights, peace issues or women's issues. It is in regular contact with local NGOs to discuss current problems and to find ways to solve these problems—and providing assistance when requested and where possible, such as accompaniment for their representatives in unsafe situations and access to, and credibility with, local authorities. The establishment of contacts between local NGOs and local authorities is seen as a contribution to a nonviolent resolution of possible conflicts.

Although Otvorene Oci has not changed its fundamental orientation since March 1994, new activities have been added to the task list and others have disappeared. It has defined for itself the following mandate: Otvorene Oci works in the fields of civil society development, human rights advocacy and peace and nonviolent conflict resolution.

Civil Society Development
Contacts and Networking. As civil society development and networking constitute an important part of the work, maintaining contact with local and international NGOs, local authorities and the international bodies on the ground such as by the UN or the EC has been an ongoing activity. Meetings are held regularly to discuss the situation and to determine what kind of cooperation is needed.

Contacts previously established with NGOs, for instance the different components of the Anti-War Campaign, Nexus, the Croatian Helsinki Committee, the Dalmatian Committee of Solidarity, and the Dalmatian Committee for Human Rights, have been maintained. Contacts with independent media (e.g. *ARKzin* and *Feral Tribune*), international bodies (e.g. the European Community Monitoring Mission ECMM, UNHCR, Oxfam and embassies) and government organizations (e.g. the government Office for Displaced Persons and Refugees or the Civil Housing Commission) have also been maintained.

Other contacts (e.g. the Croatian Helsinki Committee and the Citizens' Committee for Human Rights in Karlovac, the International Reconstruction Project in Pakrac, the Center for Peace, Nonviolence and Human Rights in Osijek, Be Active Be Emancipated B.A.B.E., MIRamid, the Serb Democratic Forum in Zagreb, the International Rescue Committee and the Women's Association in Split) have gradually received more attention.

Otvorene Oci also attempts to bring local NGOs in contact with foreign NGOs to further cooperation and secure international financial and moral support. Local organizations have been linked with Tilburg Za Mir, an organization that provides local NGOs with office materials like computers, printers, faxes and copiers and pays regular visits to the groups they support.

Setting up Offices. The Zagreb office assisted in the setting up of the Human Rights Center of the Croatian Coordination of Human Rights Groups and an NGO coordination office in Gavrinica, former sector West. The Split office is helping with the establishment of the office of the Dalmatian Committee of Solidarity in Knin, former sector South.

The Zagreb office is also involved in the establishment of a Community Information Center in Vojnic, former sector North. The Kupljensko refugee camp, the temporary home of the refugees and followers of maverick politician and warlord Fikret Abdic, is situated near Vojnic. In this area Bosnian Muslims are living with the remaining Krajina Serbs and the returning displaced Croatians. Anti-War Campaign Karlovac, Citizens' Committee for Human Rights Karlovac and Citizens' Committee for Human Rights Porec, Oxfam and Otvorene Oci are jointly establishing a Community Information Center. The Center will facilitate the reintegration of minority groups that have stayed in the area, the return of displaced Croatians to their homes, and provide access to basic services such as shelter, housing, medical assistance, social welfare and humanitarian aid. It will also support the refugees in the Kupljensko camp and mediate in conflicts which may arise between the existing population and returnees.

Exploring the Country. Both offices have been engaged in several exploratory missions to find out about the development of civil society in Croatia and the formerly occupied territories. The Zagreb and the Split offices were both involved in the Balkan Peace Team Exploratory Tour to the former "Republika Srpska Krajina" (RSK) in February 1995. Zagreb organized a Slavonia Outreach tour to explore civil society, the human rights situation and peace activities in Northeastern Croatia. d Split did the same for Dubrovnik.

Internal Organization. If requested, Otvorene Oci is also prepared to assist local NGOs with their internal organization. For example, the Split office gave workshops in "Communication and Decision-making" for the improvement of organizational processes within the Dalmatian Committee of Solidarity.

Human Rights Advocacy

Otvorene Oci is of the opinion that the protection of human and minority rights is one of the most important confidence-building measures that Croatia can perform. If people from different ethnicities are to live together peacefully, then respect for their human rights is essential.

Housing Issues. Otvorene Oci's regular work in the field of human rights advocacy changes according to the situation. For almost half a year, less attention was paid to illegal and legal evictions since the issue was being discussed in Parliament, and a moratorium on legal evictions was in force. In that period the Zagreb and Split offices attended only two evictions together with local activists.

In the courts, however, housing issues remained a major topic. During the latter half of 1995, the military authorities stepped up their efforts to take away people's apartment rights on the basis of article 102a of the April 1992 law concerning "Enemy Activity Against the Republic of Croatia." Otvorene Oci monitors the related trials together with local activists. Proving that a former JNA member was actually engaged in enemy activity is a difficult task, with the legal necessity to accuse the family members often leading to ridiculous allegations.

Together with the local activists, Otvorene Oci talked to an attorney to get more background information on this law and asked judges about their opinions and about the criteria for enemy activity.

Since the amendments to the *Law on Privatization of Apartments Under Tenancy Right* came into effect, a new wave of illegal evictions descended upon Croatia. As the role of the Croatian military (Military Housing Commission, military police and soldiers) in these cases became increasingly negative, Otvorene Oci and local human rights NGOs came together to discuss a new strategy. In response to the law, an international fax campaign was started by local groups with Otvorene Oci's assistance. The aim was to protest at government levels on the basis that it contains discriminatory provisions. It was decided to talk to different local authorities, such as the head of the civil police and a military commander concerned with housing issues, and to be more energetic in pressuring the military police to take action.

Miscellaneous Human Rights Violations. Trials dealing with cases of job dismissals because of ethnicity and conscientious objection have also been monitored. Local NGOs and the Split office have tried to provide support for a large number of employees from the Splitska Banka who were fired because of these factors. Otvorene Oci Zagreb has also assisted the Croatian Helsinki Committee in Karlovac with its problems concerning a group of pensioners of Serbian ethnicity who have been facing difficulty in obtaining their pensions.

A relatively new development is the Croatian government's intention to strip Bosnian refugees and displaced Croatians of their respective status and send them back to areas which cannot yet be considered, in accordance with UN conventions, as genuinely safe or even appropriate for resettlement. Otvorene Oci intends to follow up on these developments with a concern for the rights of refugees and displaced persons and to pass on the information to organizations in countries that accept Croatian and Bosnian refugees upon their request.

Former Sector West. The Zagreb office cooperated intensively with local NGOs during the aftermath of the Croatian Army's Operation "Flash" in Western Slavonia. The work included monitoring the human rights situation, accompanying threatened Serb leaders and frightened Serb inhabitants, establishing contacts with international organizations such as the UN and ECMM, setting up a human rights office, accompanying Serb inhabitants to local authorities to arrange their documents, and giving the local population advice on their rights. The Zagreb office wrote an extensive report on the events in Western Slavonia and the role of local NGOs.

Former Sector South. The Croatian Army's Operation "Storm" was not only a human rights violation in terms of the killing of hundreds of people and driving 150,000 people from their homeland, but it also triggered additional human rights violations.

The Split office arranged a meeting with the Dalmatian Committee of Solidarity, the Croatian Helsinki Committee and the Dalmatian Committee for Human Rights to discuss what strategy to adopt concerning the events in Krajina. Together with Otvorene Oci, these three NGOs undertook monitoring missions in the area to assess and document the situation. Otvorene Oci established contacts and cooperation between local human rights activists and international organizations like UNHCR, ECMM, the UN and their Human Rights Action Teams, and the International Committee of the Red Cross. The Dalmatian Committee of Solidarity decided to open an office in Knin to tackle these problems and the Split office assisted in the process. This office has been available to people who may need assistance concerning their documents, rights, missing relatives or the humanitarian situation. Otvorene Oci and the local NGOs have worked on the problems of the hundreds of Krajina Serb refugees in the UN compound in Knin and have followed up on the situation of the 38 POWs from the same camp. Through 1995,

Otvorene Oci had provided a regular presence in Knin at the request of the local NGOs.

Peace and Nonviolent Conflict Resolution
Otvorene Oci perceives its work as a form of nonviolent conflict resolution. Together with local NGOs, it seeks ways to nonviolently solve conflicts that arise from the current political and social situation. Otvorene Oci tries to be a mediator between two sides in a conflict by bringing them together, if possible, and providing both sides with "the other side of the story."

Activities in this area have compized the organizing of workshops in nonviolent conflict resolution, nonviolent communication and a lecture in peaceful civil intervention in conflict situations. Other activities have included the growing involvement in the peacebuilding project of the International Reconstruction Camp in Pakrac, the dealing with cases of conscientious objection, participation in a meeting in Osijek with "displaced Persons from Vukovar" in order to prepare them for talks with (displaced) Serbs currently living in Vukovar and participation in meetings in Mohács with NGOs from Serbia, Croatia and sector East.

Trip to the "RSK". The trip to Krajina was not merely to gather information for the Balkan Peace Team and to investigate the possibilities of setting up an office in Knin; it was also intended to spread information about the findings to inhabitants of Zagreb-controlled Croatia. Such information was generally lacking so as to make people unaware of, and insensitive to, feelings and opinions from "RSK" inhabitants. Peaceful reintegration presupposes at least a fundamental knowledge of the state of mind of the other side. People in Krajina had seen Croatian television, so they knew approximately what the other side thought. This fact necessitated an as-wide-as-possible distribution of the Knin report. Otvorene Oci not only distributed the report to all the NGOs that it cooperates with and authorities that it has contacts with, but it also wrote a press release which was sent, along with the report, to major dailies and weeklies. Two reports, in the weekly *ARKzin* and in the independent daily *Novi List*, were the result. Lengthy follow-up discussions were instituted as part of the Krajina fact-finding mission.

"Committee for the Peaceful Reintegration of the Occupied Territories". When president Tudjman announced the withdrawal of the UN Protection Force (UNPROFOR), the whole world assumed that Croatia's leading party had opted for a violent reintegration of the Knin controlled territories and that war would break out. In an attempt to deny

such intentions the HDZ established a "Committee for the Peaceful Integration of the Occupied Territories." Otvorene Oci was interested to find out about the aims of this committee and spoke to three of its representatives. The president of the committee, Mr Drago Krpina, a well-known HDZ-hawk, Mr Mdirko Tankosic, the vice-president of the committee and Mrs Snjezana Biga-Friganovic, who has a Serbian ethnic background and belongs to the opposition party SDP, were interviewed. The results of these interviews were then published.

Although hardly any concrete steps or measures were on the minds of the committee members, a positive aspect was that all three representatives appeared to be open to discussing peaceful reintegration with any NGO working towards the same goal. One outcome of this was that Croatia's Anti-War Campaign invited a representative to its assembly which dealt with these issues. Furthermore, the vice- president of the committee was interested to know what Otvorene Oci could do. In the aftermath, representatives of the committee even encouraged Otvorene Oci to set up an office in the region.

Sector East. Currently, Otvorene Oci and local NGOs are engaged in an initiative concerning the normalization of relations between the Serb population of sector East and the displaced persons from the area. This action increased the possibility of a peaceful solution of the conflict between the Croatian government and the authorities of sector East. To achieve this objective, Otvorene Oci, BPT Yugoslavia and BPT-International undertook a mission to the sector in November 1995.

Office Work
Source of Information. Otvorene Oci sees itself as an independent source of information and therefore the writing of reports remains an important activity. In December 1994 the first Otvorene Oci field report was written and updates were compiled in May and November 1995. Accounts were published of the exploratory tours to Slavonia and Dubrovnik and contributions were made to the Balkan Peace Team report on the exploratory mission to Krajina. Reports were compiled on the inquiries into the intentions of the Peaceful Reintegration Committee, on the killings in Krajina, the situation in the Kupljensko refugee camp in Vojnic, the evictions and the role of the military in Split, a conscientious objector's case in Karlovac, the fate of Krajina POWs from the UN compound in Knin, the explosion in an attorney's office in Dubrovnik and the burning of copies of *Feral Tribune* in Split. A comprehensive report on the events in Western Slavonia was also completed.

Being an independent source of information has meant the sharing of this information with journalists or members of international peace and human rights organizations interested in the current developments in Croatia or in the Croatian NGO world. *BBC* and *Radio Dalmacija* have broadcasted interviews with Otvorene Oci members, *Novi List* and *Stina* interviewed its members, a US journalist made a video interview with Otvorene Oci Zagreb, and a Dutch TV station has filmed a documentary on the work of the Split office.

Otvorene Oci Summit. A relatively new activity is the periodical Otvorene Oci summit. Every two to three months both offices get together in a third place to evaluate the past months work, update the strategy for the next period, and assess the personal performance of each team member. The summit also prepares for a coordinating committee (CC) meeting or general assembly (GA), a report from a CC/GA, and discusses the more philosophical aspects of Otvorene Oci's work.

Miscellaneous. Through 1994/1995 the office work has consisted of designing and printing new business cards and ID's, designing a new Otvorene Oci letterhead and writing a new information sheet. Otvorene Oci has reorganized its database (containing every organization that it has contact with) and its filing systems; and compiled a "new volunteer packet" containing practical information about life and work in the field that introduces new volunteers to Otvorene Oci. A document on burn-out and Otvorene Oci field reports have also been prepared. And finally, new evaluation form concerning the volunteers' performance has been compiled.

Workshops, Trainings, Lectures and Conferences

The Split office ran a workshop on "Communication in Decision-making" for local NGOs. The Zagreb office gave a lecture at an Austrian Peace Services training course for volunteers preparing to work in former Yugoslavia. A lecture on civil intervention in a war-zone was given at a conference in Italy and a workshop in nonviolent communication for the Croatian Peace Research Association in Zagreb. Two workshops were held in Tuzla for Oxfam staff to train them in skills centering around the concept of the "rights of the child." The workshop focused on children's identities and breaking down barriers between local and refugee children, abled and disabled children and children of different ethnicities. A workshop in nonviolent conflict resolution was organized in Split for varied local NGOs. The Split office is currently preparing a workshop in organization, management and information for local NGOs.

As a way of keeping itself informed about current events and keeping up, or establishing contacts, with other local and international NGOs, Otvorene Oci had attended conferences, round tables and press conferences. Otvorene Oci was present at the "School for Democracy" held in Crikvenica and at the Osijek "Days of Peace Culture." It attended a conference of the "Centers for Pluralism" in Bratislava which examined the possibilities of promoting democracy in post-communist Eastern Europe, it was represented at a human rights NGO conference in Ljubljana, at the conference of the American Development Foundation in Zagreb where it introduce itself to the Croatian NGO world, at the Croatian Helsinki Committee's round table on problems within Croatia's judicial system, and at a conference in Mohács on possible alternatives for a nonviolent resolution of the conflict in sector East. Otvorene Oci also attended the annual assemblies of Croatia's Anti-War Campaign, the Dalmatian Committee of Solidarity and Peace Brigades International. Press conferences by Mazowiecki and Serb leader Pupovac about the human rights situation in Western Slavonia were attended, as well as press conferences by Croatian army and government representatives concerning "Operation Storm." Otvorene Oci participated in a working meeting with Croatian and Serbian NGOs in Mohács about the Oxfam project in the former Krajina.

Future Intentions
Otvorene Oci's activities during the 1994/1995 period have included the maintenance of regular contacts with all the relevant NGOs, the discussing and following up on problems that these NGOs are confronted with, and the providing of local and international media and organizations with information concerning the situation in Croatia. These activities will remain integral to the work of Otvorene Oci.

But the work of Otvorene Oci also changes in keeping with the changing situation in Croatia. For instance, the situation and activities of local NGOs "dictate" Otvorene Oci's participation in the establishment and maintenance of the centers currently being founded in the former UNPA sectors South (Knin) and North (Vrhovina, Vojnic). The conflict concerning sector East leads to yet another exploratory mission.

The improvement of the work itself has its own dynamics, stimulating an engagement in new activities. Regular meetings with lawyers to keep up with developments within the judicial system are foreseen as well as an increase in workshops in nonviolent communication and nonviolent conflict resolution and more activities in towns on the Dalmatian Coast (for example Zadar, Sibenik and Dubrovnik). Activities are also influenced by individual volunteers' interests. In the near future,

Otvorene Oci aims to spend more time on women's rights and on issues concerning refugees and displaced persons.

In the long run, the future of Otvorene Oci depends on the length of time domestic NGOs think they need its support. For the time being Otvorene Oci knows that this support is still necessary and appreciated, but the sooner the need for its presence disappears, the better.

11

CRY FOR JUSTICE IN HAITI, FALL 1993

Ed Kinane

PART I: BACKGROUND TO ACCOMPANIMENT

My partner, Ann Tiffany, and I first learned about Cry for Justice in September 1993 through Peace Brigades International. Both Ann and I were in Haiti with CFJ from mid-October, 1993, until the project came to its scheduled close in mid-December, 1993. We were not involved in CFJ's gestation or administration. Except that we were in the field longer than most CFJ volunteers, we did not have any privileged perspective. These notes then aren't "official."

Besides being in Port-au-Prince, the capital, we were both on CFJ teams in two of CFJ's five hinterland sites. First we worked for two separate weeks in a hamlet near Hinche on the Central Plateau. I then worked for three continuous weeks in a Catholic parish in Jérémie in the far southwest and Ann worked in Verette, northwest of the capital. Two other CFJ sites (which neither of us visited) were Cap Haitien on the north coast and Bassin Bleu in the northwest.

Our interest in CFJ derived from our close link to Peace Brigades International, a member of the CFJ coalition. Ann had been very active in our local Sanctuary Movement and we both were active in Central American solidarity work. I had served six month tours on PBI accompaniment teams in Guatemala, El Salvador and Sri Lanka.

For these PBI tours, besides room and board, there was a $50 a month stipend. But for CFJ volunteers there would be no stipend or salary. Each volunteer paid $1,200 toward CFJ expenses, regardless of how long he or she would be with the project. Our personal expense also included transport between home and Washington, DC, our embarkation point for Haiti.

As one who deliberately lives below taxable income, I had to rely on the generosity of friends and relatives to cover my share. The fundraising letter I circulated was a success: friends unable to go to Haiti themselves felt I was going on their behalf.

At the outset, our commitment was to PBI and to international accompaniment as much as to solidarity with the Haitian people. Even so, it was their harrowing plight—and our knowledge that the US was largely responsible for it—that made us respond immediately. We had both been inspired by Fr Jean-Bertrand Aristide's book, *In the Parish of the Poor*. Like many other CFJ volunteers, upon returning home we plunged into Haiti solidarity work.

Although Ann and I knew little about Haiti before Cry for Justice, we began doing our homework. The key thing we learned was that Haiti has been profoundly shaped by its huge neighbor to the north.

"Pearl of the Antilles"
Haiti is in the Caribbean about 700 miles southeast of Miami, Florida. Most of Haiti's seven million people are peasants of African descent. Five million of those live on incomes of less than $1 per day.

Most Haitians have never slept in a bed. Most are illiterate; few rural children go to school. Three quarters of pre-school children are malnourished. The infant mortality rate is nine times that of the US and neighboring Cuba. Haiti is the most desolate country in the Western Hemisphere.

Haiti's woes began in 1492, when Columbus first cast covetous eyes on the island. Since that year, Haiti has been in thrall to economic forces beyond her borders and beyond her control. Since that year, Haiti has played a single invariable role within the world economy: providing slave or cheap labor for the profit of others. Within decades of 1492, thanks to Spanish slavery and disease, the indigenous Taino people were wiped out. For the next three centuries Haiti, which is the size of the state of Maryland, had a lucrative sugar export economy. Known as "the Pearl of the Antilles," it was the richest colony in the New World.

Haiti, then known as St Domingue, was run first by the Spanish and then by the French, and worked by African slaves. Worked to death within a few years, the slaves had to be constantly replaced by imports from West Africa. In 1804, after protracted guerrilla struggle, the Africans defeated Napoleon's army and expelled the tiny strata of plantation owners and managers.

Haiti's was the first successful slave revolt in history and Haiti became the second republic in the New World, after the US, to achieve "independence." Haiti was the first New World republic in which at independence everyone, at least nominally, became a citizen. In actual fact however, at independence many Haitians graduated from slavery ...into serfdom under mulatto masters.

The 1804 revolution did not amuse the US or those European colonizers in the New World who thrived on slave economies. France delayed recognizing Haiti diplomatically until 1838 and only after extorting a crippling indemnity for French properties seized by Haitians during the revolution.

Although the US traded with Haiti, it kept Haiti isolated politically. The US did not recognize Haiti diplomatically until 1862 during its Civil War. Thereafter US gunboats continually enforced unfavorable trade terms. In 1915, under President Wilson, the US Marines invaded Haiti and several other Caribbean countries. The Marines harshly suppressed guerrilla resistance, occupying Haiti until 1934. They enforced racial segregation and built roads with coerced labor. They disarmed the people...and armed, trained and centralized the military.

During the occupation the US rewrote Haiti's constitution to allow foreign investment. For most of the time since the invasion, the Haitian military—under one dictator or another—has made sure the work force remained docile and unorganized.

This, of course, has been a boon for investors, whether domestic or North American. Another boon has been Haiti's tax system: most government revenue has come from taxing peasant produce. The land- and business-owning class, both domestic and foreign, has not been subject to income or property tax.

For generations, the comprador Haitian government has been almost totally corrupt. With the exception of the recent Aristide administration, the government has always lacked the will to invest in infrastructure. Rural areas, the source of almost all wealth and taxes, were particularly neglected. In the mountainous hinterland there are few paved roads. Inner-city phone service is sporadic at best. Foreign NGOs and missionaries provide the few social services.

In February 1991, elected by 67% of the vote, Jean-Bertrand Aristide became president of Haiti. Aristide, then a Catholic priest, was the first president in Haiti's turbulent history to be elected democratically.

Prior to his presidency, Fr Aristide, an outspoken and eloquent practitioner of liberation theology, had survived several assassination attempts. As president, Aristide threatened the military, Haiti's ruling elite, and certain foreign interests. In 1991 USAID, the US aid agency, spent millions countering Aristide's attempt to raise Haiti's abysmally low minimum wage.

US firms were, and are, Haiti's main investors. If tiny, weak Haiti succeeded in raising its minimum wage, labor elsewhere in Latin America—not to mention the US itself—might follow suit. Multinational profits would suffer. On 30 September 1991, US-trained officers deposed Aristide. Aristide went into exile. Until these Haitian officers were themselves forced into exile three years later, human rights in Haiti were rendered extinct; all dissent was snuffed out or forced underground.

Under General Raoul Cédras, several thousand Aristide supporters were murdered. Multitudes were tortured and maimed; punitive rape became wholesale and systematic. Reportedly, sons were forced at gunpoint to rape mothers, and fathers were forced to rape daughters. Tens of thousands of "boat people" fled overseas or next door to the Dominican Republic. Meanwhile within Haiti itself, hundreds of thousands went into hiding.

Cry for Justice
It was in this context that, in mid-1993, Pax Christi/USA conceived Cry for Justice (CFJ). It then had appeared that Aristide, as per the July Governors Island accords brokered by the US and UN, would be returning to Haiti on 30 October.

Cry for Justice would be a temporary coalition of US peace, faith-based and solidarity groups. It would provide international nonviolent accompaniment during Haiti's transition back to normalcy. CFJ would place small teams of unarmed, camera-toting volunteers in several sites across Haiti to accompany vulnerable individuals and communities. They would go where international presence was scanty and where human rights abuse was severe.

The several weeks preceding and following Aristide's return would be a volatile time. CFJ hoped protective accompaniment would deter violence, hearten those activists still alive within Haiti, help generate US grassroots solidarity and provide internationally credible witness.

Cry for Justice founders were both Haitian and North American. The Haitians included Fr Antoine Adrien, Aristide mentor and Governors Island negotiator; Necker Dessables of the Human Rights Platform; and Claudette Werleigh, Aristide's Prime Minister from October 1995 to February 1996.

US organizations represented on the CFJ steering committee were: Pax Christi/USA, Washington Office on Haiti, Peace Brigades International, Christian Peacemaker Teams, Fellowship of Reconciliation Task Force on Latin America and the Caribbean, Global Exchange, Haiti Communication Project, Sojourners and World Peacemakers, Inc. Other US organizations cosponsored CFJ: American Friends Service Committee, Baptist Peace Fellowship, Clergy and Laity Concerned, Conference of Major Superiors of Men, Fellowship of Reconciliation, Maryknoll Fathers and Brothers, Quixote Center/Haiti Reborn, War Resisters League and Witness for Peace.

For most of the project the CFJ coordinators in Port-au-Prince were Jozet Perard and Nadja Papillon—two dynamic, sophisticated Haitians who had both lived in the US.

Sponsoring organizations used their own mailing lists and newsletters to recruit volunteers and raise funds for the project. Most CFJ volunteers came from the eastern US, especially Washington, DC, a center of US/Haiti solidarity work. One volunteer was English, one Dutch, one Jamaican-American, one Sri Lankan-American and six were Canadian. About 50 volunteers were female and about 25 male; 15 were either Catholic nuns or priests (including, briefly, Bishop Thomas J.Gumbleton of Detroit). Most volunteers were white. A few were in their twenties, but many were over 50. Almost none spoke Creole.

Most went into the countryside. A few, however, did media or other support work in Port-au-Prince. Many of us had worked in Latin America or had taken part in delegations there, but for most, this was our first time in Haiti and the first time doing international accompaniment.

International Nonviolent Accompaniment

International accompaniment means that individual volunteers, protected by their international status, escort or repeatedly visit vulnerable local people in order to deter violence against them. To get at the target, the death squad must go through the volunteer. Given the volunteer's privileged, international status, violence done to either the volunteer or those accompanied would have international repercussions. Usually perpetrators decide that harming such targets is not worth the cost.

Accompaniment entails risk. Accompaniment volunteers enter, unarmed, political minefields fraught with violence. Often they do so with only a partial understanding of the players and particularities of each situation.

It may be costly to kill a foreigner, but there is no guarantee the thugs will act rationally or out of a prudent grasp of geopolitical realities. The foreign volunteer may accidentally (or not so accidentally) get caught in crossfire. After all, it is not necessarily in *everybody's* interest that the foreigners remain unharmed. That in certain contexts (like Haiti) such foreigners rarely get killed or wounded suggests, however, just how controlled and calculated death squad violence may be.

In Haiti, the volunteers' risk seemed slight compared to that of those they accompanied. Nor, except perhaps for the volunteers' cameras, was their property subject to extortion, confiscation or destruction.

In Haiti, CFJ volunteers stayed in the "hotspot" only a few weeks or months and then rotated home. Unlike those they accompany, they do not have to continue living where civil strife may persist for years or decades. Rarely if ever are their loved ones nearby and subject to reprisal. However, as we shall see, accompaniment can endanger locals associated with the volunteers, raising the issue of what happens to vulnerable locals when, for whatever reason, accompaniment can no longer be provided.

Accompaniment requires volunteers to *take a stand*. Such "standing" involves various features:

Understanding (consciousness). Prior to arrival volunteers need to do homework. They must have some grasp of the relevant history, economics, culture, politics, factions, current events and class and ethnic structure. They must be able to situate the country in the world political and economic system.

Upon arrival, volunteers must continually study what Latin Americans call the *coyuntura*, the correlation of domestic and international forces bearing on current events. Without such understanding, volunteers can easily be used or misled. They probably will never know what local people, even those they accompany, *really* think about them and their role. They need to be keenly aware of the limits of their understanding.

Ideally volunteers are fluent in the local language. If not, they must use effective, trustworthy translators. These are not necessarily easy to find.

Standing For (conviction). Cry for Justice and similar organizations are committed to nonviolence. Often they primarily accompany members of the unarmed popular movement. In Haiti, however, CFJ tended to accompany communities rather than specific individuals. The accompaniment was not provided to those who used arms or who worked for those employing arms (governments, militaries), nor was it provided to those seeking police protection or who otherwise use armed security.

Standing Between (interposition). In Haiti and elsewhere, perpetrators are frequently members of the military or paramilitary, both in and out of uniform. Often, like Haiti's FRAPH, they operate as death squads.

FRAPH is the Front for the Advancement and Progress of Haiti. With chapters throughout Haiti, FRAPH did much of the army's dirty work, killing hundreds, if not thousands, of Aristide supporters. According to human rights journalist Allan Nairn, "FRAPH is an arm of the brutal Haitian security system, which the United States has built and supervised and whose leaders it has trained, and often paid."

As unarmed bodyguards, accompaniment volunteers become human shields seeking to foil such death squads. Volunteers literally come between the potential target and would-be perpetrators. Volunteers cultivate vigilance, monitoring doorways and passing motor and pedestrian traffic; they are alert for ploys which might divert their attention from those they are accompanying. When providing accompaniment in public places, often they make sure they are highly visible and try to place themselves where they have a good overall view.

Standing With (solidarity). The very presence of the international volunteers and their organization is a tangible expression of solidarity. Knowing they are not alone helps keep vulnerable activists and populations from losing heart.

Knowing that in some modest way "the eyes of the world are upon them," local activists are emboldened to continue their liberation struggle. Accompaniment, then, does more than reduce overt violence and save lives. By helping to open space for liberatory action, it becomes a player in the historical process. The liberatory action accompaniment facilitates counters the slow, silent, systemic violence afflicting society. It is this systemic violence—in the form of hunger, discrimination, enforced illiteracy, maldistribution of resources and so on—that takes an even greater toll than overt violence. Systemic violence also includes racism, sexism and classism.

The two types of violence are intimately related. Overt violence is deliberately used to prop up systemic violence. Systemic violence, in turn, spawns the broken people who frequently do the dirty work for those directing, and profiting from, the overt violence. FRAPH rank and file, for example, consisted mostly of such people.

Standing By I (nonintervention). Nonintervention need not contradict solidarity, at least as solidarity is described above. In classic accompaniment, volunteers often avoid advising, doing tasks for, or materially aiding the local activists or local communities. Accompaniment enables or facilitates rather than intervenes. It avoids even the appearance of paternalism. It is careful not to spawn dependence.

The international community may tolerate a hostile government deporting volunteers if they are perceived as meddling in internal politics. Often it is only fear of international censure that keeps the government from deporting accompaniment volunteers.

Standing By II (nonpartisanship). Some models of accompaniment are explicitly nonpartisan (whatever that may mean. Nonpartisanship, like "objectivity," is an ideal hard to define). Other models are partisan. The Cry for Justice coalition fielded volunteers from organizations operating with one or the other model. In Jérémie (see below) this led to tension within our team.

By being nonpartisan, volunteers may better consider all sides of issues: seldom are these simply "black and white." Nonpartisan volunteers may better be able to relate respectfully to all parties involved. They can better see "the God within" even those with dubious histories or who seem immediately threatening. By remaining nonpartisan, volunteers may be better able to provide accompaniment to various ethnic communities or to rival factions within the popular movement.

Under the Cédras regime, public political activity would have been suicidal. Thus, CFJ volunteers seldom had occasion to accompany rallies, marches or demonstrations. Elsewhere however, accompaniment of such events is frequent. It may be prudent for volunteers to be present just beyond the periphery of the crowd and avoid any appearance of participation; otherwise their nonpartisanship might be compromised. The regime might use their apparent participation as a pretext for expulsion.

Whether or not explicitly nonpartisan, organizations like Cry for Justice do see themselves as partisans of such values as peace, justice, democracy, and human rights.

Standing By III (witness). Accompaniment entails being an eyewitness. Both nonintervention and nonpartisanship help volunteers maintain credibility for this essential role. Using the media and other public forums (e.g. speaking tours back home), volunteers play a vital role in telling the world what they have seen and heard. Such telling can get media play and frequently provides an alternative to the mainstream media's version.

Standing Out (privilege). Cry for Justice, like PBI and other accompaniment groups, ran on WSP—white skin privilege. We volunteers were super-citizens. The vast majority of Haitian citizens were and are sub-citizens.

Given the global distribution of power and given where civil strife tends to occur, accompaniment usually takes place among people of color. Most volunteers in Haiti visibly stood out thanks to our light skin. This salience protects volunteers and those they accompany. Without white skin privilege, accompaniment as we know it would surely be much less effective.

Besides skin color, volunteers' nationality may help shield them from political violence. Most volunteers doing accompaniment, whether or not with Cry for Justice, come from so-called first world nations. These nations often have leverage over the local regime. Sometimes those same nations aid the local regime as it targets people the volunteers are accompanying.

First world governments (the US, for example) may prefer that the volunteers not be present. They may not want their citizens to see firsthand their foreign policy at work. Nor is it in these governments' interest to have their citizens harmed. Attacks on such citizens cause diplomatic headaches and make it harder domestically to justify supporting the client state. These first world governments may make this clear to their client, thereby making accompaniment more effective.

Some argue that international accompaniment, by relying on white skin and first world privilege, perpetuates racism or imperialism. Given that a hallmark of nonviolence is that means must be consistent with ends, this is a vexing issue. Others counter that accompaniment justifiably employs "moral jujitsu": it turns evil against itself. Rightly or wrongly, using white skin or first world privilege to facilitate accompaniment is often an effective way to exploit an ugly reality.

The volunteers' first world origin is not always an advantage. Members of popular movements have reason to be wary of US and other first world citizens, even those offering accompaniment. Haitians, for example, widely believed the CIA/US Embassy/Bush Administration was responsible for Aristide's overthrow. Haitians also believed that the CIA controlled FRAPH, a fact later documented by Allan Nairn.

While local activists may seek accompaniment and believe the sponsoring organization is acting in good faith, they might doubt its ability to screen volunteers. And what protection is there against volunteers' naivete or indiscretion? For those in hiding, a volunteer's indiscretion could be fatal.

Standing Firm (steadfastness). Accompaniment can involve escorting someone or some group on a single occasion. But often it involves a more or less ongoing, sometimes round-the-clock, presence for a prolonged period. Those being accompanied may need to be assured that it will persist as long as the danger looms. Otherwise accompaniment, by raising their profile, may also raise their risk.

It can be helpful then, if the accompanying project can commit to being present as long as necessary. Once it became clear that Aristide was not returning on 30 October 1993, CFJ knew it lacked the funding to continue in Haiti until the end of the crisis. We had to share this with

216 *Nonviolent Intervention*

Haitians associating with us lest they be jeopardized by becoming too identified with us.

Standing Down (withdrawing). As the flipside of steadfastness, a project needs to know when to pack up and go home. It needs to know how to discern when the crisis has sufficiently subsided so that its service may cease. It needs to build an "off button" into its process.

Like any organization, these projects may fall prey to inertia, vested interest and other self-perpetuating dynamics. Also, some in the project may come to over-identify with a particular site, faction, ethnic group or liberation struggle. Closing a project may require immense maturity. The withdrawal needs to be carefully thought-out and paced so as to leave local associates as safe and independent as possible.

PART II: ACCOMPANIMENT IN HAITI

Ann and I joined CFJ in mid-October 1993, two weeks before Aristide was scheduled to return to Haiti. Haiti was extremely tense. Just before Ann and I left home, our local daily carried the page one headline, "HAITI COLLAPSES."

During his exile in the US, Aristide's communications were covertly monitored by the National Security Agency. During October the CIA intensified its disinformation campaign against him. Supported clandestinely by the CIA, the Cédras regime was then reneging on the Governors Island accords and refusing to step down by its October deadline. Nonetheless the US media and the US Embassy in Port-au-Prince continued to treat Cédras with deference.

On 11 October, a few dozen FRAPH thugs staged a raucous demonstration on the dock at Port-au-Prince. Out in the harbor was the *USS Harlan County*, carrying 200 Canadian and US military instructors meant to help pave the way for Aristide's return. Instead of delivering these lightly armed "peacekeepers," the *Harlan County*, apparently intimidated, steamed out of the harbor never to return.

Many foreigners, fearing that the regime's terrorism might now target them, immediately fled Haiti. Some had been providing an official international presence to forestall endemic "Haitian on Haitian" violence. These included Canadian Mounties and MICIVIH (the unarmed UN and OAS Civilian Mission monitoring group). Before evacuating, MICIVIH had been gathering affidavits on human rights abuse throughout Haiti.

The Haitians who worked as cooks, clerks, drivers or translators for the decamping foreigners became highly vulnerable. Most Haitians felt the international "community" had abandoned them. They felt extremely isolated. With the US caving in, it became clear Aristide would continue in exile well beyond the Governors Island timetable.

With the flight of the *Harlan County* it became clear that Cry for Justice would proceed under a more emboldened and belligerent tyranny. That made our accompaniment very timely, as well as more dangerous and possibly less effective. Cry for Justice would be one of just a few international human rights organizations left in Haiti at this time of mounting terror.

Training and Role-Plays
For its several month duration, CFJ was structured in successive two-week cycles. CFJ volunteers could sign up as short-termers (in Haiti for a single cycle) or as long-termers (two or more cycles). Short-termers got two day's training; some long-termers got four day's training. Training took place stateside, immediately prior to the volunteers' departure for Haiti.

The volunteers responding to this crisis generally were mature, disciplined and motivated. Most had experience with Third World situations and were already grounded in nonviolent values. The training would be supplemented by orientation when we first arrived in Haiti.

Trainings were held at Queen of Peace Catholic Church in Arlington, VA. Ours was conducted by PBI/USA trainer, Liam Mahony. Working with him were Sr Mary Healy RSM and Cinny Poppin, of the Washington Office on Haiti. Training included presentations on Haiti's history and current situation by prominent Haitians in exile. Returned short-termers also gave briefings. But drawing on the PBI model, training was mostly experiential. It included exercises for team building and for exploring the nature of nonviolence.

Most importantly, training involved role-plays. These are essential preparation for work in areas of civil strife. Based on recent incidents, the role-plays simulated tense or dangerous situations we might meet in Haiti. In one role-play, our luggage was searched by hostile customs agents. In another, soldiers at a roadblock detained our Haitian driver. In a third, Willie Romelus, Haiti's only progressive Catholic bishop, and his entourage were assaulted by murderous thugs on the street in Port-au-Prince.

Role-plays pose moral and tactical dilemmas. They show potential volunteers how we ourselves and our team mates might act under stress. They help trainers assess the suitability of volunteers for the project. Role-plays can generate intense emotions and can seem very real. They help bring home just how dangerous things might get, and bring fears to the fore to be acknowledged and dealt with. This needs to happen *before* going into the field. By the end of our training, one trainee, a new father, decided not to go to Haiti.

By playing various roles, volunteers get to put themselves in the place of adversaries, thereby seeing how things might feel from a drastically different perspective. Because its mandate requires non-partisanship, Peace Brigades volunteers in particular need such empathy.

Not all CFJ organizations shared PBI's commitment to nonpartisanship, but all CFJ volunteers had to commit to nonviolence. This meant all volunteers had to strive to respect all parties; the empathy generated in role-plays helps achieve this elusive ideal.

Each member organization screened its own applicants for the training. But CFJ made no commitment to accept applicants until after their interview with one of the trainers, at the close of training.

Arriving

Before leaving the States, our group set up a buddy system to get us through the rigors of Haitian customs. Identifying ourselves, implausibly, only as tourists, we all got through airport customs with unexpected ease, with few questions asked.

Except to our hosts and to certain others, we would not be identifying ourselves as "Cry for Justice" while in Haiti. This was a matter of security for ourselves, for those housing us, and for the Haitian drivers and translators accompanying us. (We also needed certain kinds of accompaniment. It is not a one-way street.)

From the airport two vans took us, circuitously, to our lodgings. First thing, lest we think we were on a lark, we were taken on a sobering drive through Cité Soleil—"the worst slum in the western hemisphere." That exposure helped center us and frame everything else we would see while in Haiti.

By contrast, our lodging was a pleasant pension, the Hotel Ifé, in Pétionville. Pétionville is the notoriously affluent suburb on the slopes high above Cité Soleil. The Ifé, modest by North American standards, was the CFJ headquarters for the duration of the project. Volunteers stayed there whenever we were in the capital. As far as I know, and for reasons I do not understand, the owners of the Ifé weren't harassed for hosting us.

Our group of 18 or 20 was not the first CFJ group in Haiti. Some volunteers had already arrived in September and earlier in October. Our group's work began with orientation and with exposure to Cité Soleil,

Pétionville and Port-au-Prince. Then, typically, we would divide up to go out to our designated site where we would stay for eight or nine days before returning to the capital for debriefing and helping to orient the next cycle's new volunteers.

Orientation
Our orientation, spread over two or three days, began immediately. It was conducted by Carla Bluntschli, a North American Mennonite and longtime Haiti resident. Carla was assisted by Ari Nicolas, a young Haitian who had previously been a political prisoner in Cap Haitien. Carla and Ari helped found Cry for Justice, and coordinated the project in its first formative weeks. They did much of the scouting for sites and local hosts that volunteers would be sent to.

Orientation included carefully arranged, secret interviews with members of the popular movement. These included Fr Jean Juste, formerly an activist among Haitian exiles in the US, and Evans Paul, then mayor of Port-au-Prince (both were in hiding at the time).

Orientation included lots of drumming and dancing—after all, we were in Haiti! Somewhere I had read that "Haitians don't smile, they laugh; Haitians don't walk, they dance." Carla and Ari prepared us for the nudity that was common in the rural areas, and modelled the touching—between both genders and within the same gender—which is much more common among Haitians than among North Americans. In Haiti, as in Africa, same-sex friends often hold hands. Haiti soon came to remind me very much of Kenya where I used to teach.

Carla and Ari taught us some basic Creole, the mix of mostly French vocabulary and mostly West African grammar which every Haitian understands. Only about 10% also speak French, the language of schooling and government and of the social elite. Each of our teams would be equipped with a driver and translator. These were mostly young men who might or might not speak good English. Fortunately, however, some CFJ volunteers knew French. This came in handy in Hinche where communication got quite cumbersome: our translator would translate from Creole into French and then pause as one of our team members translated the French for the rest of us.

Security...and Truth
Our first night at the Ifé we could hear machine gun fire out on the street. At first we walked in the neighborhood in foursomes; with time we would go out in pairs, or even on our own. It was comforting that in Haiti since the 1804 Revolution, the blood of white foreigners had seldom been shed. That was little comfort, of course, for those few volunteers who

were not white. The two people of color in our group chose not to risk going into the countryside.

In fall 1993, Haiti was a hot topic in the States. Upon returning home then CFJ volunteers had a great opportunity to publicize what we saw and experienced. But we had to be very careful not to do anything publicly that might jeopardize the vulnerable. Often we could not identify specific individuals or communities, even for publication abroad. To protect our drivers and translators we were not given their last names.

Even now as I write this, I am still careful about mentioning names. In Haiti things could revert quickly. Most FRAPH members and former military who went underground when Aristide returned in October 1994 (as a result of the US invasion) have yet to be detained and disarmed. They remain a dispersed Contra-like army ready to be mobilized if international attention wanes...or if US policy slides back into its historic groove. Fortunately, however, such mobilizing will be harder since Aristide disbanded the military in 1995.

Security issues also applied to travel. On the road there were military checkpoints, especially upon driving in or out of any town. At these our driver did all the talking. We did not even indicate, if such were the case, that we knew any French. If the soldiers were to discover our mission they might detain us. Typically they were told we were going to visit the Bishop, or the foreign priests, or certain development projects—whichever seemed right at the time. We were going to make such visits, but that was only part of the truth.

In situations like these, telling the whole truth could neutralize our effectiveness or even jeopardize lives. For those committed to a doctrine of nonviolence requiring full honesty and transparency, such fudging presents an ethical dilemma. Individuals and groups must be exposed to such scenarios in training before encountering them in the field.

I believe nonviolence proscribes fibbing or lying. These after all, following Gandhi, are forms of violence. I wince when I hear people, especially those representing organizations committed to nonviolence, playing fast and loose with the truth. It would be good if nonviolence training explored the dishonesty/violence equation. Nonetheless, to protect life I would judiciously fib or lie to illegitimate or malevolent authority. Fortunately, except at roadblocks or filling out visa forms asking for the purpose of my visit, dissimulation has never been necessary. When curious locals ask why I am in their country, I say I am visiting friends and want to see how things are here.

While US citizens do not need visas to enter Haiti, at roadblocks we were asked to produce passports. Sometimes we would be questioned and our luggage searched. We could carry no literature in which certain words (especially "Aristide") appeared. Even in foreign language periodicals such words might catch the eye of a barely literate, but intensely suspicious soldier. At one roadblock on the way to Hinche a soldier going through our luggage scrutinized my box of stationery. He methodically opened each empty envelope. Such was the goldfish bowl we were now immersed in.

On October 15 the Clinton administration, ostensibly to dislodge the coup regime, resumed its halfhearted embargo against Haiti. Petrol continued to flow across the porous Dominican Republic boarder but now the Haitian military controlled the entire supply and reaped vast black market profit. To speed delivery, it paved the road from the Dominican border to Port-au-Prince.

Throughout CFJ's time in Haiti our tiny fleet of rented four-wheel drive vehicles depended on black market petrol. Petrol was scarce and extremely expensive, further, the supply was erratic and sometimes hard to find. When we left for our weeks in the countryside we had to be sure petrol tanks were full enough to get us back. The military's monopoly wrought havoc both on the country and on CFJ's modest budget.

Because of the petrol shortage and because travel could be so time consuming, some long-term volunteers stayed at their sites and did not return to the capital every two weeks. The round trip to Jérémie, for example took us over 24 hours.

PART III: JOURNAL EXCERPTS

Hinche
October 27. Ann and I are in a hamlet a few kilometers beyond Hinche. Hinche is about 60 air miles from the capital but due to two intervening mountain ranges and the crude unpaved road, getting here took six hours. We came with our team: our driver, Jimmy our translator, and Hazel Tulecke and Bill Houston from Yellow Springs, Ohio.

Around Hinche, government terrorism is intense. The Central Plateau was the seat of the MPP, the Peasant Movement of Papaye, a national grassroots organization, now underground. The coup regime had persecuted it ruthlessly. We had been forewarned not to mention the MPP to anyone, even our hosts.

We arrived at our lodging, a Roman Catholic religious community, in the late afternoon. Except in the capital, volunteers stay almost exclusively with Catholic religious communities. There's no commercial lodging available in the countryside. If we stayed with private individuals, they would later be vulnerable to reprisal.

We don't meet our host; he's in hiding. He had given CFJ a note of introduction for us to take to his colleagues, but, for security reasons, it was brief and cryptic.

He was the only one who knew who we were or that we were coming. Our problem in explaining ourselves isn't simplified by the fact that Jimmy's English turns out to be much more limited than it first seemed. No one here has heard of Cry for Justice. And there's no way to check us out. The only contact with the capital is via the two-way radio of a Canadian nun living miles away.

Our hosts are concerned that our presence may lead to trouble with the local *macoutes* [political thugs]. Fortunately, in this community hospitality is ingrained. But there's a hesitancy, a reticence, about our welcome. That may persist until our presence can be put to a test. That test would be whether our hosts are attacked after we've left.

October 29. In these few days before 30 October, the date of Aristide's scheduled return, the terror on the Central Plateau is palpable. The people aren't fearful of Aristide, the most popular political figure in Haiti's history. They fear what FRAPH and the *macoutes* and the military might do to Aristide and to his supporters. Or to anyone. To paralyze the population at large, terrorism is frequently arbitrary and indiscriminate.

As we walk through the area the local people keep their eyes downcast. Our hosts advise us not to try to talk to local people for fear it will endanger them. Our hosts don't hold talks with us in the evening because there might be eavesdroppers right outside the house undetected in the dark. Instead we meet during the day in a nearby grove which no one could approach without being seen.

Three Weeks in Jérémie
November 26. Arrived in Jérémie yesterday after a 13-hour, nearly nonstop drive from Port-au-Prince. Lots of rain on treacherous mountain "roads." Jérémie is Cédras' hometown. It's been the scene of some of the most severe *macoute* violence.

We're staying in the rectory of St Helene parish as guests of Fr Joaquim Samedi. Fr Samedi is an absentee host. For his own safety he has taken shelter in Bishop Romelus' residence across town. Many in St Helene are in various degrees of hiding. Some appear in the neighborhood by day, but avoid home after dark. Some spend their nights on the roof of the rectory.

The rectory, a virtual fortress, is a two-story cement building on a summit overlooking Jérémie and the coast. For security, CFJ pays two gatekeepers to keep a 24-hour watch on the compound and make sure the iron gate stays locked. The rectory is in the midst of a hilly and densely populated slum. St Helene is the poorest section of Jérémie.

The fact that we're lodged here, obviously with Fr Samedi's endorsement, gives us immediate credibility in the parish. Of course, such lodging also automatically dispels any pretense to non-partisanship.

Besides Luckner, our Haitian driver, our team includes Ned Smith and Andy Petonak, both of Pax Christi in Pennsylvania, Sister Elizabeth Walters, IHM of Michigan, and Anita von Wellsheim, a 74-year old Sister of the Sacred Heart. CFJ members already here are Stacy Taeuber and Joel Classen, and our Haitian translator, Jean Role. Like Sister Anita, Stacy is affiliated with Washington, DC, Pax Christi. Joel, a young tree planter from Kitchener, Ontario, is the CFJ "long-term" team member here. He's affiliated with Christian Peacemakers, part of the CFJ coalition. He's the only *blan* (foreigner) among us who speaks Creole.

Over Cry for Justice's time in Jérémie, team size has varied from two to six members. Some volunteers have stayed as few as eight or nine days and were only replaced by more short-termers about a week later. Other volunteers were able to stay several weeks. Joel is the only volunteer who will be with the team for the project's entirety.

Short terms were intentional. This delegation-like approach exposes more *blans* to the situation in St Helene and to Haitian realities in general. Clearly a plus. But it leads to more coming and going between Jérémie and the capital at a time when, because of the economic blockade, petrol is scarce. Short terms mean that much time, mostly Joel's time, is spent orienting new volunteers and introducing them to the community. The transience fosters the tendency of locals to relate primarily to Joel, the least transient member of the team.

After breakfast Anita, Liz and I join Joel on his rounds. Twice a day he walks the neighborhood greeting dozens, being greeted by scores and chatting with many. Joel makes a point of dropping by the houses of those who may be under threat. The aim is to advertise that there's international interest in the people of St Helene generally and in certain individuals and households specifically. To maximize exposure the route gets varied with each walk.

Joel points out the culvert, just below the rectory, where the amputated corpse of an old woman was recently found. She and her husband had disappeared a couple days earlier. People say "Pastor" Bonhomme, the local FRAPH leader, wanted their little plot of land adjoining his compound and they had refused to negotiate.

FRAPH Strikes
November 28. Last night just after dark, as we were sitting down to supper, someone shouted for us. A man had just then been abducted right outside the rectory. Joel, who was outside having a cigarette, challenged the several abductors. They claimed they were only going to a meeting. Joel remembers saying, "It looks like there's someone who doesn't want to go with you." The thugs then brandished pistols and fled down the hill on foot with their hostage, a young man named Abner Joseph.

The abductors apparently grabbed Abner when he didn't heed their order to move off the church steps where he was hanging out. Abner is hearing- and sight-impaired and lives just a few feet from those steps. His mother, Anista Joseph, a seamstress, followed the abductors as they took him to the FRAPH office in downtown Jérémie about a mile away. Later she told us that en route the abductors beat her to the ground three times. She believes that if she had not followed them, they would have taken Joseph elsewhere and killed him.

While Abner was being taken we joined Joel in the street and hastened on foot to the *cazerne* [military base] across town to demand intervention. At the *cazerne* an officer said he couldn't intervene until we provided him with the victim's name (which we then didn't have). He asked why we should be concerned with a mere Haitian.

One of us then went off to get the name and the rest went immediately to FRAPH's local headquarters, on the main street a couple hundred yards from the *cazerne*. Formerly a health clinic, their office had been given to FRAPH by the military. Upon our arrival there, ten FRAPH members, some armed, blocked the driveway entrance to their compound.

As we discussed what next to do, scores of townspeople—barely visible in the moonlight—gathered nearby in silence to watch the drama. Soon, a Haitian man approached and, in good English, asked if there was anything he could do. The man identified himself as Rev. Jean Wilner Guerrier, "a Delegate of the Prime Minister" (i.e. former de facto Prime Minister Bazin, supported by the US Embassy). The *delege* told us he would go into FRAPH headquarters to seek Abner's release.

Joel and I decided to try to join the *delege*. I asked Sister Anita to join us as I figured she would be a calming presence in such a tense situation. As we eased into the compound FRAPH guys kept screaming at us. Pastor Bonhomme, the most aggressive, menaced us with his long knife. The *delege* seemed fearless; his firm position that, "We can't let the foreigners see us acting this way," prevailed. He entered the office while we three *blans* had to wait outside, a few feet from the open door.

We sat there 30 or 40 minutes while the rest of the team remained blocked from view in the street. At any given moment there were from ten to 20 FRAPH members, mostly young men, between us and the office doorway. They threatened and red-baited us, and frequently cursed Fr Samedi. One sidled up to us with a pistol protruding from his pocket. Nonetheless we felt secure. We figured, on little evidence, they must know that if a foreigner were mistreated this would be bad PR for FRAPH. Our attitude was reinforced by a certain visitor to the compound. A four-wheel drive vehicle with smoked windows pulled up to the side entrance. We didn't see any occupant and none got out. But some of our "hosts" gathered around the driver's side facing away from us. Joel said the vehicle looked like the local US Embassy rep's vehicle. Soon it drove off.

Then the *delege* came out of the office leading Abner. Abner wouldn't or couldn't speak; he seemed in shock. He had a large lump on his jaw; his left arm was bruised and dangling. Later Abner said that when the *delege* entered the FRAPH office, the thugs had put a noose over a rafter and were preparing to hang him.

Fr Samedi Celebrates Mass
November 28. This morning we accompanied Fr Samedi from the Bishop's residence to St Helene for 6:30 Mass. This was his first time back to St Helene since he was forced to seek refuge at the Bishop's months ago. I found this magazine account of that incident:

> The army often surrounds the Jérémie Cathedral, harassing worshipers as they leave services. On April 26, 1992, the soldiers surrounded the Church of St Helen's, not far from the Bishop's house. They tried to tear gas the congregation and demanded to see one of the priests, Father Joachim Samedi. When the soldiers found out that the parishioners had hidden their pastor, they killed some of them, beat and arrested others. [Jérémie Bishop Willie] Romelus finally arrived at the scene and drove Father Samedi to safety, knowing that if the military had captured him they would have beaten him nearly to death.

For security, three of us (not me) take our pickup to the Bishop's around 5am and drive Fr Samedi back to the rectory under cover of darkness. He remains out of public sight until Mass begins in the rectory compound, within the iron gate. Before we take our posts, Jean Role tells us our alert signal: first, forearms crossed; second, point in the direction of any threat; then, hold up fingers indicating number of thugs approaching. Anita and Liz attend the Mass; Andy and a couple of the local guys watch out from the roof; Ned and Stacy are stationed just outside the compound on the hillside approach; Joel and I are in front of the church watching the street.

Neighboring people begin filtering into the compound some 30 minutes before Mass is to begin. The congregation doesn't know Fr Samedi is here. When he emerges, there is a ripple of amazement and delight. I wish I could be in the compound at that moment! I also wish I could witness Fr Samedi's sermon. Like Aristide when he was a parish priest, Fr Samedi is famous for his fiery outspokenness. During Mass he strongly endorses our presence and asks people not to pester us for money.

After Mass Fr Samedi is swarmed by well-wishers. The older women kiss him and stroke his head. I don't see him until he comes out the gate. Soon Fr Samedi and most of our team and some local guys pile into the back of the pickup for the ride back to the Bishop's. I particularly want us on that trip, fearing that the *macoutes* may lay an ambush. Fr Samedi waves to people as we pass through the center of town. En route, he gets out with three of the local guys, telling us *blans* to wait in the pickup. When he returns moments later he tells us he went to the Commander's residence, but didn't find him in.

Visits
We meet with Bishop Willie Romelus, Fr Samedi's host. He tells us St Helene is fortunate our team is there; otherwise the parish would be under more pressure. He says it would be good to replicate our presence elsewhere. I ask the Bishop if he thinks we should meet with the military. He says it couldn't do any harm and might even do some good. It might soften them up. He tells us not to meet with FRAPH: FRAPH and the military are "like fish in water," i.e. hand in glove. The Bishop doesn't think it's necessary for him to be at any meeting with the Commander, but he'd be willing to be there.

We visit Fr Samedi nearly daily. He also thinks it would be a good idea for us to meet with the Commander, but cautions we must be diplomatic. We ask him about his parish. He says that before 1991, St Helene was a community center where political meetings were held. Before the coup there were 22 catechists; 13 are now in hiding.

We ask Fr Samedi about liberation theology. He says he can't speak like a pope, but only out of his own experience. For him Matthew 25:40 ("..least of my brethren...") sums up the Bible. Further, he says, you could rip up the rest of the Bible if you kept that verse. He says many clergy are into much talk and little action. He draws a balloon to illustrate the point:

Fr Samedi says, in the wake of Abner's abduction, he's afraid for the community. He fears our leaving while the situation is still unresolved. He doesn't see an increased risk for himself, however. He thinks that because of our presence, there will be less brutality. I wish I had thought to ask him if our presence had somehow *led* to Abner's abduction. Was FRAPH trying to show St Helene that foreigners couldn't protect them? If so, this time the scheme backfired. Would there be more such episodes?

Fr Samedi says he welcomes our accompaniment when he comes over to St Helene to say Mass, but not if he goes out on quick errands. One reason, he says, he wouldn't avail himself of accompaniment is that he doesn't want to appear scared. Later I ask Joel why Fr Samedi doesn't return to the rectory now that there's an international presence. Joel says the people of St Helene told Fr Samedi they are safer if he's not there.

W__ lives in the shadow of St Helene and, clandestinely, is one of our main contacts/advisors here. He says our presence reduces FRAPH violence against St Helene. He adds, our presence also means that the young men of St Helene are less likely to initiate any mischief or to respond violently. It seems our role in deterring violence cuts both ways.

In St Helene the streets are steep and muddy, footing is tricky. But we seldom use our pickup. By walking everywhere we maintain a conspicuous presence. As few *blans* are seen on foot in Haiti, we stand out. Our inconvenience is minor compared to that endured by the vast majority of Haitians throughout their lives. Our ambulatory ways keep us more accessible to those we accompany. In a world divided between those who have and those who don't have cars, our walking is itself a form of accompaniment. It also assures that our presence isn't sought for the transport we might provide.

Resisting Charity

Cry for Justice approaches accompaniment differently from PBI teams I've been on. Here we accompany the *community* as opposed to any individual leader or organization. Accompanying a community seems to call forth greater empathy.

Is there an element of triumphalism, of white-knight-in-shining-armor, in our walks and in our very presence in Jérémie? We're often swarmed by kids, of which St Helene has a vast number. Joel is immensely popular. He has the gift of lingering and schmoozing and listening. As we walk together people greet Joel. He stops to talk to many of them. Mostly he's exchanging pleasantries, but also gleaning info about persons, conditions and incidents. I appreciate all the translating he does for my benefit. Many tell tales of woe and seek some kind of aid, usually financial.

It's CFJ policy not to give any thing or any money to individuals. It's a tough but sound policy. People attach themselves to internationals sometimes for what can be gained from them. This distorts the human interaction; it also leads to false feedback about our work. People who want us to stay for their own reasons tell us our presence is needed for political reasons. Not speaking the language and being birds of passage, it's hard for us to sort out the messages. These are tough lessons for volunteers to learn. Joel is clearly struggling with this one. So many needy people seek him out so often.

Today as we walk, Jean Role points out how, by working with us, he's caught in the middle. If there's violence, he's much more likely to be the target than any *blan*. He also catches flack from another direction. Some—including, perhaps one or two of those working at the rectory—see him getting in the way of inflating their charges for various services (like laundry, gatekeeping, etc.)

Madame Enid, our cook, is unhappy with the wage CFJ pays her. This divides the team and reminds me of all the team discussion about Karuna, our housekeeper at the PBI house in Sri Lanka. Both women live in extreme poverty. Both work for whites who pay them well above the local wage, but well below white wage standards. Both women lobby for a better deal, get raises, then lobby for more. One team member is played against another. In both cases the issue takes up an inordinate amount of team time. Madame Enid's wage has even become an issue between Fr Samedi and the CFJ coordinator back in Port-au-Prince.

Dabbling in social work and charity here in Jérémie undoubtedly springs from decent intentions. Yet Fr Samedi wants us to refer people to the parish welfare committee. That committee is in a much better position to assess individual/family needs. Our here-today gone-tomorrow, no-reciprocity-required charity risks circumventing the committee's work. Our charity makes it harder for community and the local grassroots leadership to develop.

Such charity unintentionally resembles the USAID scheme of importing cheap US rice into Haiti in the guise of humanitarian aid. Such "generosity" undercuts the local rice producers. That forces farmers to leave the land and flock to the capital where their wives and daughters join the pool of cheap labor supplying local and international assembly plants. With no more local competition, expensive imported rice, from the US, comes to monopolize the market.

Another issue we deal with here is whether to help local people arrange political asylum. In 1989, in El Salvador leaders of the popular movement asked the PBI team *not* to help people leave the country. Given the repression in countries like El Salvador or Haiti, it may feel good to facilitate someone's getting out. But that can contribute to brain drain and leadership drain at a time when the popular movements in these countries need all the brains and leadership they can muster.

Resisting Solidarity
When we get back from our afternoon walk, W__ and K__ are waiting for us. They're excited about doing a clandestine postering campaign tonight and want us to buy them some of the materials. By North American standards the money involved is minuscule. I respond, however, by saying that PBI, the group I came with, has a strict nonsubsidy/ nonpartisanship policy. W__'s face tightens and he dismisses the request as no big deal. Then he and K__ abruptly leave.

Joel says he feels sick: he has put such care into maintaining these links with the local underground. He declares that as a Christian Peacemaker he would have responded differently. I didn't mean my comment to be definitive, but now there's no chance for further discussion with W__ and K__. For the next few hours Joel and I avoid each other.

The temptation to subsidize is strong. We have so much; they have so little. But I believe, for reasons similar to those that apply to personal charity, accompaniment teams should avoid making such contributions. Haitians, I tell myself, have to find their own solutions. Our role is to help provide the space for that to happen. Our role isn't to make clumsy interventions or foster dependencies, or give advantage to any particular group. This is true no matter how many points we score with our local contacts. Further, in the event of an assassination or other atrocity we may be useful witnesses. To the extent that we become entangled in local politics, to that extent our witness may be discredited.

In a country where political activity is necessarily clandestine, our financial subsidies would have to be clandestine. This undermines the *transparency* that is a hallmark of nonviolence. It is also a good way of being sucked into a trap that could lead to the team's being expelled from the region or country. These arguments convince me. But I recall Fr Samedi telling us that for him solidarity is the true sign of accompaniment. I wonder if I'm being doctrinaire.

December 4. All of the team, except Joel and I, have now recycled back to Port-au-Prince. It's good that they got off before dawn this morning. That way fewer people, both good and bad, will know they've left. Joel and I make a point of lingering in the neighborhood today, and then walking around town. We want to forestall any rumor the *blans* have up and left. This might be a real anxiety given the way the UN/OAS abruptly left Haiti back in October.

We deliberately walk by a downtown shop, a known FRAPH hangout. When we get 30 yards past it, a guy lounging in front of the shop shouts after us (in English), "Fuck you!" We ignore him and keep walking.

December 12. It's been 16 days since we've had any contact with CFJ in Port-au-Prince. We seem to have had more than our share of misunderstandings and lapses in communication with our coordinators there. It didn't help that CFJ switched coordinators midway through the project. We volunteers and the new coordinators had little prior acquaintance and little experience in common. We hadn't even shared the several-day CFJ training back in the States. There's been little chance for trust to develop. Because of Jérémie's isolation, communication is infrequent and dialogue rare.

Cry for Justice terminates in mid-December. A Christian Peacemaker team is supposed to succeed CFJ in Jérémie and arrive here before we leave. But even if it arrived tonight, the new team will have precious little overlap with us before we return to Port-au-Prince. That's *not* a good way to begin their project.

Joel especially, has learned a lot about St Helene in the three months he's been here. There is so much he could share if only there were more time. We realize we should have done a better job of developing our "institutional memory." We could have kept written records on contacts, meetings, incidents and procedures instead of trusting to our oral tradition. Ideally we would have had some standardized formats for ease of recording and reference. Then when new team members (or a whole new team!) arrive, they could use the files as part of their orientation.

There is good reason, however, for not accumulating paperwork. The rectory has no secure place to keep files. In case they got in the wrong hands, any notes would have to have been carefully written so as to in no way expose or endanger those we work with.

December 15. The Christian Peacemaker team (Cole Arendt, Lena Siegers, Kathy Kern, and Miriam Maik) has finally arrived. They're replacing us now that Cry for Justice is wrapping up here and in Haiti generally. To get closure, last night Joel and I evaluated our work here. We drew up a list of the project's strengths and weaknesses.

This morning the new team joined us for a meeting with Fr Samedi. With Joel translating, I reviewed last night's list. Fr Samedi said the negative points weren't so bad. He emphasized that our presence *did* reduce violence in St Helene and probably in Jérémie as a whole. Of course it's hard to assess what political space, if any, has been opened by our accompaniment. Nor is there any way to quantify or demonstrate the violence that's been deterred. But Fr Samedi asserted that *anything* could have happened if we weren't here.

Fr Samedi advises the new team to "begin like a turtle": go slow, learn about the community first before plunging in. This was right after Cole commented that one of Christian Peacemakers' distinguishing characteristics is commitment to nonviolent direct action. For their next meeting, Fr Samedi asked them to reflect on what direct action might be appropriate here.

Jean Role Detained

December 15 cont. Before leaving town I go to the Sisters of Charity hospice to say goodbye to the nuns I've met there. But this last visit is interrupted. Lena and Kathy have come for me. Jean Role has been detained and taken to the *cazerne*.

Soon we're inside the crowded, confused *cazerne*. We're all there, plus an officer, a bunch of soldiers, and the corporal who, at gunpoint, detained Jean Role. The corporal, who was in civies, accosted Jean Role a few minutes ago as he and some of the new team were passing through Jérémie's main outdoor market. The corporal demanded to know why he was always hanging out with these *blans*. Jean Role told him it wasn't any of his business. The corporal then pulled a gun and demanded that Jean Role go with him to the *cazerne*. Of course our people went right along with them.

We physically hold on to Jean Role. Under his breath he's urging, *"Don't leave me alone."* In a few minutes JR, the officer, the corporal and all of us go upstairs to the Commander's office. We insist on going with JR upstairs, but aren't permitted to accompany him into the Commander's office. At this point our old friend, the *delege*, emerges from the Commander's office. He assures us it would be okay to let JR go in alone. When we hesitate, the *delege* gives us an annoyed look. "Don't you trust me?" We respond, perhaps dishonestly, "Yes we trust you."

Standing outside the Commander's closed door we hear how well JR handles himself, hear him stand firm in the face of the corporal asserting that he has been "insolent." After the corporal tells his story, JR insists on telling his. The *delege* then declares that since both are Haitian, and that since their two stories are consistent (an obvious fiction), this must simply be a misunderstanding, and therefore they should both shake hands. JR is willing, but the corporal takes some urging. Soon though, bowing to the *delege*'s influence, he reluctantly agrees. JR is then released to us. We all go in and shake the smiling Commander's hand. His name is Carus.

Freeing Jean Role was the new team's baptism of fire, a fine orientation to Jérémie...and to the power and ambiguities of accompaniment.

The night before Joel, Jean Role and I head back to Port-au-Prince, our neighbors gather on the rectory balcony. There's dancing and drumming deep into the night. As I watch by candlelight I think how fortunate I've been to live, if only briefly, amid these people. I'm privileged to witness their grace and resilience despite extreme poverty and enduring oppression.

While I've accompanied them for a few weeks, their example will accompany me always. Cry for Justice volunteers have sought to help open space for Haitians in their struggle for liberation. Our payback is ample: the courage of the Haitian people will always be there as an example for our own struggles.

REFERENCE

Nairn, Allan. 1994. "Behind Haiti's Paramilitaries,"*Nation Magazine,* 24 October.

NONVIOLENT INTERCESSION

Intention: to be present in a zone of political, social, economic or ecological violence; to highlight the suffering the violence is causing; to generate solidarity action (sometimes limited to lobbying elites) by grassroots activists and networks in other parts of the world; and, if possible, to stop the violence directly.

12

THE SAHARA PROTEST TEAM*

April Carter

Introduction

The French Government announced in the summer of 1959 that the first French Atom Bomb would be exploded in the Sahara desert. Many African countries protested about the danger from nuclear fall-out. Africans were also angry at this further manifestation of French colonialism, which made Algeria the testing ground for the symbol of French national prestige. Jules Moch defended the proposed test at the United Nations. In France the new Gaullist regime discouraged open dissent, and few people even wished to oppose the French Bomb. So French technicians went ahead with building the atom town near the test site at Reggan, and the French authorities—who claimed that the area was deserted—made plans to send the people living round the local oases to "camps de regroupment."

In a last minute challenge to the French authorities, an international team left Accra, capital of Ghana, in December with the aim of travelling 2,100 miles to the test site. The team represented African opposition to the Bomb—11 members were Ghanaians—and included peace movement representatives from Britain and the United States. There was one French woman in the team at this stage. Spokesman for the team was the Reverend Michael Scott, then widely known for his work at the United Nations for the people of South West Africa. The departure of the team was the culmination of six months' prior negotiation and planning between Accra, New York, and London; journeys to France; deputations to African embassies in London; and debate about politics, route, personnel, and financing of the team.

The aims of the protest were to arouse the conscience of the French people and the people of other nuclear powers; to simulate further active opposition in Africa; and to halt the bomb tests—or at least to embarrass the French Government. Achieving these aims meant the team must make a serious effort to reach the test site. Three possible routes were considered. The first possibility was to start from Morocco, follow the clearly defined route to Reggan, and use the oases and official staging posts along the way. But French military passes were needed to use this route. French paratroops also patrolled the zone between Reggan and the Moroccan border, and often shot unauthorized travellers on sight. The other possible approaches lay from the south through French West Africa, starting from either Nigeria or Ghana. This journey was three times as long as the route from Morocco, and the last part involved crossing the bleak and stony Tanezrouft desert. But the likelihood of eluding the French authorities for much of the way was greater, and the risks less.

The decisive reasons for choosing to start from Ghana were, however, political. An early memorandum written in London summarized the reasons for preferring Ghana to Morocco:

> (1) We have contacts there who have promised us support; (2) We think the Ghana Government is less liable to pressure from the French to hand the team over, or to deport them; (3) In Morocco we are more likely to become involved with the FLN, which from the point of view of the European and American organizations, and especially the French, would be a great mistake.

Independent Ghana was also better able to give support than Nigeria, which in 1959 could only make representations about the French tests through the British Government. The Prime Minister of the Nigerian Federation wrote in reply to a request for help for the Sahara team: "With the achievement of independence next year, the Federal Government will be free to take necessary steps by itself and in co-operation with others, to bring direct pressure to bear in the matter."

There were also positive reasons why Ghana provided a hospitable base for the team. Anti-French feeling in Ghana was high because of the ruthless conduct of the war against the FLN [nationalist movement] in Algeria, and because of the recent French treatment of Guinea. When Guinea chose complete independence, instead of membership of the French Community in Africa, the French stripped the country of all technical and administrative equipment, down to the typewriters and light bulbs. Hostility to France added to popular anger about the Sahara test. But there were other elements in Ghanaian foreign policy which encouraged a more comprehensive dislike of nuclear strategies, and which blended with the protest team's avowed opposition to *all* nuclear bombs and tests. Ghana had become independent in 1957 and was committed to support principles which were the antithesis of imperialism and militarism associated with the colonial powers. Nkrumah had also avoided taking sides in the Cold War and stood for nonalignment along the lines enunciated at the Bandung Conference in 1955.

In addition, the fact that Ghana's campaign for independence had been based on Nkrumah's strategy of "positive action" meant that the protest group's commitment to nonviolence could be identified with the idea of positive action. It was not therefore necessary to defend nonviolence against advocacy of violence. Because Ghana's expressed ideals of disarmament and nonviolence were in harmony with the fundamental principles of the team's policy, they were able to avoid compromising these principles, despite the need to adjust to the political circumstance inside Ghana, and the attitude of the Government there.

A further advantage was the fact there was a Ghanaian Campaign for Nuclear Disarmament set up at the end of August 1959. The Ghana CND included representatives of the main organizations in the country and was in fact an unofficial government body. But its status and ostensible independence made it an ideal body to sponsor the protest team in a way politically acceptable to both the team and the Ghana Government. Ghana CND decided to co-operate in the Sahara direct action plan at the end of August. An important personal link between Ghana CND and the British and American organizations promoting the team was Bill Sutherland, a black American previously active in peace and civil rights campaigns. He was at that stage personal assistant to the Ghanaian Finance Minister, Mr K.A.Gbedemah.

Bill Sutherland also helped to persuade the initially reluctant Committee for Nonviolent Action in New York to support the venture. CNVA had promoted a number of civil disobedience actions against American military policy, including the 1958 voyage of the *Golden Rule* into the Pacific nuclear testing area at Eniwetok. They sent two of their most experienced members to Ghana: Bayard Rustin, veteran of many civil rights and peace campaigns, and A.J.Muste, then in his seventies, the leading figure in the American movement for radical nonviolent action. Both played a crucial role in the political negotiation preceding the final departure of the team.

The organization which launched the Sahara team, the London-based Direct Action Committee Against Nuclear War, already had close links with CNVA. The DAC itself had originated with an attempt by a British Quaker to enter the British H-Bomb testing zone in 1957. The Committee had gone on to organize the first Aldermaston March in 1958 and demonstrations at Thor missile bases. The DAC sent out their twenty-five-year-old chairman, Michael Randle, to Ghana to initiate practical preparations for the team. Once the British and American team members were in Accra the Committees in London and New York ceased to play an active role. Ghana CND raised the funds to equip the expedition, and the team members made the political decisions.

Build-up in Ghana
When two British team members arrived at Accra airport early on 9 October, they received in Michael Randle's words: "an almost royal welcome." The Chairman of Ghana CND, E.C.Quaye, was there to greet them, along with other notables from the ruling Convention People's Party. A Daimler plus chauffeur and public relations person were put at their disposal.

In the afternoon the two British volunteers attended the final session of the All African Peoples Conference Steering Committee, and were introduced to Dr Nkrumah's parliamentary secretary. The Steering Committee passed a resolution urging all governments to stop testing nuclear weapons and to dismantle their stocks of bombs. The Committee also expressed support for "Africans and humanists" protesting against the French tests.

Michael Randle and his colleague—twenty-nine-year-old artist Francis Hoyland—continued to receive VIP treatment. They were driven to observe some Urban District Elections, and were entertained to a lavish dinner by the Regional Commissioner. Michael Randle conveyed his first impressions in a letter to London:

> Ghana radio has been making regular broadcasts about our activities, even to announcing our schedule for the next day. We have become unofficial ambassadors for radical Britain and if absolutely nothing else came of our visit, the fact that we shall have brought home to people here that there are many in Britain who are concerned about the French tests and nuclear weapons in general could be of historic importance...there is real disappointment here that Britain has made no official protest.

Ghana CND met to hear the plans for the protest team, and agreed to arrange meetings and film shows. Among the meetings subsequently organized was one at the University College of Legon, where 300 students came to listen to the volunteers. In Kumasi, the second largest city in Ghana, men and women, many with babies strapped to their backs, crowded into the small Council Chambers there. While in Kumasi the team met the Asentehene, the traditional leader of the Ashanti people, and later that day spoke with the paramount chief at Kibi, some 80 miles from Accra. Two days later this chief called an emergency meeting of the Council of Chiefs specially to hear the team. Sunday 18 October was observed in churches throughout Ghana as a day of prayer for nuclear disarmament. The timing had been arranged to coincide with the launching of the team. There was a mass meeting in Accra nine days later.

Bayard Rustin arrived in Accra on 20 October. His arresting personality and political skills enabled him to persuade the Ghana Government to move beyond official gestures—despite their royal welcome the British volunteers were feeling somewhat trapped—and to give genuine backing to the team. He began working too on promoting opposition to the Sahara tests throughout Africa. The Secretary General of the Ghana Trades Union Congress invited Rustin and Randle to address a plenary session of the All African Trade Union Federation that met in Accra on 7-9 November and passed a resolution in support of the team. The team members were also able to talk privately with a number of African leaders in Accra for this conference, including Tom Mboya and Oginga Odinga. Two weeks later the Secretary General of Ghana TUC—who was also First Secretary of the Federation—called on all African workers, especially those in the French Community, to demonstrate against the French tests.

As a result of publicity about the Sahara protest plan, Ntsu Mokhehle, President of the Basutoland National Congress Party, flew to Accra to join the team. He represented 150 volunteers from his own country, who for practical reasons could not take part. A Nigerian student, Hilary Arinze, also volunteered and was accepted.

The French volunteer, twenty-seven-year-old Esther Peter, flew in a day after Rustin. She had given up her job in the translation section of the Council of Europe to join the team. Earlier she had been active in the World Citizen movement. Because no French disarmament organization could be persuaded to support such an unorthodox venture, Esther Peter was during the preparatory stages the only French team member. But the day the team left Accra they were joined at Kumasi by a French pacifist, Pierre Martin, who had just completed a work camp mission for UNESCO there. Martin, who was also on a tour for the Service Civile Internationale, had in the past spent over a year in the Sahara working with the first French oil research teams, and still had contacts in the area. He also has a record of active resistance to French military policies.

The most sensational arrival was that of Michael Scott on 17 November. A cable to the London pacifist weekly, *Peace News*, reported:

> Scott receives tumultuous welcome. Government and Opposition supporters unite in backing Sahara Protest. Cheering crowds carried Rev Michael Scott shoulder high into the waiting room when he arrived by plane from the United States.... At a press conference the following day Rev Scott told reporters of the deliberations that had been going on at the United Nations in New York. In spite of the pressures that had been brought to bear on

her, however, France remained adamant...since his arrival the Sahara protest has become a national issue and is headline news in press and radio.

After Scott's arrival, final plans were made for the journey. Ghana CND appealed for funds over the radio and at a public rally, and with the 4,500 pounds raised, the team bought two land rovers and a Bedford truck. The whole team (then numbering 19 volunteers) planned to drive the 1,000 miles to the Algerian border, if they were able to cross the French-controlled territories of Upper Volta and the French Sudan. Beyond the Algerian border the real desert began, and the military zone near Reggan was also likely to be heavily patrolled by French troops. So only ten members would attempt the last stage of the journey taking with them enough supplies to get to Reggan.

A Quaker couple in Ghana who had made the journey across the Sahara the year before, advised that:

> To demonstrate the sincerity and the seriousness of your purpose to the French authorities, even though your hopes of reaching the desert are small, you should start with an even better equipped expedition than is required for this journey normally, as you do not wish to become a charge on the state for saving your lives or to lay yourselves open to justifiable ridicule.

The team aimed to follow this advice.

If the ten volunteers reached the test site they planned to try to persuade French technicians to stop co-operating with the preparations for the test, and to remain in the area as a deterrent to the bomb being dropped. The rest of the team in the Sudan would hope to keep in touch and to send news back to Ghana. In addition they would seek to act as a focus for promoting opposition to the test within French West Africa. In September the Premier of the French Sudan, Modibo Keita, had broken away from the united front presented by the French Community in supporting the test, and had made a statement condemning it. This was significant for the team since they would need help in Sudan in obtaining advice about the best routes and in acquiring a local guide. If it proved necessary to send a rescue party into the desert, this would also have to start from the Sudan.

But the first problem was to get past the French authorities at the Upper Volta border. Since the team had publicized their plans, and had officially applied for visas to enter French West Africa—which were refused—the likelihood of their being stopped was high. The team agreed that: "Under no circumstances would we attempt to drive our vehicles on past a manned barrier as this might easily cause danger to other people or lead to a situation of panic where soldiers or police were confronting vehicles rather than individuals..."

The First Attempt

The team set out at dawn from Accra on 6 December, and at their first stop at Kumasi were joined by Pierre Martin. The next day they drove to Tamale, where there was a rally in their honor, and 25 young men volunteered to join on the spot. In the afternoon they reached Bolgatanga at the junction of two roads leading to Upper Volta. Two members of the team, together with A.J.Muste who, acting as coordinator, conferred with several district commissioners in the area about conditions on the Upper Volta side of the border. As a result it was decided that the team should cross from the village of Bawku on 9 December, whilst volunteers would distribute team leaflets around the other Ghanaian border village of Navrongo.

Michael Randle cabled on 9 December:

> Today 9am Chief in ceremonial robes, village elders, drummers and musicians and whole town turned out for meeting. Ntsu Mokhehle, President of Basutoland Congress Party, in speech: "We go unarmed. We say to French do not weep for us but for yourselves and your children...." Team now at 21 members.... Latest members Pierre Martin and Hannah Kojo, Women's Federation, and one of the most prominent and important women's leaders in Ghana. Crossing border this afternoon. District Commissioner to lead people of Bawku to border.

As the border itself was not clearly marked, the team encountered the first French control post at Bittou, 16 miles inside Upper Volta. Despite earlier rumors that the Upper Volta people might be unfriendly, the team was cheered during their journey through Volta territory.

At Bittou the team were stopped by three white French officers, who told them that instructions from Paris forbade the team to proceed. The officers were polite and offered the team food and drink, which we refused. Michael Scott made plain that they were not prepared to leave. The officers said they had no orders to arrest the team, and would have to go to Ouagadougou 50 miles away to get fresh instructions. They asked the team not to give out leaflets or talk politics to the Africans in the area. The team agreed not to do so before the officers returned from Ouagadougou at noon the next day.

When the officers did return, they said they had not been able to contact the authorities in Paris, but asked for the keys of all vehicles, which the team refused. Muste reported the subsequent developments in an article for *Liberation* (January 1960):

From this point on tension built up. The Africans in the vicinity were plainly friendly to the Team, eagerly sought leaflets (which had a message in four languages: Arabic, Hausa, French, and English), and listened to talks. Even some of the African police showed interest. The local chief built a hut to shelter the team from the heat. The local butcher brought meat.

The response of the French officers to this infiltration of the anti-test propaganda into the native population was to tighten control. By the end of the third day at the Bittou barrier there were a hundred police and soldiers on hand, armed with revolvers, rifles, and machine guns. Not only did they surround the team on all sides, confining them to a space of only 50 yards in diameter, but they also kept the Africans so far away that propaganda by talk or leaflet distribution was shut off.

After five days of mounting frustration the team made a strategic withdrawal to Bolgatanga to rethink their position. They had found themselves unable to move forward either by vehicle or by foot, and they also felt in an ambiguous position in their relations with the French officers. Furthermore, the period of waiting had created a number of internal difficulties in the team—many of whom had no previous experience of direct action.

During this period a certain amount of hostility developed among some African volunteers towards the Western team members. One source of tension was the way decisions were made within the team. Although final decisions were made after discussion among all members, a policy planning committee was responsible for putting alternative proposals to the meeting. The members of this steering committee were: the two Americans, Rustin and Sutherland; two British, Scott and Randle; and two Africans, Mokhehle from Basutoland and Frimpong-Manso from Ghana. Since there were 12 Ghanaians on the team then, they felt underrepresented. Pierre Martin reported that there were mutterings among the Ghanaians about European and American domination.

A second source of resentment was the role played by Esther Peter in acting as interpreter with the French officers. The Ghanaians, already very hostile to the French for political reasons, were disposed to be distrustful towards individual French people even on the team. When Esther Peter talked at length with the French officers, and sometimes went away with them, some of the Ghanaians became convinced she was betraying the team and was acting as a French spy in their midst. The suspicion that she was a spy travelled back to Accra, and later she was asked to leave the country. Interestingly this suspicion never extended to Pierre Martin—perhaps because he did not play a dominant role, and was particularly aware of the Ghanaian attitudes.

The team were joined at Bolgatanga by A.J.Muste. It was decided there that only seven people should make the second attempt to enter

Upper Volta. Three other Ghanaian volunteers were to base themselves on Navrongo to keep contact with the team, and to give all travellers into Upper Volta leaflets to be distributed there. The rest of the team returned to Accra to promote activity against the test there, or went home. Rustin was needed in the Untied States to work on a civil rights campaign, and Mokhehle had to contest an election in Basutoland.

The decision to split up the volunteers created a more united and flexible group for further attempts to enter French West Africa. It also enabled team members to extend the scope of their political activity. Hilary Arinze returned to Nigeria where he was energetic in seeking support for the team; and Esther Peter was able to play a particularly important and necessary role in Paris in publicizing and interpreting the venture there. But the decision to engage volunteers in other political work was also a guise for dropping some members from the team, and a number of the Ghanaians who found they had little real work to do in Accra became very resentful that they were no longer regarded as being part of the protest team.

The Second Attempt
The members of the seven-person team were Michael Scott, Michael Randle, Bill Sutherland, and four Ghanaians: Benjamin N.Akita, a book-keeper; R.Orleans-Lindsay, a science teacher; K.Frimpong-Manso, a private businessman; K.M.Arkhurst, a driver. They crossed the Upper Volta border on 17 December, penetrated 11 miles inside French territory, and were stopped at the military post of Po.

In accordance with decisions reached after the experience of Bittou, the team this time adopted a less co-operative course with the French officials. They applied for permission to pass through several times each day, and sat down in front of the barrier after being refused. They waited two weeks at the barrier and gave out leaflets despite threats of arrest. The leaflets were confiscated from those who accepted them. At one point a large group of Moslems on their way to Ouagadougou dismounted in the forecourt of the customs place, and chanted prayers for the success of the Protest Team's mission.

On Christmas Eve, Michael Randle and a Ghanaian team member found two people in the nearby town of Paga to make recordings of the text of the leaflet in two local languages. The recordings also announced that the Northern House of Chiefs was calling for a day of prayer on 1 January. The team started using the loudspeakers on Boxing Day. Randle's log book notes:

> The recordings...sounded as clear as if someone had been speaking into the microphone. People gathered round and seemed most interested, and in the

evening one of the Moslem guards, Kopdji, said that the African guards agreed that they were "bonnes paroles." The commandant came and told us that loudspeaking without a permit was forbidden in Volta, even for commercial firms, and threatened to confiscate equipment, prevent us from going back to Ghana for supplies etc. and stop us from using the well for water.

We broadcast again on morning of 27 December. The threats were repeated. At 3pm we broadcast again. This time the French officer in charge, M.Charriere, mounted the land rover and removed both loudspeakers. We gave a note to an English group passing through to deliver to our Pressman in Paga.

The group started dawn-to-dusk vigils on 29 December, in shifts of two at a time. On 1 January the whole group kept vigil and fasted to coincide with the day of prayer by the Northern House of Chiefs. During the morning they were visited by an African deputy from Po, who asked the team detailed questions, and indicated that though the Upper Volta Government was sympathetic they had to play things cool because of their negotiations with the French.

The French officers had agreed to transmit a message to the President of the Upper Volta Parliament, asking for transit. But eventually the team were told that the matter was not under the jurisdiction of Upper Volta, but of Paris. The team decided therefore on further action. Michael Randle sent the following report on 8 January:

> Four set off at 6am on Sunday, 3 January, on foot for Ouagadougou...mile past barrier surrounded by guards with rifles and bren guns. Told under arrest. Scott searched and keys of our vehicles seized. Vehicles impounded and team driven 90 miles under armed escort in police van from Po to Leo. Held all day, then taken back to Tumu in Ghana.
>
> Team now in Bolgatanga, north Ghana.... Another attempt imminent, form under consideration, although team heard news of action travelled to Ouagadougou, Niamey and Gao on fringe of Sahara. Learnt this from lorry drivers passing through.

Supporting Actions

While the seven-person team was at Po, Pierre Martin picketed the French Embassy in Accra for five days and then on Christmas Eve started a seven-day fast. The fast was in protest against the refusal of the French authorities to let the team through Upper Volta on their way to Reggan. It ended with a meeting addressed by Finance Minister Gebedemah, Mayor of Accra Quaye, and Minister of State N.A. Welbeck, and with a short religious service. Nkrumah sent a message of thanks. Pierre Martin received sympathetic letters from many parts of Africa and Europe. A Czech factory worker sent a cutting from *Rude Pravo* with a photograph of Martin in front of the Embassy. Letters of support arrived from France, and a number of French Embassy staff expressed their agreement with him. Citizens of Upper Volta living in Ghana joined in the demonstration in front of the Embassy, and sent a letter to the Upper Volta President asking him to grant the team visas.

The Nigerian volunteer, Hilary Arinze, also began a three-day fast on 4 January, outside the French Consulate in Lagos, to demand that the team should be allowed to continue. Arinze told the *West African Pilot* that the fast was also designed to protest on behalf of the people in Upper Volta, who could not speak for themselves because of their colonial subjection.

In London the Youth Campaign for Nuclear Disarmament picketed the French Embassy over Christmas to protest against the Sahara Bomb, and focussed on the efforts of the team. CNVA started daily lunch-hour pickets outside the Fifth Avenue French Government Tourist Office in New York after the team were stopped at Bittou. Sympathizers in Hamburg had begun picketing the French Consulate each evening the day the team left Accra.

Third Attempt
Before the third attempt to enter French territory, the Chairman of Ghana CND, E.C.Quaye, made formal representations to the French authorities, demanding the return of the team's impounded vehicles. The demand was referred to Ouagadougou.

London and New York urged another attempt, and suggested starting from Nigeria. Randle cabled back on 12 January: "Nigerian expedition impossible now, funds very low...funds and volunteers would have to be found in Nigeria itself and would take many weeks, even if same public response as in Ghana which is most unlikely."

However, money was scraped together to buy another land rover and other necessary equipment for the third entry, and the team set out again on 17 January. Randle wrote to London: "It is just possible we may get through this time, at least to Ouagadougou. Using Western road through Tuma which would normally avoid checkpoints. Quite likely that French have now closed the gap."

The team slipped across the border on foot, and hitched lifts with friendly lorry drivers as far as Tenkodogo, about 66 miles north of the frontier. There they were noticed by Upper Volta police, and were detained by the French authorities, who search them, confiscated their radio and binoculars, and then put them on a lorry and sent them back into Ghana.

At this point the team all returned to Accra. Randle cabled on 25 January:

> All possible routes in Upper Volta now under close 24 hour guard. Team and Ghana Council estimate further confrontations on Volta border ineffective following eight weeks spent there already.
> Michael Scott leaving Accra for Tunis today, to represent Ghana CND and Protest Team at All African Peoples Conference. Will appeal for Africa Day of Protest and will investigate possibility of new attempt from Morocco or other sympathetic state, by plane if possible.
> Meanwhile Bill Sutherland to contact Nigerian personalities to investigate possible action from there. Nevertheless very possible further direct action will prove impossible.
> Pierre Martin expelled from Trusteeship territory of Togoland. Informs us that border police know names of all team members and are alerted to prevent our entry. Officials at Air France showed Pierre special instructions by security police Contonou not to accept him on their air lines going to Togo or Dahomey.

A fortnight later Pierre Martin learned through a friend at Air France that if he stopped off at Adidjan (Ivory Coast) on his way to Dakar in Senegal he might be arrested there. Further evidence of the French authorities' concern was given in a letter from Michael Randle dated 4 February:

> We are still waiting for Michael Scott.... If we could mount this plane expedition it would really shake the French. Not that they are not shaken now! Every day we get more and more evidence of it. Today a Quaker couple here asked permission to cross French territory on their way to Kenya and there was a great deal of discussion to the effect that they mustn't be allowed to stop here, or take such a road...and Embassy people are in fact completely jittery.

The team was still a focus for some expressions of opposition to the French test. Hilary Arinze had announced to the press in Enugu in January that 300 Nigerians had offered to take part in the next attempt to enter French territory. The Iraqi Federation of Democratic Youth cabled to Accra from Baghdad at the end of January saying 43 people from Iraq had volunteered to join the team.

In France

In Paris Esther Peter had been working to break through the barrier of silence about the team in the French press. Muste noted that at the time of the first confrontation in Bittou a French Government representative told reporters that he had "no knowledge" of anti-bomb protesters being "arrested" at the border. The absence of any French organizational backing for the team, and the fact that only two French nationals were involved reduced the news value of the team. In addition the French press was very nervous of printing any material which indicated opposition to the test. However, Esther Peter did get *Le Monde* to print a long letter about the team in its issue of 2 January. She reported to London that *France Observateur* and *Le Canard Ecnhainé* had carried stories. So did the Communist *Liberation*. *Témoinage Chrétien* were persuaded to go as far as to print a map of the Sahara to show that Reggan was the last of a chain of oases. (The French Government had withdrawn all maps of the Sahara and Esther Peter found one by chance with the help of a French ethnologist, who had been trying since the previous summer to publicize the fact that the test area was not uninhabited desert.)

Esther Peter also contacted about a dozen French peace groups and formed an *ad hoc* committee for nonviolent direct action to demonstrate outside a nuclear center near Paris. She also began to organize parades in Paris against the French test. She wrote to London on 5 February: "Am sending out tonight letters asking for participants in public demonstrations in Paris. It will be difficult. People are only getting over the Algerian shock and very reluctant to speak against anything De Gaulle wishes to do."

General agitation about the bomb test mounted in the weeks just preceding the expected date of the explosions. There were officially supported mass demonstrations in Tunis on 25 January and in Tripoli, Libya, on 31 January. In Rabat, Morocco, about 2,000 demonstrators gathered outside the French Embassy despite a Government ban on the demonstration. While in Paris 500 African students from French Community countries were arrested on 11 February, when they gathered to present a petition against the test to Premier Debre.

At dawn on 13 February the French Bomb was exploded at Reggan. There were immediate protests by President Nasser of Egypt and the Arab League Council. The Moroccan Cabinet met to discuss measures against France and the Istiqlal Party called for the breaking off of diplomatic relations. Ghana froze the assets of French firms in retaliation, and Julius Nyerere of Tanganyika congratulated Ghana on her action. However, the French Community states, including Sudan, refrained from overt protest, and Ivory Coast and Chad went so far as to congratulate France on the test.

The team had been frustrated in their last minute hope of flying into the test area. Instead, team members still in Ghana diverted their energies to calling a special All African Conference to co-ordinate action against further French tests. The idea was put to Nkrumah by Michael Scott, and the Ghana Government took the initiative in calling the Conference which was held in Accra from 7-10 April 1960.

The Accra Conference
The conference itself was immediately caught up on inter-African politics. Although Nkrumah's speech and some of the final resolutions

reflected the ideas and aims of the American and British team members, their real influence was rapidly declining.

Nkrumah had broadened the conference agenda to cover the "balkanization" of Africa, and the two priorities in the African liberation struggle: Algeria and South Africa. The Conference was attended by representatives of all the nine independent African states and of many countries still awaiting independence. The FLN supported the Conference despite the emphasis on nonviolence in the original invitation, and fears that after their victory at Tunis in January in getting endorsement of their proposals for an African Brigade to fight in Algeria, they would either ignore the Conference or try to remove the emphasis on nonviolence. The main gap in participation was the absence of most French community leaders.

The Conference brought out some of the difficulties of getting joint African action. Tom Mboya made a powerful speech in which he pleaded: "Let it not be said that all we can do is embark on expensive conferences and talk, and then go back home to await the next conference." The Conference passed resolutions for action on South Africa, and endorsed again the proposal for an African Brigade to fight in Algeria. Ghanaian volunteers paraded outside the Conference Center. Simultaneously, however, the Conference passed a resolution to set up training centers in nonviolent positive action to launch demonstrations against the French tests, and train participants in liberation struggles.

But no practical organizational or financial provisions were made to implement this resolution. So in effect any Center would be sponsored by the Ghana Government, or not at all. An initiative by Ghana alone would, in view of the rivalries between leaders of different states, be distrusted. The Center might be treated as a prestige symbol in inter-African power struggles.

A more serious danger, however, was that the Center would never be set up at all. After the Accra Conference Nkrumah, who was no doubt aware of this danger, asked Scott, Sutherland, and Randle for suggestions. Nkrumah said he was willing to find funds to cover the running costs for the first year, and offered use of a school at Winneba, 30 miles from Accra. The General Secretary of the Convention Peoples' Party was to have final responsibility for choosing staff and a board of governors. It was agreed that Winneba would be a suitable site. But no further progress was made for three months. Nkrumah and other Ministers attended a Commonwealth Prime Ministers' Conference, and then in June a Conference of the Heads of Independent African States. Events in the Congo had become the center of attention by July 1960. A proposal to send a Positive Action reconnaissance team into the Congo, and perhaps to bring volunteers from the Congo back to the Center, was not accepted by the President. But in July Nkrumah announced publicity that a CPP training school to be called the Kwame Nkrumah Institute would be set up at Winneba. It would have two sections: one dealing with the training of Party and Trade Union members; the other for training in Positive Action.

By this stage the protest team members still in Ghana viewed their possible role in the Center with considerable doubts. They had three main worries. First, they felt that the leading members on the staff of the Institute should be African, not outsiders. It was not clear, however, that there were any candidates who combined commitment to nonviolence with sufficient experience and personal standing to steer the Center through the intrigues of Ghana politics.

Second, they became increasingly concerned that a Center under the direct control of the Ghana Government would either have to abandon its commitment to individual civil rights, and to other beliefs associated with nonviolence (for example a general concern to decentralize power), or else sooner or later come into direct conflict with the Government. This dilemma was becoming acute by the end of August 1960, after the introduction of press censorship, the issuing of preventative detention orders against leading members of the opposition United Party, and the police harassment of the Chairman of the United Party in a by-election in Accra.

Third, they were concerned whether the Center could maintain any kind of commitment to nonviolence. It was likely to be closely associated with the Bureau of African Affairs, set up in September 1959 under the Minister of the Interior after the death of Nkrumah's special advisor on African Affairs, George Padmore. Several members of the Bureau's board were bitterly opposed to nonviolence, and might try to divert the Center to specifically violent action related to Algeria or South Africa. Nor was there any guarantee that the Board elected for the Winneba Center would necessarily be concerned to stress or maintain a commitment to nonviolent action.

The immediate aim of the Center had been to organize massive demonstrations against French tests, and this idea had been incorporated in Nkrumah's opening speech to the Accra Conference. Nevertheless a few weeks later Ghana unfroze French assets, and Nkrumah gave the impression that he did not expect further French tests in the Sahara. But in September the news that France was planning a new series of nuclear tests caused a stir in Ghana and led to immediate protests.

Reports suggested that the first underground test was scheduled to take place in the Hoggar mountains—the site was about 350 miles from the nearest point on the Niger-Algeria border. Randle and Sutherland proposed that a team should attempt to reach the site through French-controlled Niger. They also suggested co-ordinated protests in African capitals, and a charter flight of Africans to Paris to stage a demonstration there. They urged the need to put the Center into operation immediately to promote these plans. Despite their reservations about the Center they felt that it was worth pursuing attempts to organize direct action against the French tests.

Nothing came of these proposals. So Michael Randle flew back to England in October to take over the secretaryship of the newly formed Committee of 100 for mass civil disobedience against nuclear policies. He had been in Ghana a year. Michael Scott, who had already returned to Britain, was a co-sponsor of the Committee of 100. The Sahara Protest Team had, after more than 15 months of planning and activity, finally come to an end.

Political Effects of the Protest Team
The impact of the Sahara Protest Team varied considerably. There was almost no response to the venture in France, and even peace groups were reluctant to express support. The lack of internal support and the lack of publicity in the French press clearly constituted a major failure—even if it could be ascribed in part to the wider political situation in France.

There was virtually no publicity in the United States about the Team either. Muste commented on the absence of coverage in the American press despite reports filed by Reuters and other correspondents in Ghana. The British press, both national and local, did carry news items from the time the first volunteers flew to Ghana until the end of the third attempt to enter Upper Volta. But the team was never treated as a major news story.

On the other hand the team did have major impact in Ghana, and served as a focus for opposition in other parts of Africa. Bayard Rustin commented at the time that the Sahara team was the most significant pacifist project he had been associated with:

> In the past most of our projects have been moral protests in an atmosphere where there was no possibility of political accommodation. This project was in an atmosphere where most of Africa was already aroused and was waiting for a project round which it could rally. It had profound political implications in that it tied together the whole question of militarism and political freedom in a way that people could understand and respond to (*Peace News*, 1 January 1960).

Within Africa the team's main political failure was the absence of any organized support from the countries of French West Africa. Rustin explained to *Peace News* (1 January 1960) that:

> The chief reason for this is that a good deal of French West Africa is coming up for independence. The leaders in these areas, such as the Mail Federation, were in fact in Paris at the time negotiating for independence and for economic ties with France, and it was too much to expect them to defy France at that point.

The team's attempts to enter Upper Volta were nonetheless revealing. Muste reported that a Ghanaian official in Washington had said to him that the team's exposure of the illusory character of the "self government" granted by the French to Africans was one of the most significant achievements of the project. (Interestingly the President of Upper Volta contacted Esther Peter when in Paris, and spoke to her about the nuclear test before meeting De Gaulle—though this did not prevent him from being the first African head of state to congratulate France on the nuclear explosion).

There was some individual opposition to the French test in Community countries. A Youth Conference held in the French Sudan in August had proposed that demonstrations should be held against the test throughout West Africa. The team may also have helped slightly to crystallize opposition. The government of the Ivory Coast canceled grants to all its students opposing government policy in January 1960, following action by students in Paris calling for the protest team to be allowed to proceed, and for the abandonment of the Atom test. The Niger Government warned its officials in January that anyone opposing Government policy would be sacked immediately. But popular opposition never became significant.

More puzzling than the actions of French Community governments was the attitude of Guinea. President Sekou Toure publicly opposed the French tests when it was first announced. But his attitude appeared to change during 1959. Muste observed in *Liberation* (New York):

> It had been assumed that Guinea and its leader Sekou Toure would give substantial support to the Sahara Team. Early in December, however, a number of African papers quoted Toure as saying in Morocco that personally he was neither for nor against the test, but that Africa was against it. Toure made no effort to deny this report.

Muste speculated that the reason might have been Guinea's dependence on Soviet economic aid. He noted that the team had received indications that Communists in Africa had little sympathy for the protest team, and suggested that Moscow was not interested in making an issue of the

French Bomb, which might be seen as a divisive issue in NATO and irrelevant to the overall balance of nuclear power.

An additional factor was the very complicated relationship between Ghana and Guinea. The team made soundings to discover whether it might be possible to start from Guinea, and met with a courteous but cautious response from the Embassy in Accra. When Bill Sutherland and Esther Peter flew to Guinea they were not able to meet Sekou Toure. They had an interview with the Vice President, but received no concrete offers of assistance.

However after the Bomb test the Political Bureau of the Guinean Democratic Party, the supreme governing body in Guinea, did issue an official condemnation, stating that the French Bomb was "an intolerable threat to the African peoples struggling for independence."

In Ghana the team could claim not only to have focussed opposition to the tests, but to have influenced the tone of public pronouncement about it, and to have spread both nonviolent ideas and methods. Rustin noted in his *Peace News* interview of 1 January 1960:

> Another interesting thing about it is that when we arrived (in Ghana) there was fantastic anti-French feeling concerning everything, but when we left they had responded to our view that we have nothing against France and the French people as such, but we are opposed to the testing of weapons wherever they are.... The moral contribution which we gave came because we were able to operate from their political assumptions, bringing in our own point of view.

Muste estimated that in the opinion of many Ghanaians the idealism and the enthusiasm of the struggle for independence had been revived among supporters of Nkrumah's Convention People's Party:

> Moreover, an immense propaganda job for the idea of nonviolence has been done among the masses and a considerable amount of intensive training in nonviolent philosophy and strategy has been give the 20 or so volunteers who were able to attend training sessions regularly (*Liberation* January 1960).

Ghanaian leaders and newspapers began to emphasize nonviolence. Nkrumah's message to Pierre Martin at the end of his fast said that this sacrifice would "go down in history as one of the first of such nonviolent acts against imperialist aggression on the people of our continent." The *Daily Graphic* reported on 25 January: "About 600 students...staged a nonviolent and peaceful demonstration in front of the French Embassy in Accra in protest against the test." The *Ghana Times* carried a story on 1 February that: "The vanguard activists of the Convention Peoples' Party carried out a 'non-violent' demonstration in front of the French Embassy...." The style of action demonstrated by the team was also imitated. For example a fifty-year-old Ghanaian chief, the Omanhene of Nkoranza, undertook a week's fast in protest against the tests a month after Martin's fast.

Lessons from the Sahara Protest
The relative success of the protest team in getting across their aims and ideas contrasts with their failure to launch a training center in nonviolence. The difficulties involved in promoting the Center suggest that the enthusiasm generated for nonviolence and disarmament was temporary and superficial. However the team could scarcely expect to exercise any profound influence on Ghanaian culture or politics, and the nature of the problems confronting the Center have been outlined.

It may be more instructive to ask why the difficulties which beset the founding of the Center did not sabotage the protest team. The answer lies partly in the fact that the protest team was a short-term action with limited aims. The team's goals of opposition to the French tests coincided with the policy aims of the Ghana Government. Secondly the protest team was an independent initiative which had already got under way and defined its own methods and objectives when the first volunteers reached Accra. And once the team left Accra it had complete discretion in planning its tactics. Therefore, the role of the Ghana Government was restricted. Indeed, although the team was dependent on the co-operation of the Government, each had a mutual interest in not becoming too closely identified. For the team, any government backing was to some extent compromising. The Government did not wish the team to be interpreted as an officially backed "invasion," or to be committed to an embarrassing support of their own nations should they get into trouble in French-controlled territory. While there is bound to be some ambiguity in governmental support of nonviolent direct action, agreement on immediate aims and mutual interests may make co-operation acceptable to both sides.

On the other hand there is an inherent incompatibility between the idea of a permanent training center for nonviolent action and government control. The Center also depended, for both financial and political reasons, entirely on governmental initiative, so the team members were unable to take independent action.

It could be argued, too, that when the team moved away from the realm of direct action, where it did have the initiative, to the realm of conference politics and of bidding for long term official support, it was likely to lose out to the rivalries governing that level of political activity. The team could no longer inject their own moral and political concepts into the situation. While the element of daring and simplicity which is appropriate to direct action it is quite inappropriate to conventional political manoeuvering.

There was, however, a useful balance between the direct-action protest and more orthodox propaganda and political activity. The team did considerable educational work in Ghana about the effects of nuclear bombs. Michael Scott was personally presented at the United Nations during the November General Assembly debate on the French tests, and had circulated a memorandum on the proposed protest team. Indian Foreign Minister Krishna Menon quoted during the UN debate an article from the British *Observer* on the nature of the Sahara testing area—an article printed through the efforts of the Direct Action Committee. Michael Scott flew to Ghana to join the Team after a majority at the UN General Assembly had backed a resolution calling on the French to refrain from nuclear testing.

The Sahara Team and Ghana CND both engaged in exchange with the British government about the dangers arising from the February atomic test at Reggan. The French Embassy distributed an official publication claiming that the tests would have no harmful effects. In their reply Ghana CND and the Team contested the scientific validity of the French claim that Ghana could not be affected by the fallout because of the direction of the winds.

When British Prime Minister Harold Macmillan stated at a press conference in Ghana that the Sahara test would not harm the people of Ghana, Ghana CND immediately reproached Macmillan for encouraging the French to test the bomb on African soil, and urged Macmillan not to repeat his statement in other parts of Africa. Michael Randle said for the team that he was ashamed as a British citizen that a British Prime Minister should make such an untrue statement. Ghana papers gave prominence to this refutation of Macmillan, illustrating Michael Randle's early comment that he had become an ambassador for radical Britain. Two days later, Macmillan in a speech to the Nigerian Parliament declared his opposition to nuclear tests in Africa and anywhere else in the world. The chairman of Ghana CND immediately cabled thanks for this statement, and suggested that Macmillan should use his influence to restrain the French.

NOTE

* Reprinted with permission from A.Paul Hare and HerbertH.Blumberg (eds.), *Liberation without Violence: A Third-Party Approach* (Totowa, NJ: Rowman and Littlefield, 1977) pp.126-148.

NONVIOLENT SOLIDARITY

Intention: to be present in a zone of military violence to share the danger with local people; to highlight the suffering the violence is causing; to generate awareness of, and support for, grassroots initiatives to halt the war; and to generate solidarity action by grassroots activists and networks in other parts of the world.

13

ONE MILLION KILOMETERS FOR PEACE, RECONCILIATION AND HOPE: THE DHAMMAYIETRA MOVEMENT IN CAMBODIA*

Yeshua Moser-Puangsuwan

Introduction

Before and after the United Nations' most costly peace initiative has come and gone, ordinary people continued to pursue the path of peace-making in Cambodia. The most visible and inspiring manifestation of this pursuit of peace by peaceful means is the annual Dhammayietra, a mass cross-country walk for peace and reconciliation. The Dhammayietra movement began as a onetime event in April of 1992 when a month-long walk of reconciliation by refugee Khmer living on the Thai-Cambodian border was organized into the interior of Cambodia. The walks have since been maintained and developed by newly emerging people's movements within Cambodia. This chapter takes a brief look at the development, methods and achievements of this movement. It assumes a basic familiarity with the rich and complex political situation in Cambodia. (For further background information, see Shawcross, 1979; 1984.)

Dhammayietra is a Pali word combination, and translates into "pilgrimage of truth." (Pali is a language of ancient India and the language of the Buddhist Canon of the Therevadin school.) Through positive action, the Dhammayietra movement teaches peace, reconciliation and compassion for all beings and exemplifies an alternative, nonviolent way. It is an exceptional event because it can provide a space that is free of war, conflict and partisan politics as it moves across the violent and narrow political landscape of Cambodia. Most important of all, it visits the people who are suffering the most, the victims of war. It keeps the hope that peace is possible alive for people who live on the edge of despair.

Cambodia is a majority Buddhist country, and the message of the Dhammayietra is presented in simple Buddhist teachings by venerated

258 *Nonviolent Intervention*

Cambodian Buddhist elder Maha Ghosananda.[1] Maha Ghosananda has served as spiritual leader of the peace walk for all its five years. Although his entire family was killed during Khmer Rouge rule, when he speaks about how to respond to the Khmer Rouge, his being emanates compassion:

> I do not question that loving one's oppressor—Cambodians loving the Khmer Rouge—may be the most difficult attitude to achieve, but it is a law of the universe that retaliation, hatred and revenge only continue the cycle and never stop it.... Reconciliation does not mean that we surrender rights and conditions, but rather that we use love. Our wisdom and our compassion must walk together. Having one without the other is like walking on one foot; you will fall. Balancing the two you will walk very well, step by step (Ghosananda, 1992, pp.68-69).

The Dhammayietra walks for peace do not just occur, but have slowly built up through action and reflection as strategic nonviolent and spiritual events. Compassion, nonviolence and remaining nonpartisan are the key elements that make up this path of action. Since the beginning of these events, each of these elements has been evaluated and modified in the face of political challenges, but all have remained at the core of the Dhammayietra method.

Training for Nonviolence

Training for nonviolence is necessary in all cultures because few human social institutions teach us how to deal constructively with conflict. Usually we are taught to avoid it or to leave it to the authorities. Neither of these paths are open to people who directly confront violent conflict. The Cambodian organizers of the Dhammayietra have developed preparatory nonviolence training programs to help prepare walkers for foreseeable difficulties. Experience gained through the annual walks has been used to improve each subsequent preparatory training.

The pre-walk nonviolence trainings are held in different locations throughout Cambodia and are made available to as many people as possible. During a three day intensive live-in program, potential walkers and interested others receive an introduction to the philosophy of the walk and to meditation for peace. This is to make sure that all participants have an understanding of basic Buddhist concepts, with a particular emphasis on their application to daily difficulties of life. This introduction is followed by sessions with stories of individual peacemaking, both from within Cambodian society and from other cultures, which are illustrated with examples and experiences. Training continues with an introduction to the theory of nonviolence; stressing the need for nonviolent discipline in an area of conflict, including visual presentations of discipline/rules for the Dhammayietra. Participants undergo exercises for handling fear; they role-play situations which the walk might encounter; take a practice walk around town; and undergo mine awareness training.[2] The training sessions end with an evaluation.

During the 1996 pre-walk preparations the Dhammayietra Center planned to organize eight trainings, but demand necessitated 12 trainings in eight provinces (about half the provinces in the country). Over 600 people—almost twice as many as had been trained in the previous year—attended the pre-walk trainings. The component on dealing with fear in particular was expanded this year, as the principle trainer noted: "Our biggest obstacle to working for peace is fear. We have to help people continue to act and confront their fears if we will ever make peace" (report to funders on Dhammayietra 5 by Center for Peace and Reconciliation and the Dhammayietra Center, June 1996).

These trainings are not only an essential part of preparation for walkers, but have built up a core of Cambodian citizens trained in nonviolent action. This is extremely important in a society where the primary teaching for the past 20 years has been that "peace comes out of the barrel of a gun." There is now an expanded network of people available for peace action throughout Khmer society, and the Dhammayietra trainings have also been used as an occasion for local people to discuss nonviolence and peacebuilding within their own communities.

Developing Compassion
As a component of a mass movement, the focus on the development of compassion is certainly unique to Asia. The Dhammayietra movement believes that no other skill is as important as the development of compassion in personal preparation for the walk or social action because only compassion gives staying power in a protracted nonviolent struggle. Compassion is considered the key virtue in Buddhism—both a method and a result—on the path of personal and social liberation.

Needless to say, development of compassion is a long-term process, but clear tools and techniques for its practice are available within Buddhism: particularly the meditations on the Brahma Viharn of Karuna (limitless space of compassion) prescribed by the Buddha 2,500 years ago as the most potent method of combating fear. As a tool of nonviolence this is very important because people are usually manipulated to violence by their fears. A personal commitment to the long-term cultivation of compassion helps condition a long-term commitment to social struggle. This dual focus and linking of personal change and social change is perhaps one of the most unique aspects of the Dhammayietra as a mass movement. Another tool for cultivation of compassion is mindful walking mediation. The result of mindfulness is a mind that is active rather than reactive. With enough practice the serious student of these practices of the mental cultivation can confront extremely difficult situations and respond quickly and with great clarity of mind, or with patience according to the situation. Without the clarity of mind which can come from such an intensive practice, experience shows that people generally only react; they are still controlled by the event which precipitated the reaction. The cultivation of non-reactivity does not mean inactivity, however, it means we have broken the chain of being controlled by the event, and can truly act creatively. Only the mind free of reactivity is truly capable of peace in action.

Staying Nonpartisan
Situations of violent conflict are highly polarized. Nonpartisan action treads the fine line of neither endorsing nor opposing any party in a conflict, while often making clear statements of opposition to policies being used. Within Buddhist terminology, the path of nonpartisan action is the Middle Path: neither joining the fight nor hiding from it. Within a Gandhian framework it is the method which exemplifies the Mahatma's prescription to "oppose the evil, not the evil doer."

Nonpartisan action is the most difficult path in conflict situations as it calls for a very clear awareness not only of the actual effect of our actions, but of the perception of these effects by the combatant parties.

In past Dhammayietras political parties would attempt to join the walk holding the banners of their cause. This could not be allowed, as it would make the Dhammayietra appear to be mobilized by, or supportive of, their cause. Specifically, the organizers will not allow civil or military personnel of either the Cambodian Government, the legal opposition, or the armed counter-government organizations to join—or even appear to join—the walk. The participants learned how dangerous this was at a terrible price during the third Dhammayietra. The walk had to leave the main road on a narrow path. A patrol of government soldiers came to walk on the same path at the same time, and they wove in and out of our walk line in an attempt to pass the Peace Walkers. It was at this time that the soldiers saw opposition armed forces in the tree line and opened fire, resulting in Dhammayietra walkers being shot and killed in the ensuing firefight. Since then, the walk has had a clear policy of asking all soldiers not to escort the walk, nor to have any walker wear what could appear to be military clothing. Since the Fourth Walk, this difficulty has continued to arise because the central government sends messages to provincial authorities to "protect" the walk. In practice, this means they will order an armed patrol to accompany, lead or follow the walk. The walk committee, a group of monks, nuns, laypeople and organizers who make decisions during the walk, meet with local military or police authorities and explain the nonviolent nature of the walk. It is explained that nonviolence cannot be protected by violence, but is its own protection. This is frequently difficult for military personnel to understand. When they fail to understand this, as a last resort, the walk will stop and not move until all military or armed police escorts are removed. As a compromise, to allow the officials a path to carry out their duty, they are allowed to come on the walk provided they are unarmed and out of uniform.

A lesser difficulty arises when governors or politicians try to escort or lead the Dhammayietra for their own aggrandizement (frequently for ten minutes during which they will have ten cameras filming them). As the walk is a line with ordained clergy in the front and lay people following to the rear, the walk committee devised a strategy based on experience, whereby the would-be leaders are asked to "lead the section of laity in the rear" (no provincial authority would be ordained). This method works due to cultural esteem for the ordained in South-East Asian society. During the Fifth Walk a provincial governor breached the rules by walking in front, leading the Walk, before anyone approached to ask him to walk in the back with the laypeople. The mistake led to immediate meetings and discussions. As the walk was just outside the capital, the walk committee used the experience to improve on strategies for dealing with such incidents upon entering the city, where they were bound to multiply. Later, when a major opposition politician joined the walk, the Committee immediately asked him to respect the walk pledge and in addition remove his armed bodyguards, refrain from distributing party flyers, and walk in the back with the laypeople.

Solidarity and Organization
Maintaining a nonviolent discipline among 400-700 people as they walk for a month and perhaps into life threatening situations is no small task. It also takes a lot of organization. The Dhammayietras seek to reassure the Cambodian population through a strong presence of fearlessness and compassion, all of which requires great spiritual strength. As previously mentioned, the core of this strength is built around Buddhism. Religion however, was totally removed from Cambodian society during the period of Khmer Rouge rule and was only reinstituted during the following Communist regime under the tight control of the state. Today many Buddhist monks are quite young and have perhaps joined the order only as a means of escaping military conscription or as a path to an education.

Lack of access to spiritual teachers has also hurt the Buddhist Order in Cambodia. It is thus ironic that the while Buddhist teaching provides the essential power of this peace action it is the ordained clergy who are the most likely source of internal problems for the Dhammayietra. Particularly in the past there was a difficulty with young monks who sought rides on vehicles once they tired of walking, rather than building stamina through perseverance. This activity, although harmless on first appearance, was found to be very demoralizing for other walkers. Some of the ordained clergy used the walk to solicit money in the name of religion for their own personal enrichment. These two behaviors, plus a general lack of understanding of Buddhism by many newly ordained clergy, and the experience of the Third Dhammayietra (during which two walkers were killed and others were injured) has led to the development of a discipline program based in nonviolence for the walk. The following guidelines have evolved:

> 1) Participant must attend a pre-walk training or is not allowed to walk;
> 2) Each monk or nun presents a letter of approval from the abbot of his or her temple to join the walk;
> 3) Each participant verbally agrees to respect the five point pledge :
>   a) All walkers will undergo a pre-walk training scheduled by the Dhammayietra committee;
>   b) All walkers commit themselves to nonviolence, neutrality and walking in a spirit of compassion;
>   c) Riding on vehicles, or use of drugs or alcohol is forbidden;
>   d) Carrying weapons of any kind is forbidden. Civilian dress is required and emblems and flags other than religious ones are prohibited;
>   e) Walkers must follow these points. The Dhammayietra Committee can and shall ask those who do not follow these points to leave the Dhammayietra.
> 4) Participants not respecting the pledge are given three chances. At the first violation of the guidelines, their group leader is asked to explain the problem their behavior is causing. If problems continue with a second violation, then a member of the walk committee is asked to talk with them and remind them they could be asked to leave the walk. In extreme case they receive a third chance during which they are asked to sign an oath in front of the entire walk committee promising to stop the disruptive behavior or agree to leave the walk.
> 5) Walkers are asked to leave the walk and return to their temples or homes if necessary.

When the organizers and walk committee implemented these new guidelines it resulted in a Dhammayietra with clear nonviolent discipline. A direct result of this was a much greater level of faith in the Dhammayietra, both amongst the walkers and by the communities through which the Dhammayietra passed.

Another structural improvement in the walk was the way in which walkers were organized into groups and group leaders chosen. Informed by previous experience, small groups of approximately ten walkers instead of 20 as before, were formed. The larger groups had communication problems, especially in times of difficulty or danger. Each group selected a leader, an assistant and representatives to help with distribution of supplies, food and water, medical attention and information dissemination. Over the years of the walks, more substantial training and meetings were held with the group leaders at the start of the walks as well as follow-up support throughout the event. Sub-committees of volunteers were also formed in the areas of transport of supplies and personal belongings, food and water, mine awareness and campaign, medical assistance, receiving donations, and distribution of leaflets.

Perhaps one of the most radical changes to take place in the organizing of the Dhammayietras was in the structure of the pre-walk organizing group. The First Dhammayietra was entirely organized by western expatriots working on behalf of Cambodian refugees in the camps on the Thai border. That pre-walk committee of non-Khmer turned leadership of the walk over to a delegated committee of refugees once the event crossed the border into Cambodia, but several of those expatriates remained involved as advisers, pre-walk organizers on later walks, or as walkers.

The walk committee was small in the early days, and functioned informally and often without coordination. This method broke down completely during the Third Walk after the walkers were killed. Since that time, through painful reflection and evaluation, a new collective has been built which consists entirely of Cambodian monks, nuns and lay people living inside Cambodia. From the previous five or six people who made all essential decisions for the walk, the walk committee now contains 17 people who are far more representative of walkers, as a whole. This group meets frequently with a much larger gathering of group leaders, which numbers about 70 on a walk of 700, to discuss walk policies and to hear input. The most impressive aspect of this new leadership structure is its democracy, which has evolved in a country with a noted lack of democratic institutions. Now the Dhammayietra committee, in coordination with those running the nonviolence trainings before the walk, identify many potential leaders and invite them to join in the leadership structure of the walk. Some of those people identified will have participated in previous walks, but never in a leadership capacity. Leadership experience on the walk has empowered several of them to take a more active role for progressive change in their own communities on return. In this way, the Dhammayietra is contributing to peacebuilding not only by keeping hope alive in the war-torn country through which it walks each year, but also by creating and empowering a network of people whose ongoing work will bring about change in Cambodian society.

Public Education

Since the Fourth Dhammayietra, an element of conscientization or public education has been added to the Dhammayietra walks. This has taken a number of forms. One is the development of simple illustrated Peace Health messages (so called because the ongoing civil war in Cambodia has been declared the number one health problem by organizations working in the field of health care). By 1996, 90,000 of these messages had been printed and distributed along the walk route. They provided information on the issue of deforestation, land mines, the Dhammayietra and reproduced the Prayer for Peace:

> The Suffering of Cambodia has been deep—From this suffering comes Great Compassion—Great Compassion makes a Peaceful Heart—A Peaceful Heart makes a Peaceful Person—A Peaceful Person makes a Peaceful Family—A Peaceful Family makes a Peaceful Community—A Peaceful Community makes a Peaceful Nation—And a Peaceful Nation makes a Peaceful World—There is No Happiness Higher than Peace —May All Beings Live in Happiness and Peace.

Public talks are held at three to four village temples or other public spaces per day during the Dhammayietra. Maha Ghosananda uses the opportunity to stress Buddhism as a basis for social reconciliation and compassion, encouraging the listeners to "remove land mines of hatred from our hearts." Land mine awareness trainers who have accompanied the walk for several years then explain the need to avoid the land mines in the fields and forests by giving talks, setting up displays, and distributing and hanging up posters, offering trainings on how to remove victims from mined areas and in recent years even showing videos on the dangers of land mines. In addition to these educational activities, the Dhammayietra has gathered a substantial number of the over 400,000 signatures collected thus far in Cambodia on petitions calling for a total worldwide ban on antipersonnel land mines. These petitions have been delivered abroad by Cambodian amputees to governmental forums taking decision on the regulation and use of weapons.

The Dhammayietra has walked through some of the provinces experiencing accelerated deforestation. Although officially there is a ban on logging within Cambodia, documents leaked to the press show that corrupt government officials have sold foreign corporations the right to cut in *all* remaining timber stands within the country (Global Witness 1996). The evidence shows that mismanagement and corruption within the Royal Government of Cambodia (RGC) is now responsible for the destruction of Cambodia's forests on a scale that dwarfs all activity in the years prior to 1995. Documents obtained by Global Witness show that the RGC is in the process of allocating all of Cambodia's remaining forest in 19 massive concessions to mainly foreign companies. The Dhammayietra has focused attention on the ongoing deforestation in Cambodia, and the link between deforestation and the ongoing war. It also planted 2,000 trees along the walk route. "These trees are a symbol for renewal and an objection to the destruction of our environment," explained Kim Leng, one of the walk's central organizers.

Buddhism and the health of forests are closely linked. Buddhist renunciates have lived under the trees and wandered in the forests of Asia for 2,500 years and it is the environment which has fostered it's greatest teachers. The Buddha is also believed to have been born, reached enlightenment and died under a tree. Sitting peacefully under a canopy of leaves at a rest stop along the walk, Maha Ghosananda explained the gift which comes from the trees. "Breath," he said, "In Buddhism, peace means to breathe, in and out. To live is to breathe, without this peace, there is no life. We walk every day," he added, "This peace walk is the same. Without walking, you have no life" (Ghosananda, 1996). Initially officials attempted to dissuade the Dhammayietra organizers from planting trees along the route, but they persevered.

While planting a few trees seems harmless enough, criticism of the powerful in Cambodia has resulted in attack, imprisonment, exile or death. The current regime, brought to power under the UN program, will tolerate little criticism. The Dhammayietra recruits a small contingent of walkers from surrounding nations to join its activities in Cambodia each year. In 1996, two participating Thai Buddhist monks gave talks encouraging Cambodians to heed the lessons of Thailand, where the environmental destruction is great, forests are disappearing, and rivers have been polluted. They urged the Cambodians to protect their natural resources before it is too late. In this way, the Dhammayietra attempts to raise awareness of global issues on the local level.

A Model for Change?

Does this walk, and it's methods outline above, have any lessons for the world beyond Cambodia's borders? The Dhammayietra walks for peace have begun to receive international attention. *CNN*, the *New York Times* and regional news magazines have run short articles on the walks, but without any meaningful analysis of the method. A Canadian anthropologist has called the Dhammayietra a "new cultural ritual of re-membering through the creation of new collective memories, it will allow some Cambodians to emerge from the culture of violence created by the last 20 years of war and the Khmer Rouge era" (Skidmore, 1993-94, pp.35). This report suggests that the Dhammayietra is extremely culture specific, which would rule out the transference of this *form* to another conflict situation. However an analysis of the function of the Dhammayietras reveals useful lessons for activists elsewhere. An Australian nonviolence trainer has concluded that the Dhammayietra's work is a form of "Nonviolent Solidarity" (see the typology chapter by Robert Burrowes in this volume) with the intention to be present in a zone of military violence to share the danger with the local people and to highlight the suffering the violence is causing. This further generates awareness of, and support for, grassroots initiatives to halt the war. It also generates solidarity actions by grassroots activists and networks in other parts of the world.

While the methodology is one of solidarity with those suffering oppression, the fuel for this is compassion and wisdom. It is on these qualities in particular that Buddhism can offer clear guidance in the struggle for a nonviolent world.

Dhammayietra veterans and others have now set up the Dhammayietra Center for Peace and Reconciliation in Cambodia as a positive symbol for what ordinary people can do for a more peaceful and just nation. The Center is committed to using every opportunity to encourage empowerment of the people through nonviolence trainings and peace actions such as the walk. Almost as soon as one walk ends, villagers ask when the next walk will happen. "It is the only thing that gives us hope. Every other day all we know is war," claimed one from a village near the front line. The Dhammayietra Center and the walk Committee have responded:

> Our steps have given us courage. We will not stop now. We vow to continue the Dhammayietra, walking and working for peace every day, everywhere, throughout the entire country and world. We will not wait for foreigners to bring us peace. We have to persist in peacemaking every day, ourselves (report to funders on Dhammayietra 5 by Center for Peace and Reconciliation and the Dhammayietra Center, June 1996).

Powerful mass actions like the Dhammayietra can only manifest from powerful human experience. When a journalist asked organizer Kim Leng to talk about what sustains her through the hard work of preparing a Dhammayietra and the often blistering heat and other difficulties of walking in Cambodia, she grew quiet and then broke into tears and said, "Everywhere I have been I have met so many orphans," she sobbed, "so many widows, so many crippled by mines...now I ask the rulers of Cambodia to see the sorrow of the people and to stop their war." When asked how she could continue walking five times when they had not yet reached their goal of peace, she answered: "We know the road to peace is a long one, and there are many obstacles. But it is the only road. What is the alternative in the midst of all this violence? Do nothing? Then it's as if we're just lying around waiting to die."

NOTES

* An earlier version of this paper appeared in *Social Alternatives* (1997, vol.16, no.2, pp.18-22) under the title "One Million Kilometres for Peace: Five Years of Peace Action in Cambodia." The title refers to an average of 500 walkers multiplied by an average 400 kilometers per walk, times the five year history of the Dhammayietra, giving one million kilometers.

1   Samdech Preah Maha Ghosananda is a Pali scholar and respected Buddhist teacher. He is one of the only individuals of Cambodian descent who was able to move freely between all four combatant factions during the 1980s. He survived the Khmer Rouge time by being out of the country, practicing meditation in a forest monastery in Thailand. Although he lives in a temple in central Phnom Penh, he frequently travels abroad to meet with leaders of other religions, such as the Pope or the Dalai Lama. In 1996 he was nominated for the third year in a row for the Nobel Prize for Peace for his tireless work for the reconciliation of Cambodia, and for his ecumenical work around the globe.

2   Mine awareness training is usually given by nongovernmental agencies operating in Cambodia whose sole function is to educate the population on the danger of mines and unexploded ordinance in the country. They have devised a set of instructions as to how to judge a safe path or area, how to mark an area if mines are found, and how to evacuate victims from mined areas. The Dhammayietra has enjoyed a close relationship with these NGOs, and for the past few walks they have accompanied the Dhammayietra to further their outreach to the public. The Dhammayietra endorses the International Campaign to Ban Land mines, and mine awareness campaigns.

REFERENCES

Ghosananda, Maha. 1992. *Step by Step* (Berkeley: Parallax Press).
——. 1996. "On the March Again for Nonviolence," *Phnom Penh Post*, 31 May.
Global Witness. 1996. *Corruption, War and Forest Policy: The Unsustainable Exploitation of Cambodia's Forests* (London: Global Witness).
Shawcross, J. 1979. *Sideshow: Kissinger, Nixon and the Destruction of Cambodia* (London: Deutsch).
——. 1984. *The Quality of Mercy: Cambodia, Holocaust and Modern Conscience* (London: Deutsch).
Skidmore, Monique. 1993-94. "The Politics of Space and Form: Cultural Idioms of Resistance and Re-Membering in Cambodia," *Sandte Culture/Cultural Health*, vol.10, no.12, pp.35-59.

14

MIR SADA: THE STORY OF A NONVIOLENT INTERVENTION THAT FAILED

Christine Schweitzer

Introduction

About 3,000 people from Italy, France, USA, Mexico, Japan, Germany, Britain, Belgium, the Netherlands, Poland, Greece, Sweden, Norway and the Czech Republic arrived in the Croatian town of Split in the first week of August 1993. They went in response to an appeal to go to Sarajevo to stop the war in Bosnia. "Mir Sada—Peace Now," as the action was known, was prepared by two organizations: the Italian Catholic group *Beati i costruttori di pace* ("Blessed are the Peace-makers") which had organized the peace caravan to Sarajevo in December 1992, and the private French relief organization *Equilibre*. Independently, before joining forces, both had been organizing activities around the war in Bosnia: Beati planned three peace camps, in Sarajevo and in Croatian and Serbian dominated towns near Sarajevo, and Equilibre organized a demonstration of 100,000 people in Sarajevo.

If, after the rather symbolic visit of solidarity in Sarajevo the previous December, Mir Sada had been a success, it would have been one of the first direct nonviolent interpositions in a war. It would have been a big step forward in the discussion about alternatives to military interventions. However, the action failed almost completely. Not only did we not reach the goal, Sarajevo, but after a few days, organizers and participants split hopelessly. The rest of the story consisted of 14 days of discussion until almost everybody was close to nervous breakdown, and all returned home with the feeling "never again anything like this." But more is learned from mistakes than from successes, and so there is the hope that a thorough evaluation of the action (as is being carried out in the countries of most of the participants), will subsequently give some sense to Mir Sada.

Mir Sada: A Brief History

The meeting place of the Mir Sada action was a park area on the outskirts of Split. It had been transformed into a military base by the Croatian army and given to us partly as a camping site. The fact that there were not enough buses for everybody, as well as reports about severe fighting in Bosnia, delayed the departure of the first group for a day. Finally, transport secured for everyone, we left for Prozor in the south of Bosnia, where we erected a new camp on the shore of a beautiful lake. Prozor could be considered the limit of the war region. Behind Prozor there was intense fighting going on between Croatian and Bosnian ("Muslim") troops. From our camp we could watch, at short distance, grenades being shot towards the Bosnian-held area of Gornji Vakuf. This fighting finally caused the organizers at first to doubt the advisability of, and then to cancel, travel to Sarajevo.

The first to leave were Equilibre (who were responsible for the logistics of the action) with the majority of the French participants. They called those of us who stayed behind suicidal and a bunch of murderers. On that Friday evening a part of the second group of participants arrived (another part had decided to stay in Split after receiving information concerning security). Our relief on seeing the rear lights of Equilibre, in spite of them taking all logistical equipment with them, soon disappeared as the realization dawned that Beati was also only making half-hearted attempts at organizing the continuation of our trip. The proposal of several affinity groups to resume talks with the Croatian and Moslem commanders of the region, in order to inform them about our passage, were not even taken up in discussion. Instead, after two days, a proposal to return to the next UNPROFOR base to demand from the UN that they somehow open up a safe route for us was passed by a majority. It was at that point that the often mentioned unity of the project finally broke: some French participants wanted to go on their own to Sarajevo, others seriously threatened a "nonviolent" blockade of their cars, and six people from the American-international affinity group got their back packs out of the bus and started walking towards Sarajevo. (Eventually, after the Croatian military had threatened to arrest and deport them, an act that may have endangered the whole group, it was possible to persuade them to return.) Spreading the information that the road via Mostar to Sarajevo might be opened the next day, after one night at the UNPROFOR base, the organizers managed to convince the group to return to Split. Approximately 60 people decided at this point to leave the project and, in a bus, to go directly to Sarajevo. The majority of this group (some returned later to Split) made it eventually to their destination after facing some very dangerous moments on the journey.

In the meantime, the group which had remained in Split (along with Equilibre who, as we found out, had not really left) had planned an alternative action in Mostar. In front of a church in the Croatian part of Mostar a one-hour demonstration was held. Those who could not secure seats on one of the buses stayed behind, 20 kilometers from Mostar, and participated in a silent march towards the town, returning when they met the buses coming back from Mostar.

Mostar was the last action of Mir Sada. The next day some of the participants returned home, others spent four more days planning a second attempt to leave for Sarajevo, finally capitulating in the face of too many unsolvable organizational problems and the tacit resistance of the organizers. On the way back to Italy there were two demonstrations, in Aviano and Geneva, to protest against a possible military intervention by NATO.

Why Mir Sada Failed

The reasons for the pitiable failure of Mir Sada included the following factors:

Imprecision About the Goals of the Action. Looking at the original appeals of Beati and Equilibre as well as the common Mir Sada appeal, it is obvious how vaguely the goals were formulated. The Mir Sada appeal stated:

> Mir Sada is a nonviolent international action of humanitarian intervention, that has the following aims:
> • To stop the war, starting with a "cease fire" during the Mir Sada period,
> • To be in solidarity with each person suffering from this war, regardless of his/her ideology, sex, religion or ethnic origin,
> • To represent civil interposition against violence,
> • To support and encourage a multi-ethnic population to live together in Bosnia,
> • To implement negotiations that will go beyond armed conquest and will impose both respect for, and the safeguard of, human rights under international law.

Nowhere was the aim of stopping the war elaborated. For some it meant an appeal to the United Nations to make a ceasefire on our behalf. Others prepared a nonviolent interposition, that might have meant passing through Gornji Vakuf after informing both warring parties about our coming, or trying to reach the Serbian occupied part of Sarajevo.

Although it was discussed in many affinity groups and preparatory circles, the term "nonviolent interposition" in general remained quite vague for the group as a whole. The confusion became clear for everybody when the secretariat saw it as reason enough to send an urgent fax asking if the action should be further pursued when, one week before Mir Sada, the UN informed us that they did not support the action and counselled us not to go to Bosnia!

It also remained unclear what we would do in Sarajevo once we arrived there. Many affinity groups had prepared certain activities, for example working in a hospital, giving blood or doing direct actions, but nobody, with the possible exception of the organizers from Beati, had a clear idea which of those things could be realized.

Uncertainty About the Political Base and Positions Towards the War in Bosnia. To support multi-ethnic coexistence meant for some to support the Bosnian government, for others it meant strict neutrality and expressing solidarity with the victims of all sides. Only two weeks before Mir Sada, there was no agreement on talking to the heads of the Serbs and Croats in Bosnia since they were not internationally recognized! After this was finally done and Karadjic had answered that we should take Serbs with us out of Sarajevo, this demand was rejected outright by the negotiating people from Equilibre, without asking the opinion of the participants. Out of fear of being used by one side, the group rejected a later offer of the "Serbian Republic of Bosnia" to travel via Dubrovnik through its territory to Sarajevo, but without having information about the negotiations which had been going on.

In general the question of neutrality occupied many participants, especially those who had decided their participation when there was still the original plan of Beati of organizing three camps in all three parts of Bosnia—a plan which failed mainly because the hosts in Sarajevo, the International Peace Center, did not agree with it. Mir Sada never left the Croatian-dominated part of Bosnia and did not manage to manifest a critical stance toward this warring party. (The only exception was a demonstration in Split.) During our stay in Prozor there was the lasting rumor that the Bosnian troops did not attack Prozor because of our camping there. But we did not actually do anything for the Bosnian side which was shelled every day with grenades from a place about two miles from our camping site. A "half" interposition is not a successful example of interposition, but taking sides in a war!

But there were even more fundamental differences between the participants. There was no consensus on the principle of nonviolence. This was demonstrated in differences over the question of military intervention in Bosnia or an armed escort by UNPROFOR. The latter was again and again brought into the discussions and only rejected by a part of the group, while the other part did not see a contradiction between participants in a nonviolent intervention asking all sides to lay down their arms while protecting them with weapons. That there were different positions about military intervention had already become clear in the preparatory meetings of Mir Sada. When, during the Mir Sada action, that possibility became real for the first time, the result was that some of the participants (mainly the Americans) wanted to be present in Sarajevo to prevent an intervention, while others decided not to go to Sarajevo in order not to inhibit such an intervention. Whether this was one of the real reasons the organizers made us return to Split remains an open question. However, it is obvious that our hosts in Sarajevo feared exactly that.

Given such great lack of clarity, and the fact that it was built into the structure of the action from the beginning, it was not surprising that there were different opinions and positions on other issues as well. For instance, many people wanted to ask the UN, their own governments and local commanders, for permission to conduct the action, while others pointed out that governments never liked nonviolent actions and that at home they only informed the power holders of their decisions, rather than make themselves dependent on their permission.

To an annoyingly high degree I found sexist overtones showing up from time to time. This can be illustrated by a proposal in Prozor that the women should sleep in the busses since drunken soldiers might enter the camp, or by the refusal of the organizers to accept women as night guards.

The Preparation of the Participants. Beati asked for participation in a training course; Equilibre and the international secretariat did not. The level of preparation of the participants differed markedly depending on the office with which the national preparation committees had most contact. However, as had been the case in the previous December, the trainings of Beati were not sufficient to guarantee unity in the Italian group which split on the question of goals and methods in the same way as the group as a whole did. The best prepared group probably was that from the US, which assembled a large number of Plowshare activists. They had undertaken a long and thorough preparation for a direct nonviolent interposition with all its possible consequences. Many other participants had arrived with a similar attitude as people have when they go to a demonstration with possible police action: a little risky but the organizers will see to it that nothing happens. Again others had private reasons for going to Sarajevo, being attracted by the adventure or the desire to see what war is like. There were also differences among those who came to participate in a direct nonviolent intervention: some wanted to witness against the war and showed at least superficial indifference towards the risk of being killed. For others the effectiveness of the project was the main motivation. Many showed a strong religious motivation (mostly Catholic or Buddhist). Across all these categories there was a minority of those who knew the situation in Bosnia and had a realistic knowledge of the war while the majority lacked this experience.

The Flawed Structure of Organization and Decision-Making. As in their previous action, Beati pushed for work in affinity groups, and managed to persuade the French participants who arrived without affinity groups to organize their own. Nevertheless the speakers' council worked without imperative mandate of the speakers, being more of a parliament making its own decisions. The fundamental problem, however, was that over this democratic structure there was a second one, the structure of the organizers. There were the leaders of Beati, including a group of "permanents" willing to stay for three months (one group of six persons had already been in Sarajevo since the beginning of June), and the leaders of Equilibre. There was also the international coordination, consisting in theory of one delegate per country plus the representatives of Beati and Equilibre, which had met twice for the preparation of Mir Sada. This coordination had founded an international secretariat run by both organizations, but did not do much more than send out letters and contact UN and Bosnian politicians. On site in Split and Bosnia this coordination functioned only rudimentarily: after one day only French and Italians met, the other delegations were no longer invited. After the withdrawal of Equilibre, Beati increasingly took the sole leading role; after the action in Mostar Mir Sada officially was declared dead and all further activities were taken under the name of the original Italian action "We share one peace."

My impression, which was shared by many people, was that this inner circle of organizers manipulated the speakers' council and the ordinary participants. They were the only people to have all the information and very often it seemed that they gave us only those bits necessary for us to make a certain desired decision.

A big problem for the organizers probably was that of the responsibility they bore. Since they initiated the project they felt more responsible than those who came following their appeal. And of course it would have been them who were blamed by others, especially the media, if something had happened to participants of the action. When it became obvious that travelling on after Prozor bore a high risk, they did not feel capable of taking the responsibility for it. I think that this was also the result of an organizational structure which does not guarantee real equality between all participants.

Communication. Although consecutive translation in the plenaries and speakers' councils was organized, the dominance in numbers of Italian participants meant disadvantages for non-Italian-speakers. And, as already mentioned, the flow of information did not work. Rumors could spread without hindrance. And the answers to some questions are to this day unclear: for example, what happened during Mir Sada in Sarajevo? When did hosts in Sarajevo stop expecting us? Were we welcome or not?

More serious were the mistakes made in relation to the media. Here Equilibre must bear the major part of responsibility: they spoke of the fantastically high number of 100,000 people coming to Sarajevo. During the first coordination meeting they still said they expected 20,000 people, and two weeks before Mir Sada their information said 7,000. Finally, a few hundred people came from France! Perhaps it is useful when collecting money for humanitarian actions to give high numbers in order to get high donations, but peace actions are planned differently—nothing is more disastrous then giving higher numbers of participants than finally attend the action.

Mistakes in Relationship to Peace Groups in the Former Yugoslavia. Croatian peace groups were not even informed of the action although Mir Sada started in Croatia. On the other hand the cooperation with a certain group in Sarajevo, the International Peace Center, was perhaps too close. When this group criticized the plan of Beati to have camps also in the Croatian and Serbian part of Bosnia, Beati did not manage to adequately get across its independent position of solidarity with all victims on all sides to its Sarajevan partner. A task which admittedly would have been very difficult.

The Lessons from Mir Sada
How could things have been done differently? In preliminary discussions the following elements emerged:

- have an unambiguous and very clear formulation of the goal or goals of the action and see that those goals are realistic;
- have a shared and clear understanding of a common base like nonviolence before the action;
- see that everybody is conscious of the risk of such an action;
- only admit participants who share goals and the common base of the action;
- plan for as many problematic situations as you can think of before doing the action, for example: what to do in case of heavy fighting on the road? (who returns? who continues?) what to do

if stopped at a checkpoint? what possible alternative actions are available if the original plan cannot be realized?

• build a democratic structure which guarantees access to all information to everybody and gives equal responsibility to everybody. Determine specific roles where necessary (not everybody can negotiate with commanders or at checkpoints), but have a clear agreement on the limits of competencies before the action (as it is done with police and press representatives in nonviolent actions in home countries). Form groups of supporters responsible for media information and infrastructure before and during the action.

• ensure control of the participants over media, transport and logistics.

Of course those above-mentioned points (which may well need to be added to) cannot be a guarantee of success of an action. They are not solely based on the mistakes of Mir Sada, but also on experiences gained from other nonviolent actions, from the actions to stop nuclear tests in Nevada to the International Nonviolent Marches for Demilitarization. A direct nonviolent interposition in a war zone is not so different from those actions once the threshold of doing such an action has been stepped over. That this is possible was proved by Mir Sada—here were 3,000 people willing to risk their lives for peace, not for war.

Conclusion

The failure of Mir Sada is not proof, although some critics would like to see it that way, that pacifists are helpless once a war has started, and that in that case intervention is better left to the military. Even though it might sound paradoxical, Mir Sada was too badly prepared to allow for such a conclusion. There are examples enough that military actions fail. But pacifists still need to prove that they have got an alternative to violence. We said goodbye to each other in Split and Ancona being sure that we will meet again, better prepared next time and avoiding all the mistakes we made this time.

NONVIOLENT INTERPOSITION

Intention: to position nonviolent activists between conflicting parties to help prevent or halt war.

15

WITNESS FOR PEACE*

Ed Griffin-Nolan

On the Border of War

WANTED

Non-violent Christian women and men, immoderate in opposition to militarism and foreign intervention, for peace mission to Nicaragua-Honduras Border. Must speak fluent Spanish, have previous rural living experience in Third World, be of sound mind and body, and be prepared spiritually to stand and if necessary risk death alongside a people threatened with armed invasion by forces trained and outfitted in the U.S., Subsistence salary. Must be over 21.
draft of a Witness for Peace recruitment ad

On the night of 8 April 1983, the Contras all but destroyed *El Provenir* ("the future"), a tobacco farm that sat right on the border. Civilians and defenders were wounded in the shelling, which forced the eventual evacuation of the farm, one of the most productive in the country.

On the afternoon of 9 April, a yellow school bus pulled into what remained of the settlement. The tobacco warehouse was in cinders and smoke still rose from the gauze that shielded the tobacco fields. Spent shells lay all over the ground, and huge holes were dug out where the mortar shells had hit. Many of the brick homes, newly rebuilt following an earlier attack, had been hit again.

The militia guarding the rubble and the few remaining civilians stared as 30 dazed North Carolinians piled out of the bus. The group, representing ten religious denominations, had flown to Managua the night before for a one-week fact-finding tour. When they heard of the attack on El Provenir, they decided to set out in the early morning in the hope of reaching the border region that day to see for themselves. They had been on the bus since 4:00am. El Provenir was the last of three stops. The six-hour ride from the capital, the 100-degree heat, and the emotional devastation of their visit to war-ravaged communities had left the group exhausted.

As the group wandered from building to building, one of them, Jefferson Boyer talked to a few soldiers, youngsters who had come to work the crops and were now defending the farm. One of them pointed to a zinc-roofed hut on the horizon, across the border. It was Suicida's headquarters. Through the binoculars Boyer could see khaki-clad Contras strolling about.

"Why aren't they shooting now?" he asked.

"Because you're here," the soldier replied.

It was after 3pm. A three-hour ride still separated the group from the relative safety of Ocotal. "The bus driver is getting very nervous," said Gail Phares, a former Maryknoll sister who organized the trip for CITCA, the Carolina Interfaith Task Force on Central America. "It is not a good idea to be on that road after dark." It was an uncharacteristic understatement for Phares, who ran such study tours with the same loving but stern hands she once used as a young schoolteacher in the distant mining town of Siuna, in Nicaragua's northern rain forest, two decades ago.

That was before the war. Now her main concern was getting a bus load of exhausted gringos safely back to Managua. The sun sets quickly in Central America. Suicida's commandos were within a few miles. It was time to say goodbye to El Provenir.

Boyer and some of the others were already thinking about staying. "It really got to us," he says. "The tobacco warehouse had gone up in smoke, the gauze was on fire, [and] all the buildings."

The visitors were ordinary, middle-class Americans from the United States. They were mostly churchgoers from North Carolina: eight pastors, a few academics, a housewife, one congressional aide, and a retired IRS employee. Their average age was over 40. Most of them had children. Most were seeing Central America for the first time. The Nicaraguans did not want them to leave. They brought the group to a tin-roofed house on the edge of the property. Blood coated the floor, and a child's pair of shoes sat in the middle of the room. More bloodstains marred the walls.

A young mother stood trembling in shock inside. Her three children and her mother had been taken away in an ambulance that morning. An infant, two toddlers, and their grandmother were all injured in the overnight attack. She didn't know if they were dead or alive. The fear and anguish on her face told the delegation more about the war in Nicaragua than a week of meetings or years of reading.

The driver was calling them. They started slowly toward the bus, saying goodbyes, shaking hands, embracing these people they had just met, making pledges not to forget. The woman began to cry. Men and women of the delegation cried with her. Boyer held her. "What the hell are we doing?" he called out to no one in particular. "We can't just leave these people."

Yet the bus was about to leave. "I knew that the most important thing that group of people could do would be to get back to the United States and to tell the story of what had happened," said Phares. That didn't make leaving any easier.

"Holding that woman was the most empty gesture I've ever made in my life," remembered Boyer. "I said, 'cuidese, señora' [take care, ma'am]." The bus driver wanted to go. Boyer went to the back of the bus and broke down. Phares tried to comfort him. "To this day," Boyer said solemnly five years later, "I think we failed those people. We should have stayed."

That day, looking at the faces of his companions, he could see they were all feeling the same combination of rage, helplessness, and a measure of culpability. The eyes of the woman who was trembling inside that house would not leave them. Their government had provided the mortar shells and trained the men who aimed them at that house. The bus engine came to life and the odor of diesel feul mixed with dust as the driver hurriedly put them back on the road south, away from the border.

Inside the bus, Phares kept repeating just one thing, "Somehow," she said, "we have to find a way to stop this war." Boyer thought back on the soldier's words. The Contras, funded by the United States, would not dare attack while US citizens were in town. In his anger he blurted out, "If the United States is funding this, then let's put fifteen hundred... volunteers here to stop this fighting. If all it takes to stop this killing is to get a bunch of Americans down here, then let's do it."

"We kinda laughed at first," says Boyer, "but out of that we started talking about having a vigil." By the time they were back on the paved road and darkness had set in, the mood on the bus shifted from horror and outrage to anger and determination, and as the night settled, an exhausted sense of hope.

Back in Managua, Phares told Sixto Ulloa what had happened and raised the idea of a peace vigil on the border. Ulloa, a radical teetotaling Baptist, was a founding member of CEPAD, the Evangelical Committee for Aid to Development, and now directed the agency's international relations. A flowery speaker who loved earthy parables and new ideas, Ulloa lit up when he heard the idea. He imagined it as a prayer vigil for peace at the very heart of the war. Sixto immediately set to work arranging meetings with government and church leaders.

By this time the imaginative Carolinians had in mind an invasion of 1,000 US Christians. Over the next week they met with leading government figures Ernesto Cardenal, Sergio Ramirez, and Interior Minister Tomas Borge.

It was a hard sell. The meeting with Borge took place beside a pool at a fancy house in the hills outside Managua. When the group presented the idea, Borge, a short, stocky, enigmatic man who can be kind and poetic or tough and crude, leaned back with his cigar in air for just a moment. "I myself would go to that place on the border and risk my life there. But I won't permit any North American to die in that place. It would be wrong for us to allow any one of you to receive a bullet that was meant for us."

The ever-optimistic Phares remembers that he also suggested that perhaps in another place, where the situation was a bit more controlled, such a vigil would be possible.

Ulloa then set up a meeting with Daniel Ortega, then head of the governing junta. Ortega's response was less ambiguous. "One thousand people? Why not 5,000?" The Sandinistas had always felt that the more international visitors who came, the better, but they did not yet fully understand the implications of this proposal. Nor did those who were doing the proposing.

Through the muggy Southern spring of 1983, Gail Phares, Jeff Boyer, and the others confronted the task of organizing an international pilgrimage within two months. They sought a national organization to sponsor what was now being called Action for Peace in Nicaragua, but no existing peace group, Central American organization, or denomination could carry the ball. It was too much, too soon, and a bit crazy to boot.

They organized a battery of volunteers who worked the phones at the CITCA office day and night for weeks. "I have no idea what the phone bills were those two months," says Boyer, "but it paid off." Working with networks such as the American Friends Service Committee and Clergy and Laity Concerned, with numerous regional and local task forces concerned with Central America, and with the New York-based Interreligious Task Force on Central America, they recruited, screened, and trained 153 people from 40 states, people willing to go to the border and risk their lives to "stand with the Nicaraguan people."

Laying the Foundation
> To develop an ever-broadening, prayerful, biblically based community of United States citizens who stand with the Nicaraguan people by acting in continuous nonviolent resistance to US covert or other intervention in their country. To mobilize public opinion and help change US foreign policy to one which fosters justice, peace, and friendship. To welcome others in this endeavor who may vary in spiritual approach but are one with us in purpose.
>
> Original statement of purpose, Witness for Peace

The mail at the Resource Center in Santa Cruz made for some interesting reading once applications for the first Witness team of long-term volunteers started to arrive. It was one thing to ask people to give up a week and travel to a war zone; quite another to ask people to give up their job, their family, maybe their life, and go live there. But applications poured in, and their pages told the stories of challenging lives salted with a willingness to risk.

Four applicants were ready, willing, and able to go on the first of October. Among them they had more than 30 years of experience living in Latin America. Russ Christensen, a burly, bearded lawyer from Maine, had served in the army as a paratrooping medic during the Korean War. Since then he had worked with the development agency CARE in Central America and Chile, married and had two children in Costa Rica and run for state office in Maine. Rose Dalle Tezze was a non-nonsense Sister of Mercy from Pittsburgh. As a community organizer and administrator, she had worked in Peru and in Puerto Rico. South Dakotan Dan Anderson had worked as a Peace Corps advisor to the Honduran Boy Scouts during the 1970s. From that vantage point he watched Nicaraguan refugees fleeing the war and learned of the brutality of the Somoza regime. Janet Wenholz was a middle-aged housewife in Corpus Christi, mother of three grown children, and formerly a partner in a family insurance business. In 1968 she had moved her family to Colombia when her draft-aged son decided he would not go to Vietnam.

In their pre-trip planning the Witnesses tried to anticipate every possibility they might face in Nicaragua. During endless hours of training in a Quaker Peace Center in the Redwoods, volunteers from the Resource Center tried to help them recreate the tenor of life in remote Central American town like Jalapa. They rehearsed dozens of scenarios they might face. The preparations took on the atmosphere of protracted frenzy usually associated with Apollo moon launches. After the Santa Cruz training, they were ready to fly to Managua when word came that the steering committee had put them on hold until after an organizational meeting planned for 8 October in Philadelphia. The delay meant that the promise of David Sweet, a professor of Latin American history, and member of a large group of North Americans peace vigilers who made a second trip to Nicaragua in July, of having a team on the ground by 1 October would not be met.

Philadelphia
The Philadelphia meeting proved to be the time of definition for Witness for Peace. In one long weekend, disparate concepts of the organization's goal and purpose were discussed and debated by 20 people.

In a marathon session at the Convent of the Good Sheppard a statement of purpose and plan of action were distilled, a national coordinator hired, and the principles that would guide the organization into the '90s —faith basis, nonviolence, and political independence—were set out in a covenant.

The steering committee contained members from a variety of political and religious cultures, who were veterans of struggles as old as pre-World War II pacifism and as current as the nuclear freeze. Each brought the culture and the issues of the struggles that had been central to their lives over decades. Middle-aged Presbyterians concerned with structure and order had to learn to work with New Age Westerners who worried such concerns threatened to imprison the very spirit they sought to set free in Witness. Modern evangelicals and activist Catholics found themselves at home together as they looked for ways to focus attention on Nicaragua and to channel that attention into creating a movement to change US policy.

The most important person at the meeting was a woman who hadn't planned to go, whom few of the participants knew, and who slept through many of the sessions. Yvonne Dilling, from Fort Wayne, Indiana, had been working until recently with Salvadorean refugees in Honduras. She was in the United States for treatment of a recently diagnosed case of Hodgkin's disease. In Washington between chemotherapy treatments, she wanted to visit friends in Philadelphia and hitched a ride with Jim Wallis and Joyce Holliday, who told her on the way about Witness for Peace.

"My hair was one-fourth of an inch long," remembers Dilling,

> I had to take a nap every two hours. All I wanted was to see some friends and relax. Jim said, "Why don't you stick around?" So I stayed for a couple of hours. After the first night I called my friends to tell them I wouldn't be there until tomorrow. For the rest of the weekend all I did was listen, sleep, and call my friends every half hour to tell them I was still busy. And then at the end of the weekend they asked me to be the national coordinator.

Dilling accepted, despite worries about the strain on her health. "It was just that kind of thing. You knew you had to do it," she said later. Her presence on the staff helped give the project the credibility it needed to make the leap from the wild idea to viable undertaking.

The group had just enough experience to know that there were philosophical issues that had to be faced, and enough impatience to get things moving. They tackled three key philosophical issues that were to undergird Witness for the rest of the decade.

Faith Basis. One of the thorniest questions was religious identity. The April CITCA delegation and the July Action for Peace had been explicitly and exclusively Christian in their language, style of worship, and public image. Sojourners felt strongly that the Witness, born of an ecumenical delegation and married to Christian agencies in overwhelmingly Christian Nicaragua, should be "Christian and welcoming to others." In a memo prior to the meeting, Jim Wallis wrote:

> The stronger the religious identity, the stronger will be the Witness. The concern for a "prayerful, biblical approach" and ...a strong Christian character is, I think, critical.... If the identity were more liberal and secular, or, even more problematic, left or Marxist in character, it would be easily written off by the U.S. government and press and would not attract the numbers and kind of people whom we need.... And [the] risk factors of the vigil require a strong spiritual rootage, as well as keen political perspective.

John Collins, a Methodist, disagreed, arguing from his experience of coalition work in the struggle against the war in Vietnam. He cited two elements of the issue: (a) to identify the organization as religious would alienate secular activists; (b) to identify it strongly with Christian churches would alienate Jews, Buddhists, Unitarians, and other non-Christians or "post-Christians."

Collins and other felt that the use of specifically Christian language and symbolism was wrong in principle because it would exclude people who were important to the social justice community and foolish in practice because it unnecessarily limited the support base. They suggested an alternative statement noting that participants derived strength from a number of sources, including Rabbi Abraham Herschel, King, Gandhi, and Christ. Wallis countered that the core of the Reagan administration's arguments against Nicaragua was its appeal to fundamentalist Christian values and an attempt to equate Sandinismo with an "evil empire." Only from a position as credible church people, he argued, could they muster the public attention and moral authority to combat such charges. It was pointed out that the administration also labelled the Sandinistas as anti-Semitic, a charge best answered by groups with a strong Jewish identity. The administration also pointed out Sandinista mistreatment of the Miskito people, a charge that might best be answered by Native Americans, who might be reluctant to work with a Christian group.

Based on her work in Honduras, Dilling believed that the team in Nicaragua would need a common language and resources for prayer and reflection, and that a fuzzy identity might inhibit the vital spiritual life essential to the project. "The last thing you want to be doing when people you love are getting killed is worrying about whether your prayer is going to offend someone," she offered. That sentiment carried the day.

After much debate, a statement of purpose drafted by Bob Bonthius was adopted. It described Witness for Peace as a "Prayerful, biblically based community." Witness delegations to Nicaragua accepted people who were "comfortable" with a prayerful, biblical approach, even if they were not identified with any particular faith.

The final sentence of the statement of purpose committed Witness for Peace "to welcome others in this endeavor who vary in spiritual approach but are one with us in purpose." In practice, however, the profile of the organization remained decidedly Christian for several years. Every newsletter for the first year carried New Testament scripture readings or a reference to Witness participants as Christians on its front page. The press release for the first delegation was titled "U.S. Christians Launch Witness for Peace in Nicaragua." The internal correspondence, the prayers that began each conference call, and reflections at the various gatherings, both in the United States and in Nicaragua, had an almost unanimously Christian flavor.

Nonviolence. Witness for Peace embraced just-war theorists, crusading absolute pacifists, and a collection of struggling souls somewhere in between. Gail Phares was concerned that the Witnesses not go to Nicaragua "preaching" nonviolence. She worried that "first-world pacifists" might impart a judgmental or holier-than-thou attitude toward the Sandinistas, which she found particularly enraging given that the United States was making war on them. There was consensus that Witness was to focus its peacemaking efforts on silencing the US guns.

Everyone agreed that participants, at a minimum, had to agree to practice nonviolence while involved in Witness for Peace activities. This "lowest common denominator" approach allowed room for people who viewed nonviolence as a way of life and for those who saw it as just as a tactic. While they resolved the issue in the negative sense, by making it clear what could not be done (e.g., pick up a gun in case of attack), the discussion did not get far on the positive side. The covenant committed each participant "to nonviolence in word and deed as *the essential operating principle* of Witness for Peace." The question remained open as to how actively nonviolence was to be employed as a means to achieve the organization's goals.

Dick Taylor felt that risky nonviolent actions, including interposition, should be at the core of the Witness experience. Gail Phares took the opposite tack, arguing that risking the lives of Witnesses was foolish; it would only scare people away and deprive the movement of valuable activists. This difference in conception had been visible behind the scenes at the July vigil. Before going to Nicaragua in July, Dick Taylor had talked over the idea of interposition in Jalapa with Mennonite author Ron Sider, who has a keen interest in the subject. In June the *National Catholic Reporter* referred to the upcoming Action for Peace as a "human shield." Meanwhile Joe Moran, associate director of CITCA, was telling the press that he would make absolutely sure that the road was safe before he let the group travel to Jalapa.

The conferees got down to more practical matters, such as the length and number of trips to Nicaragua. David Sweet had envisioned a long-term team living in Jalapa for months at a time as the essence of Witness. Paddy Lane and Scott Kennedy of the Fellowship of Reconciliation tended to agree. Gail Phares pressed for an avalanche of short-term visits, some as brief as seven days, "to tear open people's hearts, open their eyes, and blow their minds." She wanted to start organizing these visits right away.

The question of risk arose again. Dick Taylor, Jim Wallis, and Buddy Summers stressed that willingness to risk was essential to the experience, and that the prayerful vigil in a war zone was what made Witness different from the many other groups already sending study or work groups to Central America. Phares felt that risking was irrelevant. "Expose people to the reality," she said, "and they'll come back rarin' to go. That road is too dangerous to be out driving on unless we absolutely have to." Buddy Summers felt that delegates absolutely had to share the risk in order to understand and faithfully convey what the Nicaraguans lived through every day. Dick Taylor went further and expressed his hope that, if a Witness bus were blown up by a mine one day, "we would be willing to be back on the road again the next day."

Long-time Latin America activists had suspicions about nonviolent activists. Phares felt the urgency of getting people to Nicaragua and back again and had little time or patience for the idea of a nonviolent crusade. She saw the key to changing US policy as the careful selection of delegates who would bring pressure on Congress to cut off the Contras. "Some people had this romantic idea," said Phares, "that we'll go to Jalapa, and just sort of be there at the border—crazy! We didn't see ourselves as martyrs. We needed organizers, not dead people."

Phares and others like her in movements of solidarity with Latin America had not looked at nonviolence seriously, particularly after the mortal failure of Salvador Allende's Peaceful Way to Socialism in Chile when the military overthrew his government in 1973. When the US-backed coup brought General Augusto Pinochet to power, thousands were killed or disappeared, and the progressive movements were decapitated. It was taken as a lesson by the left throughout Latin America that state power equalled military power—liberation movements were not interested in hearing about nonviolent means.

To a generation of Latin America activists who had come of age in the '60s and '70s, pacifism was a weapon used against the poor, a means of maintaining the status quo. The political culture of pacifists seem to them ill-suited to the rigors of a struggle where torture and disappearance could happen at any time. "We had problems," Phares recalled years later, "with people being soft, being nice all the time. Then I hear about Gandhi saying that violence was better than doing nothing," she says, "and that didn't sound so bad." Just-warrior Phares heard that from Dick Taylor, of whom she once said, "Dick taught that true nonviolence in not preaching.... I learned that it meant creativity."

Dick Taylor helped to open ears. A white haired, six-foot-two-inch teddy bear of a man. Taylor had spent part of the 1950s as a development worker in El Salvador and most of his time since then as an organizer for nonviolent projects or as an author writing about them. An avid canoer and champion body surfer, Taylor was particularly fond of action on the high seas. He had written a book about the efforts—similar to Greenpeace actions—of a group of his friends to stop the shipment of US arms to Pakistan by using canoes to blockade the arms vessels in the Philadelphia harbor back in 1971. In the early 1970s he miraculously escaped death when a train carrying arms bound for Vietnam passed over him as he knelt and prayed on railroad tracks at a New Jersey arms depot.

In a 1984 memo he defined nonviolence as:

> a way of fighting for human liberation which involves the following elements:
> 1. Faith and trust in God.
> 2. Active struggle against evil, injustice, or oppression.
> 3. Removal of support or cooperation from unjust structures.
> 4. Refusal to use violence or killing to achieve ends.
> 5. Willingness to suffer personally, rather than to inflict suffering on others.
> 6. An effort to express goodwill toward all, including opponents, as persons made in the image of God.
> 7. Openness and truthfulness, guided by love.
> 8. Constructive program of concrete work to create and point to a new social order.

Words like these were food for thought to people who tended to associate nonviolence with passivity. To hear of nonviolence as a form of fighting for something and not just a personal life-style choice was a revelation. There was movement in both secular and religious circles to develop the use of nonviolence as a means of conflict resolution. Almost simultaneously with the founding of Witness, the Mennonite and Brethren churches began to work on selecting and training recruits for Christian Peacemaking Teams, ready to move to areas of conflict to serve as a nonviolent witness against war, even positioning themselves in harm's way if need be. No group had ever been able to sustain such a presence in a war zone in a foreign country, though the World Peace Brigades had tried in East Africa during the Zambian and Namibian independence struggles of the 1960s. Witness was seen by some as a continuation of that tradition.

Bob Bonthius was still concerned with making Witness a witness for pacifism rather than a witness to the need to change US policy. A former pacifist, he took pains to elucidate his own vision of nonviolence and to insist that the organization not assume that all who partook at the table were absolute pacifists. He wrote that "vocational pacifism has an important role in societal change but...is not an option for nation states." He worried that the organization might focus more on means than ends, or that it would exclude people other than absolute pacifists.

The group agreed that the long-term team would be supplemented by short-term visits on a rotating basis. The long-term team would maintain a permanent vigil and would host the short-termers, referred to as "rotating vigilers." There were to be two types of short-term delegations: a one-week, fact-finding trip for those whose time was short and propensity for risk low, and a two-week trip for people ready and willing to share the perils of riding to Jalapa and standing with the people.

The week-long delegations were soon discontinued. More people signed up for the "risky" two-week delegations than anyone had expected. Their willingness to risk travelling to the heart of the war and accompanying the people most at risk came to distinguish Witness from other groups. As it turned out, the greatest risk was not facing death but facing conversion, as they encountered what Henri Nouwen called "the most heartrending suffering and the same time an incredible hope."

Political Independence. Feelings at the Philadelphia meeting regarding the Sandinistas ranged from enthusiasm to skeptical support. The July experience had generated such good feelings about Nicaragua and such awful feelings about the Contra war that it seemed obvious who wore the white hats. Nonetheless, the founding few found the wisdom to make a distinction between opposing US policy and supporting the Sandinistas.

While most had high hopes for the Sandinista program, and some had played prominent roles in solidarity activism, the group agreed that Witness for Peace would attract more people and ultimately have a greater impact if it were careful to preserve its independence from the Sandinista government.

Nicaragua's most prominent evangelical leader, Gustavo Parajon had reminded the July group that his loyalty was not to the Sandinistas but to their *actions* on behalf of the poor. "Put not your trust in princes," he had said, quoting from Psalm 146. Jim Wallis warned in a memo that

> the U.S. government...will attempt to dismiss the vigil simply as a group of Sandinista sympathizers.... The project must be independent enough to include those who are very sympathetic with what the government in Managua is trying to do, as well as those who have legitimate concerns about its current direction, and of course, those who feel both things.

This bothered some, particularly John Collins, who felt that what Nicaragua most needed was people willing to clearly state their support for all the revolutionaries were trying to do—land reform, state control of vital resources, literacy, health care, and so on. Merely opposing US policy did not go far enough; he, like many in the Central America movement, felt that defending the intrinsic value of the revolution in Nicaragua was one way to highlight the need for such changes here in the United States.

Dick Taylor countered that if the organization were to call itself pro-Sandinista, "we would spend all our time defending the government in Managua rather that focusing on what our government is doing." Meetings with Miskito leaders and *La Prensa* had made him feel that the Sandinistas, while their program contained many positive points, should not be placed above criticism.

In the end, the group recognized that even among those in the room, there was no shared impression about the Sandinistas. This, as much as the force of any argument, pushed the group to affirm an independent course. Witness for Peace became an anti-intervention organization, quite distinct from a solidarity group.

Three days of debate produced a statement of purpose that remained unchanged for more than five years.

For many, the sense of community that grew within delegations, among the long-term team, and within local support groups back at home was the most attractive feature of the organization. Activists who had burned out during the war against Vietnam found that the commitment to working as a community, with all its difficulties, was enough to make the difference between sticking with it or jumping ship when the going got rough.

The community had limitation that would have been striking to anyone who peered in the window of the convent in Philadelphia. First, like many peace groups, the founding group was all white and highly educated. The programs they devised, the culture, and the image that began to evolve made Witness appeal to white, educated people. In later years Witness struggled to overcome this limitation by conscious outreach and inclusion efforts, which produced mixed results.

Second, no one from Nicaragua was present. This omission made it very difficult to get a reading from the Nicaraguans about the appropriateness of the group's actions. Since a basic value held by all was that Nicaraguans should have say in what happens to them, this omission now seems all the more glaring. Failure to incorporate Nicaraguans into decision-making roles left Witness for Peace permanently exposed to the dangerous virus of paternalism.

After the Philadelphia meeting, Witness for Peace was here to stay. A six-member executive committee (Bonthius, Holliday, Phares, Summers, Sweet, and Dick Taylor) agreed to meet each week by telephone. Wallis agreed to organize an advisory committee of religious leaders. National offices were established in Washington, DC, Durham, North Carolina, and Santa Cruz, California. Buddy Summers became the first executive secretary. Within a month, 17 delegations were on the schedule, extending into mid-1984, and the names of 19 advisory committee members adorned the letterhead.

By mid-November Witness had $25,000 in hand, $13,000 in grants expected, and four regional pledges totalling $1,100 per month. CITCA also donated $2,000 for the Durham office. Twenty-seven local support groups were functioning around the country, and seven regional Witness for Peace offices soon opened to support the local work, recruit volunteers to go to Nicaragua, publicize the Witness, and carry our public policy work.

The Philadelphia meeting demonstrated that the organization was able to tolerate diversity of opinions. Individuals who differed could find ways, in their local or regional activities, to carry on in ways consistent with their own priorities, keeping the main purpose in mind. Geography may have been their saving grace. If everyone who came together for the founding had lived in the same town, Witness might never have gotten off the ground. Distance and cumbersome memos and conference calls that became standard fare in Witness caused their share of miscommunication, but they had their up side. There was too much leadership experience and too much history, but when those leaders were given specific functions to perform and spread around the country, they found they could work together and stimulate one another. Without decentralized operations, Witness for Peace might never have survived its birth.

Jalapa's Open Heart

On 18 October 1983, Sixto Ulloa drove to the Managua airport and picked up the first team of long-term volunteers. He steered Dan Anderson, Russ Christensen, Rose Dalle Tezze, and Janet Wenholz through the maze of customs and immigration, helped them change money and find their luggage, and then lodged them with his in-laws, a prominent Baptist couple, Eugenio and Candalaria Zamora.

Just as the team got to Nicaragua, the war ended. Or so the US public was led to believe. On 20 October, Congress voted for the second time to cut all aid to paramilitary groups fighting in Nicaragua. In practice, aid shipments to the Contras barely skipped a beat, as the administration took its war underground. The vote didn't make any difference in the countryside, where the attacks continued and the death toll was rising every day.

The new arrivals spent a week finding their way around Managua, one of the world's most confusing cities, and getting acquainted with government agencies, the US Embassy, opposition political parties, and the Catholic Church hierarchy. They would later be taking many short-term delegates to visit these same organizations.

Ulloa and CEPAD were the lifeline for the team, supporting them emotionally as well as logistically. Ulloa fervently believed that the US churches had the potential to prevent a US invasion and to turn the war around, and he worked feverishly to get Witness off the ground.

At the end of the team's first week they were jolted by news of the US invasion of Grenada. Managua was gripped with a sense of fear and defiance—the government believed Nicaragua was next on the Reagan hit list. The new team went to a rally of tens of thousands of Nicaraguans protesting the invasion. Activists around the United States reacted with rage. More than anything else, the Grenada invasion brought people active on other peace issues to the recognition that the Nicaraguan revolution was in mortal peril as long as Ronald Reagan occupied the White House.

On 27 October, Witness for Peace arrived in Jalapa. As the group rode through the Segovia mountains, two Spanish nuns, Sister Marimer and Sister Esperanza, narrated the history of each bend in the road, a chronology of the triumphs and travails of four years of revolution. Their stories of ambushes and mine explosions, accompanied by the visual evidence of rusting hulks of vehicles, were grim reminders of how precarious life in Jalapa could be.

The sisters, along with a Basque priest, Father Lucinio, and a Sacred Heart sister from Boston, Liza Fitzgerald, quickly became guides and soul mates for the new team. The team was impressed by their pastoral work, which was rooted in an evolving liberation theology that identified closely with the revolution. Though the Catholic church in Latin America had shed some of its reflexive conservatism in recent decades, the Nicaraguan bishops, who had opposed Somoza, viewed the Sandinistas with suspicion and did not look kindly on pastoral workers mixing religion with revolutionary politics. From the start, Witness for Peace was identified with the base communities and the progressive sectors of the Catholic church.

The Witness' "job description" was still a bit vague: to witness and document the impact of the war and to share the life of the people. The threesome (Janet Wenholz had returned to the United States) quickly put flesh on those words. At dawn the next day Dalle Tezze and Anderson went with the nuns to pick corn at the community of Santa Cruz while Christensen travelled to another cooperative to pick coffee.

Anderson and Christensen often worked the coffee brigade organized by the evangelical churches, and they began a friendship with the pastor of the Assembly of God church, Nicaragua's most conservative. They worshipped with that church, one of four evangelical congregations in Jalapa. The pastors were key figures in the rural areas and good sources of information because they often ventured into areas where they had contact with both Contras and local farmers. Winning the trust of conservative evangelicals, many of whom had family and fellow church members in the Contras, was no easy task, but by working and worshiping with them, they were making headway.

Dalle Tezze worked with the nuns tending to the needs of the many refugees pouring into town. They held classes for the children and helped distribute food and medicine within the six refugee communities forming outside of town. She soon began to feel as if she never wanted to leave.

Christensen began to organize an exchange of children's drawings between Nicaraguan and US kids. Anderson made plans for a photo essay documenting the work in the tobacco fields. The team went about trying to fit themselves into everyday life as best three gringos can in a small rural Central American town. They learned to eat ice cream and sip Coke from plastic bags—bottles and cups were in short supply. They came to know where and when the best fruits showed up at the marketplace, they spent hours chatting with people at the local eating place run by a woman named Reina, and they attended church, school graduations, parties, and, increasingly, the wakes of young men killed in the mountains.

On the one hand, they wanted to be as inconspicuous as possible, to fade into the woodwork and become part of the town, the share the trials and joys of everyday life. On the other hand they were supposed to make their presence as visible as could be, both to publicize the impact of the US-backed war and to deter attacks.

Each morning the team met for biblical reflection and, during most of December, they held a nightly vigil in the town square. Russ Christensen, who was reacquainting himself with Christian rituals and was learning about nonviolence for the first time, remembers those nights looking out into the darkened mountains where the Contras were moving about as a time of personal transformation and healing. "We held candles. We were always surrounded by Nicaraguans. There was a strong sense of solidarity, of standing up to an immense power that was wrong. And you did it by love, not shaking a fist. It was a message of love. That was very good for me."

And always they carried a question with them. Did the fact that these few people were there, holding candles and writing letters home, actually stop Contra attacks? Honduran jets and helicopters were flying over the nearby village of Teotecacinte every day. At night strange, shiny, silver, lighter-than-air balloons floated over the valley from the north. Their purpose was never determined, but they spooked the population. Reagan had invaded Grenada just days earlier. That same week a Contra force devastated the town of Pantasma, killing 37 people and scrawling "for God and country" on the walls with the blood of their victims.

"I came to believe that [our presence] was [a deterrent]," says Russ Christensen. "Most of our friends in Jalapa, in the trucks on the way to the fields, with us living in Jalapa, they felt safer...."

"Some of them came with the idea that their presence alone would be enough to stop the war," recalled Francisco Machado, a soldier stationed in Jalapa who later became a government leader in town. "But they quickly learned," he adds with a smile. Like many Nicaraguans, he saw their support as more symbol than substance.

Sixto Ulloa says without hesitation that the presence of Witness for Peace kept the Contras from mounting another assault on Jalapa. "Witness for Peace...made the counterrevolution move away [from Jalapa]," he said. By visiting the resettlement communities, Witness extended a certain amount of protection to those areas as well. On the chance that visitors from the United States might be in the community, he believes, the Contras had to avoid attacking. Dr Parajon, too, found the idea of the Witness being a deterrent "very logical."

Most Witnesses saw their role as being somewhere in between. "I don't think anyone came down looking to be a martyr," remembers Doug Spence. "The idea of standing up and taking a bullet never appealed to me. I never thought it was a smart idea. We perceived ourselves as a presence that would make the US government think twice before attacking. If it didn't stop them, they would at least have to take responsibility for whatever happened."

Arturo Cruz, who served for a time as one of the directors of the FDN (Nicaraguan Democratic Frorce, a part of the Contra organization), said in an interview six years after Witness took up its role in Jalapa that he would not expect the presence of North Americans to make a difference in the plans of the Contras. By his analysis, some field commanders cared nothing about civilian casualties of any nationality and others were very careful to avoid endangering civilians.

The presence of US citizens may have been more of a deterrent against a direct US invasion than in deterring hostilities from any particular Contra group. Contra troops typically owed their loyalty only to a single field commander. The field commander would not know precisely just who was or was not in a town they planned to hit. Pentagon planners, on the other hand, had to consider long and hard the implication of invading a country so thoroughly overrun with North American civilians.

After the Grenada invasion, the Committee of US Citizens Living in Nicaragua began weekly protests at the US Embassy to say that they did not want to be rescued by Marines. Francisco Granados, who succeeded Ulloa as bus drivers for the delegations, said in 1988, "I think that this Witness has been fifty percent of the reason that this señor [Reagan] has not invaded us." It is hard to calculate the impact of this kind of deterrent act. Claims of triumph are easy to discount; the reality that the US Marines never landed is not.

Short-Term Delegates

The long-term team fulfilled David Sweet's idea of a small community of US citizen's living at the open end of the barrel of US militarism. But that was just part of the Witness idea. Gail Phares's proposal for a perpetual, rotating presence of US citizens to go to Nicaragua and come back to tell what they had seen and heard was the other half. Over the next seven years nearly four thousand people travelled to Nicaraguan war zones as part of what became the biggest exchange of church people between the United States and Latin America since the Catholic church launched the Papal volunteers program in the 1960s.

The first short-term delegation arrived on 2 December 1983, the third anniversary of the murder of the four US churchwomen in El Salvador and the beginning of Advent. They had left Washington, DC, after an emotional commissioning service at which family and community members bid farewell to their loved ones and prayed for God's blessing upon them.

Vincent Harding, a veteran in the black freedom struggle, referred to the delegation as joining the "cloud of witnesses" that the apostle Paul refers to in Hebrews 12. Harding sounded a theme of faithful defiance. "The message," he said, "to the people of Nicaragua, is that there are men and women of love and compassion who refuse to give consent to our government's intervention. Regardless of what our government does, we are filled with the spirit of another authority and we will act on that authority as long as we are able."

The Washington service marked Witness for Peace's debut in the national media. Dennis Marker and Sojourners carefully cultivated an image counterposing the mainstream background of the participants with the risky nature of what they were doing. "These were US Christians going into a war zone—ordinary people motivated by conscience to do a radical thing," said Marker. "That's the image we wanted to get across."

Ordinary people—extraordinary risk: that is exactly what the media conveyed. *Newsweek* referred to them as "Christian soldiers" in a full-page article. The *Washington Post* said the

> team of Church members will leave tomorrow for Nicaragua's war-torn northern province where they plan to form a 'human shield' along the border. They hope their presence in the area will discourage attacks by U.S.-backed counter-revolutionaries.

The initial press release, controversial within the steering committee because of the emphasis on interposition, read as follows:

> The aim of the witness is to provide...a "protective shield" between the Nicaraguan people and the U.S.-sponsored contras.... The group hopes that the constant presence of North American church people in the war zone will hamper the operations of the contras.

It was the clearest statement before or since of Witness as a shield. It was also widely successful and drew the media like flies to honey. An NBC camera crew made the whole trip with the delegation, and at one point three TV crews were covering their time in Jalapa. Most of the coverage focused on the risk and the hope of preventing attacks.

Some Witnesses resented the implication that instead of "standing with" the Nicaraguan people they were standing between them and the attacking Contras. "That phrase 'shield of love' drove me right up the wall," recalls John Collins. "We would be just silly if we didn't recognize that the real shield for the Nicaraguan people was the Nicaraguan army. The army had strengthened its position in Jalapa, and no one could seriously assert that attacks had dropped off due to the visits of delegations or the presence of a few long-termers."

To some, the idea of standing between the Nicaraguans and the Contras smacked of paternalism and superiority, precisely the attitudes which had justified so many instances of US government and corporate intervention in Latin America. Douglas Schirch, a Mennonite biochemist who came to work on the long-term team, was attracted to Witness because of the shield idea but later rejected the idea as "condescending, first world-ish." Anything that is done has to be done with the Nicaraguans, not for them," was his conclusion.

Getting Organized
Witness' great strength was the burning moral outrage of its returnees. Its most frustrating weakness was an inability to focus those energies. From the latter part of 1983 through 1985, Witness sent more than 1,000 people off into the most important experience of their life, but it had no national organization or strategy to involve them in upon their return.

Stateside organizing went on, but support from the national and regional organizations was spotty. The lion's share of the steering committee's efforts in 1984 and 1985 focused on setting up the Nicaragua portion of the Witness. In fact, it would be an exaggeration to call Witness for Peace in the United States a "movement" before 1985.

After the Philadelphia conference in October 1983, the steering committee did not meet again in person until February 1985, in Santa Cruz. Monthly meetings of the full committee and more frequent meetings of subcommittees were held on the telephone. Membership on the national steering committee was serious business. The term lasted three years, and the job required a commitment to dedicate substantial time, energy, and resources. It was a working body, and anyone who didn't put in their time was asked to leave. A number of members were full-time volunteers.

While Witness was getting organized, other Central American organizations, both religious and secular, gladly put the returned Witnesses to work. A Central America movement had been growing for years before Witness for Peace.

The Central America Resource Center in Texas listed more than 500 US groups dealing with Central America in 1985 and more than twice as many two years later. These groups maintained audiovisual resources, speaker's bureaus, telephone trees, and information hotlines; held regular vigils and leafleting; visited editorial boards of newspapers; set up tables on street corners and at community events; and conducted teach-ins, sit-ins, and campaigns of civil disobedience.

What Witness did in its early years was energize people, providing a ready supply of activists for other organizations concerned with Central America. It also redirected toward Nicaragua the energies of many groups that had been focused on El Salvador. Returnees sometimes formed their own Witness chapters, but more typically they worked with an existing local group. In North Carolina it was CITCA; in Nebraska, Nebraskans for Peace. In northern California, the Resource Center for Nonviolence was the focus. In Texas and Oklahoma the American Friends Service Committee (AFSC) played a major role, as it did in New England. In St Louis the Catholic Worker community became the focus of Witness for Peace activity; in Cincinnati the New Jerusalem Community offered its support. Activists in the Midwest came to rely on the Chicago Religious Task Force and Detroit's MICAH (Michigan Interfaith Task Force on Central American Human Rights).

Washington-based organizations like the Washington Office on Latin America, the Coalition for a New Foreign and Military Policy, and the public policy offices of religious denominations provided information on legislative developments. As the war escalated, dozens more national organizations formed or dedicated their ongoing efforts to the Central America struggle.

The decentralization of Witness, which some participants advocated and others accepted reluctantly, created its share of confusion. Returned Witnesses received mail from Santa Cruz, from Durham, from Washington, DC, and in some cases from regional offices as well. In addition, national Witness for Peace eventually opened a development office in Syracuse, New York, mailed its newsletter from Ellsworth, Maine, and later from Berkeley, California, and asked that contributions be sent to 198 Broadway in New York City or to any one of 11 regional offices.

A satellite photo of Witness for Peace in the United States in 1984 would probably have shown something resembling what TV meteorologists refer to as "scattered storm activity." The number of local Witness groups grew from 27 in November 1983 to 90 in April 1984. Responding to the call of the spirit and the pleas of the Nicaraguans, veteran organizers and social-action novices worked together with every last ounce of energy to expand their base of supporters, to recruit more volunteers for delegations and the long-term team, to gain access to the media, and to protest an endless series of aggressions against Nicaragua.

No one knew how long the war would go on, but already Witness was committed to staying on the border as long as the war continued. As time passed and it became clear that the struggle would be a long one, the process of recruiting, training, and sending a delegations to Nicaragua became more routine and organizers were able to dedicate more time to the war at home.

A real spirit was moving, a rebel spirit battling the complacency, the materialism, the militarism of the times. In churches and religious communities across the country, small voices were questioning the right of a mighty nation to bully its smaller neighbor, and more people began to listen.

They tugged at the edge of the nation's conscience while powerful forces sought to put conscience to sleep. But individual witness was not enough. Witness for Peace faced a challenge in the United States as daunting as facing the Contra threat. Could they organize the necessary political pressure to change the policy? Would the same people who were drawn to such risky witness be capable of and willing to build the type of organization to sustain what was clearly going to be a prolonged struggle? Translating moral outrage into effective political pressure is one of the most difficult areas faced by religious groups.

Effectiveness Versus Faithfulness
Activist participants promoted organizing for direct political action right from the start; they faced uneasy resistance from those who stressed the primacy of prayer, out of which would grow witness and symbolic action. Some believers insisted that planning actions solely on the basis of immediate impact was inappropriate. They felt that symbolic actions had a great potential to inspire even if the immediate consequences could not be measured, and that to focus only on strategic goals placed the soul of the organization at risk. "God gives the increase," or, as the Nicaraguans would say, "Uno pone, y Dios dispone" (You do your part, and God decides how it turns out).

Radical Christians are easily motivated to symbolic witness, but often ambivalence about power makes organization building and strategic planning tough going. The cloud of witnesses referred to in Hebrews 12, and which Vince Harding referred to at the first commissioning service, was also a cloud of losers by earthly standards. The New Testament is a story in which the good usually come up on the short end of the stick, and their ancestors in Israel did not fare much better. Consciously or not, many Christian groups feel ambivalent about power and about winning. The religious wing of the Central America movement often seemed more comfortable commemorating martyrs like Archbishop Romero than standing with victors like the Sandinistas.

From a very different perspective, long-time leftists like David Sweet wanted Witness for Peace to explicitly reject attempts to influence either Congress or the media and to let the message from the border work its way into the hearts of people and effect change at the grass roots. The results, he agreed, were unpredictable, but the results of traditional political organizing, while predictable, were unsatisfying.

Such attitudes often led to a reluctance to jump into the "messy deal" of politics. As political organizers pointed out, the religious right suffered no such reluctance.

Nothing trains people as well as experience. The difficulty of working with the power structure in the United States on a foreign policy issue was drummed into Witness for Peace by hard experience. From the *Cleveland Plain Dealer* of Tuesday, 12 June 1984:

> *Washington*—When a group of Ohioans went to Nicaragua this year they risked their lives in territory contested by U.S.-funded rebels.
>
> When Ohioans, part of the non-denominational Witness for Peace program, returned to Cleveland they were met by 200 people carrying palm branches and praying for peace.
>
> But when the Ohioans took their story to Capitol Hill yesterday they were seen by only a handful of congressional staff members. One meeting to which 135 staffers were invited was attended by half a dozen.
>
> "Congress seems a much harder nut to crack than the average American," said Doug Van Auken of Cleveland.

Confronting this hard reality convinced many that to be faithful they must learn also to be effective, and it led to some of the most spirit-filled and effective campaigns that Witness conducted.

Reform Versus Revolution

"Witness for Peace," says Bob Bonthius, "is as reformist as you can get. That may not be a good thing, but it's about the best thing we [progressive movements] have going for us."

The focus on legislation, effectiveness, and "respectability" had important long-range implications for Witness. It won acceptance and cost a bit of prophetic zeal. Witness gained a spot in the national debate about Contra aid but had no chance to challenge the assumptions underlying foreign policy. It gained adherents in the East and lost them in the West. It truncated the nature of the dialogue occurring between US and Nicaraguan people of faith by reducing many issues to a question of how they affected votes on Contra aid. As the need to dialogue with and curry favor with legislators became more prominent, Witnesses found that they had to be on top of the legislator's agenda (US National Security), which was a world away from the agenda they heard expressed by the Nicaraguan campesinos (peace and life for them and their children).

It also kept Witness primarily within a middle-class constituency and may have been an important reason why Witness "won" the battle against Contra aid and the most important reason they "lost" the struggle to change US policy at its core. As it entered the nineties, Witness for Peace began to work more and more with third world communities in the United States.

The more radical members bemoaned the fact that Witness, as it grew, came to focus on short-term goals. Father D'Escoto, while not proposing to change Witness strategy, concurred that the problem went far beyond the Contra war. "The question," he said, "is not what is the future of Nicaragua, but where is the United States going, and what is the future of the world with this monstrosity developing in the US? Someone has to stand up for the sake of world peace and for the sake of your very nation itself. You find so many good people in the United States talking about helping to save Nicaragua, and I say, `My God, please save your own country.'"

But was there ever another realistic option? The Nicaraguan government as well as CEPAD and the other partner agencies were encouraging US groups to work to defeat Contra aid as a first priority.

The challenge was to harness the energy without cooling the fire of Witnesses who returned from Nicaragua like burning embers of moral outrage, to convert that outrage into effective political pressure without diluting the message. The future will tell how many Witnesses transfer their insights gained in Nicaragua to other struggles.

Means Versus Ends—The Experiment in Nonviolence
Witness for Peace struggled to develop more effective use of nonviolence. Some believed that the experiment in nonviolence was an end in itself and an important part of the organization's identity. They pushed for ever more risky and visible forms of direct action, in the tradition of King and Gandhi.

Others advocated more traditional forms of political action, which were seen as appropriate to the predominantly middle-class constituency that they hoped to attract. They felt that people who would cringe at throwing blood on the Pentagon wall but who would be glad to write a letter to Congress should still be able to feel comfortable within Witness. No one disputed the value of the letters, but many within Witness felt that it had the potential to be more than one more generator of mail to politicians and editors, to be a moving force at the edge of the resistance movement.

At is happened, Witness held together both nonviolent activists and traditionalists. A synthesis of political strategies began to emerge as the organization started to gel. The May 1984 newsletter gave a hint of the synthesis of organizing styles that Witness was to become:

WFP is beginning to build on our nonviolent strategy in Nicaragua for nonviolent actions in the U.S. But we are not forgetting the wide range of traditional political actions needed to convince candidates that U.S. foreign policy in Central America is an issue that they cannot ignore. Support for candidates who propose change in U.S. policy, opposition to those who support the present policy, petitions, door-to-door contacts, public debate, media exposure, rallies, demonstrations, local congressional office sit-ins; these are some of the many nonviolent political means available.

The effectiveness of this combination of nonviolent direct action with more traditional political tactics may be one of those lasting lessons of Witness. Many people were arrested or otherwise risked themselves in nonviolent action as a result of Witness, and many nonviolent activists took a second look at the value of traditional reform tactics. This combination was not invented by Witness. Martin Luther King worked relentlessly on behalf of civil rights legislation as he was jailed dozens of times for civil disobedience. The environmental group Greenpeace has used this combination consistently and effectively on issues for a long time.

The movement, like a train, needed both an engine and tracks to get where it wanted to go. The nonviolent direct actions, both in Nicaragua and in the United States, provided the steam and the fire, while the legislative strategies served to assure that the train got somewhere instead of just spinning its wheels and generating smoke.

Contingency Plan
One goal of the October 1984 Citizen's Hearings [on Nicaragua, organized by Witness for Peace] was to build the "Contingency Network," a plan of action in case of a US invasion of Nicaragua. This commitment had been foreshadowed by "A Promise of Resistance," adopted at a November 1983 peacemakers retreat at the Kirkridge Center in Pennsylvania. Meeting for prayer and reflection in the aftermath of the Grenada invasion, the authors condemned the invasion and warned that it "raises the real possibility of a similar scenario in Nicaragua."

In the event of an invasion, they committed themselves to "assemble as many North American Christians as we can to join us and go immediately to Nicaragua to stand unarmed as a loving barrier in the path of any attempted invasion, sharing the danger posed to the Nicaraguan people." They also called on US Christians to surround or occupy congressional offices in a nonviolent, prayerful presence until the invasion ended.

The idea of a massive presence in Nicaragua at the time of an invasion was dramatic. It was also wildly impractical and would scarcely have been permitted by the Nicaraguan government in time of full-scale war. No one knew this better that its organizers, who hoped and prayed that the mere threat of such actions would be enough of a deterrent to force the policy planners to take them into account.

Over the coming months, the Contingency Plan was refined through discussion with the Witness Philosophy and Strategy Committee, Nuclear Freeze, the InterReligious Task Force, Fellowship of Reconciliation, and others. In August, "A Pledge of Resistance," was launched with an article in *Sojourners* magazine.

The Contingency Plan, and its later incarnation, the Pledge of Resistance, was signed by over 70,000 people and attracted national attention. It captured the imagination of people all over the country and provided an outlet for many who fiercely opposed the US policy, wanted to do more than write letters, but could not travel to the war zones themselves. With the founding of Witness for Peace, the religious community had made it clear that by attacking Nicaraguan border villages the Reagan administration risked killing its own citizens. "Now," said Jim Wallis when the Pledge was announced, "if Reagan invades Nicaragua, he's going to have to put thousands of US Christians in jail around the country."

Witness for Peace was part of the original "signal committee" charged with deciding when and what the Pledge signers should be called on to do. Pledge signers were called on many times to commit civil disobedience or to hold other protest activities throughout the years of wrangling over Contra aid votes. With the implementation of the Contingency Plan, Witness could rightly claim that the two pillars of its strategy—nonviolent direct action and traditional political action—were in place.

Looking to the Future: "We Have Only Started"
The statement of purpose committed Witness to a nonviolent presence. Witness became a pioneer in the use of nonviolence. No one had maintained an intentional nonviolent presence of such magnitude in a war zone for any length of time. Witness set up a truly permanent, flexible presence and has spent six years in the war zones. Witness expanded the uses of and explored the limits of interposition, learning that such a tactic must always be tied to a larger strategic conception of social change if it is to be effective. The nonviolent presence came to include symbolic marches and vigils, accompaniment of individuals and communities in danger, fasting, work projects, peace flotillas, and a host of other actions.

Witness combined prophetic, dramatic actions with analysis and political work to capitalize on the attention generated, and it did so *on a sustained basis*. As the situation in the war zones changed, the response changed as well. Two crucial lessons for the future can be learned from this: Prepare for the long haul, and be prepared to be flexible and to adapt to circumstance. If Witness had been married to a given tactical notion at the outset, it would have fizzled as soon as the Contra offensive against Jalapa did. And if the organizers had not been willing to stick it out for the long haul, the early actions would have remained isolated gestures having little or no impact. From the peoples' struggle in Central America they learned that work for social justice cannot be conceived in terms of single actions or campaigns. In a struggle that has gone on for centuries and where the work of a lifetime can barely be measured, we are either in it for the long haul or we are not in it at all.

Witness is not a model that can be exactly duplicated. Nicaragua was a revolutionary society open to the presence of US citizens, willing to allow them to risk, and one in which long-standing ties between the churches existed. Particular circumstances in El Salvador and Guatemala have called forth different responses, such as the accompaniment of refugees going back to El Salvador, Peace Brigades' accompaniment of human rights workers. Central American governments, with the exception of Nicaragua, have been hostile to the presence of such groups. Yet openings occur and determined people can find ways to do meaningful work.

Some elements of the Witness experience can be generalized, such as the need for careful screening, training, and sensitivity to the local culture. The development of partner relationships with local people and agencies and ongoing consultation is also key. Importantly, practitioners of their own brand of nonviolence must recognize that people of other cultures have their own experiences that can teach us about creative nonviolence.

NOTE

*   Reprinted with permission from Ed Griffin-Nolan, *Witness for Peace: A Story of Resistance* (Louisville: Westminster/John Knox Press, 1991). Selections from pp.23-9, 57-68, 70-7, 94-97, 100-102, 104-5, 230-31.

16

THE PERSIAN GULF WAR AND THE GULF PEACE TEAM*

Robert J. Burrowes

Introduction

The Gulf Peace Team had its origins in the idea of sending a team to the border between Iraq and Saudi Arabia as part of the struggle to prevent war in the Persian Gulf in 1991. The idea in one form or another had occurred to several people simultaneously around the end of September 1990. However, it was Pat Arrowsmith, a veteran peace activist in England, who took the initiative of ringing several people and organizations in order to gauge the level of interest in the idea. Subsequently, Arrowsmith and David Polden—secretary of a local Campaign for Nuclear Disarmament branch—called a meeting of interested people on 1 October 1990. The meeting discussed several possible projects including the idea of standing in for the western hostages held by the Iraqi government. From this meeting a working committee evolved. It decided on the name "Gulf Peace Team" and used the name in a letter released to the press calling for volunteers and donations. It also drafted the policy statement which included the important words:

> We are an international multi-cultural team working for peace and opposing any form of armed aggression...by any party in the Gulf. We are going to the area with the aim of setting up one or more international peace camps between the opposing armed forces. Our object will be to withstand nonviolently any armed aggression by any party to the present Gulf dispute....
> We as a team do not take sides in this dispute and we distance ourselves from all the parties involved, none of whom we consider blameless.... (Gulf Peace Team, *Constitution*, 1990, p.1).

In November the composition and objectives of the Advance Party were decided. Given the refusal of the Saudi government to respond to its approaches, the working committee decided that the Advance Party would proceed to Baghdad and attempt to negotiate an acceptable "protocol" for the peace camp with the Iraqi authorities (Gulf Peace Team, *Background Notes for 12 November 1990 Meeting*, p.1). It also decided that the Advance Party would seek a series of assurances, including the following: the camp would be located "near the border between Kuwait and Saudi Arabia, between the Iraqi army and the Saudi border;" the camp would be autonomous both logistically and in terms of internal management; the policy statement would be published in the Iraqi press and there would be freedom of communication and travel (Gulf Peace Team,*Letter to His Excellency the Ambassador of Iraq*, 13 November 1990).

The Advance Party
On 16 November the Advance Party travelled to Amman where some preliminary arrangements were made and a member of the party met Princess Zein of Jordan. The party flew to Baghdad on 18 November and was accommodated at the World Peace and Friendship Camp on al Aaras Island; this became the Baghdad base of the Gulf Peace Team.

After three weeks of meetings with officials of the Organization of Friendship, Peace and Solidarity as well as members of the Iraqi government, on 6 December the Advance Party was informed that permission had been granted to establish a camp. A few days later a site was chosen at Judayyidat Ar'ar on the Iraqi-Saudi border about 420 kilometers south-west of Baghdad. It was a pilgrims' resting place at the Iraqi border post on the road to Mecca.

It was agreed that the camp would be autonomous and that there would be media access to the camp. However, while the Team would buy its own food and pay for transport, water would have to be supplied by Iraqi tankers. Despite some obvious logistical dependency and some concern that they were accepting too much from the Iraqi authorities, members of the Advance Party felt that they had largely achieved their original objectives.

The Gulf Peace Camp
The Gulf Peace Camp was established on 24 December 1990 when the first group of camp volunteers travelled from Baghdad to Ar'ar. The camp was about 500 by 200 meters in area and enclosed by a high perimeter fence. It contained a long line of corrugated iron roofs (without walls) under which there was a line of joined tents. There were showers and squat toilets in two old caravans. A kitchen area was created in a large shed.

On 31 December, some Iraqi officials, several television crews, a member of the European Parliament and several more volunteers arrived.

During a news conference, an open letter which Team members wished to present to the "Commanders of the International Armed Forces" on the Iraqi-Saudi frontier was read out. After some initial encouragement, this proposal was blocked by the Iraqi government. On 1 January 1991, the Iraqi officials, media and many volunteers left. There were just ten activists left in the camp.

At the Baghdad base during the early days of January, there was evident fear among activists about being in the border camp at the expiry of the UN Security Council deadline on 15 January. Regrettably, the poor organization and communication which had characterized the project so far reinforced this. There were rumors about large contingents of people coming but few arrived. Accordingly, the number in the camp built up only gradually. After twelve last minute departures, at the expiry of the UN deadline at 8am local time on Wednesday 16 January 1991, there were 73 people (45 men, 28 women) from 15 countries in the Gulf Peace Camp.

At 3am the following morning the entire camp was woken by the sound of heavy bombers heading for Baghdad; the Gulf War was about to begin. It is impossible to adequately describe the impact which the outbreak of war had on the Gulf Peace Camp given its implications for the camp as a whole and for the individuals within it. Physically, it meant an immediate, indefinite and unknown threat to our collective and personal security which was complicated by our limited supplies of water, food and fuel. Politically, it challenged our commitment to nonviolence and raised new questions about the relevance of our presence. Emotionally, it was highly disturbing as people dealt with their anger, fear, sadness and despair.

Nevertheless, from the outbreak of war until we were evacuated to Baghdad on 27 January, we had the chance to discuss and explore many aspects of our nonviolent vision.

Life in the Camp
While the routine and community spirit evolved slowly in the camp as we improved our processes for working together, it was clear that particular issues as well as the special needs of some people were going to cause ongoing problems. Moreover, there was some tension in the camp between those people inclined to use traditional ways of dealing with conflict and those committed to trying more creative ones.

Most major issues discussed at camp meetings entailed both ideological and practical considerations. They included debates about the decision-making process itself and the approach to problem-solving (typified by the discussions over the diminishing food and fuel supplies).

In addition, two other important issues were discussed informally and in the affinity groups. One concerned how to deal with the personal problems caused by the stress of living through the war. The other concerned how to deal with the problems created by people with special psychological needs.

Decision-Making. Some time after the camp was established, it was decided to use consensus rather than majority voting as the basis for decision-making. While numbers in the camp were low, this was practical even at full camp meetings. However, as the numbers grew, it became apparent that a declining proportion of people were genuinely involved in camp decision-making—fewer people were attending camp meetings and relatively few had the chance to speak. This was complicated by the number of activists who did not speak English or for whom it was not their first language. In addition, several meetings were poorly facilitated or were not well focused. The latter problem was often the result of peoples' genuine fears about the war or the result of little self-discipline—the camp had its share of people, especially men, who seemed unaware of, or unconcerned about, the rights of others to public space.

At a meeting on 16 January the camp decided to form affinity groups. While the Australians and Indians had always functioned as national affinity groups, it took a day or two for the new groups to settle. Eventually, six affinity groups emerged: they became known as the Australian-American group, the Circle Song group, the Dutch group, the Indian-Japanese-Belgian (Indian) group, the Rainbow group and the Tent group. The next day the camp decided to form a Steering Committee: it consisted of one representative from each affinity group and its purpose was "to make decisions between camp meetings." It was agreed that affinity groups would rotate their representative every few days and that attention would be paid to national and gender balance. In practice, this committee subsequently took responsibility for coordinating camp activities. From this point onwards, more emphasis was placed on involving people through their affinity group. However, six people were never involved in any affinity group and several others only participated on the margin.

While the process of discussing issues in the affinity groups and reporting group decisions through the Steering Committee representative worked quite well, and several issues were satisfactorily resolved in this manner, the camp was never able to reach consensus on the question of how to make decisions if and when this process did not work! Only one affinity group was against using "majority vote if necessary"; it favored persevering with the affinity groups and steering committee structure even when consensus was difficult to achieve. We were evacuated before this issue was resolved.

Problem-Solving. Dealing with problems in the camp entailed a great deal of emotional and practical energy. This was characterized by the problems related to the declining food and fuel supplies. The food shortage had an increasing impact on camp life. At the outbreak of war, and given the uncertain duration of our stay, we decided to ration food stocks by having only two meals each day. These meals became progressively lighter. With time and increasing hunger, disputes over how long our food stocks would last, disagreement over how much food should be cooked at any one meal, and concern over whether we could replenish our supplies (which effectively depended on whether our main Arabic speaker, Saadallah Atrib, could get permission and a vehicle to travel out of the camp) were all causing tension and arguments in some quarters.

After several attempts to deal with elements of the food problem, the matter came to a head one week after the war started when it became clear that there were serious problems associated with the food supply. Specific concerns included the fact that cans of food were "disappearing" and that some people were feeding the stray cats. The people concerned were unresponsive when approached by members of the Food Committee and were largely outside the affinity group structure. Members of the Food Committee were obviously frustrated and clearly felt that attempts to use trust had failed. The Food Committee was now strongly suggesting that the kitchen be locked and the Steering Committee wanted feedback on this suggestion. Again, the camp was evacuated before this issue was resolved.

Coping with the Stresses of War. While living in the camp, people dealt differently with the stresses of war. Some appeared largely unaffected; at least in the sense that they were clearly functioning normally. Others were deeply affected and responded in different ways.

One popular response was to keep busy by performing a range of camp tasks. Others participated in some of the many workshops on such topics as nonviolence, Middle Eastern politics and learning Arabic. Some played games—including table tennis or soccer with the Iraqis—and others engaged in a sunset routine of singing and dancing. Some meditated or put more time into their religious practices. A tent was set aside for meditation and prayer. Junsei Terasawa, the Buddhist monk, spent each sunrise and sunset chanting. Father Bob Bossie SJ and Uniting Church Reverend Neville Watson organized a daily bible study session. Peggie

Preston offered her time as a listener for anyone who wanted to share their feelings privately.

In contrast to the military which presumably copes with the stresses of war by relying on such factors as discipline, obedience and routine instilled through training, it was clear that in our participatory and egalitarian community whatever discipline and routine evolved had to do so in a very different way.

People with Special Psychological Needs. The camp routine was regularly disrupted by the activities of some people with special psychological needs. This caused considerable frustration and tension at times and complicated attempts to deal with a range of issues from the camp decision-making processes to the food shortage.

While it may have been possible to marginalize those people with special psychological needs in the same way that mainstream society had done, this would have further complicated camp life. And it may have been disastrous. Because of the confined space our community occupied, it was not possible to escape from the problems within it. Moreover, there was considerable energy in the camp to listen to these people in order to find meaningful ways of addressing their particular needs. In this way, some became contributing members of the camp community within the short duration of the camp's life.

For the camp to evolve into a genuine community, it was clearly imperative that its structures and processes were designed to satisfy the needs of the people within it. In addition, we needed a process designed to restore people's sense of responsibility for their personal behavior. Some members of the camp were committed to trying to facilitate this.

Evacuation
Ten days after the outbreak of war, two buses and a truck arrived to evacuate us. We left the Gulf Peace Camp at 11am and arrived at the Al Rasheed Hotel in Baghdad that evening. There was an excited reunion with 11 team members still in the capital. There was no electricity; water was only available in the hotel for one hour each day. We had a very light meal in the dining room which made us immediately aware that there was a severe food shortage in Baghdad as well.

After dinner we were urged to go immediately to the bomb shelter. Several of us decided to return to our rooms first and when we did so we were immediately caught by the display outside our heavily soundproofed windows. We could see the bombing and the anti-aircraft fire right across the horizon. We could see plumes of black smoke where bombs hit and the red line of tracers racing into the sky. Sometimes the noise was so loud that we could hear it despite the sound-proofing; on at least one occasion we all ducked instinctively for cover as a loud bang went off near the hotel.

During our four days in Baghdad we asked the Iraqi officials to show us civilian damage caused by the war. We were taken on a tour of the milk factory—supposedly a chemical weapons plant—destroyed by US bombing. We were shown around Yarmuk Hospital where we saw civilian victims of the war and noted the severe shortage of instruments, bandages, medicines and anesthetics. We were also shown a suburban shopping center and other buildings that had been bombed. A brief expedition to a Baghdad bazaar gave us the chance to talk to Baghdadis and gauge their reaction to the war. They were still very warm towards the "peace messengers." We shopped briefly which allowed us to gauge the sudden increase in price of some commodities; bananas were now $1.50 each!

On 31 January we travelled west along the secondary highway to Jordan; there were several bomb craters in the road as well as several burnt-out vehicles including a truck carrying grain that was still burning. We arrived in Amman at 3am on the following day.

The Gulf Peace Team: An Assessment

The Gulf Peace Team experience allows the opportunity for a new and wider round of debate, as well as a critical reassessment. Like its historical antecedents, the Gulf Peace Team raised several issues which are critically important to the theory and practice of nonviolent interposition. These include vital questions in relation to politics, strategy and organization. Some of these questions are discussed below.

Political Questions. The Gulf Peace Camp raised at least three important political questions. The first relates to the camp's purpose. The existence of the Gulf Peace Camp represented the idea (and the ideal) that a peaceful solution to the Gulf crisis was possible if appropriately selected nonviolent actions and problem-solving processes were employed. Was it merely symbolic? Or did it have real potential to intervene? Is the main impact of interposition physical or political?

Was the real aim of the camp simply physical interposition, intended, as the policy statement and constitution suggested, "to withstand nonviolently any armed aggression by any party"? Was this even realistic—particularly given the numbers involved? Or was the aim of the interposition primarily political—designed to help build a global consensus against war? To the extent that these questions had been considered, there were clearly different views in the camp itself. For example, 13 activists—presumably committed to the importance of the physical nature of their interposition—chose to resist evacuation on the basis that they might be able to physically resist violence by the Iraqi army at least. It was patently clear however that 73 people were not going to be able to physically resist the violence of two military forces totalling a million combat personnel, although, in some circumstances, there would have been political and symbolic value in trying to do so. The difference in numbers does not, in itself, make physical resistance impossible nor morally inappropriate. However, it does raise important questions about strategy and tactics and the wisdom of these.

It is evident that the Gulf Peace Camp was primarily a symbol that carried political, psychological and moral weight. And it was clearly the physical location of the symbol which gave it power. It was a symbol of nonviolence that challenged the legitimacy of war. It was a symbol of courage that inspired people to act. And it was a symbol of morality that touched the conscience.

The second question concerns the camp's precise location: should the camp have been nearer the Kuwaiti-Saudi border? While the Advance Party's concern that such a site may have been seen to be defending the Iraqi occupation of Kuwait, it seems clear (at least in retrospect) that the final site offered and accepted on the Iraqi-Saudi border was too far from Kuwait, particularly if physical intervention during the land war was seriously envisaged. More fundamentally however, did the Gulf Peace Camp, located on a land border between two armies, serve the interpositionary purpose in the context of a war fought essentially in the air? The early "battles" of the Gulf War were bombing raids on the cities of Iraq and Kuwait; they were not land battles fought across territorial boundaries. Should there have been several Gulf Peace Camps located in Baghdad, Kuwait City, Riyadh and Tel Aviv?

The third question concerns the camp's neutrality. Given that the Saudi Arabian government refused to respond to requests for a camp on the Saudi side, was the Gulf Peace Team genuinely neutral? Was it seen to be neutral? The *Shorter Oxford Dictionary* defines "neutrality" as "not assisting either party in the case of a war between...states" and the Gulf Peace Team's constitution made its neutrality explicit: "We ...do not take sides in this dispute." But the question of neutrality is not a simple one. What constitutes "assisting either party"? The camp was clearly located on the Iraqi side of the border. Did that compromise our neutrality? The Gulf Peace Team was not on the side of any government; but that did not stop various parties trying to use it for their own ends. Did that compromise our neutrality? As a camp, we were clearly not on the side of the

Iraqi government, but we were logistically dependent on it. Did that compromise our neutrality?

It is evident that the location of the camp at the Iraqi border post—rather than on neutral territory or in conjunction with a second camp on the Saudi border—was a second best option given the refusal of the Saudis to negotiate. But, in itself, this did not constitute a violation of our neutrality: it was not "assisting either party." Nevertheless, the camp's location did improve its potential as a propaganda tool. While there is little evidence to suggest that Iraqi officials used the Gulf Peace Team explicitly or widely for this purpose (perhaps because there were too few people in the camp), it clearly had some value in this sense. More importantly perhaps, some critics (including some in the media) associated with the US-led coalition were keen to discredit the camp on this basis or to use it for wider criticisms of the peace movement generally. It is clear that the camp had some propaganda value for both sides but it would be difficult to substantiate the claim that this compromised its neutrality.

The most difficult aspect of the neutrality question concerns the Gulf Peace Camp's logistical dependency on the Iraqi government; this was clearly less than desirable. However, while this may have been seen to compromise our neutrality in the opinion of some observers, it did not effect the declared political neutrality of the camp. In this sense, the camp was little different from a Red Cross operation: dependent on a host government for a range of services, but politically neutral. What seems clearer is that once the war broke out, our continuing dependency on the Iraqi government for supplies and transport used increasingly scarce Iraqi resources and, in that sense, we were obviously assisting (in a very small way) the US-led forces. At this point, it seems clear, the camp was no longer technically neutral.

Strategy. While the Gulf Peace Team had a stated policy of "working for peace...in the Gulf," it never had a strategic aim and a strategic plan to guide its efforts. Moreover, the conditions necessary to make the project practicable—including knowledge, skills, independent access to resources, high degree of philosophical cohesion, organizational framework, communication channels (especially links with grassroots networks) and determination—were insufficiently met. In addition, the Gulf Peace Team did not attract enough participants who were deeply involved in, and representative of, their local grassroots networks and who, by their presence, could provide the rallying point necessary to galvanize substantial numbers of people to resist the war. How was the Gulf Peace Team supposed to help stop the war?

At no stage did the Gulf Peace Team consider formulating a strategy of its own or consider how its initiatives fitted any wider peace movement strategy to stop the war. The goal of establishing the Gulf Peace Camp was always the focus of attention. And while the camp itself did have a vaguely worded aim—"to withstand nonviolently any armed aggression by any party"—as the main tactical expression of the Gulf Peace Team project it was devoid of strategic guidance. Nonviolence theory would suggest that the power to stop the war rested largely with the domestic constituencies of the nations in the US-led coalition. The Gulf Peace Team's power hinged on its capacity to influence and mobilize those constituencies. Lacking a clearcut strategy for doing so, any successes in this regard reflected the initiative of particular support groups back home or were incidental.

Despite these shortcomings, the anecdotal evidence suggests that the Gulf Peace Team still had impact on grassroots consciousness in some parts of the world and that this stimulated greater nonviolent resistance to the war. In the eyes of some people, whatever it lacked in strategic conception, the camp made up for with integrity, courage and vision. As the history of nonviolent struggle clearly demonstrates however, while inspirational examples have their role to play in galvanizing greater spontaneous resistance to violence or injustice, this is rarely enough to compensate for the lack of a comprehensive strategic orientation. Good nonviolent struggle, like any struggle, requires a sound strategic plan.

Organizational Issues. A major shortcoming of previous attempts at nonviolent interposition has been the lack of an organizational infrastructure. The Gulf Peace Team suffered the same shortcoming. In part, this reflects the lack of a well-developed and worldwide nonviolent action network which, it seems clear, is necessary if initiatives such as this are to have the organizational foundation to be successful.

An organizational infrastructure provides the framework in which ideological, political, strategic and moral questions are resolved. It is also the foundation on which action planning, networking, communication, recruitment, nonviolence education and financial matters are based. Without an adequate organizational framework, the Gulf Peace Team had immense difficulty dealing with basic policy questions and various practical matters such as recruitment and education of activists. Moreover, it directly contributed to a range of complications in the camp itself. Consider, for example, the question of camp membership.

It is clear from the historical record that the preferred organizational unit for effective nonviolent action is the affinity group. An affinity group is a group of five to 13 people which performs a range of task and personal support functions in an atmosphere of trust developed through periods of time working together. In contrast, the Gulf Peace Camp was essentially a collection of individuals from 15 countries; there was no single language which everyone spoke. Few had experience of working in affinity groups; not all had experience of nonviolent action. Moreover, there was neither shared cultural identity nor ideological cohesion to bind camp members together. In addition, and typically of social movements which have a tolerant social milieu, the Gulf Peace Camp attracted a disproportionate number of people with special psychological needs. Given the complexities of camp life under conditions of war, all of these factors were challenging complications.

But the organizational problems did not stop at the camp; consider the problems of communication and finance. It is clear that communication is vitally important and should allow regular contact between members of the organization and with grassroots networks. It requires the use of various types of open channels, accurate and adequate information, and conscientious use. On all of these points, however, the record of the Gulf Peace Team—and particularly the London office—was poor. For instance, the London office lacked adequate communication channels—and had none with the camp once the war broke out; it lacked access to grassroots networks; it consistently circulated inaccurate information, particularly in relation to the estimate of the number of activists going to the camp; and it consistently failed to supply reliable information to national support groups.

In relation to finance—given the cost of $2,000 to $5,000 (depending on their country of origin) to support one activist—there are several important questions to be considered. How do projects such as this raise the necessary money? Is this the best use of money raised to support activist causes? Is this a good use of money for someone who can think of nothing better to do to express their anger? How much local activism could be financed with this money? How much equipment or food or medicine could be bought? Whatever the answer to these questions, it is clear that the financial constraint alone means that such projects cannot involve many ordinary (and particularly African, Asian or Latin American) activists.

It is evident that if key organizational problems cannot be resolved, then the action itself must be questioned. Integrity of the action alone is not enough.

Conclusion
Whatever its shortcomings, the Gulf Peace Team was profoundly significant both historically and politically. First, after decades of proposals

and abortive attempts, it was only the second nonviolent interposition in history. Second, it did constitute a nonviolent presence in the war zone which drew public attention to alternative and peaceful solutions to the Gulf conflict. Third, it did inspire some grassroots resistance to the war. And fourth, it rapidly accelerated our learning in this vital area of nonviolent struggle.

However, it is equally clear that its shortcomings were legion and that the Gulf Peace Team raised a series of questions in relation to politics, strategy and organization which need to be systematically addressed. It is now time for activists and scholars to reflect upon this experience in order to attempt to answer the fundamental question: is nonviolent interposition a viable and effective nonviolent tactic as part of a strategy to prevent or halt war?

NOTE

* I thank John Steel, fellow member of the Gulf Peace Team, for his meticulous efforts to identify and locate much original GPT documentation, on which sections of this chapter are based. I also thank the Victoria Regional Meeting of the Religious Society of Friends (Quakers) in Australia for a grant from the Otto Marx bequest to fund the writing of it.

CONCLUSION

17

NONVIOLENT HUMANITARIAN INTERVENTION: A FRAMEWORK FOR THE FUTURE

Yeshua Moser-Puangsuwan and Thomas Weber

During the last two decades of the twentieth century, cross-border nonviolent action initiatives, specifically focused on intervening in civil conflict, have been pursued with greater energy, resources and organization than at any other time in human history. These small-scale, voluntarily organized, nongovernmentally initiated projects have been more numerous than governmental efforts such as the United Nations Peacekeeping program. New initiatives are being proposed on an almost weekly basis by both governmental and nongovernmental groups.

Regional efforts, such as Michigan Faith and Resistance are sending volunteers to be a presence in Haiti, while religious groups such as the Quakers' Friends Peace Teams Project have focused on funnelling their members into existing peace teams. World Peace and Relief Teams, mobilized out of Austria by a former member of the Gulf Peace Team (GPT) seek international volunteers to do civil reconstruction in Iraq. The Swedish Council of Churches has brought together a diverse group of individuals involved in humanitarian, UN, governmental, military and peace team work to discuss the possibility of a Global Peace Service. United Nations Volunteers (UNV) has agreed to start a new program, based on the examples of nongovernmental organization (NGO) efforts like Peace Brigades International (PBI). The UNV is seeking volunteers for new programs in Burundi, Bosnia, and in the Trans-Caucasus region of the CIS to encourage a peaceful resolution of the civil conflicts there. Every political party in Germany now backs some form of Civilian Peace Service.

However, due to the resources at its disposal and the sheer number of people it places in the field, UN peacekeeping far overshadows the peace teams with their limited resources and small members. Rather than being staffed by highly visible armed forces, the low-profile ordinary citizens who make up peace teams, more often than not, come together in an *ad hoc* fashion and are plagued by a chronic lack of resources, both financial and human. Inadequate infrastructure, poor communications, and limited training opportunities are major impediments to mobilizing a large scale effort. Minimum public exposure in the mass media, combined with little popular understanding of the dynamics and history of this type of nonviolent action, has also hindered growth.

Moreover, current peace team organizations have limited global participation. Almost all their members are from the segments of western society that have demonstrated against their own governments' policies in foreign military adventurism: the North American and European peace movements. Nevertheless, these movements have gained from the experience of past efforts. Better organization, more public exposure and more thorough volunteer and project preparation will eventually overcome these obstacles and provide a people's peace action plan to replace the current military-based intervention scenarios.

In this final chapter we will look at some of the limitations and recurring problems experienced by the types of initiatives documented in this book, and examine a few options for future growth and development, including a new category of humanitarian assistance: *humanitarian political intervention*.

The Lure of Large-Scale Nonviolent Interposition

While attractive from an ideological perspective, large-scale nonviolent interposition, as attempted by the Gulf Peace Team and Mir Sada, appears to be logistically and politically extremely difficult to accomplish and its strategic goals have often been confused or vague. Yet the idea of "peace armies", that is large-scale nonviolent interventions, continues to persist. If the primary consideration of interposition is the maintenance of internal consistency by living out the principles of nonviolence that are held to be intrinsically good, then interposition is a useful tactic.

Mahatma Gandhi had quite a lot to say about large-scale nonviolent action in response to the threat of war. The most famous example came during a public meeting in Geneva on 10 December 1931, when he was on his way back to India following his attendance at the Second London Round Table Conference to discuss India's future. Gandhi was brutally clear about his vision of unarmed nonviolent interpositionary peacekeeping when he outlined his ideal of civilian defence. He was asked: "How could a disarmed neutral country allow other nations to be destroyed? But for our army which was waiting ready at our frontier during the last war we should have been ruined." At the risk of "being considered a visionary or a fool," Gandhi stated that,

> what I would have done would be to refuse passage to the invading army by refusing all supplies. Secondly, by re-enacting a Thermopylae in Switzerland, you would have presented a living wall of men and women and children, and inviting the invaders to walk over your corpses (*Young India*, 31 December 1931).

This "living wall" method of peacekeeping was central to Royden's attempt, and possibly to Non-Violent Action in Vietnam (NVAV), Witness for Peace, Mir Sada and the Gulf Peace Team. For Gandhi the rationale for such an approach rests on the assumption that voluntary suffering is a creative process, the role of which is to break a deadlock, to "cut through the rationalized defenses of the opponent" (Bondurant, 1967:228).

For Gandhi a belief in human reason and human goodness allowed for a faith in the possibility of converting or shaming a belligerent so that they desisted because of the creative self-suffering of such acts. Even if psychological simulation exercises demonstrated that self-suffering to "melt the heart" of an attacker is a gross oversimplification, or if they showed that it may even "elicit a negative reaction towards the victim" (Pelton, 1974, p.143; Weber, 1993) it would not have greatly troubled the Mahatma. His belief in the underlying unity of humanity meant that accepting suffering was far more dignified than inflicting in on another who was merely mistaken, and additionally it was the path to self-realization (see Naess, 1965:28-33, Naess, 1974:54-55; and Weber, 1989).

Those who do not share Gandhi's spiritual world view may still advocate interpositionary peacekeeping because of a desire to protest against evil, because of a hope that nonviolent action will generate favorable world-wide publicity and achieve a reduction in violence through international pressure, or simply because, as pacifists, they can see no other alternative and still maintain internal consistency. It would appear, however, that many of the advocates of these attempts have given little thought to the dynamic process which they hope will bring about the desired change, and have not clearly thought through their strategic goals (see Roberts, 1967:277-278).

During the Gandhi centenary the BBC broadcast a program of reminiscences about Gandhi. One of the interviewees, a young Gandhian, noted that the Gandhian movement relinquished a potential leading role in the popularization of unarmed interpositionary peacekeeping (and even nonviolent invasion) on at least two occasions. In 1955 approximately 15,000 satyagrahis were about to illegally enter the then still Portuguese territory of Goa when the Indian government stopped them.

The Portuguese had badly beaten up smaller earlier contingents but it was thought unlikely that they would fire on such a large unarmed nonviolent crowd. If they had, he continues:

> There would have been a tremendous upsurge of public opinion at international level, and I think that would have meant adding a new dimension to international politics—an unarmed people resisting a power that was fully armed. That was the first case where I felt that we bungled it. The second case was the Chinese attack, which was a crucial test for the Gandhians. I am afraid they did not rise to the occasion. If in October 1962, when the Chinese attacked, a few thousand Indians committed to non-violence had marched to the front and said, Well, it doesn't matter, let the Indian soldiers shoot us down or the Chinese soldiers shoot us down, we are going to stand here and try to separate these two armies, it would have looked a little foolhardy, but I think it would have caught the imagination of people all over the world and it would probably have made a large number of people in different parts of the world, the young at least, say, well, we are going to India now to join this international brigade for peace (Watson & Tennyson, 1976, pp.155-56).

It is difficult not to agree. Such acts would certainly have popularized the idea and provided a model for those calling for the establishment of unarmed nonviolent interpositionary peacekeeping forces. However, being realistic, one must recognize that the opportunity for such actions will not present themselves in the foreseeable future. While some of the debates around the role of Witness for Peace echoed Brinton's vision of over half a century earlier, the conclusion that Witness prevented a US invasion of Nicaragua is equivocal at best. Furthermore, the return of the Gulf Peace Team with nothing physically, and very little politically, tangible to show for its efforts means that there is still no available successful blue-print of this model of interposition, and it does not appear that one will emerge in the near future.

Moreover, fielding a large number of people in order to have a major impact may not be required, and could be a result of militaristic thinking within the peace movement. The International Committee of the Red Cross, one of the largest and most effective international organizations to intervene in civil war situations, and one which receives both governmental and private funds, often fields only a dozen expatriate staff to carry out their invaluable activities in zones of conflict and maintains a neutral but very powerful presence. The recent attempt and failure by Mir Sada/One Peace in ex-Yugoslavia may spell the end of attempts at raising "Peace Armies." In reflection on the results of this action, a local Bosnian activist wrote:

> Our common stand is that mass actions of visiting these territories...are ineffective and a waste of energy. During a short period, a large number of participants can't really understand what has happened, nor articulate

any political message except general opposition to war, which is commonplace. Those who come...in small groups and who cooperate with us on concrete projects help us much more. Hard long-term work is understood. Delusions that fast and easy solutions are possible must be rejected (quoted in Schirch, 1995, pp.65-66).

A More Realistic Approach

While it is clear that interpositionary forces could serve a valuable symbolic function, as well as the hoped for immediately practical one, this may hold even more true in the case of other forms of interventionary actions. For example, while the sailing of protest vessels into nuclear test zones did not immediately stop testing, they helped to focus the world's attention on the issue. They also brought the concept of nonviolent action into the public arena. And both of these played a part in the stopping of (at least atmospheric) nuclear tests and paved the way for the now common interpositionary efforts carried on by groups such as Greenpeace. Also—if effectiveness in the more immediate and physical sense is desired, that is if nonviolent interposition is seen as instrumental in stopping hostilities—then these somewhat modified tactics may be more applicable.

Maude Royden and her colleagues gained a great deal of publicity for the idea of nonviolent interpositionary peacekeeping but the proposal was stillborn. NVAV, a less well publicized endeavor, managed to send a small team towards a war zone. The Gulf Peace Team, the latest and probably least well thought through effort, actually managed to place a team of volunteers in a position of interposition in a war zone. It would appear that with the passing of time gains have been achieved on the physical plane: the attempts are increasingly getting volunteers closer and closer to the interpositionary ideal; however the corresponding intellectual and analytical gains have not been made. The attempts continue to suffer from the same problems with finances, logistics, communications, the number and quality of volunteers, international credibility and unity of purpose within the teams, as well as from unrealistic expectations about what can be achieved (and a tendency internally to believe rhetoric that was originally designed to achieve publicity). Learning does not necessarily come from experience but from an analysis of experience. And an assessment of the viability of nonviolent unarmed strategic large-scale interpositionary peacekeeping, based on an analysis of previous attempts, and measured in terms of physical effectiveness, seems to suggest that the concept is not a viable one.

Analysis of experience indicates that the approach should be modified and that other variations on the theme, such as small-scale tactical intervention, especially in the form of nonviolent witness and accompaniment initiatives, should be developed more thoroughly.

Turning the Vision into Reality: Difficulties Experienced

Current smaller-scale initiatives, although based on more attainable material and human resources, face most of the same problems in implementation. Their struggle for political legitimacy has been hindered by a general lack of understanding of their purpose. This lack of understanding has come from confusion within the movement itself as to various goals, methods of operation and effectiveness, which in turn has fed suspicion or noncooperation with other, more traditional governmental humanitarian and relief agencies working within the crisis situation. As well media reports on peace team activities are frequently vague or dismissive. All too often aid or relief agencies see actions as interfering in the internal affairs of sovereign nations, and therefore keep their distance so that their own activities are not "tainted."

Peace team development has suffered from lack of resources and capable personnel as well as clear strategic goals. This also appears to foster a cycle of lack of support from more traditional groups because these shortfalls make the voluntary groups appear unprofessional or naive. More intensive training may help alleviate this deficiency, but this too costs resources and assumes training capacity is available. Logistically, there appear to be recurrent problems connected with the initiatives reviewed in this book.

The case studies point to several areas that need consideration. For example, the experience of the *Lusitania Expresso* shows how actions that require media coverage for success can end up being media driven; the Cyprus Resettlement Project illustrates the problems of communication with locals that can beset teams that come from outside the region of operation; Mir Sada and the Gulf Peace Team, highlight the problems of communication among team members themselves when the team is multinational; the Sahara Protest Team demonstrates how tensions and misunderstandings can develop between local and international activists and the problems that can arise when the peace team agenda becomes enmeshed with larger political issues such as decolonisation; and the Mir Sada and GPT actions show how the strategic objectives of a team can be confused—was the action a means to an end or an end in itself? Witness for Peace raises other questions—what role is there for returned peace team participants? Is it enough that actions are symbolic, or should they have immediate impact? Should the support team on the home front focus on influencing elites or changing the hearts of people at the grassroots? The experience of the Gulf Peace Team also presents some challenging problems: how are of questions lity can surround a peace team's neutrality be dealt with? How do team members cope with the stresses of war, and what can be done with people exhibiting special psychological needs who cannot simply be sent elsewhere? Project Accompaniment also raises issues about the personal and emotional qualifications necessary for being a successful accompanier, while Peace Brigades International examines the issue of personal danger. and Cry for Justice clearly illustrates some of the ethical dilemmas faced by team members.

The following appear to be the main areas where problems appear to be common:

Organization and Decision-Making. Some years ago in Canada, during a meeting on the structure and functioning of peace teams, a retired military man who was in attendance was asked how the military would respond to a peace team type effort, and he answered, "We wouldn't need to. You are totally disorganized" (interview with George Willoughby, former International Secretary for PBI and the World Peace Brigade).

While this was perhaps overly harsh, it should be noted that most international humanitarian aid and development agencies have relatively hierarchical structures (though some are fairly open and have built in participation and feedback for some internal decision making). By comparison, the structure for decisions in organizations like PBI, Mir Sada or the Gulf Peace Team looks anarchic. Peace teams at the level of the in-country units frequently try to function on consensus. Enormous amounts of time, energy and expense can be spent on even minor aspects of the operation when seeking agreement to proceed. Questions have frequently occurred about team lifestyle maintenance (for example, the Cyprus Resettlement Project), gender needs, minority needs (especially pertaining to language) and project direction. These concerns provide ample opportunity for internal conflicts.

By way of comparison, if one is working for a traditional aid agency, most of these decisions have already been made by the central organization. Some peace teams place a great amount of importance on the connection of means and ends, and believe the organization's structure should reflect the democratic society their actions are meant to foster. This difference in decision making process is a result of an important difference in ideology between most humanitarian aid agencies and peace teams. It also reflects the roots of development of the peace team ideal as a foreign policy instrument of the western peace movement. A balance still needs to be struck on when responsibility can be delegated, and when the issue is related to general policy and should be considered by the larger organization.

Economics. Obtaining adequate funding has been a major source of frustration for all groups which have wished to send intervention teams. All interventions discussed in this book, with the exception of new projects opened within Peace Brigades International and Witness For Peace, have been *ad hoc* efforts or newly formed groups. All major efforts since 1990 have been coalitions: Balkan Peace Teams, Cry for Justice, SIPAZ, have included Peace Brigades International in all three, and Witness for Peace and Christian Peacemaker Teams in the last two. This is partly to gain legitimacy from the past actions of their predecessors, as well as to tap their expertise in the form of trainers and gain access to an experienced volunteer pool. But this has also meant an inability to demonstrate a successful track record that will inspire major donors. This fact alone effectively prohibits the possibility of large-scale efforts where groups want to field hundreds or thousands of volunteers, usually in a last minute attempt, to interpose between fighting units. Without governmental support, large-scale efforts will always be impossible.

Traditional philanthropic patterns also pose an obstacle to the widespread growth of peace team initiatives. Generally speaking, it has been considered a breach of protocol for the major international philanthropic agencies to fund, or be involved in, programs that are believed to interfere in a sovereign nation's internal politics. This attitude is changing, but not quickly enough. Most citizen-based intervention initiatives are clearly in the realm of political intervention. Although the teams may declare themselves to be nonpartisan in internal party politics, their support of the oppressed, who are almost always opposed to the State, usually makes them appear to support one political stance or side in a struggle. WFP walked a fine line of non-endorsement of the Sandanista government, and instead supported the right of the Nicaraguan people to have a government of their own choice. (This issue was complicated by the fact that some of the WFP volunteers were obvious Sandanista supporters). PBI has worked hard to maintain their nonpartisan position. In a case in which aggressive propaganda portrayed them as allied with the opposition to the government, PBI teams even took out newspaper advertisements to publicize their mandate and activities. CPT openly sides with activities of the oppressed, which has led to their expulsion from a West Bank city, a situation others have attempted to avoid (not always successfully) by cultivating a nonpartisan appearance.

Nonpartisan and non-interventionary policies also make an organization more donor friendly, but donor education is still needed. This will be a long term effort, and a clearly detailed track record of successes over a long period of time is probably the only way to elicit strong support from the international oriented philanthropic community.

In the meantime, as long as these programs have difficulty being perceived as non-partisan, few major donors will wish to be associated with them. For similar reasons governments are extremely reluctant to back programs—such as the Civilian Peace Service, proposed in 1994 as an alternative to military service by evangelical churches in Germany— which involve intervention in another country.

As a last resort, it might be reasonable to expect volunteers from the economically overdeveloped countries to be self-funding. Actually they have been for most of the initiatives within this book. But such a policy confines peace team organizations and volunteers to the wealthy and elite nations, which, with few exceptions is currently the case.

Personnel. The recruitment of quality team members has been difficult for initiatives which depend totally on volunteers. As previously noted, almost all come from Europe and North America. There has been no serious organized attempt by any of the initiatives detailed in this book (with the exception of the Dhammayietra in Cambodia) to find, train and fund volunteers from the non-elite nations. This has economic roots, and in some cases it simply was never pursued as a matter of policy (see more on this below). Within the first-world pool of volunteers a general observation can be made about the age groups: those in their early to late twenties; people aged 30-50; and people past their mid-fifties. By and large, the participants in the past have come from the first and last of these social groups. People in the middle group are usually too committed to family-raising responsibilities or securing their niche in the capitalist economy, to be able to take off the time necessary for such service.

Youthful volunteers tend to be richer in ideology and enthusiasm than life experience, which is both a strength and a liability. One of the authors has served on three peace teams on which the team came to the decision to expel a member, and the member was always in the twenties age group and the problem one of maturity or ideological inflexibility. Experience of this type has compelled some organizations to make rules about minimum age requirements for service. Elderly people, on the other hand, have far more life experience and are less given to arguments over ideology. However most of their life experience is not directly relevant to peace team work. Elders also have more established networks of friends and family, and are usually more financially secure than younger volunteers, but are frequently less open to new and experimental ways of working.

Financial support for service on an overseas nonviolent intervention program is not available for most potential volunteers, few of whom can demonstrate prior intervention expertise in another culture's conflict.

Securing a leave of absence from an established occupation is difficult. Although most employers must agree to allow men to have leave from their place of employment, with the possibility of return, for military obligations, they would look on volunteer service for a peace team with suspicion or incomprehension. While there are some progressive trends in businesses in the West which allow for childcare by parents of either gender, it has yet to reach the point where businesses will allow workers to take leave time for activities that provide nonviolent service to society. Even the most progressive businesses, while perhaps sympathetic, would probably point to cost reasons for not granting such leave. However, a recent law has been passed in Italy which would allow for the funding of government civil servants on overseas development projects. This law is apparently liberal enough to have allowed university professors to join a project of social reconciliation at a peace house in Kosovo.

As peace teams are not a generally recognized form of social service abroad, and are more often than not an extension of the volunteer's activities within a local peace movement in Europe or North America, family members frequently voice opposition to service on a peace team. This adds to the team member's emotional isolation while serving in an environment which offers very little in the way of support for the volunteer but does make many stressful demands.

In addition, volunteers available to peace team organizations often have mixed reasons for offering their services. Their personal objectives can be different to those of the project. When volunteers with mixed motives are on a team, all too often it leads to friction and disharmony rather than a focus on the main issue of concern, the people in need in the country. Some inappropriate motives for serving on a peace team observed by one of the authors have included: adventure tourists or people looking for a socially acceptable holiday; people looking (only) to create credentials to work abroad; and people running away from bad marriages or wishing to gain space from other undesirable relationships.

These factors have led to more stringent screening policies and interviews before and during training to weed out clearly inappropriate cases. However, but more in the way of volunteer pre-selection needs to be done. While the same problems affect international development and aid agencies, their requirement of prior experience usually (but not always) weeds out those with severe problems. This selection predicament faced by peace teams is partly traceable to their birth within the western peace movement which has difficulty "policing" itself. The problem could be addressed by further professionalizing peace teams, but it is a point of contention among several of these organizations whether their teams should become "professional" or remain voluntary and open to "ordinary" citizens. Some feel that the voluntary nature of the initiatives is part of nonviolent action and fosters a genuine attitude of service and risk-taking while professionalism curtails these attributes. There is certainly an ideological resistance within the western peace movement to funding any group which would then be seen as an elite. Other peace advocates feel that professionally hired team members would bring about a higher level of commitment and capacity and a more professional organization, since team members would be freed of the volunteers' financial and time constraints.

It is a hopeful sign that now all current and new peace teams are developing more in-depth application procedures to screen volunteers, as well as conducting longer training sessions. A summary of characteristics sought by organizations of volunteers for peace team work (which includes qualities such as self-knowledge, motivation, flexibility, discretion, a sense of humor, ability to work in a team as well as certain physical, skill and availability requirements) has been compiled by Schirch (Schirch, 1995, pp.75-79).

Internationalization of Peace Teams. In the introductory chapter to *Liberation Without Violence*, Herbert Blumberg noted that violent conflicts between communities are not likely to occur where people have a common identity and similar goals. In other words, severe conflicts are generally unlikely to occur within western democracies and so attempts at nonviolent intervention that provide practice in transcending national boundaries are for the common good. He also noted that the group involved in the intervention itself should be transnational to ensure that "the team is not a group of Canadians or a group of South Africans carrying out some action, but a group of people doing so" (Hare and Blumberg, 1977, p.12). It is important that western outsiders do not descend on places they know little about and attempt to control conflicts without the guidance of local contact groups. It is also important for more prosaic reasons.

As noted above, currently all peace teams are based in the northern Euro-American, wealthy countries. With the exception of PBI, which considers itself international, none has an outreach program to recruit members from the economically deprived countries. To some extent members of the Euro-American based initiatives believe they are engaging in a kind of reverse racism, because white skin is frequently given respect in southern nations. This is a complex issue, and contains elements of both racism and elite economic power interests. On the level of race, one Columbian involved with a PBI initiative noted that,

> We of the South are perceived by our northern compañeros as people of lesser capacity. This is true, as we have not had access to many of the advantages available to those in the North. However, judging us this way does not help us get out of this situation and offer our services (interview with Marcel Rodriguez, a Colombian volunteer of the PBI El Salvador team).

An Amnesty International and PBI sponsored multi-racial exploratory team which went to the Philippines in 1997 to assess a request of an indigenous human rights organization for an international presence during a politically risky event, also sought information as to what race of the monitor the local activists believed would offer the best protective presence. Unanimously the local activists asked for "Internationals. You know, people from America or Europe." When asked if people from other Asian countries could also provide accompaniment the reply was "No. They look too much like us and their governments don't care about human rights." Asked if African volunteers could serve, one replied after a pause, "Dark people are not paid attention to. The whiter the better."

Peace teams acknowledge that being visually different is important in situations in which the presence of a "foreigner" is hoped to deter violence. However this can also be accomplished by focusing on the volunteer's connection to a larger organization rather than the skin color. Uniforms (as worn by the UN) or symbols (as employed by the Red Cross) can also achieve this. Most peace team members find it ideologically inconsistent to profit from local racism, aiding and abetting it as it were, but racism is real and will die slowly. Perhaps more importantly, most peace team volunteers come from the nations, and local client elites frequently rely as much or more on the support of the ruling class of elite nations, than they do on their own people for their power. Therefore using volunteers who come from elite nations does make sense from a power perspective.

Development of a common symbol for peace teams, along with public education about their goals and methodology, should be pursued. It will be difficult, due both to some operational differences between organizations and also the knee-jerk reactions to authority symbols among some members of the western peace movement. However introducing a symbol is the only way to switch from reliance on the color of a peace team's skin to reliance on the power of the organizations as an institution, thereby increasing the power of the method.

Training. In his concluding essay in *Liberation Without Violence*, Paul Hare makes the assessment that "if you wish to solve conflicts without violence, use the best theories [of social change] available, combined with valid facts, so that a multi-disciplinary team can make a day-to-day application of principles with sensitivity and understanding" (Hare and Blumberg, 1977, p.285). This, in turn, calls for training.

Training is something that has been totally lacking in the beginning of almost every peace team venture in the past. Like volunteer pre-screening, it has developed as organizations have grown—out of necessity and to solve problems of poorly prepared volunteers. Training takes time and money, which most organizations feel they cannot afford, preferring to immediately place people in the field to "do something now." While pre-service training is presently on the agenda of all existing peace teams, still no program offers more than a week of training before sending volunteers into the field. Currently, a five day preparatory training by PBI, which has the most complete training program of any of the peace team organizations, includes the following: learning the history of the conflict of the country to which the volunteers will go; studying the history of PBI's activities there; roleplaying of various situations which have occurred or could happen while the team is in the field; and acquiring a series of learning experiences to develop cultural sensitivity, team work and trust, and an ability to deal with stress and fear.

Established overseas aid programs and voluntary service organizations such as the VSO or US Peace Corps intensively prepare their staff for up to three months in language, culture, and organizational mandate; introduce them to local contacts; and give them clear lines of communication and a budget. Peace team volunteers require far more training than they currently receive: at a minimum it should match that of the programs mentioned above, but at this stage such a goal is beyond the financial and resource capacity of any peace team organization.

Logistics. Not only do the physical resources require more money, they also mean additional training. For example, it takes time to learn to operate packet radio communications equipment, or even to drive a car.

Being more ideologically driven, some peace teams find it a major organizational struggle to determine if they will even use some types of tools. This internal struggle also consumes time and energy. For example, one team in PBI debated whether it should attempt to procure a car to maintain a presence in several villages where public transportation had been suspended. Some team members felt that this was a legitimate way to fulfil the accompaniment need, while others felt that it set the team apart, as an elite, from the general population, none of whom could own a car. This debate flowed over from the team and its project office into the larger organization, finally affecting projects in other countries for the precedent that this decision might set within the organization. It took almost six months to make the decision, by which time the urgency had passed, yet the positional differences between team members had meanwhile reached the point that outside mediation was required. The car was eventually rented from a local trade school, which had found it abandoned by guerrillas in the jungle, and had rebuilt it as a class project. It was used by the team for a few months before the project was closed in that area of the country due to lack of staff and internal tensions on the "peace" team.

Decisions of this type in most overseas service organizations have already been made for the volunteers. More discussion and thinking about the types of tools an organization will use or will not use should be debated at the policy level rather than by the team in-the-field, which should focus its energy on addressing the immediate problems of the local people it is working with. However, peace teams are still in their developmental stage, and are only discovering how to respond from their direct experiences. Drawing on the years of experience of established organizations such as Médecines Sans Frontièrs and the International Committee of the Red Cross would be extremely helpful and should be sought.

Long-Range Strategic Thinking. If the aim is to avert the endless chain of remarkable but frustrating programs, then the above mentioned areas and the following questions need to be addressed:

- What is the best intervention scenario for a given conflict?
- What are the goals and aims of a proposed project of intervention?
- How many people will need to be placed in the field to have an impact, and what skills and training will they need in order to be of service?
- Is the budget for sustaining the above attainable?
- How can the effectiveness of projects in a fluid conflict environment be evaluated in an ongoing way so as to facilitate responsive or proactive change?

To ask these questions suggests the existence of an ongoing organization pursuing the establishment of independent international crisis intervention teams with clear strategic goals. Currently there is no such organization. PBI has set up a new project exploration process that asks approximately these questions, but the scope is circumscribed by the organization's current focus: protective accompaniment (see Mahony and Eguren, 1997, pp.247-49; and Schirch, 1995, pp.59-60).

Development of good analytical capabilities within the peace team movement is crucial not only for knowing how to be most usefully involved, but to know how and when to disengage. This has proved more difficult than anticipated, and none of the peace team organizations examined in this book has developed clear procedures on how to evaluate when it is time to disengage and close a project, and then to follow them.

Nonviolent Cross Border Actions as Engaged Third Party Actions
There is no consensus among the organizations chronicled within this book about the level of engagement in the local struggle. Some of the approaches appear to be mutually exclusive. Solidarity actions such as those of the Christian Peacemaker Teams in Hebron are incompatible with the noninterventionist and nonpartisan approach of Peace Brigades International in Guatemala. Each approach is philosophically sound as nonviolent action, but they cannot be pursued by a team in a country simultaneously. It is not possible to represent an organization as being nonpartisan while doing partisan actions and yet maintain credibility. Both approaches are actually a tactical decision based on an analysis about how to support the local activist groups and the struggle for social justice in an appropriate and effective way. These two approaches are most sharply shown by the activities of PBI and CPT, but the tension between active involvement in the struggle and a noninterventionist approach exists to some extent in all the teams documented in this book.

PBI epitomizes the nonpartisan approach. It is described in *Unarmed Bodyguards* as partial but nonpartisan: "We will be at your side in the face of injustice and suffering, but we will not take your side against those you define as enemies" (Mahony and Eguren, 1997, p.236). Christian Peacemaker Teams, on the other hand, believes that a nonviolent and just solution to a given problem is impossible until a balance of power is attained, and that there is a role for its peace workers in addressing the imbalance. CPT volunteers have thrown themselves into such actions with Palestinians as tearing down gates erected by Israeli settlers or troops and encouraging Palestinians to take part by saying, "If you get arrested we get arrested too" (interview with Art Gish, CPT team member in Hebron, Palestine). CPT states that it stands in the middle in a conflict, and points out that the middle ground shifts according to the situation, but the organization clearly takes a side. One volunteer on a CPT team in Hebron described this choice by explaining, "We stand on the side the guns are pointed at, that's the side we take" (Art Gish interview).

Peace teams differ dramatically in the focus of their work from the international agencies for relief and development aid which provide what is called humanitarian crisis intervention and humanitarian assistance, respectively. Humanitarian aid groups frequently state that aid must not be politicized. Peace teams, on the other hand, frequently see aid and relief programs as mere bandaids which do not address the underlying social problems that caused the situation to which the humanitarian aid and relief agencies are responding. This difference in analysis has caused a lack of understanding and support between peace team organizations and the development and relief community. On the other hand, many workers for aid and development agencies see that their activities are not addressing structural problems and seek ways they can support initiatives by local people that will resolve them. Some aid workers have been very helpful and supportive to peace teams for this reason. Aid organizations like Oxfam and Quaker Peace and Service do have wings of their organization which are more politically active and actively attempt to address structural issues.

A path through this antagonism would be the joint development of a new concept which is cast in the response pattern of humanitarian concern. Perhaps it could be called *humanitarian political intervention*. Even this phrase would probably be contentious, initially, within the traditional humanitarian assistance community as it is considered a violation of a basic tenet: noninvolvement in the political affairs of sovereign nations.

However, as documented within these pages, the services that peace teams offer are tangible. They have served as one-on-one human rights monitors offering some protection to local activists from political violence, and on a larger scale as cease-fire and border monitors. In some circumstances they have acted as mediators, as advocates for groups under oppression, as process observers (for example monitoring conduct at demonstrations and strikes, or during elections), and as messages bearers between groups unable to maintain contact (for example between refugees and their families who have remained behind). Nongovernmental volunteers have overseen the safe passage of people fleeing violence or resettling in tense areas, and they have overseen the exchange of prisoners of war.

While these actions in themselves have not stopped wars, they have certainly provided good service in the cause of peace and peacebuilding, and at the very least proved inspirational for others. In desperate cases perhaps the most important service that peace teams contribute is letting people know, by their very presence, that their suffering is not forgotten—that they are not alone. And this is a precious gift for people who are often living on the edge of despair. The belief in principled nonviolent action is one of the key aspects which differentiates peace teams from development agencies. And this demands a willingness to directly address the political situation in a manner of a concerned, third party with the intent that their presence will reduce fear, build trust, and create a space where aggressive actions are less likely, and political struggle or negotiation, rather than armed struggle, will become the norm.

Peace Teams as a Movement
The path towards development of both practical and sustainable methods of nonviolent conflict intervention will require growing beyond the base of the western peace movement. To draw upon the expertise developed by traditional humanitarian aid and development organizations and to become recognized as a legitimate international institution, peace team activists should begin working on building a multi-sectoral movement which seeks the involvement of diverse sections of the world community. A first step would be for both humanitarian aid organizations and peace team activist to work together to seek a joint method of nonpartisan political intervention. This is already beginning to happen by chance in the field, but not as a matter of policy. There is a great need to incorporate the constructive programs of the aid agencies and educate their donor community about humanitarian political intervention. A precedent for this type of joint action can be based on the movement to bring about a global ban on land mines. Handicap International (HI), an international agency providing prosthetic devices to civilian and military victims of land mines became one of the first humanitarian assistance agencies to cross the line into political action when they joined with a human rights organizations and a veterans' group to found the International Campaign to Ban Land mines. HI now feels that it is working on the *cause* as well as the *result*. It is also working on an issue usually considered the domain of peace movements: disarmament. The ICBL has forged a worldwide coalition of humanitarian agencies, peace and religious organizations and other civil society groups to become a powerful lobby against national military policies.

This movement is setting an important precedent for humanitarian agencies to move beyond direct aid into nonpartisan political action, and is an example of a coalition action in which groups usually separated by methodology or concern are working together to address both the cause and the solution.

Arising independently, but benefiting from the ICBL, are the new humanitarian de-mining organizations. De-mining was once considered the province of governments and the military. Distinguishing humanitarian de-mining from military de-mining (de-mining to reach a military objective) and commercial de-mining (plowing a single path through a mine field to lay a pipe), the humanitarian de-miners have approached the problem from a people's perspective ("this well was mined and now we have to walk four hours to the next village for water") which is not on the agenda of governments, militaries or corporations.

Guidelines for humanitarian political intervention by NGOs will be criticized by some nations as a violation of sovereignty, or foreign interference and manipulation. Fortunately, many of the guidelines needed are already enshrined in principle in UN and regional conventions, such as the instruments on human rights, the rights of women, children and the environment and the right to development.

Like all other intervention, humanitarian political intervention is a double-edged sword. As Mahony and Eguren point out, from PBI's experience outside political intervention is apt to be misused or inadvertently abused. However, the vision of a compassionate and realistic method of nonviolent conflict intervention has proved to be an enduring and recurrent idea. With more careful preparation of staff to develop the ability to respond creatively, compassionately and wisely to changing political situations in the field and a wider community to draw upon for resources, social power and wisdom of experience, it is a vision that humanity should be capable of realizing.

REFERENCES

Bondurant, Joan V. 1967. *Conquest of Violence: The Gandhian Philosophy of Conflict* (Berkeley: University of California Press).

Hare, A.Paul, and Herbert H.Blumberg (eds.). 1977. *Liberation Without Violence: A Third Party Approach* (Totowa, NJ: Rowman and Littlefield).

Mahony, Liam, and Luis Enrique Eguren. 1997. *Unarmed Bodyguards: International Accompaniment for the Protection of Human Rights* (West Hartford, Con.: Kumarian).

Naess, Arne. 1965. *Gandhi and the Nuclear Age* (Totowa, NJ: Bedminster Press).

——. 1974. *Gandhi and Group Conflict: An Exploration of Satyagraha* (Oslo: Universitetsforlaget).

Pelton, Leroy H. 1974. *The Psychology of Nonviolence* (New York: Pergamon).

Roberts, Adam. 1967. "Civilian Defence Strategy," in Adam Roberts (ed.), *Civilian Resistance as a National Defence: Non-Violent Action Against Aggression* (Harmondsworth: Penguin) pp.249-294.

Schirch, Lisa. 1995. *Keeping the Peace: Exploring Civilian Alternatives in Conflict Prevention* (Uppsala: Life & Peace Institute).

Watson, Francis, and Hallam Tennyson. 1976. *Talking of Gandhi* (New Delhi: Orient Longman).

Weber, Thomas. 1989. "The Satyagrahi as Heroic Ideal," *Gandhi Marg*, vol.11, no.5, pp.133-153.

——. 1993. "From Maude Royden's Peace Army to the Gulf Peace Team: An Assessment of Unarmed Interpositionary Peace Forces," *Journal of Peace Research*, vol.30, no.1, pp.45-64.

APPENDICES

Appendix A

FROM THE PEACE ARMY TO SIPAZ: A CHRONOLOGY OF GRASSROOTS INITIATIVES IN UNARMED PEACEKEEPING

Yeshua Moser-Puangsuwan

Introduction

This brief chronological summary of nongovernmental efforts at sending peace missions, known as "peace brigades," "peace teams" or "peace armies," chronicles citizen-based, voluntary and unarmed programs of intervention in international or civil war conflicts.

Where accessible references are available, they are listed under "Further Reading." Interested readers should also scan current issues of peace newspapers such as *Peace News* and try looking on the Internet for up-to-date information on peace team activities. (The Balkan Peace Team, Christian Peacemaker Teams, Eirene, Friends Peace Team Project, Pastors for Peace, Peace Brigades International, Project Accompaniment, SIPAZ, Witness for Peace and the *Peace Teams/Peace Services Information Networker Directory* have extensive postings on the Net).

FURTHER READING

Robert J.Burrowes, "Cross-Border Nonviolent Intervention: A Typology," (this volume).

Gene Keyes, "Peacekeeping by Unarmed Buffer Forces: Precedents and Proposals," *Peace and Change,* (1978) vol.5, no.2/3, pp.3-10.

Mark Shepard, "Peace Brigades," in *World Encyclopedia of Peace* (Oxford: Pergamon, 1986) vol.2, pp.178-180.

Thomas Weber, "From Maude Royden's Peace Army to the Gulf Peace Team: An Assessment of Unarmed Interpositionary Peace Forces," *Journal of Peace Research,* (1993) vol.30, no.1, pp.45-64.

1932-1939
The Peace Army

The Peace Army proposed to intervene in the fighting between Japan and China in Shanghai. It was mobilized by British Anglican minister Maude Royden who wanted to initiate a Gandhian "Living Wall" of unarmed national defenders standing against external aggression. The force was offered to the League of Nations, which did not give it any substantial support. The Peace Army failed to raise enough recruits and finances to intervene before the crisis in Shanghai passed. The organization did follow up with a few less ambitious proposals, eventually fielding a team of volunteers in Palestine for a couple years. At the outbreak of WWII the Peace Army was shelved as most of its proponents began working on the Pacifist Service Corps, an alternative to armed service in the British Forces during WWII.

FURTHER READING

Thomas Weber, "Gandhi's 'Living Wall' and Maude Royden's 'Peace Army'," *Gandhi Marg*, (1988) vol.10, no.4, pp.199-212.

1948-
V.I.D./Peaceworkers

V.I.D was began by students and veterans. It built a file of a few hundred volunteers to serve on a "UN Peaceforce." Unable to find institutional backing they sent a team of four volunteers to Egypt shortly after the Suez crisis under the name Volunteers for International Development. In 1979 the organization changed its name to Peaceworkers, and has cosponsored training for peace action teams in Europe, Africa, Central and North America.

1957-
Eirene

Eirene is a European-based ecumenical Christian peace service founded as a project of the International Fellowship of Reconciliation and the Mennonite and Brethren churches. Combining peace work and development, Eirene places both short- and long-term volunteers in North and Central America, Europe and Africa. Although most Eircne work focuses on development activities, volunteers in Chad in 1997 helped facilitate the growth of the *Association Tchadienne pour la Non-Violence*, an indigenous group seeking ways to reduce growing social violence resulting from civil war. They have fostered the growth of a similar group in Niger. A particularly innovative idea in the European Voluntary Service, in which Eirene is involved, is support for "reverse service" in which opportunities are created for partner countries in the South to serve in European situations. Eirene is actively trying to promote international service as an alternative to military service.

1959-1960
Sahara Protest Action (SPA)
The SPA attempted to interrupt the first French nuclear weapons test scheduled to be held in French controlled Algeria. A multinational group of Africans, Europeans and Americans gathered in Ghana, from where it sent three teams across the desert to enter French West Africa to interrupt the test. All were apprehended by French military forces. This action had the support of several neighboring African nations and peace action organizations in Britain and the US. Supporters in France were publicizing the actions of these teams, and organizing public pressure in Paris. An all-Africa conference to coordinate nonviolent action to stop the tests was convened in Accra, which established a center for "positive action" against French nuclear tests, and led to the freezing of French assets by the Ghanaian government.

FURTHER READING
April Carter, "The Sahara Protest Team," (this volume).

1960-1961
San Francisco to Moscow Walk
The San Francisco to Moscow Walk was made up of a multinational group which traversed both North America, West and East Europe to Russia, taking the people's voice to end nuclear testing to three nuclear capitals. It managed to organize the first "uncontrolled" demonstration in Red Square. It was an act of intervention in the Cold War which was bold and international in perspective. The SF-Moscow Walk was organized by the Committee for Nonviolent Action (CNVA), which organized several boats to the US South Pacific nuclear test sites and an international protest within Vietnam. Several of its members became active in the World Peace Brigade.

FURTHER READING
Barbara Deming, "San Francisco to Moscow: Why they Walk," in Barbara Deming (ed.), *Revolution and Equilibrium* (New York: Grossman, 1971) pp.51-59.
——, "San Francisco to Moscow: Why the Russians Let Them In," in Barbara Deming (ed.), *Revolution and Equilibrium* (New York: Grossman, 1971) pp.60-72.

Bradford Lyttle, *You Come with Naked Hands: The Story of the San Francisco to Moscow March for Peace* (Raymond, NH: Greenleaf Books, 1966).

1961-1964
The World Peace Brigade (WPB)

The setting up of a WPB was proposed at the War Resisters' International meeting in India in 1960 to "internationalize the Shanti Sena idea." Many western attenders of this meeting were inspired by the work of the Shanti Sena (lit. "Peace Army") established by Gandhi's followers in India. The Shanti Sena's work in riot prevention and disarming of bandits were particularly spectacular. The WPB was founded in Beirut in 1961 and soon established a training center in Dar es Salaam, Tanganyika, where it attempted to coordinate an international Freedom March into Northern Rhodesia to support nonviolent calls for independence from British rule. The March became unnecessary due to changing political events which turned the tide in favor of the pro-independence movement. A second program was mobilized in 1963 by the Indian section to address conflict on the Indochinese border. A pilgrimage from Delhi to Beijing was organized, which met with hostile reaction from both governments. The last action officially undertaken by the WPB was a follow-up on antinuclear actions by CNVA. It involved sailing a boat to Leningrad and the Arctic sea to protest Soviet nuclear testing. The name of the voyage was *EveryMan III* (1962). The WPB drifted into oblivion by the mid-60s without fulfilling the goal of regionally developed crisis response teams. During its life, the WPB did achieve much through the international exchange in ideas, materials and trainers, and development of the "peace team" concept. The WPB left behind several empowered activists who helped mobilize later initiatives.

FURTHER READING

Barbara Deming, "International Peace Brigade," in Barbara Deming (ed.), *Revolution and Equilibrium* (New York: Grossman, 1971) pp.92-101.
Theodore Olson, "The World Peace Brigade: Vision and Failure," *Our Generation Against Nuclear War*, (1964) vol.3, no.1, pp.34-41.
Devi Prasad, "The World Peace Brigade," *Peace News*, 6 August 1971, 2-3.
Earle Reynolds, *The Forbidden Voyage* (London: Cassell, 1962).
Charles C.Walker, "The Delhi-to-Peking Friendship March," *Friends Journal*, (1963) vol.9, no.23, pp.517-518.

——, "Nonviolence in Eastern Africa 1962-4: The World Peace Brigade and Zambian Independence," in A.Paul Hare and Herbert H.Blumberg (eds.), *Liberation Without Violence: A Third Party Approach* (Totowa, NJ: Rowman and Littlefield, 1977) pp.157-177.

1966
Non-Violent Action in Vietnam (NVAV)
NVAV was a British-based initiative to intervene in the US war with Vietnam which proposed sending hundreds of nonviolent volunteers to North Vietnam in an attempt to halt the bombing (as international noncombatants would be injured). It went ahead although NVAV had not received the support of the North Vietnamese government, and was only able to send a token team of about 20 people. It did not get further than Cambodia but some of the NVAV team stayed in Asia to stage a protest outside a US airbase in Thailand, after which it was forcibly evicted.

FURTHER READING
Pat Arrowsmith (ed.), *To Asia in Peace: The Story of a Non-Violent Action Mission to Indo China* (London: Sidgwick and Jackson, 1972).

1968
Czechoslovakia Support Actions (CSA)
CSA was an *ad hoc* effort coordinated by War Resisters' International to support the "Prague Spring" and to protest the Russian invasion of Czechoslovakia. The CSA "intervention" was at the level of information and authority challenge. CSA set out to "put into practice precisely those freedoms which the Czechoslovaks were attempting to defend" according to the organizers. CSA sent volunteers to leaflet in most Eastern Bloc capitals in an act of solidarity with both Czechs and local acts of protest within East Berlin, Moscow and Leningrad. In all, four teams were sent out with representatives from seven different nationalities.

FURTHER READING
Michael Randle and April Carter, *Support Czechoslovakia* (London: Housemans, 1968) pp.17-23.

1966-1971
A Quaker Action Group (AQAG)
AQAG was founded by a group of US nonviolent activists, including some former members of the WPB. It mobilized volunteers to complete several small overseas actions. One of these was support of people displaced, harassed and sometimes wounded by a new US military target range set

up on the island of Culebra, Puerto Rico. The Puerto Rican Independence Party called for citizens to engage in "pacific militancy" or nonviolent action. They set up encampments on the target range and swam in a lagoon to reclaim it from target practice. Over 600 of the 730 inhabitants took part in these actions. When the people of the island attempted to rebuild a former chapel, AQAG sent a team to help them, and provided a foreign presence for several months. Later AQAG team members carried a model of this chapel around embassies in Washington, DC, to publicize the islanders plight. AQAG also sailed the *Phoenix* to Vietnam in 1967 in an attempt to deliver medical supplies to noncombatants in both North and South Vietnam. In all, three different voyages of aid *and* intervention to Vietnam were attempted. AQAG volunteers were arrested by South Vietnamese naval forces when they attempted to breach a blockade off Danang harbor. In 1971 AQAG sent a team to Panama in protest of US support for counterinsurgency strikes in South America.

FURTHER READING

Charles C.Walker, "Culebra: Nonviolent Action and the US Navy," in A.Paul Hare and Herbert H.Blumberg (eds.), *Liberation without Violence: A Third-Party Approach* (Totowa, NJ: Rowman and Littlefield, 1977) pp.178-195.

1971-1973
Operation Omega
The organizers of this multilateral action were Indian Gandhians, members of War Resisters' International and staff from its British journal *Peace News* in Britain. Some of the organizers had experience as WPB and NVAV activists. In India the Shanti Sena met with a number of refugees to organize a 50,000 strong column of refugees to return to East Bengal (Pakistan) as "a nonviolent liberation force." International volunteers were sought to join the column. The advent of the Indo-Pakistan war prevented the march from going ahead. Meanwhile, the international and local volunteer groups who had organized under WRI's initiative attempted to take relief supplies directly into East Bengal, while North American activists blocked arms shipments to Pakistan in Montreal, Philadelphia and Baltimore harbors. The relief teams, with trucks of supplies but no visas, got to the border of East Bengal (later Bangladesh). One group was arrested by the Pakistani army, but the others got through with relief supplies well ahead of established aid agencies working through official channels. This was done in collaboration with, and strong support from, the *Mukti Bahini*

(Bangladeshi liberation fighters). Two team members from these missions were arrested, tried and sentenced to two years imprisonment before being liberated by the Indian Army. Some Operation Omega volunteers stayed on working in Bangladesh until 1973.

FURTHER READING

"Operation Omega," in A.Paul Hare and Herbert H.Blumberg (eds.), *Liberation without Violence: A Third-Party Approach* (Totowa, NJ: Rowman and Littlefield, 1977) pp.196-206.

Richard K.Taylor, *Blockade: A Guide to Non-violent Intervention* (New York: Orbis Books, 1977).

1975

Cyprus Resettlement Project (CRP)

The CRP set out to respond to the needs of people displaced by the communal fighting between Turkish and Greek Cypriots. This program was put together by several WPB veterans and others with support from the International Peace Academy. During the life of the Project, three trained volunteer groups were placed in Cyprus and succeeded in arranging negotiations between Greek and Turkish communities where even the UN had failed. Several communities joined together under the international presence and encouragement of the CRP to rebuild and resettle their villages before the project was brought to a halt by two major political events: the coup in Greece followed by Turkish military invasion of the island. Although the CRP did not achieve its goal, it was particularly inspiring in the care and preparation it took before committing volunteers to the area of conflict.

FURTHER READING

A.Paul Hare, "Cyprus Resettlement Project: An Instance of International Peacemaking," (this volume).

—— and Ellen Wilkinson, "Cyprus—Conflict and its Resolution," in A.Paul Hare and Herbert H.Blumberg (eds.), *Liberation Without Violence: A Third-Party Approach* (Totowa, NJ: Rowman and Littlefield, 1977) pp.239-247.

1977

Operation Namibia (ON)

Operation Namibia grew directly out of Operation Omega, with additional involvement of AQAG activists from the US. ON was a political challenge effort, underlining the failure of the UN to act according to its mandate to replace the South African occupation of

Namibia. ON proposed taking books that were banned by the government of South Africa into Namibia aboard the *SS Golden Harvest*. After an initially promising start with press coverage as it sailed from Europe to Africa, ON experienced difficulties. The ship ran into rocks off the coast of Gambia and the crew ran afoul of authorities in the African countries of Nigeria and Togo. Time taken dealing with these difficulties, and changing situation in Namibia, led to an early end of the voyage. (The books themselves did arrive later through an overland route.) Later, the *Golden Harvest* sailed on to South America and now serves as a floating center for social and environmental activism in "French" Guiana.

1981-
Peace Brigades International (PBI)

Peace Brigades International was founded at a meeting in Canada as a second attempt to "Internationalize the Shanti Sena idea" by former activists from the World Peace Brigades and Cyprus Resettlement Project. PBI's first action took place in 1983, with the placement of volunteer peace teams in Guatemala and a short-term presence in Nicaragua. The PBI peace team sent to Guatemala developed what is PBI's most distinctive feature: international protective accompaniment of local human rights activist living under threat of abduction or assassination. PBI volunteer human rights monitors are placed directly in the homes and offices of local activists who have reason to fear for their lives because of their social change work. The presence of an international monitor raises the cost of "disappearance" or extrajudicial execution of local activists by ensuring that there will be international witness of any such events. PBI has now grown into an international organization with sections in 17 countries. Each section recruits and trains volunteers to serve on one of PBI's current projects, produces publications about PBI's work, does fundraising and coordinates the national section of PBI's global Emergency Response Network. PBI is the most successful effort to date to create and sustain multinational peace teams in conflict situations. PBI has carried on projects in El Salvador (1987-1992) and Sri Lanka (1989-present). PBI teams and short-term delegations have monitored and accompanied the return of refugees in Honduras and Southern Mexico. PBI also had a short-term project in Israel/Palestine (1989) and was cooperating with the government of Nicaragua to develop a program of nonviolent civilian-based defense until the change of government in 1990. In 1992 the North American Project opened to provide support for native communities facing external violence in North America. In late October 1993, PBI sent a team to Haiti as part of the Cry for Justice coalition. In November 1994, PBI began accompaniment activities with activists in Colombia, and in November 1995 opened a project in Haiti. Recent Exploratory Teams were sent to Chad and the Philippines in response to requests from indigenous activist organizations. PBI has also taken part in the Balkan Peace Team

FURTHER READING

Patrick G.Coy, "Protective Accompaniment: How Peace Brigades International Secures Political Space and Human Rights Nonviolently," in V.K.Kool (ed.), *Nonviolence: Social and Psychological Issues* (Lanham, Md: University Press of America, 1993) pp.235-245.

Piet Dijkstra, "Peace Brigades International," *Gandhi Marg,* (1986) vol.8, no.7, pp.391-406.

Barbara MacQuarrie, "Nonviolent Action in El Salvador," in Graeme MacQueen (ed.), *Unarmed Forces: Nonviolent Action in Central America and the Middle East* (Toronto: Science for Peace/Samuel Stevens, 1992) pp.52-61.

Liam Mahony, "Peace Brigades International: Nonviolence in Action," (this volume).

—— and Luis Enrique Eguren, *Unarmed Bodyguards: International Accompaniment for the Protection of Human Rights* (West Hartford, Con: Kumarian Press, 1997).

1981-
Witness For Peace (WFP)
WFP organized a permanent border and conflict monitoring program in Nicaragua by bringing teams of previously trained US citizens for short-term tours of duty. Each group was coordinated so that as it left another group took its place, providing a continuous foreign presence. This US-based initiative was administered by several US offices, and a permanent office in Managua. WFP has the dual focus of: 1) providing a foreign observer presence and 2) creating a growing number of American citizens with direct experience of the results of US foreign policy in Nicaragua. The later were expected to organize domestic resistance to, and demand change of, US policy. In 1989 WFP expanded its focus beyond Nicaragua. WFP has begun accompaniment of Guatemalan refugees from southern Mexico. In 1990, with the International Fellowship of Reconciliation, WFP sent a team to the Middle East. This helped initiate what later became an independent organization, Mideast Witness. WFP has developed a powerful model of organized grassroots response to international conflict by its development of a standardized

training program, evaluation and improvement procedures, overall organization and the numbers of volunteers it has placed in the field (thousands during the 1990s) in Colombia, El Salvador, Guatemala, Mexico, Nicaragua and Haiti.

FURTHER READING
Ed Griffin-Nolan, *Witness for Peace: A Story of Resistance* (Louisville: Westminster/John Knox Press, 1991). Extracts in this volume.
Ronald Sider, *Exploring the Limits of Non-Violence* (London: Spire, 1988) ch.2, pp.36-54.
Witness for Peace, *Ten Years of Accompaniment* (Washington, DC: Witness for Peace, 1994).

1988 -
Pastors for Peace (P4P)
Pastors for Peace is a US-based initiative which has sought to directly challenge US government foreign policy towards Central and Caribbean America. P4P began with a focus on the immorality of a blockade of Cuba, sending in, most notably, a yellow bus of medical supplies. Since its founding in 1988, it has delivered over $10 million worth of equipment donated by US citizens for hospitals, churches and development projects in Nicaragua. Over 20 aid caravans have been organized, and have gone to Mexico, Guatemala and El Salvador in addition to Cuba and Nicaragua. En route to delivering the material aid, the caravans travel through hundreds of cities in the US as an awareness raising method, and to develop further support. The caravans demonstrate foreign policy from below and add pressure for change on the US government by example and by the amount of aid they are capable of generating. P4P began a program of support for indigenous self-determination in Chiapas in 1995 and provided emergency relief for over 20,000 people. In 1997 P4P organized a high profile Caravan for the Children of Cuba, and were attacked by a right-wing Cuban-American group during their exit from the US.

FURTHER READING
Robin Hayes, "'Wave After Wave They Went Crossing the Border': Friendshipments by Pastors for Peace," (this volume).

1989-1991
Citizen Refugee Repatriation Accompaniment
Citizen Refugee Repatriation Accompaniment is not the name of a single organization, but several independently mobilized community-based initiatives. Their focus was providing international monitors for refugees

returning from Honduras to El Salvador in an attempt to protect the returnees from reprisals by armed forces. The largest group to send volunteers was an umbrella organization in the US called Going Home, which coordinated volunteers recruited through Central American Solidarity networks throughout North American. Some local communities (for example the Rocky Mountain Peace Center in Denver) organized their own complete teams and solidarity networks in Europe also sent several repatriation monitors.

1989-
Project Accompaniment
Project Accompaniment is a Canadian-based initiative that responded to a request by Guatemalan refugees living in Mexico to organize an international presence during and after their return to Guatemala. Returns and accompaniment continue.

FURTHER READING
Beth Abbott, "Project Accompaniment: A Canadian Response," (this volume).

1990-91
The Gulf Peace Team (GPT)
The GPT was an *ad hoc* initiative mobilized out of Britain by a former NVAV veteran and others to respond to the anticipated war against Iraq for its invasion of Kuwait. Like Royden's Peace Army and NVAV, the GPT hoped to place a massive number of noncombatants between opposing forces to stop a battle. On short notice, the GPT placed a team of over 70 people from a wide variety of countries in the war zone. This is the most multinational team of any effort to date. The GPT suffered immensely from lack of preparation, but a peace camp was established at a small caravanserai on the Saudi/Iraq border. The GPT maintained an international presence there until it was evacuated by the Iraqi military to Jordan ten days after the air strikes began. Several of the GPT members stayed on in Jordan providing an international presence on local aid convoys entering Iraq for the remainder of the war.

FURTHER READING
Robert J.Burrowes, "The Persian Gulf War and the Gulf Peace Team," (this volume).

1990-1992
Mideast Witness (MEW)

MEW provided teams based on the WFP model and from which it received its initial support and expertise. MEW volunteers lived with Palestinians in the occupied territories. The US-based MEW folded due to lack of both money and volunteers.

1990-
Christian Peacemaker Teams (CPT)

First chartered in 1984 at the US General Conference of the Mennonite and Brethren Churches, CPT was not mobilized in the US until late 1987 when its activities focused on training and disarmament issues. CPT began its first activities abroad by seeking hostage release in Iraq in 1990. It has since sent teams to the Gaza Strip on a frequent basis, and to Haiti as part of the Cry for Justice coalition. In October 1993 it launched the Christian Peacemaker Corp, a ready reserve of people trained and ready to enter situations of conflict quickly. Several CPT members maintained a presence in Haiti after the pullout of the UN, and later, Cry for Justice. In early 1995 the CPT responded to a request from Palestinians to accompany them to blockade projects by settlers from Israel.

FURTHER READING
Kathleen Kern, "Christian Peacemaker Teams," (this volume).

1991-1992
Peace Mission for East Timor [Lusitania Expresso]

This Portuguese-based effort was mobilized in response to the Dili massacre in East Timor. Organizers sent a ship with students from 21 nations in an attempt to land without Indonesian visas to challenge Indonesian sovereignty claims to East Timor. The ship did consciousness raising during its voyage to Indonesian territorial waters, and made it to within sight of Timor before being forced to turn back by Indonesian navy warships.

FURTHER READING
Andrew McMillan, *Death in Dili* (Sydney: Sceptre, 1992).
Andrew McMillan, "The Voyage of the Lusitania Expresso," (this volume).

1991-
Memorial Human Rights Observer Missions (MHRS)

Memorial has trained and sent observers to several areas of conflict in the former Soviet Union to provide an outside nonpartisan observer presence. Set up by the Human Rights Section of the organization MHRS, it is primarily a Russian initiative, but with members in several other, now independent, republics. Memorial was formerly a dissident organization in the Soviet Union, dedicated to the social reinstatement of former political prisoners and the victims of Stalin. The new Human Rights Section monitors the current situation of human rights in the Commonwealth of Independent States. MHRS has brought together social reformers from Armenia and Azerbaijan to promote "reconciliation from below" and publishes its observations of the conflicts in the CIS in Russian and foreign journals. A joint exploration from PBI and Memorial received permission from Azerbaijani inhabitants to put an international monitoring group in the disputed Nagorno-Karabakh region, but the initiative was aborted (before the Armenian side could formally agree) by the shooting down of a helicopter with 40 civilians aboard. MHRS continues to send missions, especially to the volatile trans-Caucasus region.

1992-
Dhammayietra

This Walk for Peace and Reconciliation into Cambodia was organized by peace activists and former aid workers in conjunction with Cambodian refugees living in camps in Thailand. The Walk's objectives were to break down the enemy image that the estranged populations of Cambodians living within the country, and those living in the refugee camps, had of one another. Travelling by foot to the capital, it was hoped that meetings between the refugees and populations of the towns in Cambodia would help dispel the fear of the other which had been perpetuated during the previous 15 years of war. A small international contingent, mainly from regional Buddhist nations, was also recruited to accompany the walk and provide it a nominal protective presence and neutrality. Reconciliation was achieved. Many walkers met family they did not know had survived the Pol Pot regime. The walk reached the capital with ten times the number of people walking than had left the refugee camps, and was the first people's-based event which Cambodia had witnessed for 20 years. The Dhammayietra walks have continued to be organized on an annual basis by a coalition of indigenous Khmer NGOs, addressing issues of societal healing and the ongoing violence within the country.

FURTHER READING

Elizabeth Bernstein, "Walking for Peace and Reconciliation in Cambodia: The Third Dhammayietra," *Nonviolence Today*, (1994) no.40, September-October, pp.11-13.

—— and Yeshua Moser, "Washing away the Blood," *Nonviolence Today*, (1992), no.29, November-December, pp.5-7.

Yeshua Moser-Puangsuwan, "One Million Kilometers for Peace —Reconciliation and Hope: The Dhammayietra Movement in Cambodia," (this volume).

1993
Mir Sada

Mir Sada was a joint effort of an Italian faith-based group, We Share One Peace, and a French aid delivery initiative, Equilibre, to set up an international peace encampment in Sarajevo. Like the GPT and several of its predecessors, Mir Sada hoped to place as many noncombatants as possible (Equilibre publicly called for 50-100,000) in an attempt to stop aggression through third-party interposition. Mir Sada did manage to get an international team of Italian, French, and other volunteers to the town of Prozor in southern Bosnia before the project collapsed due to unforeseen political changes, disagreements within the group and stress.

FURTHER READING

Christine Schweitzer, "Mir Sada: The Story of a Nonviolent Intervention that Failed," (this volume).

1993
Cry for Justice (CfJ)

CfJ sent it's first team to maintain a nonviolent presence in Haiti in late September of 1993, the anniversary of the 1991 coup. CfJ was a coalition of groups pooling resources and volunteers to put together a presence during a political crisis. Originally this program hoped to ease internal fear and to reduce the increase in repression prior to the scheduled return of former president Aristide. CfJ provided a foreign presence near rural grassroots organizations which suffered increased attacks upon their members when the UN program was abandoned. Conceived of as a short-term effort, more than 20 US-based groups including Christian Peacemaker Teams and Peace Brigades International managed to keep the project afloat long after their initial pullout date, but lack of long-term commitment ended the program in December 1993.

FURTHER READING

Ed Kinane, "Cry for Justice in Haiti, Fall 1993," (this volume).

Liam Mahony and Luis Enrique Eguren, *Unarmed Bodyguards: International Accompaniment for the Protection of Human Rights* (West Hartford, Con: Kumarian Press) ch.14, pp.218-224.

1993-
Balkan Peace Team (BPT)
BPT is a German-based initiative with organizational support from WRI and BUND (Federation for Social Defense). Almost a year in development, it fielded a peace team in Zagreb in early 1994. Volunteers came from Europe and North America, and within six months they opened a second team in Split and sent a second exploratory mission to Kosovo with hopes of opening a new team there. BPT teams have been involved in preventing evictions by para-militaries, and personifying international concern by being a presence with local human rights and social change activists at refugee camps and in meetings with officials in conflict regions.

FURTHER READING

Dave Bekkering, "Balkan Peace Team in Croatia: Otvorene Oci (Open Eyes)," (this volume).

1993-
Friends Peace Teams Project (FPTP)
This initiative began as a support organization within the Society of Friends (Quakers) in the US seeking volunteers for some of the above-listed peace teams. FPTP now offers financial support to Quakers who volunteer with PBI and CPT and runs its own peace teams training program. In January 1999, FPTP sent a 12 member delegation to the Great Lakes Region of Africa in response to local requests for an international peace team presence and to work on the development of FPTP's own overseas service project.

1995-
Servicio Inernacional Para La Paz (SIPAZ)
SIPAZ is a coalition of California-based organizations. It has launched a project in response to an invitation by peasants living in the Chiapas state of Mexico. SIPAZ has established a permanent presence in Chiapas, and recruits and trains volunteers for it's non-partisan observer teams in the region.

Others

For each of the efforts mentioned above, there were many proposals that never managed to get volunteers to the field, and died in some stage of growth. These include the Women's Peace Army (1917 Australia); Active Nonviolent Resistance Army (1959 UK); Peace Guards (1960 Madariaga and Narayan/Spain and India); Nonviolent Peace Keeping Corps (1965 US); Northern Ireland Peace Force (1971 IFOR); International Peace Contingents (1971 US); World Peace Army (1981 US); and World Peace Guard (1981 Walker/US) to name a few. Other groups have organized supportive networks for peace teams. The Global Peace Service, for example, has developed a three month training program for civilians intending to do peace service work in situations of war, and the German-based Liaison Center for Ecumenical Services issues a directory listing some 340 voluntary service agencies, many doing peace team work.

FURTHER READING

Thomas Weber, "A History of Nonviolent Interposition and Accompaniment," (this volume).

Appendix B

NONGOVERNMENTAL ORGANIZATIONS CURRENTLY SEEKING VOLUNTEERS AND PLACING PEACE TEAMS

BALKAN PEACE TEAM
Marienwall 9; D-32378 Minden, Germany
tel +49 571 29456; fax +49 571 23019
<balkan-peace-team@bionic.zer.de>
www.igc.org/pbi/bpt.html

CHRISTIAN PEACEMAKER TEAMS
PO Box 6508; Chicago Ill. 60680-6580 USA
tel/fax +1 312 455 1199
<cpt@igc.apc.org>
www.prairienet.org.cpt/homepage/html

EIRENE
Postfach 1322; D-56503 Neuwied, Germany
tel +49 2631 83790; fax +49 2631 31160
<eirene-int@oln.comlink.apc.org>
www.eirene.org/

GUATEMALA ACCOMPANIMENT PROJECT
59 East Van Buren, Suite 1400; Chicago Ill. 60605 USA
fax +1 312 939 3272
<nccord@igc.org>

PASTORS FOR PEACE
IFCO402 W 145th St; New York, NY 10031 USA
fax +1 212 926 5842
<p4p@igc.apc.org>
www.igc.apc.org/cubasoli/pastors.html

PEACE BRIGADES INTERNATIONAL
(National Sections in 17 countries)
International Secretariat: 5 Caledonian Road; London N1 9DX UK
tel +44 171 713 0392; fax +44 171 837 2290
<pbiio@gn.apc.org>
www.igc.org/pbi

PROJECT ACCOMPANIMENT
2606 Commercial Dr; Box 78080, Vancouver, BC, V5N 5W1 Canada
tel +1 875 6003; fax +1 872 0709
<accompany@web.apc.org>
www.island.com/vglobe/gconprac.html

SIPAZ
PO Box 2415; Santa Cruz, Ca. 95063 USA
tel/fax +1 831 425 1257
<sipaz@igc.org>
www.nonviolence.org/sipaz

WITNESS FOR PEACE
1229 15th St. NW; Washington, DC, 20005 USA
tel +1 202 588 1471; fax +1 202 588 1472
<witness@witnessforpeace.org>
www.witnessforpeace.org/

MULTINATIONAL GOVERNMENTAL PEACE TEAMS:

UNITED NATIONS VOLUNTEERS
HUMANITARIAN RELIEF UNIT
Palais des Nations; CH-1211, Geneve 10, Switzerland
www.unv.org/index.html

SUPPORTIVE ORGANIZATIONS:

ENTREPUEBLOS
Plaza Ramon Berenguer el Gran n° 1,3ª-1°; 08002 Barcelona, Spain
fax +34 3 268 4913
<epueblo@pangea.upc.es>
www.pangea.org/epueblos

FRIENDS PEACE TEAMS PROJECT
c/o BYM, 17100 Quaker Lane; Sandy Spring, MD 20860 USA
tel +1 301 774 6855; fax +1 301 774 7087
<fptp@igc.apc.org>
www.quaker.org/fptp

PEACEWORKERS
721 Shrader St; San Francisco, Ca. 94117 USA
tel +1 415 751 0302; fax +1 1415 7515 708
<peaceworkers@igc.apc.org>
www.webcom.com/~peace/PEACETREE/pworker/homepage.html

DIRECTORY OF PEACE TEAMS

The *Peace Teams/Peace Services Information Networker Directory* is an open networking project which aims to serve the growing community of individuals and organizations who wish to develop an alternative to armed intervention in local and global conflicts. It is located at:
495/44 Soi Yoo-omsin, Jaransanitwong 40 Road;
Bangkok, 107000 Thailand
tel/fax (66-2) 433 7619 or 374 1671
<ahimsa@ksc.th.com>
www.igc.org/nonviolence/niseasia/ptsin

Index

Accompaniment, 3, 10-11, 39, 58; accepted, 153-54; assessment of, 174; as conviction, 212; defined, 58, 211; difficulties of, 228-29; in El Salvador, 148-50; 214; in Haiti, 216-21; as interposition, 212-213; logic of, 141; as nonintervention, 213; as nonpartisanship, 214; and PBI, 139-42; as privilege, 214-15; problems with, 140; by Project Accompaniment, 167, 169-70, 172; purpose of, 211; saves lives, 144; as solidarity, 213; in Sri Lanka, 150-54; as steadfastness, 215-16; under attack, 144-47; as understanding, 212; withdrawal of, 216; and witness, 39 324.
Acland, Sir Richard, 21.
Active Nonviolent Resistance Army, 21, 356.
Affinity groups, 308, 314-15.
Aid agencies, humanitarian, 3.
Alatas, Ali, 74, 77-78, 81.
Algeria, 342-43; people power in, 7-8.
Allende, Salvador, 287.
American Friends Service Committee, and Cry for Justice, 210; discussions in Cyprus, 116; and Witness for Peace, 282, 298.
Amnesty International, 4, 139, 191.
Anabaptist churches, 175.
Antarctica, 61.
Aristide, Jean-Bertrand, 156, 177-79, 209-10, 221, 354; deposed 210, 215; in exile 217; return to Haiti 220.
Armies, international, 3.
Armenia, 353.
Arrowsmith, Pat, 305.
Atom bomb, see French atom bomb.
Auschwitz, 54.
Australia, 53, 73-5, 78, 89, 99.
Austrian Peace Service, 204.
Azerbaijan, 353.

Balkan Peace Team, 7, 38, 59, 326, 341, 349, 355, 357; and civil society development, 192; conferences, 205; in Croatia, 191-206; field work of, 198; future work of, 205-06; goals of, 191-92; and human rights advocacy, 192, 200-02; internal organization of, 199; networking by, 198-199; and nonviolent conflict resolution, 192, 202-03; offices of, 199; office work by, 203-04; and PBI, 153, 349; summit, 204; workshops, 204, in Yugoslavia, 192.
Bangladesh, 24, 50, 53, 55, 346.
Baptist Peace Fellowship, and Cry for Justice, 210.
Beati I Costruttori de Pace, 269-70, 273-75; camps in Bosnia, 272; and Mir Sada, 269-70, 273.
Bell, Rev. Ralph, 21.
Bhave, Vinoba, 22; and Delhi-Peking March, 33, 35; and Shanti Sena, 36; and Sino-Indian War, 32-33; and UN, 35; and World Peace Brigade, 37.
Bigelow, Albert, 22.
Blumberg, Herbert H., 9.
Bluntschli, Carla, 219.
Bonthius, Bob, 286, 289, 291, 300.
Borge, Tomas, 282.
Bosnia 62, 354; Beati in, 272.
Boulding, Elise, 7.
Brethren churches, 252, 342.
Brinton, Henry, 23, 39, 322; peace army of, 19-20.
Buffer actions, 8.
Buffer forces, 7, 16, 63.
Burrowes, Robert J., 11, 266.

Calixto, Mario, 155.
Cambodia, 48, 61-62, 64, 353; and Dhammayietra, 257; and NVAV, 36; UN in, 257.
Canada, 25, 37, 140, 143; Pastors for Peace networks in, 105.
Cannon fodder, viii, ix.

Cardenal, Ernesto, 282.
CARE, 283.
Carolina Interfaith Task Force, 280, 282, 285, 287, 291, 298.
Catholic Worker, 298.
Cédras, Raoul, 177, 210, 214.
Centeno, Humberto, 149.
CEPAD, see Evangelical Committee for Aid to Development.
Cerezo, Vinicio, 141-42, 144-45.
Chad, 247, 342, 349; PBI in, 153.
Chicago Religious Task Force, 298.
China, 7, 52, 63, 342; Cultural Revolution, 8; Japanese invasion of, 17; JP's view of, 33; people power in, 8; war with India, 32, 34-35, 54, 322.
Christian Peacemaker Corps, 177, 352.
Christian Peacemaker Teams, 175-90, 326, 341, 352, 357; campaign against violent toys, 188-89; Christian Peacemaker Corps, 177, 352; and Church of Brethren, 189; and Cry for Justice, 58, 177, 210; and Gulf War, 177; in Haiti, 58, 177-81, 189; Haiti routine, 178; 177; in Hebron, 177-80, 189, 333-34; Hebron routine, 182; in Iraq, 177; mandate of, 176-77; and Mennonite Church, 189; and Pax Christi, 177; and PBI, 177; and Quakers, 189; in Quebec, 177; volunteers attacked, 184-86; in Washington DC, 6-7, 38, 177, 186-88; and Witness for Peace,177; in US 180.
Church of Brethren, and Christian Peacemaker Teams, 189.
CITCA, see Carolina Interfaith Task Force.
Citizen Refugee Reparation Accompaniment, 350-51.
Civil Disobedience, 50.
Civilian Peace Service, 327.
Clergy and Laity Concerned, and Cry for Justice, 210; and Witness for Peace, 282.
Clinton, Bill, 177.
Cole, Edith, 134.
Colombia, 349-50; PBI in, 153-55.
Committee for Nonviolent Action, 237, 343-44.
Conference of Major Superiors of Men, 210.
Conflict, in India, vii.
Constructive program, 49, 56.
Contras, 103, 279-81, 293-94, 299; deterred from attacking, 294-95; US support for, 64, 103, 281, 287, 292, 300-04; and Witness for Peace, 296-97.

Croatia, 62; , and Balkan Peace Team, 191-206; human rights in, 194-97; NGO work in, 194, 196-98; Oxfam in, 196; Red Cross in, 201; refugees in, 196; UNHCR in, 196, 201.
Cross-border intervention, criteria for, 46-47.
Cross-border nonviolent intervention, a typology of, 45-69.
Cry for Justice, 38, 32-26, 348-49, 352, 354; and American Friends Service Committee, 210; arrival in Haiti, 218-19; and Baptist Peace Fellowship, 210; and Christian Peacemaker Teams, 58, 177, 210; and Clergy and Laity Concerned, 210; and Conference of Major Superiors of Men, 210; different to PBI, 227-28; disbanded, 178; and Fellowship of Reconciliation, 210; formed, 210; and Global Exchange, 210; in Haiti, 207-32, 354; and Haiti Communication Project, 210; long-term volunteers, 217, 223; and Maryknoll Fathers, 210; and Pax Christi, 210; and PBI, 153, 210; and PBI model, 217; and Quixote Center, 210; short-term volunteers, 217; and Sojourners, 210; team in Hinche, 221-22; team in Jérémie, 222-32; team orientation, 219; volunteer detained, 231; volunteers, 207; volunteer training, 217-18; and War Resisters League, 210; and Washington Office on Haiti, 210; and Witness for Peace, 210.
Cuba, 54-55; friendshipments to, 105-07, 109, 111; Lucius Walker in, 105; Pastors for Peace in, 55-56, 350; US embargo of, 106-07, 110.
Cuevas, Rosario de, 136-137.
Cyprus, 25, 27, 50; American Friends Service Committee discussions in, 116; Charles Walker in, 115; Cyprus Resettlement Project in, 115-129; refugee situation, 117; Turkish invasion, of 123; UN representative in, 116.
Cyprus Resettlement Project, 25-27, 36-37, 50, 57-58, 115-29, 324-25, 347-48; and American Friends Ser-vice Committee, 116; budget, 115; evaluation of, 125-29; first team, 115-18; fourth team, 12-23; Hare's report on, 124-25; history of, 124-25; limitations of, 125-29; proposal endorsed, 118; second team, 118; success of, 126; termination of mission,123-25; third team, 119-20; work camp, 121-23.

Czechoslovakia, 37, 46.
Czechoslovakia Support Actions, 345.

Dayton Peace Agreement, 196-97.
Death squads, 47-48; in Guatemala, 164.
Delhi-Peking Friendship March, 115, 344; and JP, 54, 63; and Michael Scott, 33-34; and Vinoba, 33, 35, and World Peace Brigade, 30, 32-33, 35.
Dellums, Ronald, 110.
Denktash, Rauf, 117-19, 123, 128.
Desai, Narayan, 115-116; and Shanti Sena, viii.
Dhammayietra, 62, 257-268, 327, 353; and Buddhist monks, 261, 263, 265; Centre, 266; and compassion, 259-60; definition, 257; and forests, 264-65; guidelines, 262; and land mines, 259, 264, 267; and mindfulness, 260; as model, 265; movement begins, 257; and nonpartisanship, 260; and nonviolence, 258-59; organization of, 261-63; participants killed, 260, 262; and politicians, 261; prayer for peace, 264; and public education, 264; training for, 258-59.
Dilling, Yvonne, 284-85.
Direct Action Committee Against Nuclear War, 237.
Drummond, Sir Eric, 18.

Eanes, Antonio Ramalho, 74, 80, 88.
East Timor, 352; human rights abuses in, 79. See also Mission for Peace in Timor.
Egypt, 342; and Israel, 21.
Eirene, 357, 341-42.
El Salvador, 55, 134, 288, 304, 348, 350-51; nuns murdered in, 295; Pastors for Peace in, 55, 350; PBI in, 58, 148-50, 229; PBI in, 58; 148-50, 156, 229, 298; PBI workshops in, 156; peace in, 150; US-supported violence in, 104.
Emergency response network, 58, 140-41, 145.
Entrepueblos, 358.
Equilibre, 270-72, 274-75; 354; and Mir Sada, 269; in Sarajevo, 269.
European Voluntary Service, 342.
Evangelical Committee for Aid to Development, 281, 292, 301.
Evans, Gareth, 76, 80.
Everyman I, 32-3, 60.
Everyman II, 32, 60.
Everyman III, 30, 32, 34, 54, 344.

Federation for Social Defense, 355.
Fellowship of Reconciliation, 23, 287, 303; and Cry for Justice, 210.
Fereira, Alfredo, 89.
France, 60, 74, 344; atom bomb of, 235.
FRAPH, 180, 212-13, 220, 222; controlled by CIA, 215; demonstration by, 216; kidnapping by, 224-25, 227, 230; relationship with Haitian military, 226.
French atom bomb, 235; detonated, 247; opposed by Britain, 254.
Friendshipments, to Cuba, 103-112; to Nicaragua, 104-05; by Pastors for Peace, 55; stopped at border, 107-09; as violation of US law, 105.
Friends Peace Teams Project, 319, 341, 355, 359.
Friere, Paolo, 156.

Gandhian movement, 32-33; and Sino-Indian war, 35, 322.
Gandhi, Indira, 36.
Gandhi, Mahatma, 17, 19, 20, 22, 139, 220, 285, 288, 301, 320; and creative self-suffering, 321; on defense, 320; on resisting invasion, vii-ix, 321.
Garcia, General Romeo Lucas, 164.
García, Nineth de, 136, 139, 140.
Ghosananda, Maha, 258, 264-65, 267.
Global Exchange, and Cry for Justice, 210.
Global Peace Service, 319, 356.
Goa, 50, 60, 321.
Golden Harvest, 55, 347.
Golden Rule, 22, 59, 237.
Gomez, Bishop Medardo, 148.
Gramajo, Hector, 141-42, 145.
Gray, Dr Herbert, 17-19, 24, 63.
Greenpeace, 4, 50, 54, 60-61, 65, 288, 302, 323.
Grindstone Island, 133.
Grupo de Apoyo Mutuo (GAM), 134-136, 140, 142-43, 145-46, 154-55; attacked, 138; member of killed, 136-38.
Guatemala, 304, 349-51; death squads in, 164; history of, 163-64; Pastors for Peace in, 350; PBI in, 58, 134-144, 146-47, 158, 333, 336, 348; PBI workshops in, 155-56; peace accords, 167, 171; Project Accompaniment in, 163-74; refugees in Mexico, 165-66; refugees return to, 147; Witness for Peace in, 59, 349; US-supported violence in, 104; US support for military, 164.

364 *Index*

Guatemala Accompaniment Project, 358.
Guerra, Yuri, 104.
Gulf Peace Team, 9, 16, 37-39, 46, 50, 64, 305-16, 319-25, 351, 354; affinity groups, 308, 314-15; assessment, 311-315; in Baghdad, 306-07, 310-11; camp, 306; camp life, 307-10; communications, 315; decision-making, 308-09; evacuation, 310-11; finances, 315; and Gulf War, 307; and interposition, 311; location of camp, 312; and logistical dependency, 313; neutrality of, 312-13; organization, 314-15; origins of, 305; policy statement, 305; and problem solving, 309; and psychological problems, 310; strategy of, 313-14; and stresses of war, 309-10; as symbol, 312.
Gulf War, and Christian Peacemaker Teams, 177; and Gulf Peace Team, 307.
Gumbleton, Bishop Thomas, 211.

Haiti, ix, 38,348,350,352, 354; accompaniment in, 216-21; Christian Peacemaker Teams in, 58, 177-78, 189; CIA involvement in, 216; Cry for Justice in, 207-232, 354; demonstrations in, 179; *Harlan County* in, 216-17; history of, 208-10; PBI in, 153, 156; USAID in, 228; US involvement in, 209-10.
Haiti Communication Project, and Cry for Justice, 210.
Hammarskjöd, Dag, 22-23.
Handicap International, 335.
Harbottle, Michael, 26; and Cyprus Resettlement Project, 119.
Hare, A.Paul, 9-10, 115-16,120, 331; proposal by, 117; report of, 124-125.
Harlan County, 177, 216; leaves Haiti, 217.
Harrison, Red, 98.
Hebron, Christian Peacemaker Teams in, 177-80, 182, 184-86, 189, 333-34; Christian Peacemaker Team volunteers attacked, 184-86; history of, 181-86; opening university gates in, 184; water truck incident, 182-83.
Herschel, Rabi Abraham, 285.
Hislop, Ian, 84, 86-87.
Hiroshima, 54, 62.
Hitler, Adolf, 20.
Honduras, 279, 284-85, 348, 351.
Humanitarian aid caravans, see Friendshipments.
Humanitarian political intervention, 320, 334.

Human rights, 3; political cost of abusing, 141.

IFCO, see Interreligious Foundation for Community Organization.
India, conflict in, vii; war with China, 32, 34-35, 54, 322.
Intercession, 3.
Intercessionary peacekeeping, 10.
Interfaith Pilgrimage for Peace, 54, 62.
International Campaign to Ban Land Mines, 335-36.
International Fellowship of Reconciliation, 342, 349.
International Longshoremen's Association, 53.
International Nonviolent Marches for Demilitarization, 276.
International Peace Academy Institute, 115-16.
Interposition, 3, 39, 316, 320-23; and accompaniment, 212-13; and Gulf Peace Team, 311, nonviolent, 46; and PBI, 38.
Interpositionary peacekeeping, 10, 37; and PBI, 38.
Interreligious Foundation for Community Organization, 103; Central America week of, 104.
InterReligious Task Force on Central America, 282.
Intervention, 10; by children, ix; coercive, 45; direct, 11; humanitarian, 45; non-official, 45; non-coercive, 4, 45; non-governmental, 4; nonviolent, 46, 48-49; official, 45; physical, 49; political, 49; third party, x; third party humanitarian, 10; typology of, 8, 10, 45-69; unarmed, 6.
Invasion, viii-ix, nonviolent, 11.
Iraq, 15, 64, 305-06, 319, 351; Christian Peacemaker Teams in, 177.
Israel, 10, 54, 348, 352; and Egypt, 21.
Italian Peace Association, 54.

Jackson, Jesse, 110.
Japan, 74, 342.
Jolly George, 53.
Jordan, 64, 306, 351.

Kaunda, Kenneth, 31.
Keating, Paul, 89.
Kemp, Kate, 125.
Kennedy, Robert F., 155.
Kern, Kathleen, 184-85, 230.
Keyes, Gene, 7.

King, Martin Luther Jr., 107, 285, 301-02.
Kohan, Randy, 172.
Kosovo, 355.
Kuwait, 15, 38, 64, 306, 312, 351.

L'Abate, Albert, 10.
Land mines, 335-36.
League of Nations, 5, 17-19, 22, 342.
Lewer, Nick, 10, 45.
Liaison Center for Ecumenical Services, 356.
Liberation movements, 47.
Liberation Without Violence, 9, 329, 331.
Little Yellow School Bus, 110-11.
Local nonviolent actions, defined, 51.
Loretto Sisters, 7.
Lusitania Expresso, 73, 76. 54, 324, 352; arrives in Darwin, 85; buzzed by helicopters, 97; confronted by Indonesian warships, 92; description of, 85; leaves Darwin, 87; leaves Lisbon, 80; sights Timor, 93; voyage of, 73ff. See also Mission for Peace in Timor.
Lutrin, Zena, 126.

Madariaga, Salvador de, 22, 356.
Magee, Raymond, 28, 37.
Mahony, Liam, 217, 336.
Marti, Jose, 107.
Martin, Pierre, 239, 241-42, 244, 246, 252-53.
Maryknoll fathers, and Cry for Justice, 210.
Mazoweicki, Tadeusz, 195-96, 205.
McLean, Jean, 77, 93.
Médecines Sans Frontièrs, 332.
Melbourne Rainforest Action Group, 52.
Memorial Human Rights Observer Missions, 38, 353.
Menchú, Rigoberta, 110, 142, 145.
Mendez, Amilcar, 143, 147, 155.
Mennonite and Brethren Churches, 58, 176-77, 342, 352; and Christian Peacemaker Teams, 189, 289; peace monitors, 7.
Mennonite World Conference, 175.
Mexico, 55, 348-51, 355; Guatemalan refugees in, 165-66; and Pastors for Peace, 55, 106, 110, 350; and Witness for Peace, 59, 349.
Michigan Interfaith Task Force, 298.
Mideast Witness, 38, 349, 352.

Mir Sada, 62, 269-276, 320-22, 324-24, 354; and Beati, 269-70, 273; communication in, 275; decision-making, 274; and Equilibre, 269; failure of, 271-75; goals of, 271; history of, 27-71; lessons of, 275-76; organization, 274; and peace armies, 322; preparation of participants, 273-74; and UN, 271-73; and UNPROFOR, 270, 272; and Yugoslav peace groups, 275.
Mission for Peace in Timor, 73, 76, 353; indemnity form, 84; purpose of, 86; relationship with media, 99-100; US view of, 86. See also Lusitania Expresso.
Mobilization actions, 11; defined, 53, 71.
Montt, General Efrain Rios, 164.
Moser, Yeshua, 151.
Muste, A.J., 30, 237, 241; and Sahara Protest action, 242.

NAFTA, 166.
Narayan, Jayaprakash (JP), 22, 24, 29, 356; Chinese view of, 33; and Delhi-Peking March, 35, 54, 63; and World Peace Brigade, 30, 33.
NATO, 6, 15-16, 252, 271.
New Jerusalem Community, 298.
Nicaragua, ix, 55, 105, 349-50; friend-shipments to, 104-04; Lucius Walker in, 103, 105; and Pastors for Peace, 55, 104, 350; PBI in, 348; US invasion threat, 295, 302-04, 322; US-supported violence in, 104; and Witness for Peace, 59, 64, 282, 289, 349.
Nkrumah, Kwame, 236-38, 244, 246-49, 252.
Nobel Peace Prize, 4, 16.
Nonviolence, 3; defined, 288; and Dhammayietra, 258-59; as means of liberation, x; training, 258-59; as way of life, x; and Witness for Peace, 286-89.
Nonviolent action, 46; as noncooperation, 49; as nonviolent intervention, 49; as persuasion, 49; as protest, 49.
Non-violent Action in Vietnam (NVAV), 9, 36-37, 64, 321, 323, 345-46, 351; and Michael Scott, 36.
Nonviolent cross-border intervention, typology of, 8, 10, 45-69.
Nonviolent defense, viii, 46.
Nonviolent humanitarian assistance, 11, 54, 101.
Nonviolent intercession, 11, 59, 207.

Nonviolent interposition, 9, 11, 46; defined, 62, 177.
Nonviolent intervention, 7, 9, 46, 48-49, 51.
Nonviolent invasion, 11, 50, 64-65.
Nonviolent reconciliation and development, 11, 56, 113.
Nonviolent resistance, ix.
Nonviolent solidarity, 11, 61, 255.
Nonviolent witness and accompaniment, 11, 58, 131.
Northern Ireland Peace Force, 23, 356.
Northern Rhodesia March, 24, 30, 63, 344; and World Peace Brigade, 30-31.
Nyerere, Julius, 247.

Olson, Theodore, 31, 33.
Operation Desert Storm, 16, 38.
Operation Namibia, 55, 347-48.
Operation Omega, 50, 55, 346-47.
Ortega, Daniel, 282.
Osorio-Tafal, Mr., 116,119.
Otvorene Oci, see Balkan Peace Team.
Oxfam, 4, 48, 334; and Balkan Peace Team, 204; in Croatia, 196.

Pacifists, 5, 20.
Pakistan, 50, 53, 55, 288, 346.
Palestine, 10, 54, 348, 352.
Pastors for Peace, 55-56, 103-11, 341, 350, 357; Canada network, 105; and Castro, 106; in Cuba, 55-56, 350; in El Salvador, 55, 350; friendshipments by, 55; in Guatemala, 350; hunger strike, 109-11; at Mexican border, 106, 110; in Mexico, 55, 350; in Nicaragua, 55, 104, 350; and solidarity activism, 103; US network, 105.
Pax Christi, and Christian Peacemaker Teams, 177; and Cry for Justice, 210.
Peace armies, 5, and Mir Sada, 322.
Peace Army, 342; of Brinton, 19-20, 23; of Royden 9, 17-20, 23, 63, 342, 351.
Peace brigades, 5, 133.
Peace Brigades International (PBI), 6-7, 9, 16, 25, 48, 50, 65, 133-61, 319, 325-26, 330-31, 333, 336, 341, 354, 358; and accompaniment, 139-42; attacked, 145-46; and Balkan Peace Team, 153, 349; begins escorting, 137; and Burma, 153; and Canada, 156; in Chad, 153; and Christian Peacemaker Teams, 177; in Colombia, 153-55; communications, 159-60; country groups, 159; and Cry for Justice, 153, 210; decision-making, 159-60; different to Cry for Justice, 227-29; in El Salvador, 58, 148-50, 156, 229, 298; emergency response network of, 58, 140-41, 145, 348; and England, 147; in former Soviet Republics, 153; founding of, 37, 133; future challenges, 160; General Assembly, 153, 159; and Germany, 147; in Guatemala, 58, 134-44, 146-47, 155, 158, 333, 348; in Haiti, 153, 156; and Holland, 147; International Council, 159; and interpositionary peacekeeping, 38; long-term escorts, 140; in Nicaragua, 348; North America Project, 156-58, 348; and Philippines, 153; short-term escorts, 140; and SIPAZ, 153; and Spain, 147; in Sri Lanka, 58, 150-54, 158; steering committee, 158; and Sweden, 147; and Switzerland, 147; task of, 37; and Turkey, 153; and UN Human Rights Monitoring Mission, 156; in US, 147; volunteers detained, 148-50; workshops, 155-56.
Peacebuilding, 5, 10, 24, 335.
Peace Corps, 28, 34, 331; in Philippines, 117.
Peace enforcement, 15.
Peace guards, 22-23, 356.
Peacekeeping, 5-6; international, 21, interpositionary, 10, 37; and soldiers, 26; UN, 15, 24 39, 319; unarmed, 9, 46.
Peacemaking, 5, 10, 24.
Peace teams, 5, 7; decision-making, 325; development of, 324; directory of, 341, 359; economics of, 326; internationalization of, 329-31; logistics, 332-33; as movement, 335-36; and neutrality, 326-27; organization, 325; personnel, 327-29; questions for, 324-25; and reverse racism, 330; and strategic thinking, 332-33; and symbols, 331; training, 331; and uniforms, 330.
Peaceworkers, 24, 28, 342, 359.
Peter, Esther, 239, 242-43, 246-47, 251-52.
Phares, Gail, 280-82, 286-88, 291, 295.
Philippines, 46, 349; and PBI, 153; peace corps in, 117; people power in, 8.
Phoenix, 59, 346.
Phyllis Cormack, 60.
Pinochet, General Augusto, 287.
People power, 7; in Algeria, 7-8; in Bangkok, 8; in Beijing, 8; in Belgrade, 8; in China, 8; in Jakarta, 8; in Moscow, 8; in Philippines, 8.
Portugal, 73-74, 76, 78, 85, 89.

Prague Spring, 37, 345.
Prasad, Devi, 30-32.
Premadasa, Ranasinghe, 152.
Project Accompaniment, 6-7, 38, 163-74, 341, 351; 358; accompaniment and, 169-70; Canadians in, 167-68; ends accompaniment, 172; founding of, 167; goals of, 168; in Guatemala, 163-174.
Pt'chang, 7.
Puerto Rico, 346; Culebra action, 56.

Quaker Action Group, 57, 345, 347.
Quaker Peace and Service, 334.
Quaker Peace Center, 283.
Quakers, 6, 133, 355, and Christian Peacemaker Teams, 189; mediation by, 45. See also Friends Peace Team Project.
Quebec, Christian Peacemaker Teams in, 177.
Quebec-Washington-Guantanamo Walk, 54.
Quixote Centre, and Cry for Justice, 210.

Rabin, Itzhak, 183,186.
Rainbow Warrior, 5, 60.
Ramirez, Sergio, 282.
Ramsbotham, Oliver, 10, 45.
Randle, Michael, 237-39, 241-45, 250, 254.
Rangel, Charles, 110.
Ravara, Antonio, 77-79, 98-99.
Reagan, Ronald, 285, 292, 294-95, 303.
Red Crescent, 124.
Red Cross, 4, 45, 124, 139, 313, 322, 330, 332; in Croatia, 201.
Refugee Escort Services, 38.
Resource Center for Nonviolence, 298.
Richard, Alain, 137.
Rider, Lorne, 78, 81, 88, 94.
Rigby, Andrew, 10.
Rikhye, General Indarjit, 116.
Romelus, Bishop Willie, 217, 222, 226.
Romero, Archbishop Oscar, 135, 299.
Royden, Maude, 5, 8, 16-19, 24, 39, 323; peace army of, 9, 17-20, 23, 63, 342, 351.
Rustin, Bayard, 237, 239, 250-52.

Sahara Protest Team, 22, 50, 60, 235-54, 324, 343; actions in France, 246-47; ends, 250; first attempt, 241-243; in Ghana, 238-44; leaves Accra, 235, 242; lessons of, 253-54; Michael Scott as spokes person for, 235; political impact of, 250-53; route, 236; second attempt, 243; stopped by French, 241; support actions, 244-45; third attempt, 245-46.
Salstrom, Paul, 34, 37.
Salt Satyagraha, 65.
Samedi, Father Joaquim, 178-79, 222, 225; celebrates mass, 225-56; describes clergy, 226-27; meeting with, 231; welcomes accompaniment, 227, 231.
Samitha, Baddegama, 152-53.
Sandinistas, 282, 286, 289-90, 299; anti-Semitic, 285; and Catholic church, 293; and Miskito people, 285; and Witness for Peace, 290.
San Francisco-Moscow Walk for Peace, 22, 53, 343.
Santos, Captain Luys dos, 82, 85, 90-92, 94; talks with Indonesians, 95-96.
Saravanamuttu, Dr Manorani, 151.
Satyagraha units, 21.
Saudi Arabia, 4, 16, 38, 305-06, 351.
Saurez, Rev. Raul, 105.
Schirch, Douglas, 297.
Schirch, Lisa, 10, 329.
Scott, Michael, 235, 240, 242-43 254; arrives in Ghana, 239; and Delhi-Peking March, 33-34; and NVAV, 36; and Sahara Protest Team, 235; and World Peace Brigade, 30.
Sea Shepherd, 50, 60-61.
Shackleton, Shirley, 77, 97, 99.
Shanti Sena, 22, 24, 28-29, 63, 115, 117, 344, 346; and Narayan Desai, viii; and Vinoba, 35-36; and war with China, 32-33, and World Peace Brigade, 32, 344.
Sharp, Gene, 49.
Sheppard, Rev. H.R.L., 17-20, 24, 63.
Sider, Ron, 175-76, 189, 287.
Sino-Indian war, and Gandhian movement, 35, 322; and Shanti Sena, 32; and Vinoba, 32-33, 35.
SIPAZ, 6, 341, 326, 355, 358; and PBI, 153.
Sipe, Dan, 121-23.
Sirius, 54.
Sjeme Mira, 62.
Soares, Mario, 75, 86.
Social change, 9-10; nonpartisan, 10; partisan, 10;second party approach, 10; third party approach, 10.
Social cosmology, 47.
Society of Friends, see Quakers.
Sojourners, 285, 296; and Cry for Justice, 210.

Sojourners Neighborhood Center, 188.
Solidarity for Peace, 62.
Somalia, 15,46,48.
South Africa, 34, 78, 347; apartheid in, 52.
South Vietnam, 346.
Soviet Union, 53, 353.
Spindler, Syd, 90.
Sri Lanka, 58, 348; PBI in, 58, 150-54, 158.
Stalin, Joseph, 353.
Stolzfus, Gene, 176-77.
Sutherland, Bill, 237, 242-43, 250, 252.
Sutrismo, General Try, 77.
Swann, Robert, 34, 37.
Sweden, 6, 74.
Swedish Council of Churches, 319.
Sweet, David, 283, 287, 291, 295, 299.
Syafei, General Theo, 73, 83, 89.

Tatum, Arlo, 29.
Taylor, Richard, 286-88, 290-91.
Time for Peace, 54.
Timor, see East Timor and Mission for Peace in Timor.
Torricelli Bill, 105.
Toure, Sekou, 251-52.
Trading with the Enemy Act, 107.
Typology of interventions, 8, 10, 45-69.

Unarmed Bodyguards, 333.
UNHCR, 124, 165-66; in Croatia, 196, 201.
United Nations, 3, 6, 16, 23, 47, 50,133; Article 43 troops, 15; in Cambodia, 257; and East Timor, 76; Human Rights Monitoring Mission, 156; and Mir Sada, 271-73; Peace Guard, 22-23; peacekeeping, 5, 15, 24, 39, 319; sanctions, 46; Security Council, 15; soldiers, 3, 26; standing army, 15; UNEF, 21; and Vinoba, 35, volunteer corps, 21; and World Peace Guard, 28.
United Nations High Commissioner for Refugees, see UNHCR.
United Nations Observer Corps, 21.
United Nations Volunteers, 6, 319, 358.
United States, 6, 18, 35, 60, 74, 343; Christian activists in, 64; embargo of Cuba, 106-07, 110; invades Grenada, 292; invades other countries, 48; involvement in Haiti, 209-10; Pastors for Peace networks in, 105; PBI in, 147; supports Contras, 64, 103, 281, 287, 292, 300-04; supports Guatemalan military, 164; supports violence in El Salvador, 104; supports violence in Guatemala, 104; supports violence in Nicaragua, 104; threatens Nicaraguan invasion, 295, 302-04, 322; view of Timor Peace Mission, 86.
UNPROFOR, 202, 270, 272.
Usborne, Henry, 21.

Veniamin, C., 117.
Victims, taking sides with, x.
Victores, Mejía, 135-36.
Vietnam, 64; and NVAV, 36; war, 139, 285, 290.
Vinoba, see Bhave, Vinoba.
Violence, direct, 5; structural, x, 5, 47.
Volunteers for International Development, 342.

Walker, Charles, 5-6; in Cyprus, 115; proposes a World Peace Guard, 25-26; and World Peace Brigade, 32.
Walker, Rev. Lucius Jr., 109-01; in Cuba, 105; in Nicaragua, 103,105; in Washington, 111; wounded, 103.
Walk for a Peaceful Future, 54.
Walk for Peace and Justice, 54.
Wallis, Jim, 284-85, 287, 290-91, 303.
War Resisters' International, 29, 37, 355; triennial conference, 28.
War Resisters League, and Cry for Justice, 210.
Washington DC, Christian Peacemaker Team in, 6-7, 38, 177, 186-88; crackhouse in, 186-87; Halloween, 188; Lucius Walker in, 111.
Washington Office on Haiti, and Cry for Justice, 210.
Welensky, Sir Roy, 30-31.
We Share One Peace, 354.
White Berets, 6.
Wilkinson, Ellen, 120.
Willoughby, George, 325.
Witness and accompaniment, 39, 324.
Witness for Peace, 6, 279-304, 321-22, 324-26, 341, 349, 358; and American Friends Service Committee, 282, 298; and Christian Peacemaker Teams, 177; and Clergy and Laity Concerned, 282; and Contras, 296-97; and Cry for Justice, 210; daily routine, 293-94; described, 286; described in media, 296; executive committee, 291; faith basis of, 285-86; in Guatemala, 59, 349; in Jalapa, 292-95; in Mexico, 59, 349; in Nicaragua, 59, 64, 282, 289, 349; and nonviolence, 286-89; organization,

297-98; Philadelphia meeting, 283-91, 297; political independence of, 289-90; recruitment ad, 279; and Sandinistas, 290; short-term delegates, 295; statement of purpose, 282; and US threat to invade Nicaragua, 295, 302-04.
Women's Peace Army, 356.
World government, 3.
World Pacifist Meeting, 21.
World Peace and Relief Teams, 319.
World Peace Brigade, 9, 24, 29-34, 58, 63, 115, 289, 325, 343, 345-46; and Charles Walker, 32; initiates Delhi-Peking March, 30, 32-33, 35; and Devi Prasad, 31-32; *Everyman III*, 30, 32; fades away, 34; failure of, 31-33; founding of, 29-30; and JP, 30, 33; legacy of, 28; and Michael Scott, 30; and Northern Rhodesia March, 24, 30-31, 63, 344; program for, 29-30; and Shanti Sena, 344; success of, 31; Vinoba calls for new, 37.
World Peace Guard, 5, 24-28, 356; and casualties, 26; Charles Walker proposes, 25-26; composition of, 28; future shape of, 27; mandate of, 25-26; and Shanti Sena, 344, and UN, 28.

Yugoslavia, 15-16, 38, 62, 197; Austrian Peace Service in, 204; and Balkan Peace Team, 192.

JZ
5574
.N66
2000

DATE DUE

HIGHSMITH